MW01201314

Becoming Neapolitan

Becoming Neapolitan

Citizen Culture in Baroque Naples

JOHN A. MARINO

The Johns Hopkins University Press
Baltimore

The Johns Hopkins University Press
2715 North Charles Street
Baltimore, Maryland 21218-4363
www.press.jhu.edu

Library of Congress Cataloging-in-Publication Data

Marino, John A.
Becoming Neapolitan : citizen culture in Baroque Naples / John A. Marino.
p.   cm.
Includes bibliographical references and index.
ISBN-13: 978-0-8018-9787-0 (hardcover : alk. paper)
ISBN-10: 0-8018-9787-4 (hardcover : alk. paper)
1. Naples (Italy)—History—1503–1734. 2. Naples (Italy)—Social life and customs. 3. City and town life—Italy—Naples—History. 4. Citizenship—Social aspects—Italy—Naples—History. 5. Group identity—Italy—Naples—History. 6. Rites and ceremonies—Italy—Naples—History. 7. Political culture—Italy—Naples—History. 8. Popular culture—Italy—Naples—History. 9. Naples (Italy)—Ethnic relations. 10. Naples (Kingdom)—History—Spanish rule, 1442–1707. I. Title.
DG848.12.M37 2011
945'.73107—dc22   2010011047

A catalog record for this book is available from the British Library.

Special discounts are available for bulk purchases of this book. For more information, please contact Special Sales at 410-516-6936 or specialsales@press.jhu.edu.

The Johns Hopkins University Press uses environmentally friendly book materials, including recycled text paper that is composed of at least 30 percent post-consumer waste, whenever possible. All of our book papers are acid-free, and our jackets and covers are printed on paper with recycled content.

CONTENTS

ACKNOWLEDGMENTS

This project began as an inquiry into the noble *seggi* (political wards or neighborhoods) of the early modern city of Naples. Because the *seggi* archives in the Archivio di Stato di Napoli were destroyed during World War II, primary sources had to be gleaned from wide reading in sixteenth- and seventeenth-century printed books published in Naples. Early printed books and manuscripts preserved in Naples at the Biblioteca Nazionale di Napoli and the Biblioteca della Società Napoletana di Storia Patria and in Rome at the Vatican Library and the Biblioteca Nazionale Centrale di Roma are the foundation upon which this very different book than the one originally imagined is based. Intellectual support for my research in Italy has benefited from generous friendship and conversation with Giuseppe Galasso, Rosario Villari, and Giovanni Muto.

Two Newberry Library fellowships were especially helpful at early stages of this project: a Newberry Library Exxon Fellowship in 1985/86 and a Newberry Library / National Endowment for the Humanities Fellowship in 1992/93. In 1985 I participated in a Newberry Seminar by Carlo Ginzburg on "Ritual Pillages" and began lifelong friendships with other *italianisti* at the Newberry (Albert Ascoli, John Martin, Martha Pollak, Mary Quinlan-McGrath, and Diana Robin). Important questions raised in that seminar as well as our discussions of research methods have much influenced my work. Trips to the libraries in Naples and Rome where most of the sources reside have been made possible by annual University of California at San Diego (UCSD) Academic Senate Research Grants. Grants from a six-month Fulbright Western European Regional Research Fellowship in 1986 and a Cesare Barbieri Fellowship (Trinity College, Hartford, Connecticut) in summer 1996 sustained longer research forays. I would like to thank Paul Gehl at the Newberry Library, Lynda Claassen at UCSD's Mandeville Special Collections, and all the library personnel at the many libraries I have visited.

Ritual studies of Renaissance and early modern Italian cities by Richard

Trexler on Florence, Edward Muir on Venice, and Maria Antonietta Visceglia on Naples and Rome have laid out the theoretical model and practical blueprint for my study. I am most grateful for their encouragement and suggestions along the way. Conversations and correspondence with younger scholars of ceremonies, festivals, and rituals in Naples have also been of great assistance on issues big and small, with special thanks to Sabina de Cavi, Dinko Fabris, Gabriel Guarino, Carlo Hernando, and Nick Napoli. Margaret Murata has shared her knowledge of early modern music, Renato Ruotolo and Tom Willette have shared their knowledge of early modern Neapolitan art, and Tommaso Astarita has been an insightful and meticulous critic of my manuscript.

Papers on various parts of the book have been presented over many years at conferences or seminars at the University of California at Los Angeles, University of California at Santa Cruz, University of California at San Diego, University of Chicago, University of Connecticut, University of Minnesota Twin Cities, Princeton University, the Center for Research on Festive Culture at the Newberry Library, the Renaissance Society of America, and the Sixteenth Century Society and Conference. I cannot record everyone who has commented and made helpful suggestions on these visits, but let me thank John Davis, Luce Giard, George Gorse, Sam Kinser, Jules Kirshner, Ed Muir, David Quint, Ingrid Rowland, and my UCSD colleagues, especially Jack Greenstein.

Thanks to Ana Varela Lago for translating the Juan de Garnica memorial on ceremonies, Ann Rose for research assistance on the Certosa di San Martino, Michele Greenstein for preparing the plates, and the Johns Hopkins University Press staff from Henry Tom and Suzanne Flinchbaugh to copyeditor Brian MacDonald for turning the manuscript into a much better book. Images have been provided with grateful thanks to Archivo dell'Arte / Luciano Pedicini, Naples; the Bibliothèque nationale de France, Paris; and the Soprintendenza per i Beni Architettonici e Paesaggistici e per il Patrimonio Storici, Artistici ed Etnoantropologici per Napoli e Provincia, Naples. Institutional support came from a UCSD Humanities Institute Fellowship in spring 1999 and from the UCSD Office of Research Subvention for Scholarly Publications.

Generous hospitality in Rome from Michele and Jack Greenstein, in Naples from Anna Maria Rao and from Giovanni Muto and Linda di Porzio, and in Chicago from Jeff Schamis and Eva Eves have made being away from home like being at home. Having completed writing this book over the past four years while serving as UCSD History Department chair, I would also like to thank Alejandra Ruiz, Jacqueline Griffin, and our whole departmental staff for their patience and good cheer through the many absences and distractions that have found my mind in early modern Naples rather than in San Diego. Last but not least, Cynthia Truant and our children Sara and Marc, who have suffered most from my frequent absences during the obsessive hunting for and gathering of materials away from home or the many hours spent cooped up in my study reading and writing, have been constantly in mind. Studying rituals and ceremonies public and private make one keenly aware of the importance of their form and meaning in one's own life and one's own family. I regret that I was not able to complete this project during the life of my father, Joe Marino, whose many sacrifices for my study and education deserve special remembrance and to whom I dedicate this book.

Becoming Neapolitan

Urbs et Orbis

The Problem of Identity and Solidarity

At the culmination of the French invasion of Italy that began in 1494, the French king Charles VIII was in the city of Naples to accept the fealty of its citizens and take the oath of allegiance after his conquest of the Kingdom of Naples. The *seggio del popolo* (the city ward of the commons) had been dissolved by the Aragonese conqueror Alfonso the Magnanimous forty years earlier in 1456; and when, on Sunday 16 May 1495, persons in the French king's entourage asked for the people and citizens of Naples, certain noblemen replied that *they* were the people, the citizens, and noblemen of the town. The non-Neapolitans present expressed their surprise to the king that such a town would have no citizens except noblemen.

A few days later at the Church of San Lorenzo, the seat of the city council, a native citizen and *aromatario* (a member of the spice dealer and druggist guild) named Batista Pirozo asked Carlo Mormile, a nobleman of the *seggio* of Portanova (one of the five noble city wards), what his most Christian Majesty, the King of France, had commanded regarding the city statutes and ordinances. Mormile retorted, "Why do you concern yourself about this city? We are the nobles and citizens of Naples, and you have nothing to do with it, you loathsome vermin!" Batista went around to the influential citizens and merchants of the city repeating Mormile's insult. The next morning they marched in their robes six hundred strong, two-by-two, to the Castel Capuano. They stood in the courtyard awaiting the king, who, on seeing them from the window, asked who they were. They responded that they were the citizens of the Neapolitan *popolo*, whereupon the king turned to Carlo Mormile, Lancilotto Annese, and the other noble councilors who had said there were no other citizens in Naples, who now did not know how to respond. Charles brought eight of the six hundred before him and learned from them their true number and their grievances. The king then granted them permission to unite in a council and congregation at the Church of S. Agostino, which became the center of the restored *seggio del popolo*.[1]

This famous confrontation in the city of Naples between its nobility and commons (*popolo*) recounted by the contemporary chronicle of Notar Giocamo dramatizes the problem of citizen identity and solidarity in the early modern city. Who were its citizens, and how were they made? How did the early modern city hold together? Why did its diverse social components of caste and class not pull it apart? How was civic culture created? Such conflict over urban space, civic symbols, and municipal power cuts to the quick of the ambiguity in Neapolitan urban life and of the overlapping and contending relationships within the early modern city in general: namely, voluntary and involuntary association; solidarity and social stratification; and cohesion and conflict among opposing parties, factions, clans or families, classes, and neighborhoods, as they engaged in agonistic relationships among themselves and with centralized authority.[2]

Piero Ventura's important work on Neapolitan citizenship has focused on the legal and political making of citizens.[3] Ventura cites a 1671 manuscript by Michele Muscettola, a nobleman of the *seggio* of Montagna, in which he divides Neapolitan citizens into four types: natives born or conceived in the city or its nearby villages (*casali*); children of the native-born who were born elsewhere; those made citizens by the city council representatives (*eletti*); and foreigners or residents of the Kingdom of Naples who, according to the royal decree of 1479, would buy or build a house to live in the city and marry a Neapolitan.[4] All citizens of the Neapolitan capital enjoyed exemption from direct taxation of the hearth tax paid by residents in the kingdom and from customs duties on imported and exported goods in the city or in the kingdom.[5] They were subject, however, to periodic parliamentary aids (*donativi*) and to various gabelles, which taxed consumption of flour, wine, grain, meat, cheese, salami, olive oil, fish, and other products. Citizens were eligible to hold office, had the right to vote for elected officials, and were guaranteed certain judicial privileges. As citizens, no distinction was made between noble and commoner; nevertheless, the common legal formula "cavalieri, cittadini e habitanti" did distinguish three groups: nobles of the *seggi*, commoners, and noncitizen foreigners. Aggregation into the noble *seggi* became more difficult and was virtually frozen by the end of the sixteenth century; such a closure, affecting "new men" trying to enter the exclusive ranks of the old city nobility, was widespread across all the Italian states at this time.

This book examines the making and unmaking of citizens—not their legal status or rights, but their identity and self-representation—through a study of the myths and rituals in early modern Naples under Spanish rule, especially from the mid-sixteenth to mid-seventeenth century under the reigns of three absentee Spanish kings: Philip II (1556–98), Philip III (1598–1621), and Philip IV (1621–65). This book analyzes how the rationale, invention, elaboration, mechanisms of transmission, and change over time in Baroque rituals affected authority, solidarity, and identity in Spanish Naples. Three optics—the church, the nobility, and the *popolo*—allow us to see how Spanish rule and church reform joined forces to impose themselves upon and transform commoner traditions from above. The problematic in this book derives from Machiavelli's discussion on how to gain and maintain a new state, as described in *The Prince*, chapter 3: "On Mixed Principalities"—that is, a newly gained principality "if it is not altogether new but rather an addition (so that the two together may be called mixed)" and, in particular, "when new possessions are acquired in a province that differs in language, customs, and laws."[6] For Machiavelli, the inherent difficulties stem from the changeability of the people, the offense to new subjects caused by occupying troops, the alienation of former local allies, and the necessity to avoid new laws and taxes in order to form one body from the old and new states in the shortest time possible. Machiavelli examines the opposite of gaining and maintaining a new state with his primary example: why "Louis XII, king of France, quickly occupied Milan and quickly lost it." Here we will be looking at the reigns of the three Philips of Spain, the rhetoric of good government and virtue, and solidarity among the citizens in Naples, over the sweeping trajectory from the Spanish conquest to their co-option practices and the eventual loss of Naples.

The city of Naples had a strong tradition of decentralized, neighborhood-based political organizations, both noble and popular, through the Middle Ages. Five noble neighborhood districts, consolidated from an original twenty-nine, were called *seggi* (seats) but also *tocci* (a corruption of the Greek topos), *teatri*, *piazze*, and *portici*. All these names conveyed the same meaning, that of a specific place in the city. In addition to a particular urban space, the word "seat," "place," "theater," "square," or "portico" carried with it two other ideas: one defined a political identity in Neapolitan city government; and the other, social distinctions between nobles and commoners, as well as among nobles themselves, who were divided not only by their competing *seggi* affiliations but also from other nobles who were not aggregated into the *seggi*.[7]

Who one was in Naples was inextricably linked to where one was from. One's residence or affiliation within one of the city's five noble districts (*seggio* of Capuana, Montagna, Nido, Porto, or Portanova) or its lone popular district (*seggio del popolo*), as much as one's right of precedence in the order of march in parades and processions, reflected one's status or honor among fellow citizens

and one's place in the local social and political structure. After the Spanish conquest of 1503, the streets and piazze of early modern Naples continued to be the
parade grounds for face-to-face interaction in the struggle for power among royal
officers, religious and secular clergy, resident nobles, non-noble citizens of the
popolo, and a sea of plebeians.

Other early modern Italian cities under princely or signorial regimes witnessed similar contests between neighborhood associational groups and their
rulers to control the city's social and symbolic geography.[8] Whether the six *seggi* of
Naples, the eighteen *alberghi* of Genoa, the sixteen *gonfaloni* of Florence, the seventeen *contrade* of Siena, the six *sestieri* of Venice, or the fourteen *rioni* of Rome,
the city's traditional wards or quarters wrestled with centralizing administrations
to retain their monopoly over municipal government and local affairs. The overall trend from late medieval to early modern states concerned the victory of the
central state, its bureaucratization, the power of its ministers, and the increased
authority of its ruler.

Larger territorial states might subordinate the decentralized government of
neighborhood organizations and leave them as atrophied medieval remnants.
Even in this case, though, social rivalries and violence could continue and must
be understood as normal rather than dysfunctional to the fabric of urban life if
we are to understand why the sociopolitical power structure of any particular
city persisted so long.[9] In Naples, however, the Spanish viceroy, the surrogate for
the absentee king, short-circuited "normal" conflictual relationships. The Spanish conquerors implemented a conscious policy of fortifying and reorienting the
city's urban landscape with an army and navy of occupation, as well as manipulating the social structure of the city by playing rival groups against one another.
Under the viceroys, garrisoned troops played an essential role in reshaping the
city's political fortunes; and patronage to a nonaristocratic bureaucracy of magistrates and judges (*togati*) and foreign merchant creditors (especially Genoese)
had a lasting impact on the development of citizen culture. Four contemporary
voices, two outsiders and two insiders, provide a good perspective on the fomenting crisis of political alienation in Naples under Spanish rule.

In 1559, the year that Philip II created the Council of Italy—which comprised
the three Spanish-ruled states of Milan, Naples, and Sicily—the Venetian ambassador to Spain, Michele Suriano, reported that "as for the morale of the Neapolitans, I can only repeat what they themselves always say: every government
sickens them and every state displeases them."[10] According to Suriano, Spain's
long half-century rule had "extinguished all the passions of the kingdom" to the

point that the King of Spain "could not rely on the loyalty of these subjects." In fact, "the present discontent of the nobles and *popolo*" stemmed from disaffection because of heavy taxes on the nobility, neglect of the *popolo*, and "the many defects in the government." Forced parliamentary aids (*donativi*) on the nobility and ever-increasing gabelles on city commoners, who had come to the capital to avoid direct taxes in the provinces, were impoverishing everyone with the result that the kingdom suffered three main defects: the burdensome billeting of Spanish troops, privilege and patronage given to Spaniards and so-called janissaries (the name given to the children of Spaniard-Neapolitan intermarriage), and unequal justice in not granting the nobility its rightful place of honor over an "insolent and presumptuous" *popolo*. No metaphor expresses the conflation of complaints better than the derogatory expletive janissaries for the children of Spanish-Neapolitan mixed marriages, because these elite Turkish troops and administrative servants of the sultan's household were conscripted young boys taken by force from their subject Christian families in the Ottoman Empire. The accusation of favoritism to a fifth-column offspring of foreigner-citizen marriages captures the Neapolitans' sense of political exclusion, alienation, betrayal, and loss.

An erudite Neapolitan *popolano*, Camillo Porzio, sent Don Iñigo López de Mendoza, marquis de Mondejar (viceroy, 1577–79) upon his appointment in 1575 an analysis of Naples in the same vein as that of the Venetian ambassador Suriano.[11] Porzio distinguished three kinds of men in the Kingdom of Naples— plebs, nobles, and barons—who shared a stereotypical personality profile in that they desired change, had litle fear of the law, highly valued honor, loved appearance more than substance, and were courageous and deadly; but, "on the present [Spanish] rule, they all agree they are little content."[12] Excessive taxation, lost housing, closed access to offices, and disregard for due honor to rank were the leading strands of criticism adopted by contending castes during the long prelude to the revolt of 1647.

A second foreign expert's diagnosis of the problem of Naples comes from Giovanni Botero's 1590s world history, *Relationi universali*, which includes an excursus on Naples in a section on the capital city's province of Terra di Lavoro. According to Botero, the area and population of the city of Naples would have been even larger were it not for a Spanish law against further construction.[13]

It is in compasse seven miles, but narrow: of late times it is much augmented, and would increase continually, if the King of *Spaine* had not forbidden a further increase of building; whereunto he was moved, partly by the complaints of the Barons (whose Tenants to injoy the liberties granted to the *Neapolitans*, did forsake their owne dwelling to seat themselves there): partly by the danger of rebellion, which in so mighty a City cannot easily be repressed.[14]

The motives for the law limiting urban construction and population growth are identified as twofold: baronial complaints (*querele*) against their rural subjects (*sudditi*), who were escaping both feudal jurisdiction and dues in order to gain the capital city's liberties (*essentioni*), that is, its privileges and immunities;[15] and the ubiquitous danger of popular uprisings (*sollevamenti popolari*) in so big a city.

The revised 1630 English translation, "now once againe inlarged according to moderne observation," adds a paragraph on Naples not found in Botero's original Italian that portrays Naples in a degenerative spiral from the home of Philosophy and the Muses to military occupation under the heavy hand of Spanish rule:

> *Naples* was first the receptacle of *Philosophie*, secondly, of the *Muses*; and now of Souldiery; the moderne inhabitants having their eares daily inured to the sound of the drum & fife, and their eyes to the management of Horses, and glittering of Armours. For the ambitious *Spaniard* now governeth this Kingdome by a Viceroy, directed (upon occasions) by the Councell appointed for Italy, which innovation hath principally befallen them, by their dependancie upon the Popes; who knowing (by reason of the brevitie of their lives) not otherwise to govern than by spleene, passion, and private respect, have continually disquieted the estate, until a third man hath bereaved both parties of their imaginary greatnesse. And this is the *Spaniard*, who making right use of former defaults, hath secured the peece: first, by taking all power and greatness from the Nobility, (more than titular;) and secondly, in suppressing the popular throughout the whole Kingdome by forren souldiery.[16]

From the antipapist, anti-Spanish, English perspective, Naples's former place in philosophy and the liberal arts had been replaced by an occupying army whose martial tunes and armored cavalry erased the arts and the sciences. The "ambitious" Spaniards introduced the institutional innovations of a viceroy and Council of Italy to take Naples away from its capricious papal overlord, and even from the Neapolitans themselves, by usurping local noble power and suppressing the *popolo* through force of arms. Both states, papal Rome and the Kingdom of Naples, remained bereaved in mourning for their lost "imaginary greatness." The daily presence of the sounds and sights of Spanish military occupation had ushered in wailing mourners in bereavement for lost glories.

As insiders, seventeenth-century Neapolitans themselves knew the consequences of cohesion or conflict in society at the time of the revolt of 1647. Nescopio Liponari, a pseudonym for one Scipione Napolini, published a *Relatione delle rivolutioni popolari successe nel distretto e regno di Napoli* in 1648 that compared the successful revolt against the introduction of the Inquisition in Naples one hundred years earlier in 1547 with the possibility for success in the present situation of 1647. "What greater contagion can befall a city," he asks, "than disunion among its citizens?" After citing historical examples of a city's ruin caused by factional division in ancient Carthage between the war party of Hannibal's family and the peace party of Hanno the Great during the Punic Wars, in France between the houses of Burgundy and Orleans prolonging the Hundred Years' War, in England between the houses of Lancaster and York during the War of the Roses, and in the Republic of Florence between the Whites and the Blacks after their Guelph victory over the Ghibellines, Liponari's text explains, "In sum it is this, the continued fever in a body comes from the disunion of the souls in the city and the kingdom."[17] From the image of a sick body, he turns to the traditional metaphor of the ship of state, here with leaks and holes unattended by a crew fighting among itself, such that "the ship sinks with all its goods."[18] Fission or fusion may result from the threat of external enemies or internal rivals. Solidarity is fostered by common institutions and traditions through shared stories and a history whose saints and secular heroes establish images and myths that become a part of an unspoken language of shared beliefs. Liponari reported such hidden transcripts of the private exchange of ideas and bravura in the Neapolitans' call for revolt, "What? Are we less than Palermo? Is our *Popolo* perhaps not more formidable and warlike? Don't we have perhaps more reason than others do, as we are more aggrieved and oppressed? Onward, onward to arms, resolution is needed, the time is opportune, it's no good to defer the enterprise, we ought to revolt, to hate our quarrels and disregard them is to make a promise and not keep one's word. These and similar laments made in diverse conventicles were now never public."[19] But how could such conversation be authorized and become a part of the public sphere of petition and protest?

Civic myths and rituals provided a shorthand answer to legitimate the establishment of citizen culture, as theory became practice and ideals were played out in public celebrations. Much of the argument for contemporaries in the sixteenth and seventeenth centuries centered on the city's origin myths and identifying who were the city's rightful citizens. Civic rituals and public ceremonies actualized and revivified those myths as a lived reality. Thus, myths and rituals attempted to rationalize the fissures in the body politic, but they could never really repair or remove them.

Naples was the capital of a kingdom stretching across the southern third of the Italian Peninsula with a population about one-tenth of the kingdom at large, ranging roughly from 100,000 to 300,000 city inhabitants in a population of 1 to 3 million kingdom-wide in the sixteenth and seventeenth centuries.[20] A wide array of verbal and visual sources on Neapolitan rituals, the transactions between artifacts and spectacles, and the interplay between beliefs and practices highlight the reciprocal relationship between religious and civic culture. Civic ritual became the site and circumstance for contesting the meanings of the ancient republic, and in the course of the revolt of 1647 four different theoretical models for republican government in Naples were proposed: a Dutch federal model, a Venetian oligarchic model, a ministerial model, and a military republic model.[21] The debates during the revolt of Naples in 1647 had been laid out in theory by different authors and had been embraced in practice by different constituents in the previous half century. A long tradition had contested republicanism in the five noble wards and the one non-noble ward within the town council of the city of Naples. The Spanish administration, for its part, tried to dampen and control such tendencies through a conscious policy of divide and conquer from its conquest of the city and kingdom in 1503 until the occupation of Naples by the Austrian Habsburgs in 1707 during the War of the Spanish Succession. The dispute in Naples centered on the contentious question, Who was a faithful citizen? What we must first understand are the structures and institutions of the city world of Naples, the historiographical foundation and organization of my argument, and the sources used to reveal themes running through the analysis of church, nobility, and *popolo* interactions.

The City World

The Neapolitan poet Giambattista Marino's letter upon his arrival in Paris to his friend Lorenzo Scoto back in Turin in 1615 gives some sense of how his impression of early modern Paris is, in reality, displaced writing about the great Baroque master's hometown of Naples and large urban capitals in general:

> I must tell you I am in Paris. . . . What shall I say about this country? I will tell you that it is a world. A world I say, not so much on account of its size, its people and its variety, as because it is remarkable for its extravagance. Extravagances provide the beauty of the world, for, being composed of contrasts, it is the combination of these contrasts that maintains it. So France too is full of contradictions and disproportions, and these nevertheless combine to form a concordant discord, which perpetuates it. Bizarre costumes, terrible rages, constant changes, perpetual civil

wars, disorders without rules, extremes without half-measures, tumults, quarrels, disagreements and confusions, all these things in short ought to destroy it, yet by some miracle, they keep it upright. Truly this is a world, and indeed an impossible world, even more extravagant than the world itself.[22]

Marino sees the city of Paris as a transformative world of extremes unto itself, whose extravagance is its dominant characteristic. Not only does one find there all things, material and immaterial, in the world; but, paradoxically, in Marino's aesthetic of the marvelous, the seemingly confusing and contradictory nature of such competing oppositions is precisely the glue that keeps this and all vibrant urban worlds together.

A fiscal census in 1528 after the collapse of the last of the French invasions of the Kingdom of Naples counted 155,000 inhabitants in the city of Naples. The next census, a special count to determine population for the distribution of bread during the famine of 1547, revealed a 37 percent increase to more than 212,203 inhabitants.[23] By 1606 the population of the city had grown to 270,000; and, before the devastating plague of 1656, it had reached 360,000 inhabitants to rank it about the same size as Paris as western Europe's largest city in the first half of the seventeenth century.[24] Provisioning became the first cause of alarm for its Spanish rulers by the mid-sixteenth century. Population growth, scarcity, unemployment, and crime were linked in the rationale of Spanish urban policy. An edict issued by Viceroy Pedro de Toledo in April 1550 identified vagabonds as criminals, expelled vagabonds and delinquents from the city, banned firearms, and attempted to control the working class by issuing labor permits. Such anti-vagabond decrees were again reissued in 1560 and 1586 and continued through the seventeenth century, a sure sign of the need for renewed efforts of enforcement.[25] Similarly, there was an attempt to control new construction. Between 1566 and 1718, it was illegal to build outside the city walls without a permit, although the oft-repeated building restrictions were largely ignored.[26] Spanish policy attempted to confine the city's burgeoning population within its medieval quarters and to exert authority over its extra-urban territory.

To understand the social geography of Spanish Naples, we must first visualize its sixteenth-century landscape as reconstructed by Viceroy Toledo (r. 1532–53). The old city, "an artificial theater sloping from the sea plain imperceptibly up the hills,"[27] was subordinated to an expanded city with a new center of gravity around the Spanish foundation at the Castel Nuovo. To the northeast of the Castel Nuovo, construction of the Via Toledo and its adjacent Spanish quarter was initiated in 1536 along the city wall's western perimeter and completed in 1560, while the *borgo* of Chiaia, which opened the Porta Romana to Pozzuoli, was developed along the Via and Riviera di Chiaia after 1538. At the base of this new urban development outside the dense streets of the old city's *seggi* to the west of the Castel Nuovo gardens, the viceroy's palace was built between 1540 and 1565, with a major intervention by Domenico Fontana under the viceroy Count of Lemos after 1600.[28] To the east, the heart of the old city's *popolo* quarter remained an untouched maze of streets and *piazze*. The linchpin of the sixteenth-century urban transformation was the previously vulnerable Castel Nuovo, which was fortified into a fortress impregnable from either land or sea. New city walls rose along the natural contours of the hills, integrating three old castles into one compact defensive system whose center was the new Spanish Quarter itself, which ran halfway up the hill from the two sea-level fortresses of Castel dell'Ovo and Castel Nuovo to Castel S. Elmo at the top of the hill above the city. The early modern city, then, comprised the inhabited population center in the old city, with new additions grafted onto its western periphery.

Early modern Naples can be seen in a naturalistic bird's-eye view in the 1566 map of Étienne Du Pérac (Stefano Dupérac), printed by Antonio Lafréry, the Burgundian engraver who set up shop in Rome about 1540 (fig. I.1).[29] The "Noble City of Naples," as it is called in the cartouche, and "Napoli Gentile" or "Nobile," as it appeared in numerous later copies of the Du Pérac plan over the next century, reveal the rough topography of the landscape, with the city proper at center stage.[30] The sharp boundary between city and countryside is significant. Inside its walls, Naples had no greenbelt of agricultural fields, as in Milan or Florence, and no empty, uninhabited areas as in Rome's abandoned ancient quarters. Outside the walls, open fields remained the dominant feature, except for some construction bordering the main routes east and west along the coast, and to the northeast outside the Porta Capuana and Porta San Gennaro. These dwellings corresponded to the city's seven suburbs (*borghi*), where three diverse populations sought to circumvent urban restrictions.[31] Rich nobles built sumptuous palaces and gardens on expansive sites impossible to find in the city; artisan and industrial workers set up shops to avoid guild regulations; and vagabonds, who crossed into the city as day laborers, found shelter. Not visible on Du Pérac's map is another ring of some thirty-five to forty-five nearby villages (*casali*), which enjoyed the same fiscal privileges and immunities as the capital and were juridically dependent on it.[32] They served as the city's immediate hinterland by providing agricultural and commercial needs and accounted for as many as 50,000 more people beyond the city's 212,000 inhabitants in 1547.

The Du Pérac map places the urban interventions of Pedro de Toledo into

Figure I.1. Étienne Du Pérac printed by Antonio Lafreri, *La Nobile Città di Napoli* (1566). Soprintendenza per i Beni Architettonici e Paesaggistici e per il Patrimonio Storici, Artistici ed Etnoantropologici per Napoli e Provincia, Naples.

plain view—walls, fortifications, streets, castle and marina embankments, and the new quarter for billeting Spanish troops[33]—and makes it clear that they stood guard as sentinels around the old city. Among the monuments listed in the legend are gates, castles, public buildings, churches, the *seggi*, private palaces, squares, streets, and fountains. The Du Pérac map stands as a starting benchmark to evaluate the city's social geography in the early modern period. In the mid-sixteenth century under Spanish rule, then, the *seggi* of nobles and *popolo* still had a special prominence in representations of the city.

The old city, for its part, inherited its dense habitations and characteristic streets from antiquity. The main streets, which were established by the rectilinear grid plan of the ancient Greco-Roman city, imprinted an underlying foundation of city blocks measuring 185 by 37 meters.[34] The three east-west *decumani* were wider and more prominent than the north-south *cardines*. The medieval city complicated this ordered space with a second street pattern. Religious foundations and private residences interrupted the narrower *cardines* and created a tangled web of irregular alleys and cul-de-sacs. Finally, overlaying the old city's architectural topography, numerous competing and complementary socioreligious and sociopolitical geographies (parishes versus *seggi*) defined associational spaces.

The sacred jurisdictions of innumerable churches, monasteries, and religious foundations abounded and overlapped. Religious organization of urban space proceeded from the Duomo, situated just northeast of the crossing of the *cardo* (Via del Duomo) and the *decumanus major* (Via Tribunale). In the Jesuit Giovan Francesco Araldo's chronicle from 1552–96, hundreds of churches and chapels ministered to the inhabitants of Naples: twenty-eight churches and parishes for the city's twenty-nine *ottine*, seventy other churches and chapels served by the secular clergy, about thirty other chapels inside the city's churches and monasteries, more than a hundred other chapels built by Neapolitans at the time of Charles I of Anjou (1266–85), and among them, eleven built and governed by foreign communities and thirty-one by the city's guilds.[35] From the archbishop's parochial reform of 1596, ecclesiastical organization filtered down to four major parishes (S. Giovanni Maggiore, S. Maria Maggiore, S. Giorgio Maggiore, and S. Maria in Cosmedin [in Portanova]), with thirty-three minor parishes subordinate to them.[36] In addition, Naples counted the extraordinary number of some one hundred monasteries and convents at the beginning of the seventeenth century.[37] At the same time, lay confraternities multiplied from 80 in 1603 to 100 in 1618 and 180 in 1623.[38] Most of the nobles of the *seggi* were enrolled in 5 of these confraternities, 4 of which were founded in the sixteenth century under Spanish rule—Misericordia (1532), Holy Ghost (1550), Seven Sorrows (1552), and

Immaculate Conception (1580)—but membership patterns were not at all congruent with *seggi* residence or inscription.[39]

For municipal government, the civic organization of the city's streets and *piazze* involved two contiguous jurisdictions, not next to each other, but one on top of the other. Twenty-nine noble districts were represented by the five *seggi* of the nobility; twenty-nine non-noble districts covered the same urban space, but were represented in the one commoner *seggio del popolo*. The five noble *seggi* of Naples included most of the city's noble families who had come to prominence in their own neighborhoods and then had amalgamated their twenty-nine neighborhood strongholds into larger district organizations by the thirteenth century. The *seggio del popolo*, which had been dissolved by the Aragonese in 1456, was reestablished by the French in 1495 after the episode described by Notar Giacomo at the swearing of fealty to Charles VIII. Its divisions were called *ottine*, a name that may be explained from the original election of eight of a district's best men to stand for election as captain.[40] This organization of the *popolo* under local captains reflected an earlier militia composed of nonpatrician citizens, but the curious prime number twenty-nine no doubt merely mimicked the number of original noble *seggi*.

This earlier juridical-institutional definition of the *popolo*, which referred to *all* the members of a community as was still meant by Machiavelli when he wrote of "the people," gave way to a clear difference in the connotation of the word as used by political writers in the seventeenth century.[41] This discontinuity signaled a distinction between wealthy, professional guildsmen, such as doctors, lawyers, merchants, and entrepreneurs, and the poor and working class, who were identified as the plebs and most often condemned with stereotypical characterization as vile, demonical, bestial, mad, and turbulent rabble.[42] In his 1620 commentary on Alciato's emblems, *Il Principe*, the Neapolitan city secretary Giulio Cesare Capaccio concludes his thoughts on the "best citizen" with a division of citizens into three kinds: "The best citizen is he who wishes the right for convenience; and he abhors the contrary without scandal. Euripides defines three kinds of citizens: the first are the rich, but they are useless. The second are the poor, who are envious of the rich. The third are those in the middle, who conserve that discipline which constitutes the city."[43] Capaccio elaborates on the inhabitants of Naples itself in his 1634 guide to Naples, *Il Forastiero*, by distinguishing "the nobles, *popolo*, and plebs. The first are of the *seggi* or outside the *seggi*. The second are in better or of middle condition. The third are the low people."[44] But Capaccio then further explains that the *popolo* should be understood to be divided into three kinds because "Naples has one *Popolo* in name but many in fact." The first and primary group comprised "gentlemen by antiquity, by wealth, by possession of feudal lands, and by their noble style of living." The second group included "persons promoted by the Tribunals," that is, lawyers who have become magistrates and may even be granted titles. The third group was composed of those "in trade and commerce."[45] And, likewise, Capaccio finds the plebeians divided into three grades: "artisans who live more civilly," "those declining somewhat from civility," and "those who with the lowest employment have reduced themselves to such baseness that they cannot be claimed in any way to be of true *popoli* status."[46] This distinction is not without consequence for Capaccio, whose disdain for the plebs knows no bounds: "The base-born plebs can in no way obscure the fame of so glorious a city. . . . But, as I say, that vile, seditious, and, above all, ignorant plebs can cast a stain on it; in the long run, though, they wash it off with their own blood."[47] Depending on time period and context, Neapolitan sources may refer to the *popolo* as all the inhabitants of the city; sometimes as the middling group of wealthy property owners, professionals, and merchants; and sometimes as these groups with or without the lower guildsmen.

The noble *seggi* were defined geographically in the historic city center. Four *seggi* were identified with the four quadrants of the old city within the ancient walls. The two oldest *seggi* were the most important. Capuana, in the northeast quarter, was associated with the important gate to northern Italy, the Porta Capuana, and had its "seat" on the *decumanus major* just east of the *cardo* crossing. Nido, in the southwestern quarter, commanded the old western Cumana Gate and had its seat on the *decumanus inferior*. Two newer *seggi*, Montagna, named from its location on the sloping terrain of the northwestern quarter, and Forcella, in the southeastern quarter, were amalgamated into one *seggio* after the fourteenth-century plagues. The two other new *seggi*, to the south toward the harbor, took their names from their locations, Porto at the ancient port near S. Giovanni Maggiore and Portanova near the new port.

In purely spatial terms, one could visualize the distribution of *seggi* as forming a single configuration within the walls, except for the two newer *seggi* outside the ancient city near the port. The two oldest *seggi*, Capuana (home of the Caracciolo clan) and Nido (home of the Carafa clan), dominated the important eastern and western gates of the city, while the unified *seggio* Montagna-Forcella was squeezed in the middle. The perception that the center of the city was its most sacred precinct (near the site of the Duomo) is neatly confirmed, because that was precisely the contested territory.[48]

Iconographic evidence suggests that this parallelism between larger kingdoms, or the world at large, and the city was consciously portrayed. The coat of arms of Capuana had originally been an unbridled horse (later, after 1250, a bridled one) on a blue field, and that of Nido, an unbridled horse rampant in a field of gold.[49] Not by chance, the coat of arms of the city of Naples was an un-bridled horse—free and independent. The two dominant *seggi* each claimed to be the city proper, just as the city claimed to be the world.

The city itself thus became the arena of political conflict. The members of the five noble *seggi* chose twenty-nine representatives (six each, save Nido with five) in keeping with the tradition of the twenty-nine earlier neighborhood centers. From these deputies, called the Cinque and the Sei, each noble *seggio* selected a single deputy (except Montagna, which had the right to two representatives in light of its amalgamation with the former *seggio* of Forcella). The *eletto del popolo* was the deputy of the one non-noble *seggio* that was not bound by a simple geo-graphic district but represented all the *ottine* in the city at large.[50] The *seggio di popolo* rebuilt its sixteenth-century seat in the city's southeast quarter below the defunct noble *seggio* of Forcella at the monastery of S. Agostino alla Zecca, near its original site in Via della Sellaria.[51] These seven *eletti* (six noblemen and one commoner) formed the city council, called the Tribunal of San Lorenzo, the nom-inal authority in city government named after its meeting place in the Church of San Lorenzo. In addition to being in charge of grain provisioning for the city, the city council also had jurisdiction over public works, streets and roads, water, public health, city finances, public ceremonies, and religious processions.

Not all noble families, however, were aggregated into the neighborhood dis-tricts. In addition to the primary group in the *seggi,* Giovanni Muto identifies three additional kinds of nobility in Spanish Naples: *nobiltà fuori dei seggi, no-biltà titolata,* and *baronaggio non titolato.*[52] Nobles outside the *seggi* included two categories: native families or foreign nobles (both Spanish and Italian) recently arrived in the city, and families of dubious nobility with mercantile roots or families that had recently purchased titles.[53] Titled nobles who exercised feudal jurisdiction in the countryside and had recently taken up residence in the Nea-politan capital could be inscribed in a noble *seggio* in Naples or in their respective provincial towns, such as Salerno with three *seggi,* Trani with four, and Tropea, Bari, Barletta, Cosenza, and Catanzaro each with one; but most members of the feudal nobility did not belong to a *seggio.* Finally, nontitled or small-time nobles of the baronage from the countryside who owned a feudal town or held vassals found themselves ever more subject to economic fluctuations and shifting politi-cal fortunes. Numerous noble families, both old and new, rich and poor, as well as foreigners, who were excluded from the existent *seggi* and thus from city gov-ernment, could become significant players in the urban contests for power.

When political conflicts within the city of Naples erupted in the traumatic upheaval of the revolt of 1647, we can see the fissure in the political geography of the city delineated in the 1648 map of Pierre Miotte (fig. I.2). While the *popolo* in revolt was able to secure the gates of the old city and the port as well as the access roads in and out of the city north, south, east, and west, the Spanish were able to pivot west with moorings between the pier (*molo*) and the Castel dell'Ovo onto Mergellina. The fortifications put in place by Pedro de Toledo on the western perimeter of the old city became the bulwark for the Spanish refortifying of the city by sea. Spanish troops were also able to repel the *popolo* from strongholds in the western addition, blocking the road up to the Castel S. Elmo and the Certosa di S. Martino at S. Lucia del Monte, on the heights above the royal palace at Pizzofalcone, and at the two positions just to the east of the Castel Nuovo and the *molo* at the Dogana Grande and the Posto dell'Olmo. The result was political stalemate with a clear line of demarcation between the free, old city held by the *popolo* and the Spanish-occupied new city on the west.

Historiographical Tradition and Argument

The voluminous studies of early modern Naples under Spanish rule by Giuseppe Galasso, Rosario Villari, Aurelio Musi, Giovanni Muto, and Maria Antonietta Visceglia have set the standard for scholarship on the political, social, economic, and cultural world of the Neapolitan capital and its provinces. Studies of ritual in early modern Naples have been pioneered by Franco Mancini and developed by the broad, interdisciplinary research of literary scholars such as Michele Rak, music historians such as Dinko Fabris, and historians such as Visceglia, Carlos Hernando, and Gabriel Guarino.[54] Four recent dissertations merit special mention. Guarino provides an introduction to state ceremonies in Spanish Naples, with special emphasis on the role of the viceroy in order to understand the "communication and reception of symbolic forms of power" through civic processions, state celebrations, emblems, and fashion.[55] Sean Fidalgo Cocco has studied antiquarian writings on the volcanic landscape and new eruptions around the Bay of Naples from the Campi Flegrei to Vesuvius after 1631, as they relate to the religious and political life of Spanish Naples in scientific and symbolic terms.[56] Sabina de Cavi's architectural history dissertation on Domenico and Giulio Cesare Fontana in Naples has been revised and published in a study on the use of artistic projects and public space in the cultural politics of the Spanish monarchy in Naples.[57] And Céline Dauverd has described the extensive role of the Genoese in Naples on Holy Thursday and the feast of Corpus Christi as part of a larger examination of the economy, society, and culture of the Genoese trading diaspora in Naples.[58]

More than a quarter century ago, Richard Trexler's study of ritual in Renaissance Florence and Edward Muir's in Renaissance Venice opened up ritual studies in Renaissance and early modern Italy as a way to understand politics and culture, society and personality; and, more recently, Maria Antonietta Visceglia has added Rome to the list of ritual cities so studied. All cities in Renaissance and Baroque Italy and Europe were "ritual cities," and each used similar means to make their inhabitants into distinctive citizens.[59] The unique contexts of this commonality of practices, the particulars of local topography and historiography, and the contingent interplay of castes and classes reveal configurations and characteristics of infinite variety in local stories worth telling and retelling.

This book on Neapolitan rituals and citizen culture describes citizen participation under Spanish rule in order to trace how an early modern monarchy maintained control over one of its kingdoms in the sixteenth and seventeenth centuries. Not just one of the kingdoms in Italy but the largest principality in the peninsula, and called by contemporaries "The Kingdom" (Il Regno), Naples was the name of both the country and its capital, a capital that stood at the center of the city's and kingdom's power, tradition, and ceremony. Naples had a distinctive foundation myth as the city of the Sirens; and its historical development, while still sharing the same kind of classical and Christian myths and metaphors as the other ancient cities in Italy, passed from Greek and Roman to Byzantine rule, before an independent dukedom returned it to the Latin West and medieval centuries under Norman, Hohenstaufen, Angevin, and Aragonese rulers. Naples saw itself endowed with an unsurpassed natural beauty and legendary agricultural abundance; located on the banks of the river leading to the entrance of the underworld as sung by Virgil in antiquity; infused with a deep and early Christianity that made it the New Jerusalem; built with enduring monuments, churches, palaces, and fountains; shaped by a history of successive dynasties that fostered a fierce independence; sustained by a faithful noble class renowned for its valor and comportment; and blessed with a burgeoning population as the largest city in Spain's four-continent empire.

Not by chance, in *The Prince* Machiavelli makes Alfonso V's Aragonese conquest of Naples in 1442 one of his first two examples of a newly acquired state, one grafted onto an already existing state; and Spanish ideology and practice after the 31 December 1503 conquest always presented itself as the legitimate heir and continuation of Aragonese rule in Naples. In his last years, Philip II's interest in his royal ancestry and genealogy, for example, led to two royal architectural

Figure I.2. Pierre Miotte, *Città di Napoli* (Rome, 1648). © Archivio dell'Arte / Luciano Pedicini, Naples. The city of Naples lies under the protection of the Virgin and Child flanked by the seven original and six new patron saints of the city. Miotte numbers the strongholds of the *popolo* (*circles in the light area*) and Spanish (*squares in the dark area*) with those contested or taken by the Spanish (*circle in a square*) at the end of the revolt of 1647. The *popolo* held the old city and port, as well as land access to the city (the mountain to the west separating the city from Pozzuoli and the road to Rome, the heights to the north and the road to Capua, and approaches from the east and south). The Spanish held the strategic western perimeter of the city and the sea to Mergellina as well as Pozzuoli and its Gulf.

Popolo (Old city and port)

5   Lanterna del Molo
13 Palazzo della Vicaria
14 Chiesa di S. Domenico
21 Monasterio di S. Sebastiano
22 Torrione del Carmine
23 Piazza del Mercato
30 Palazzo delli Studii Regii
35 Fosse del Grano
45 Port' Alba
46 Porta di Costantinopoli
47 Porta di S. Gennaro
48 Porta Navale
49 Porta Capuana
50 Porta del Carmine
51 All Gates along the Marina

Popolo (Control of Land Access)

15 Capodimonte passo
16 Ponte della Maddelena
31 Montagniola
32 Posillipo
34 Poggioreale
37 Vomero passo
39 Grotto di Pozzuoli
52 Fortino al Capo di Posillipo

Popolo lost to Spanish

10 Posto S. Lucia del Monte
11 Posto di Pizzofalcone
24 Posto dell'Olmo
25 Dogana Grande

Popolo fight Spanish

36 S. Maria delle Parte

Spanish fight *Popolo*

29 Houses flattened by Spanish cannon

Spanish

1   Castel S. Elmo
2   Castel Nuovo
3   Castel dell'Ovo
6   Fortino del molo
7   Certosa di S. Martino
12 Chiesa del Gesù
20 Chiesa di S. Chiara
33 Palazzo del Vicerè
38 S. Leonardo à Chiaia
40 Galleys and ships in port
41 Pozzuoli
42 Porta di Spirito Santo
43 Porta Medina
44 Porta di Chiaia
53 Cavallarizza del Re

commissions that created pantheons of the Aragonese kings of Naples in the sacristy of S. Domenico Maggiore in 1593–94 and of the Angevin kings of Naples in the cathedral in 1598–99.[60] In late medieval and early modern Italy, there was nothing unusual about monarchical rulers fabricating genealogies in order to support their legitimacy and justifying, in Machiavelli's words, their "gaining and maintaining a new state." The false assumption that an absent king necessarily weakened his control over such lands and would dilute the city's ceremonial life is contradicted in Naples by the deference afforded to the Spanish king's substitute vice-king and the proliferation of minor "courts" among the resident nobility.[61] Supposed longing for the absentee king is a vestige of the outdated teleology of the nationalist state. On the contrary, the king's absence could make foreign rule more tolerable, as local, home rule could assert itself while the king remained in his subjects' eyes an objective mediator and benevolent moderator over the actions of any viceroy and between the internal rivalries among the city's various factions.

After the failure of the Captain General, Odet de Foix, Monseigneur Lautrec's last French invasion into the kingdom in 1528 and the redistribution of titles, fiefs, and offices of pro-French loyalists to the nobility and subjects loyal to Spain under the viceroy Prince of Orange in 1530, the alliance between the Spanish monarchy and the nobility defined a distinctive feature of Naples under Spanish rule. This allegiance remained strong and unbroken for two centuries, except for the two fleeting incidents in 1510 and 1547 when the nobility and *popolo* successfully joined forces to resist the imposition of the Inquisition. The failure of any other sustained collaboration between the nobles and commons of Naples ossified the political development of the state, a fact that can be demonstrated in the disciplining and routinization of the city's ritual life.

Investigating Neapolitan ritual practices allows us to test how the factions in the city held together and came apart, and how effective the monarchy was in drawing its subjects to itself in forging a unified state. The present study of the relationship between the city's mythical representations and ritual practices is divided into two parts. Part I establishes the urban setting in a stratigraphic overview of the dramatic unities of time, space, and action in the city of Naples during the sixteenth and seventeenth centuries. Two chapters present the tradition of myth and the structure of ritual as it traces their changes over time.

Chapter 1 explicates the problem of the myth of the origin of the city in Italy in general and Naples in particular. Examining Naples in this wider context allows for an integration of the historical sweep of events and movements as they appeared in contested interpretations by local, contemporary historians. The key political moments in Naples—the 1585 bread riot; the treason of the viceroy Duke of Osuna (1616–20); the revolt of 1647; and the plague of 1656—had profound effects upon the state control of ritual practice.

Chapter 2 focuses on time and space in the playing out of the two seasonal cycles, fall-winter and spring-summer, of the Neapolitan ritual calendar. Charles V's 1535–36 winter sojourn in Naples set a determinative pattern for an amalgamation of Burgundian and Aragonese ritual practices together with local Neapolitan customs and papal or religious ceremonies. The ritual space of procession routes through the noble *seggi* and the working-class quarter of the *popolo* inscribed a map of power and possession on the city and in its citizens' minds.

Part II establishes the basis of urban solidarities in religious and civic rituals practiced on the city's major liturgical and saints' feast days and on the superimposed, life-cycle-event holidays of the Spanish royal family. It explains how the two nodes of church and state power in the city, operating within the dominant mode of a system of hierarchical exchanges and patron-client networks, provided opportunities and obstacles of engagement within the city power structure for ritual practice in the three venues of church, court, and city.

Chapter 3 shows how rituals reinforce the model of three levels of patronage propagated by the church: saintly patronage (*patronato*), cultural and artistic patronage (*mecenatismo*), and political patron-client relationships (*clientelismo*). It analyzes these three kinds of patronage in three examples: first, the Neapolitan calendar of the saints, with emphasis on the numerous patron saints of the city as recorded in the hagiographical writings of the most prolific author of the sixteenth century, the local nobleman-bishop Paolo Regio, and the example of the clientele network of the false *beata* Suor Guilia de Marco; second, the apocalyptic iconography of the New Jerusalem in the sacristy of the Certosa di San Martino and the spiritual mission of the cloistered Carthusian monks, whose prayers watched over the city; and third, the obsequies celebrated in the cathedral in commemoration of the virtues and deeds of Philip II upon his death.

Chapter 4 likewise employs three examples to emphasize the centrality of games and play in the nobility's celebrations at court and at its summer retreat in the western suburb of Posillipo in order to emphasize the wiles of fortune and the model of virtue established for good government. This chapter begins with an explication of the important fairy tale about making a forlorn princess laugh, which is placed at the center of the quintessential court poet and dramatist Giambattista Basile's *Lo Cunto de li cunti*, as a way of identifying the underlying rules of court society. The chapter further analyzes the fantasy of the meeting between foaming sea and sylvan forests in thanksgiving for the absentee king Philip III's return to health in 1620 and traces the Neapolitan celebrations upon the births of the children of the absentee king Philip IV in 1639 and 1658, both of which highlighted elaborate musical dramas with extensive dance ensembles involving noblemen and noblewomen at court.

Chapter 5's focus on *popolo* participation and expression of *allegria* during Neapolitan festivals suggests how ritual works in creating and reinforcing identity and citizenship. It compares the competing festivals of Corpus Christi and St. John the Baptist in their religious and civic rivalry, contrasts Neapolitan Carnival and its religious antidote of the Forty Hours' Devotion with the nobility's summer festival of Posillipo, and shows how ritual traditions became interwoven in the spontaneous funeral of the exhumed body of Masaniello. Here the Tridentine Church tried to use the Eucharist to tame and reclaim popular urban ritual and rebaptize it in the manner of religious reform.

Finally, in the conclusion the promotion of noble virtues displayed in chapels and palace rooms allows us to generalize on the role of spectacle (rituals and representations) in the making of citizen identity. Being and becoming Neapolitan were enacted in the city's ritual practice through noble participation in and patronage of ritual. Authentic, autochthonous local rituals were infused with Aragonese customs and Burgundian models by their Spanish Habsburg heirs in Naples and manipulated to become mannered, routinized forms that lost their original content or meaning. Just as the *palio* in Siena after its conquest by Florence in 1555 became the central ritual confirming that city's involution, the pacification of Naples in the sixteenth century under Charles V fostered a policy of "divide and conquer" among the factions in Naples, and the patronization of the Tridentine reform of the church under Philip II froze local rituals into the celebration of the city's imagined greatness. Thus, under Philip IV, as the power of the Spanish monarchy in Europe and America was weakened by the seventeenth century's internal revolts and external wars and Naples had its wealth exported to support failing imperial ventures, local Neapolitan citizen culture turned more and more in upon itself in nostalgic reverie.

Sources and Themes

In Spanish Naples during the reigns of the three Philips, public ceremonies in the streets and squares, courts, and churches of Naples—recurrent performances of fixed, movable, and extraordinary feasts in religious processions, devotional rites, civic festivals, and popular demonstrations—not only combined the religious and the secular but also most often found the two spheres inseparable

and indistinguishable. A contiguous set of contradictions—cohesion and conflict, continuity and change, causality and contingency—mirrored the congruence between the religious and secular spheres, as context and means gave way
to content and meaning.

Neapolitan religious, civic, and familial rituals provide an extraordinary prism
to examine citizen culture and to analyze the relationship between politics and religion in the formation, maintenance, and changes in citizen culture in the early
modern state. Because of its political subordination to its absentee Habsburg
monarch in Spain, Spanish Naples accommodated its local traditions to its foreign masters and their support for the program of Tridentine reform, as the political agendas of native groups colluded or came into conflict with their Spanish
overlords. Neapolitan rituals and representations promoted associational bonds
that cut across traditional alliances and group rivalries to hold the early modern
city together, at the same time that they produced new fractures and antagonisms
among monarchical, religious, noble, commoner, and plebeian organizations.
Thus, this study aims at understanding the transactions between public rituals
and the process of the rise and fall of political authority, group solidarity, and
individual identity in the Baroque city.

In early modern Naples, the Spanish viceroy, the church, and the city's various
citizen bodies of nobles and commoners employed a Baroque political lexicon
of ephemeral structures, images, words, theater, and music in religious, mythological, astrological, and political allegories through an amalgam of religious
and secular celebrations, popular and superstitious practices, and charitable and
political offices to pledge felicity and fidelity between rulers and ruled. Ephemeral decorations, the temporary urban art and architecture erected for civic and
religious holidays and celebrations—gates and arches, fountains and mechanical
paraphernalia, drapery and bunting, paintings and statues, carts and floats, placards and poems, and lanterns and fireworks—proliferated along the well-defined
parade routes that crisscrossed the premodern city. The multiplicity of media in
reinforcing registers was used to create a common civic culture among the city's
contending interest groups, but it did not drown out their often discordant and
conflicting agendas that could erupt in urban unrest, most notably during the
nine-month revolt of 1647–48 that was touched off at the feast of Santa Maria
della Grazia on 7 July 1647.[62] Through its viceroy, the self-styled beneficent and
vigilant monarchy employed the rhetoric and iconography of humanist virtue to
preside over celebrations of secular and religious feasts in the kingdom's official
holiday calendar promulgated in 1555;[63] for the absentee royals' life-cycle events
(deaths, coronations, marriages, births, and sicknesses); and in extraordinary

emergencies of famine, plague, war, earthquake, and volcanic eruption. Church and state together manipulated historical time to rewrite the past and restructured urban space to control the present through the imposition of a new ritual calendar, patronage of art and architectural programs, the mythological lore of classical erudition, the obscure language of emblematic invention, the mannered poetry of metaphorical conceits, and the conspicuous display of bourgeois pretension.

The social and spatial context of such rituals and their complex representation connected Neapolitans in a symbolic geography and a polemical history that reinforced a number of myths about Naples—namely, that it was the most noble and most faithful city,[64] that its founding preceded that of Rome and was not subject to papal pretensions,[65] that it remained independent and was never defeated or conquered,[66] and that its rich agricultural bounty not only made it a land of abundance for its own people to lead carefree lives but provided a surplus of both raw materials and tax revenue that could be exported to support the wider Spanish Empire in Europe.[67] The political debates and cultural wars contested symbols, values, and meaning, as late Renaissance culture confronted Counter-Reformation spirituality. These civic conflicts centered on the failure of political and economic processes; societal fears from external and internal enemies; social class antagonisms and social mobility; religious reform from above; and resistance from traditional practices, scientific culture, and popular superstition. The Baroque splendor of feasts and favoritism such as that of St. John the Baptist Day, propped up and patronized as they were by Spanish viceroys, ossified in the late seventeenth century as popular support wavered under pressure from church attempts to discipline and domesticate popular religiosity and as imperial power waned with Spanish rule in defensive disarray.

Diaries, guidebooks, festival books, poems, orations, eulogies, emblems, and illustrations or descriptions of paintings, sculptures, and ephemeral architectural inventions and *apparati* support my argument through five themes embedded throughout the book. First, the theme of "The Cult of the Saints" examines the social and religious geography of the city. Early modern guidebooks and saints' lives are especially helpful here in mapping itineraries locating the myriad religious relics that helped to create urban solidarity out of popular piety.[68] The number of city patron saints, for example, increased dramatically from an original seven to a total of thirty-two by the end of the seventeenth century. Two kinds of "minor" art objects are part of saint cults. First, reliquaries in Neapolitan churches preserved thirty-six complete saints' bodies, fourteen heads, twenty-eight arms, eighteen ribs, the blood of six saints, one of the nails of the Cross, five pieces of the Cross, eleven thorns from Christ's crown, the Virgin's milk, a feather of the archangel Gabriel, and countless saints' teeth, bones, hair, and skulls.[69] Second, extraordinary ex-votos were deposited at the most popular Neapolitan pilgrimage site outside the city, Madonna dell'Arco, only eleven kilometers from the Carmine Gate around to the northern side of Vesuvius. With 1,577 ex-voto images preserved from the sixteenth century (688) and seventeenth century (889), we can identify five main categories of petitions for healing: from illness, from accidents, in the life of peasants, in the life of fishermen, and from violence.[70] From this perspective, rituals act as a mode of prayer that joins the religious and civic spheres in the four kinds of prayer—praise, contrition, thanksgiving, and supplication.

Second, the theme of "The Architecture of Devotion" examines renewal of the diocesan clergy, both secular and religious, and the design and use of buildings, both parish churches and religious houses. Sixtus V's unsuccessful reform of the Dominican houses in Naples in 1586, for example, has been reinterpreted as more a political conflict between the nobility and the *popolo* than a religious matter.[71] Whether diocesan reform in 1596, which reorganized the city into thirty-three minor parishes subordinate to four major ones, or contemporary construction projects among many of the city's hundred monasteries and convents—Theatines (1583), Jesuits (1584), Dominicans (1588), Oratorians (1590), and Carthusians (1591)—religious patronage and practice flourished in late sixteenth-century Naples through the mid-seventeenth century. Such religious architectural renewal coincided with a spectacular building boom with more than 150 church and monastic projects begun between 1600 and 1650 alone.[72]

A third theme, "Spanish Good Government," depends upon ceremonial and festival books, chronicles, diaries, and histories. After Philip II's death, obsequies were held in Naples where an ornate mausoleum designed by Domenico Fontana with fifteen statues and twenty-four emblems stood at the center of the elaborately decorated cathedral with twenty-eight narrative paintings of the king's deeds and an additional thirty-three emblems and mottos—all detailed in Ottavio Caputi's contemporary ekphrasis.[73] Similarly, descriptions of the images, monuments, writings, and emblems from the celebrations of royal births and marriages, from the procession on the vigil of St. John's Day, and from Carnival underline the interaction between church and state and among the Spanish viceroy, the nobility, and commoners of Naples.[74] Notably, Francesco Orilia's 501-page book *Lo Zodiaco, over, idea di perfettione di prencipi*, with 143 engravings and 72 emblems, situates the 1629 procession of the viceroy as the sun moving through the celestial signs of the zodiac and the embodiment of princely virtues.[75] Detailed descriptions of the viceregal ceremonial is provided by three Spanish contemporary witnesses: Juan de Garnica, a doctor of law with experience in Naples who sought patronage from the Spanish ambassador in Rome (Gonzalo Fernández de Córdoba, Duke of Sessa) in 1595; Miguel Diéz de Aux, an expert on Neapolitan court protocol from the 1580s to 1622 and master of ceremonies for the viceroy Count of Benavente (1603–10) and viceroy Count of Lemos (1610–16); and Joseph Raneo, the *portero de camera* and master of ceremonies for the viceroy Duke of Alba (1622–29) and the viceroy Count of Monterrey (1631–37).[76] The travel journal of the French visitor to Naples, Jean-Jacques Bouchard, follows Neapolitan festivals from 17 March to 6 November 1632.[77] And Neapolitan diarists Scipione Guerra, Andrea Rubino, Innocenzo Fuidoro, and Domenico Confuorto, who chronicle events from 1574 to 1699, all give continued life to ephemeral art and festivals that allow us to explore the intersection of politics and culture.[78]

The fourth theme, "The Coming Millennium," draws together visual and verbal references to apocalyptic visions in sermons, spiritual writings, and religious art. A Counter-Reformation apocalypse program executed by two Spanish Netherlandish intarsia artists in the sacristy of the Carthusian monastery of San Martino overlooking the city, Naples's richest religious foundation, juxtaposes twenty-six Vitruvian images of the ideal city with an eleven-panel Old Testament and fifteen-panel Apocalypse cycle to situate the monks as intermediaries in the transformation of Naples itself into the New Jerusalem, watched over and prayed for by the monks' vigilance. And, of course, the Calabrian Dominican who studied in Naples from 1589 to 1594, Tommaso Campanella (1568–1639), had already asserted the end of the four monarchies and the death of the anti-Christ in his early draft of *La Monarchia di Spagna* circa 1593–95 and would soon thereafter complete his utopia, *La Città del Sole*, in prison in Naples in 1602.[79]

Finally, a fifth theme, "Civic Humanism and Court Society," especially extolled in the writing of four prolific literati who often published sonnets in each others' works, had a formative effect on how the cultural world of late sixteenth- and early seventeenth-century Naples saw itself. Paolo Regio (1545–1607), a member of the Accademia degli Svegliati, published two literary works before his career as a hagiographic writer; Tommaso Costo (1545?–1612), who was a member of the Accademia della Crusca, member and secretary in 1583 of the Accademia dei Sereni Ardenti, and secretary in 1586 of the Accademia degli Svegliati, published *Il Fuggilozio*, the quintessential paean to Neapolitan court culture in his collection of anecdotes for the summer festival of the Spassi di Posillipo, in 1596; Giulio Cesare Capaccio (1552–1634) served as city secretary of Naples from 1602, later at the Duke of Urbino's court at Pesaro while in short exile from Naples, and was a founding member of the Accademia degli Oziosi; and Giambattista Basile

(1566?–1632) attended the Gonzaga court at Mantua, was a founding member of the Accademia degli Oziosi, and had his celebrated court pastimes in his collection of fairy tales, *Lo Cunto de li cunti* (the so-called *Pentamerone*), published posthumously in 1634–36. The aristòcratic circles, literary societies, and academies of Naples and Venice played significant formative roles for all four authors. They all followed in the footsteps of an earlier generation of dominant cultural figures who first made their intellectual mark in Naples in the second half of the sixteenth century—the philosopher Bernardino Telesio (1509–88), the scientist and dramatist Giambattista della Porta (1535–1615), and the poet Torquato Tasso (1544–95).[80]

What we find in Naples is the jewel of the Spanish Crown, an absentee capital much more connected and much more like other large early modern urban centers than is usually imagined, a city with an ancient mythic tradition, and a deep religiosity bursting with saints and celebrations. Yet, it was a time of decline and deficits amid rapid growth and grandiose expenditures. It was a world riven by caste and class, where the delicate balancing act of Spanish rule played off one group against another and attempted in tandem with the church to take control of citizen culture. As local wealth was extracted to feed the insatiable appetite of foreign wars and as royal propaganda became more imperial, citizen culture became more involuted and imperial ideology less reflective of political realities.

PART ONE

URBAN STRATIGRAPHY AND THE SIREN'S LYRE

Myth and History

From Italy to Naples

The Myth of the Foundation of the City in Italy

Why are myths on the foundations of cities invented and propagated? What is the relationship between such myths and local rituals? How do myth and ritual work in telling the story of a city and its people?

Beginning his *Discourses on the First Ten Books of Livy* (1512–19) with a first chapter on "What have been universally the beginnings of any city whatever, and what was that of Rome" (bk. I, 1.1), Machiavelli initiates readers into the origins of republicanism in general with a steering assumption from his reflections on Rome's beginnings—namely, that the foundation principles of the city in its laws and ordering shaped its consequent storied *virtù* and subsequent long history from republic to empire.[1] With his typical binary logic, Machiavelli immediately assigns the birth of all cities to one of two groups—"either by men native to the place where they are built or foreigners." In four examples—Athens and Venice for native, Alexandria and Florence for foreign foundations (bk. I, 1.2–3)—Machiavelli expresses no critical concern for the veracity of the myth of each city's foundation. Whether Sulla's soldiers or inhabitants from Fiesole founded Florence is of no importance, for the two variant accounts agree on what is important to Machiavelli—namely, that Florence's origins date from the time of the ancient Roman republic.[2] Machiavelli concludes by returning to the foundation of Rome to negate the importance of his original native/foreigner distinction. Whether the foreigner Aeneas or the native Romulus founded Rome is immaterial, as long as the founder provided a model *virtù* demonstrated by "the choice of site" and "the ordering of laws." Typical humanist weighing of the sources for the truthfulness of the myth of the foundation of the city is simply left out in favor of what matters, the underlying fact that the city "had a free beginning without depending on anyone," except the *virtù* of its founder.[3] Machiavelli understands that the method of ancient historians such as Livy, as Paul Veyne has explained, was inquiry, not controversy, for truth is not found but created.[4]

What Machiavelli's two discrete categories of native or foreign foundations elide and then their negation denies, moreover, is the realization, as Max Weber emphasized, that "everywhere that it made its appearance—in the Middle Ages, in Antiquity, in the Near and Far East—the city arose as a joint settlement by immigration from the outside."[5] Because death rates were higher than birth rates in the premodern city, all cities were made up of mixed elements as an influx of outsiders from near and far was necessary to sustain urban populations. Thus, although myth and binary logic might argue for city foundation by *either* natives *or* foreigners, in reality, the cities of Italy grew and maintained themselves as a result of a coming together of *both* native *and* foreign peoples. Urban populations in their social structure and values were constantly being reinforced, being replaced, and under pressure from "new" men and women immigrants from the countryside.

By the time of Botero's late Renaissance treatise on *The Greatness of Cities* in 1588, a more detailed examination of the nature of cities than that found in his anti-Machiavellian *Ragion di stato* (1589), the fictional accounts of city foundations had become lies to be dismissed. Such "fables" with their feigned history, nevertheless, were thought still to contain some truths to be mined, especially the advantage of uniting all the dispersed rural people into one city with the resulting "wealth and plenty" that derived from man's association in towns, a fact that was daily verified for Botero by contemporary practice in Brazil by the Portuguese and the Jesuits, and which led to and fostered "civil conversation."[6] The subsequent "greatness" of a city, then, was measured not by the physical size of its site or the circuit of its walls but by how a city prospered, "the multitude and number of the inhabitants and their power."[7] From the ancient poets' fables, Botero derived four motives for city foundation—authority, force, pleasure, and profit.[8]

Botero's evaluation of a city by population, however important it was to be for later mercantile economic theory,[9] nevertheless proves to be a poor definition of a city. Again, Max Weber refines the notion that "size alone can hardly be sufficient to define the city" because "of what it would include and what it would exclude."[10] The city is more than the size of its area or population: its energy comes from its associational life and communal actions. Thus, for Weber, a city is a "community," as demonstrated by its institutions.

Machiavelli's and Botero's "objective" lines of reasoning were consistent with Renaissance attempts to find "realistic" rather than idealistic rules about cities. Although the myths of the foundation of the city were patently false and irrelevant stories, they could still yield important information for what we would today identify as the political and social components of urban life. But, of the myths themselves, did nothing remain? Did the stories not carry a cultural and ideological content? What can we make of the continued telling and retelling of the inherited legends of the ancients and the proudly reinvented etiologies of the moderns, even as the old stories and legends were dismissed? How should we understand these urban genesis myths in light of the Renaissance idea of myth and the Renaissance idea of the city?

Jean-Pierre Vernant's studies on the relationship between ancient Greek myth and Greek thought, tragedy, and society help frame the problem. The city should be seen not as an abstract place of sterile piazze, streets, and buildings but as collections of citizens with diverse political and social identities.[11] Myths operate according to their own logic, which codifies new rules in an ambiguous and equivocal polarity.[12] Myths are a mode of expression different from conceptual thought; they are not reality, nor are they rational. Rather, myths are a symbolic and allegorical language that is easy to remember and transmit because of their polyvalent and polysemic modes of coordinating, grouping, and organizing experience.[13]

An ideal genre to interrogate for an answer to these questions on the nature of the city and the nature of myth in the Renaissance is chorography, the hybrid geographic, topographical, and historical compendia that developed after Flavio Biondo's 1453 *Italia Illustrata*.[14] Biondo divides his itinerary around Italy into eighteen regional rubrics and identifies 264 cities; he begins in Genoa and proceeds down the coast to Latina, up to Umbria and the North, before heading down from the Abruzzi to the South. His mention of city origin myths is sparse, usually limited to one sentence and a single source in a matter-of-fact statement, in a medieval tradition of beginning the descriptions of cities with real or mythical founders that J. K. Hyde has traced back to the *artes rhetoricae* tradition in an eighth-century Lombard manuscript.[15]

Leandro Alberti, the Dominican monk who had written hagiography and a history of his native Bologna, compiled the most popular exemplar of this genre on Italy in his *Descrittione di tutta Italia*, dedicated to Henry II of France and his consort Catherine de' Medici in 1550.[16] Alberti follows a direct itinerary down the Tyrrhenian and up the Adriatic, divides Apulia into two regions, and increases his city total to more than 300. This "Descriptio"-cum-guidebook is generally considered to be an important work at the turning point between compilers of information, including legends, and source criticism. In his description of the city of Naples, for example, Alberti conflates two origin myths. The first is fable (*favola*), the story of the Siren Partenope washed ashore after the safe passage by Ulysses; and the second is history (*storia*), Strabo's account of the building of the city around the Siren's sepulcher by people from Cuma: "One of the Sirens is buried here, who (as the fables narrate) threw herself into the sea because of the deep sorrow she felt for not having been able to trick Ulysses and his companions with her allures, and then was buried in this place built by the Cumaeans; and the name of this virgin, rather prostitute (as some say), in such a way was called Partenope."[17] Alberti's goal is to weigh the evidence and get at the truth, as he emphasizes in a typical aside on the city of Piacenza that demonstrates how his method repeats "not only fables but even lies" in order not to repress anything out of "either ignorance, or negligence, or malice."[18] What he leaves for the "judicious reader to pronounce sentence"—or rather to ridicule—are tedious trivialities of other writers, who, at best, provide the raw material to sort out the true origins of a given city.[19]

Arguing over the literal truth or falsehood of legends and myths, important as it may be to discern the facts of a particular case to clear up conflicting testimony or to differentiate fact from fiction, misses the purpose of such stories—namely, why tradition was invented, and why myth-history was propagated.[20] Myths abound out of a rationale more complex than "the human desire to have honor, ancient roots, and noble blood," ascribed by Alberti.[21] In his discussion of the origins of the city of Cremona, he himself recognizes the important additional etiological purpose of myth as storytelling to explain continuing practices:

> I do not find anything certain on the origin of this city. But it is true that I have read a very ancient chronicle that says that it dates from Hercules, the companion of Jason, naming it Troy. Hercules was passing through Italy with many fellow Greeks on their way to Spain. Demonstrating marvelous displays of his strength (and especially in this place), Hercules defeated near the Po a strong and terrible Giant who carried with him a metal ball of 300 pounds, which he manipulated in such a manner that he would throw it quite easily wherever he wished. Thus, having defeated him, Hercules wished to build a city here in memory of such a victory, naming it Climena from the name of his mother (from which the city was then called Cremona). Following the building of this city, he led in some of the neighboring people to inhabit it; and to commemorate this champion in perpetual memory, a statue was erected that represents the Giant with the ball in his hand, which every year is clothed by the Cremonesi.[22]

Myths were important for collective memory and were closely tied to civic rituals; note how the statue commemorating Hercules' victory over the Giant as the foundation act of their city is clothed in an annual celebration by Cremona's citizens. As "the place of memory," myths often explained the unexplainable, rationalized the irrational, and reconciled the irreconcilable.[23]

Leandro Alberti's collection of geographic commonplaces provides an ideal text to test the late Renaissance idea and use of myth. Every one of his city descriptions begins with the story of its origins, the sources, and their evaluation. From such a review of a catalog of the myths of the origin of the cities in Italy, we learn more not only about the nature and telling of Renaissance myth but also about the most important of Italy's medieval and Renaissance institutions, the city. For as much as the city is a physical, economic, social, political, and institutional reality, it is also an ideological construct in constant comparison with the heavenly city to come at the end of time.[24]

Biondo's 264 and Alberti's 300 cities underline the fact that the Italian Peninsula was a breeding ground for cities. By 1100, the movement toward communal government was in full swing; and by 1300, one-fifth to one-fourth of the population north of Rome lived in towns with more than 5,000 inhabitants.[25] By 1300, twenty-two mainland cities having a population greater than 20,000 inhabitants were concentrated primarily in the northern communes of the fertile Po Valley and Tuscany, with only three in the South (Rome, L'Aquila, and Naples). The fact that seventeen of these twenty-two cities still had populations greater than 20,000 by Alberti's mid-sixteenth-century edition verifies the staying power of these large population centers across the decimation of the 1348 plague and its recurrences. By 1600, twenty-two mainland Italian cities once again had populations greater than 20,000; five of the largest preplague cities had lost population to fall below 20,000 inhabitants (L'Aquila, Arezzo, Perugia, Pisa, and Siena), but another five cities had grown to number above 20,000 (Bergamo, Lecce, Lucca, Modena, and Turin—albeit Turin is in French Savoy where Chambéry remained its capital until 1563 and is not included in Alberti's 1550 chorography of Italy because his original edition was published thirteen years before Savoy's capital had been transferred from Chambéry to Turin). All twenty-seven cities that had reached a population of 20,000 inhabitants, either in 1300 before the plague or in 1600 after demographic recovery (table 1.1), then, accounted for about 10 percent of the mainland cities in Italy.

To verify the importance of these twenty-seven Italian cities, we might consult a very different kind of source that began to be widely diffused throughout Italy in the third quarter of the sixteenth century, namely, printed city maps.[26] The most complete collection of city maps of this period was the six-volume edition of Georg Braun and Franz Hogenberg, *Civitatis orbis terrarum*, published in Cologne

TABLE I.I.
Mainland Italian Cities with Populations over 20,000 (1300–1600)

	1300	1600		1300	1600
L'Aquila	40,000	—	Naples	60,000	275,000
Arezzo	20,000	—	Padua	35,000	33,000
Bergamo	[14,000]	24,000	Parma	22,000	25,000
Bologna	40,000	63,000	Pavia	30,000	25,000
Brescia	24,000	36,000	Perugia	34,000	[10,000]
Cremona	40,000	36,000	Piacenza	20,000	33,000
Ferrara	36,000	33,000	Pisa	38,000	[11,000]
Florence	95,000	76,000	Rome	30,000	100,000
Genoa	100,000	63,000	Siena	120,000	[19,000]
Lecce	—	30,000	Turin	[14,000]	24,000
Lucca	[16,000]	24,000	Venice	110,000	151,000
Mantua	30,000	30,000	Verona	30,000	45,000
Milan	100,000	120,000	Vicenza	22,000	32,000
Modena	[18,000]	21,000			

Sources: Bairoch et al., *The Population of European Cities from 800 to 1850*; and de Vries, *European Urbanization 1500–1800*.

Note: The islands of Italy are not included in Alberti's first edition of 1550 but are appended to the *Descrittione* in 1561. Two Sicilian cities had populations over 20,000 during this period: Messina with 27,000 in 1300 and 50,000 in 1600; and Palermo with 51,000 in 1300 and 105,000 in 1600. Likewise, Alberti does not consider Savoy, with its capital Chambéry, as part of Italy; its capital is transferred to Turin only in 1563. Populations under 20,000 are in brackets.

and Stuttgart between 1572 and 1618 and presented for readers as a "sedentary journey," with the Du Pérac map of Naples printed by Lafreri reprinted in volume 1.[27] These maps were bird's-eye views of the city, which reproduced city sights and monuments, churches and palaces, streets and piazze, seas and rivers, city and countryside in an ideal schematization that presented the "book" of the city as a "theater" after the model of Abraham Ortelius's world atlas of 1570 and invoked Giulio Camillo's 1550 *L'idea del theatro* and its connection to the art of memory and memory palaces.[28] For our purposes, an unusual composite map printed in Rome in 1607 by Giovanni Orlandi, *Trenta Illustrissime città de Italia Raccolte da Giovanni Orlandi in Roma Anno Domini MDCVII*, collected thirty maps and presented them six across and five down, with a slight bias for northern Adriatic cities associated with the Papal States or the Veneto[29] (table 1.2). Read like a text (left to right, top to bottom), the first five maps represent the five signatories of the Peace of Lodi (1454) and arguably still in 1607 Italy's major cities (Rome, Venice, Naples, Milan, and Florence). Orlandi, from Bologna and active as an engraver and printer in Rome after 1590, includes six cities all in the northern Adriatic or Venetian orbit (Ancona, Rimini, Trento, Treviso, Udine, and Urbino) not on our list of Italian cities with populations greater than 20,000 inhabitants, and he excludes three cities that are (two that had fallen below their larger population of 1300—L'Aquila and Arezzo; and one from the South—Lecce). The twenty-four

TABLE I.2.
Thirty Cities of Italy in Giovanni Orlandi's 1607 Composite Map

Ancona	Milan*	Rome*
Bergamo*	Modena*	Siena*
Bologna*	Naples*	Trento
Brescia*	Padua*	Treviso
Cremona*	Parma*	Turin*
Ferrara*	Pavia*	Udine
Florence*	Perugia*	Urbino
Genoa*	Piacenza*	Venice*
Lucca*	Pisa*	Verona*
Mantua*	Rimini	Vicenza*

Source: Trenta Illustrissime città de Italia Raccolte da Giovanni Orlandi in Roma Anno Domini MDCVII in Bellucci and Valerio, *Piane e vedute*, map 9, 24–25.
  *Twenty-four cities in the Orlandi composite map are among the twenty-seven cities with population over
20,000 inhabitants in table 1.1.

of our twenty-seven cities represented on his single-sheet map collation thus
confirm their centrality to the story of Italian urbanization.

Such maps do not represent cities in an objective, scientific manner but employ a hierarchical rhetoric that emphasizes local buildings, streets, and monuments according to the conventions and myths of each particular city. They convey hidden messages, political propaganda, religious enthusiasm, or local pride.
Like the unities of time, space, and action in the classical rules of Greek tragedy,
these city images create the illusion of being able to see the totality of the city all
at once and to understand the unique character and meaning of each in a com-
pressed single moment. Like a portrait, these city images attempt to capture the
quality and essence of the city so that the viewer is able to intuit the logic of the
whole city, distinguish the iconic features of each individual city, and appreciate
its mythic power.[30]

If one returns to Alberti's Italy and examines the origin myths of the twenty-
six cities with populations greater than 20,000 included in his tour of Italy
(again, Turin is not included) as representative for the utility of maintaining urban genesis stories, one can begin to discern patterns and meanings in the telling
of such myths. The foundation myths of the twenty-six cities in our sample of
mainland Italy's largest cities break down into Machiavelli's two types: foundation by native peoples or foundation by gods, heroes, or colonist foreigners, albeit
nine cities have multiple foundation myths that place them in both categories
and two (Naples and Cremona) are assigned two different foreigner foundation
myths (table 1.3). Alberti identifies fourteen of the twenty-six cities as native foundations: six founded by the Etruscans alone (Genoa, Lucca, Arezzo, Bologna,
Parma, Mantua), four jointly or successively by the Etruscans and the Cenom-

ani Gauls (Bergamo, Milan, Verona, Vicenza), three others by the Cenomani alone (Piacenza, Brescia, Pavia), and one by the Latins (Romulus and Remus's Rome). In the group with foreign foundation myths, Alberti records twenty-two out of twenty-six cities: eight cities by Greeks—gods such as Janus in Genoa and the Sirens at Naples, heroes such as Hercules in Brescia and Cremona, and colonists from Cuma at Naples, from the Peloponnesus at Pisa, from Crete at Lecce, from Thebes at Mantua, and from Pergamum at Bergamo; five cities by Trojans—including the famous Roman and Ferrarese story of Aeneas, one by Piacentilo Troiano at Piacenza, and the Paduan/Venetian story of Antenor; three cities by other peoples from beyond the eastern Mediterranean to the ancient Near East—Perugia by Persians, Bologna by Scythians, and Milan by the biblical Tubal, descendant of Noah's son Japheth; after the foundation of Rome, five cities as Roman colonies (Florence, Siena, Modena, Parma, and Cremona); and one (L'Aquila) after the Lombard invasions.

These origin myths of the twenty-six cities as told by Alberti suggest that the initial objection to Machiavelli's simple binary division was, in fact, well known at the time, for variant origin myths suggest legends about different peoples in the city who remembered different ancestors. In other words, the variant myths no doubt reflected the fact that urban foundation and continuity depended upon a joining or coming together of both natives and foreigners. City foundation myths, then, can be understood as rationalizing the layers of history in a city's tradition, as its residents attempted to mediate contradictory evidence. That is certainly the argument of Alberti, as he assigns historical priority to myths in suggesting, as in the case of Bergamo, that the Etruscans came first to found the city and the Cenomani Gauls restored and enlarged it, while the Greek foundation story is a fable.

Are there other organizing principles in addition to the quest for accuracy and historicity that will help explain the similarities and differences in the city origin myths? Perhaps politics helps explain the differences? First, whether a city was a republic or principality does not appear to matter. Principalities such as Milan and Naples were founded by foreigners, just as were the republics of Florence and Venice. Second, whether neighboring cities were political rivals similarly does not appear to influence the foundation myths. Florence and Siena both claimed Roman origins; all the rival cities of Cisalpine Gaul in the Po Valley had similar roots. The myth of Siena's twin founders, Senio and Aschio, succored by the she-wolf (a myth not told by Alberti), provides a good example of the ambiguous political meaning assigned to origin myths. Often recounted as linking Siena to Rome and its ancient virtues, this parallel Romulus-Remus story could

TABLE I.3.
Mainland Cities with Populations over 20,000 and Their Myths in Alberti's *Descrittione*

	Gods/Heroes/Foreigners	Native Peoples	Romans
Genoa	Janus	Etruscans	
Pisa	Greeks (Pilii)		
Lucca		Etruscans	
Fiorenza			Colonists
Siena			Colonists
Arezzo		Etruscans	
Perugia	Persians (Perugio Troiano)		
Roma	Trojans (Aeneas)	Latins	
Napoli	Sirens/Cuma, Greeks		
Lecce	Crete, Greeks (Idomeneo)		
L'Aquila		Lombards	
Bologna	Scythians (Fero)	Etruscans	
Ferrara	Trojans		
Modena			Colonists
Parma		Etruscans	Colonists
Piacenza	Trojans (Piacentilo)	Gauls	
Mantua	Thebes, Greeks (Manto)	Etruscans	
Brescia	Hercules (not true)	Cenomani Gauls	
Cremona	Hercules (not true)		Colonists
Bergamo	Greeks (Pergamo)	Etruscans / Cenomani Gauls	
Pavia		Cenomani Gauls	
Milano	Bible Tubal, son of Japheth	Etruscans / Cenomani	
Venice	Trojans through Padua		
Verona		Etruscans / Cenomani Gauls	
Vicenza		Etruscans / Cenomani Gauls	
Padova	Trojans (Antenor)		

Note: The islands of Italy are only appended after 1561. Thus, two Sicilian cities with populations greater than 20,000 would be included: Messina, Cuma/Chalcis, Greeks; and Palermo, Carthage, Phoenicians. The tour goes down the Tyrrhenian coast from Genoa to Naples and returns up the Adriatic from Lecce to Istria.

also be used to show the temporal priority of its founding vis-à-vis Florence, or even its independence from Rome because Siena had its own suckling twin founders.[31] Florence, for its part, could change its origin myth as internal politics shifted from pro-imperial Ghibelline or pro-papal Guelph sympathies. Thus, the Florentine chancellor Leonardo Bruni rejected the imperial myth of the city's founding by soldiers of Julius Caesar and, in his *History of the Florentine People* (1415), changed it to a republican myth, with founding by soldiers of Sulla's army after the end of the Social War around 80 b.c.e.[32] In the same way, Bruni had earlier turned Caesar's assassin Brutus into a defender of republican values against the tyrant Caesar instead of leaving Brutus assigned (along with Judas Iscariot) to Dante's last circle of hell as a traitor to friendship.[33] Myths and history could clearly be manipulated to mean different things—sometimes even interpreted in completely opposite ways—but their distribution over the whole of the Italian

Peninsula does not suggest a political pattern of preference determined by a city's form of government or by neighboring rivalries.

The best and most obvious explanation for similarities and differences in the distribution of origin myths is regional geography. Southern Italy and Sicily constituted Magna Graecia, and the heroes from the Hercules or Argonaut cycles and from the Trojan War (either victorious Greeks returning home or defeated Trojans fleeing their destroyed city) made their way into the founding of more than a hundred southern Italian cities.[34] Similarly, coastal landings account for a fair share of seaborne foreign traveler foundations. Native foundations, for their part, are clustered in Tuscany and the Po Valley, the heartland of Etruria and the area of Cisalpine Gaul, homeland to the Etruscans and the Cenomani. Should we then think of these origin myths as simply geographically determined, accidentally distributed around the peninsula by the chance of proximity, without human agency?

Renaissance understanding of the nature of myth makes it clear that the city foundation myths were not random stories. Natale Conti's *Mythologiae*, published in Latin in Venice in 1567, was "an immensely popular work, which was at once the most accessible and the most learned example of those erudite treatises on myth that flourished during the late medieval period and the Renaissance, the mythographies."[35] Conti is a good guide to the late sixteenth century's tripartite interpretation of myth. Myths were first historical or literal, that is, they recounted actual events that come down to us as dictated facts. Second, myths "reveal nature's secrets" and are thus concerned with the knowledge of the physical and natural world, that is, natural philosophy or "scientific" knowledge. Both of these first two definitions explain the city origin myths' historical and geographic distribution in Italy. But Conti emphasizes, above all, an important third understanding of myth as moral or allegorical, that is, myths also had a heuristic, ethical purpose. The last sentence of book I, chapter 1: "Which Is the Argument of the Entire Work," explains Conti's ethical and intellectual goals: "We intend to gloss only those stories that raise men to the heights of celestial knowledge, that counsel proper behavior and discourage unlawful pleasures, that reveal Nature's secrets, that ultimately teach us all we absolutely need to know to lead a decent human life, that enhance our understanding of all the great writers."[36]

City origin legends recovered lost history (through their invention and details) and, at the same time, spoke to the mysteries of a world beyond the here and now, in the same way that all figural thinking worked in the Middle Ages.[37] The city origin myths were thus recounted and retold not only because they purported to reveal some unknown truths about nature and the past but also because they offered some guidance for the present and the future. That understanding is essentially where we began, with Machiavelli's conviction that a city's inhabitants—in their success or failure—carry on the moral tradition established at the city's formation. What different lessons, then, did these sample origin myths—native versus foreign foundation—teach to Italian city inhabitants?

Native foundation myths were more than etiological devices "to explain the migration from the fertile plains of the *terraferma* to the barren lagoon" of Venice or the impregnable mountain stronghold of Fiesole to the insecurities of the malarial plains of the Arno Valley for Florence.[38] Rather, native foundation emphasized the coming together of free men in common association, the quintessential claim of privilege and equality shared by urban ruling elites whether they resided in the Republic of Venice or the Kingdom of Naples. The rights and privileges of citizens distinguished them from their rural brethren and contributed to making each one of their cities a world unto itself.

Foreign foundation myths—Greek, Trojan, and Roman—highlighted new beginnings for transplanted peoples reestablishing their traditions and culture in new soil. Greek foundation myths often invented genealogies that invariably spawned eponymous founders: Genoa, Janus; Pisa, Pilii; Mantua, Manto; Bergamo, Pergamo. The emphasis is on hero founders or their ancestors (as Hercules' mother Climena for Cremona, or the Mantua variant claiming that Agnello named it after his mother Manto). The new town, thus, assumed the attributes or *virtù* of its founder in the invocation of its name in the same way that personal names appropriated the cult of the gods or later the saints as protectors and models.[39] Trojan foundation myths, originally anti-Greek myths that were fashioned as the Romans expanded into the Greek lands in Italy and the Balkans, emphasize the succession of empires—as Troy gave way to Greece, so Greece to Rome, and Rome to the new towns and empires such as Venice.[40] Trojan myths not only rationalized political leadership but also sanctioned theocratic rule as divine right passed through specially chosen hero-founders (Aeneas and Antenor) and pointed to the providential, even apocalyptic legacy that they carried with God's favor.[41] Roman foundation myths could be invoked to elicit either republican or imperial traditions or to signify either papal or antipapal allegiances. In the context of Roman hegemonic pretensions and centralization, especially after Trent, late sixteenth- and early seventeenth-century Italian city foundation myths tended to be either pro-Roman myths that shared in the Eternal City's glory or anti-Roman myths that celebrated local, independent development. An anonymous 1607–8 descriptive history of Naples, for example, emphatically trumpets this anti-Roman ideological tradition in its terse opening sentence: "Fu Napoli a ducento anni prima dell'edificio di Roma" (Naples existed for two hundred years before the building of Rome).[42]

The city as a complete world unto itself with its unique destiny and perpetual privileges—like the theology of the individual Christian soul that such civic ideology mirrors—holds its citizens together in its "mystical body" in the same way that the church does its faithful, that is, through the practice of sacramental rituals. From the twelfth through the eighteenth century, civic culture in the "ceremonial city" used the cult of the saints and public processions to reinforce civic virtue and loyalty.[43] Similarly, civic paintings such as Vasari's *The Foundation of Florence* of 1563–65 on the ceiling of the Salone del Cinquecento in the Palazzo Vecchio and Annibale Caracci's *Plowing of the Boundaries of Rome by Romulus* dating to the 1590s (one of the eight scenes representing the founding of Rome) in the main *salone* of the Palazzo Magnani-Salem in Bologna commemorated the actual foundation ceremonies of the city founder digging the furrows for the circuit of the walls behind a plow and team of oxen.[44] Even the time of city founding was propitious, whether the favored date of 25 March (as in Venice or Siena) was mystically conjoined with the founding of Rome, the beginning of the Christian era [at the Annunciation], the annual rebirth of nature, and the first day of the calendar year [on the vernal equinox], or a date to be determined by the prognostications of astrologers (as in Filarete's ca. 1460 description of Sforzinda).[45] Because the myth of the foundation of the city was less about the "story" or "facts" than the ceremonies and practices of the rituals, civic foundation myths were forged to and became inseparable from civic ritual; and, together, myth and ritual ensured civic rights and civic virtues.

Despite Machiavelli's disinterest in and Botero's disavowal of the veracity of the founding myths, urban genesis myths continued to be important for their central place as part of civic ritual. Even in his refutation of such myths, Leandro Alberti promotes them. Whereas the Hercules myth of the founding of Brescia after killing the Hydra is demonstrated to be a "false fable" and an outright "lie," a woodcut of Hercules fighting the Hydra still graces Alberti's first edition.[46] The motto surrounding the frame is *Affectus, Virtute, Superantur*. Like Hercules', the city's disposition is to overcome by its virtue.

From Myth to History: Righting History in Spanish Naples

The starting point for printed books of Neapolitan history goes back to the Italian Wars and the beginning of the Spanish Conquest of Naples with the 1498 publication of Pandolfo Collenuccio's *Compendio de le istorie del Regno di Napoli*.

The *Compendio* saw fifteen partial or complete Italian editions between 1539 and 1613—four of them commented upon, corrected, and continued by Tommaso Costo (1545?–1612) in his *Addizioni e note al Compendio dell'istoria del Regno di Napoli*.[47] The crisis of the French invasions of 1494 and the loss of the kingdom's independent monarchy lay behind Collenuccio's original inquiry back to ancient and medieval times, from the ancient Greek origins of Naples to 1459, as worked out especially in the unpublished work of medieval Neapolitan chronicles.[48]

The myth of the origin of the city of Naples is relegated to only one paragraph. According to Collenuccio, the founders of the city of Naples came from Cuma and Chalcis on the Greek island of Euboea (in the Renaissance called Negro-ponte).[49] They had first colonized Ischia, then Cuma, and had built Naples in two campaigns, one called it the old city (Paleopoli) and the other the new city (Neapoli). Originally Paleopoli was named Partenope, because of the tomb of one of the three sisters, infamous prostitutes called Sirens, found there. But Paleopoli was subsumed by Neapolis, which the poets sometimes called Partenope. This truncated mythical genealogy, however, was subordinate to the actual history of the Kingdom of Naples, which was Collenuccio's real quarry.

Collenuccio's experience as an ambassador first from his native Pesaro to Rome and Venice, later from the Este court in Ferrara to Rome and the Holy Roman Empire, and as *podestà* of Florence and Bologna led him to regard Florence and Ferrara as model states as opposed to those of the pope, doge, emperor, or king. Naples, on the other hand, had succumbed to internal chaos and foreign conquest, above all because of the papacy's meddling in the political affairs of its southern neighbor. For Collenuccio, the problem of Naples was its perceived political instability that allowed for foreign interventions.

After the political realities of the Aragonese fall from power had displaced the fifteenth-century humanist historians patronized by Alfonso the Magnanimous (1442–58) and his son Ferrante (1458–94), not even the great Giovanni Pontano (1426–1503) could find much of a popular audience in the century after his death. Only one work of Pontano, his lone history, the 1499 *De bello napolitano* chronicling the baronial revolt against Ferrante's succession (1458–64), was reissued in Naples with a vernacular translation published in 1590.[50] Why was Pontano translated in 1590 and for whom? In the introduction by the translator, Giacomo Mauro, "uno erudito giovenetto," it is clear that his patron, Don Luigi Carafa, Prince of Stigliano, had commissioned the work to commemorate the fact that he now occupied the same estate in the province of Terra di Lavoro as Pontano and that the usefulness and pleasure of history as moral philosophy and consolation against mortality were eternal truths. No correspondence to the present political exigencies of contemporary Naples is invoked. In fact, Pontano's panegyric on the city of Naples in the concluding book 6 makes the memorial character of this translation all the more clear. Naples stands out for its man-made monuments (castles, palaces, and beautiful churches) and its natural environment (mild climate, incomparable site, and abundant fertility). While Pontano's generalizations about the dark side of human nature and Ferrante's unexpected success in establishing peace after war and his outrageous fortune might conjure up the complexity of human affairs, in no way did they address the problem of instability in Naples. Especially seen from the vantage point of the new translation in 1590 after thirty-four years of the "Prudent King" Philip II's reign, that problem was long past.

The problem of instability in Naples, however, was at the center of concerns in 1498 when Collenuccio reiterated the long-term history of the kingdom and its recurrent structural defects—the character of its inhabitants, its weak or ineffectual monarchs, the legacy of Byzantine lordship, the Angevin-inspired wars of succession, and the interference of the papacy and high clergy. This stereotypical litany excludes the feudal nobility, which found itself praised as a defender of local privileges instead of blamed for its wanton self-interest. In other words, Collenuccio's thesis was the complete opposite of Guicciardini's later explanation for the origins of the Italian Wars in the "foolish errors or shortsighted greed" of rulers through their "lack of prudence or excess of ambition."[51] Quite rightly, Neapolitan humanism has been called "feudal humanism" because its patrons and their praise lie at the heart of a rhetorical program that favored rule by its military, estate-owning oligarchy, and piously faithful nobility.[52] While studies of Renaissance humanism in Naples have been limited to the discussion of Latin-based authors, Neapolitan humanist culture extended into the sixteenth and seventeenth centuries to vernacular authors with the same classical reference base and value structure as their fifteenth-century progenitors.

Little wonder, given Tommaso Costo's feudal allegiances and courtier orientation, that he took Collenuccio's compendium history, albeit correcting its errors, as the starting point for his own narrative additions, eventually extended to 1610. Costo's *Addizioni e note* began in 1563 after Collenuccio's previous continuation by Mambrino Roseo from 1459 to 1557 and Cola Aniello Pacca from 1557 to 1562. The events chronicled by Costo's first edition of 1583 continued from 1563 until 1582; the second edition of 1588 extended the history through 1586, and subsequent editions eventually through 1610.[53] The 1588 Venetian edition included the events of the 1585 *popolo* riot and murder of the *popolo*'s city council representative, Giovan Vincenzo Starace, with its provocation and organization "the work of the people," that is, in Rosario Villari's summary of Costo, "by the urban petty and middle-level bourgeoisie, and specifically by the district captains." Villari demonstrates, however, that Costo's views on the riot's origins moderated in the subsequent 1613 edition to recognize that, "if it was not entirely the work of the *popolo*, they did not fail to consent to it."[54] The real culprits manipulating the crowds were the professionals and officials known by their togas (*cappanera*).

Soon after the second Neapolitan edition of the *Addizioni e note*, Costo published a short seventy-one-page *Memoriale delle cose più notabili* in 1592. In brief chronicle form, he summarized the history of Naples in four parts from 412 to 1302 in ten pages, from 1302 to 1408 in eight pages, from 1408 to 1500 in thirteen pages, and from 1500 to 1588 in thirty-seven pages. Immediately thereafter, in 1593 with a second edition in 1595, Costo prepared a structural overview of the kingdom in schematic form, *Nomi delle provincie, citta, terre, e castella*. Lists of the kingdom's towns and castles by province, lists of the kingdom's bishops and archbishops, a short review of the kings by dynasty, and a summary of governors and viceroys from the time of the Byzantine occupation in 545, as well as a list of the Seven Great Offices, princes, dukes, marquises, counts, and extinct members of the noble neighborhood districts, all chronicle the glory past and present of Naples.

In 1596 Costo published *Il Fuggilozio*, a literary text that marked the high point of this exemplary moral literature produced for court society, a vernacular continuation of Neapolitan "feudal humanism."[55] Costo's "Leisure Flight" is a collection of 522 short anecdotes, examples, or attributed sayings, each ending in a proverb, which are organized in a Boccaccesque frame of eight days around the summer festival of the Spassi di Posillipo in 1571, told by a company of ten (eight men and two women) with a moral message "worthy to be read by every Gentleman." Costo also resided and participated in the fullness of court culture's humanistic propaganda for the ruling class. Among his early literary studies was a 1582 Neapolitan edition of Tasso's *Gerusalemme liberata*, which connected him to the frequent Neapolitan visitor and Italian literary giant, who was Naples's adopted son born in exile across the bay in Sorrento.[56] Costo served as secretary for a number of prominent Neapolitan noble families and would write a treatise on the secretary in 1602.[57]

In his 1613 book, *La apologia istorica* (Historical Apology on the Kingdom of Naples against those who blame the Neapolitans of inconstancy and infidelity), Costo adamantly declared, "I return therefore to say that the city of Naples, by not having taken care to have written its own history, is subject to the lies of foreigners; those foreign, badly informed writers with little love for Naples have spoken of her without conforming to the truth, but according to their various passions."[58] That Collenuccio, a foreigner who had never even visited Naples, holds pride of place in this historiographical tradition explains much about Costo's castigation of lying foreigners and Giulio Cesare Capaccio's later didactic instruction of the curious, pliant *forastiero*. All Costo's antiquarian lore of civic pride in a noble frame was collected, and polemical reinterpretation propounded, not to make the lessons more forceful or to instruct newly arrived Spanish viceroys on their short, three-year term, but for the ideal nobleman's education.[59] Costo's revision of Collenuccio shifted the blame of Neapolitan history from its people to its rulers, and his goal was to reinstill a sense of virtue in its ruling class.

Costo's nemesis and rival in this genre of local nationalistic history, Scipione Mazzella, himself had been publishing on the history of Naples from 1586, the same decade as Costo's first two additions to Collenuccio. Mazzella's *Descrittione del Regno di Napoli* grew in size from its first edition in 1586 to a big book of 711 pages by its second edition in 1597, as it established itself as the most popular history of Naples. The first edition was devoid of any analysis of historical events, but rather provided a descriptive historico-geographic compendium of lists and details on people (monarchs and nobility), places (towns and castles), and things (offices and administration) in the kingdom. Mazzella's initial success spawned an expanded narrative history of the lives of the Neapolitan kings, which was published independently in 1594 and later incorporated in the second and subsequent editions of the *Descrittione*.[60] While preparing *Le vite dei re*, Mazzella published a 147-page text in 1591 on ancient Pozzuoli and the Campi Flegrei to the west of Naples, where first settlement and then the origins of the capital are traced to ancient Cuma.[61] Thus, in his *Descrittione*, Mazzella summarized the founding of Naples according to the two dominant myths, "The beautiful and royal city of Naples is said to have first taken the name of the Siren, Partenope, who arrived carried on the waves; and the city had its name changed as it was reinhabited, according to the oracle of the Cumaeans, who had previously destroyed it."[62]

All this antiquarian collecting found vituperative criticism from Costo in his *Ragionamenti* of 1595.[63] Costo derided Mazzella for being neither historian, poet, nor orator. For Costo, history provided "lezzione utile, esemplare, e dilettevole." Mazzella was instead a derivative chronicler who copied from other writers by usurping from them and attributing to himself errors, lies, thefts, and exclusions. Costo engaged in a long discussion on rhetoric, both writing in general and history in particular, only to find himself hauled by Mazzella before both civil and ecclesiastical courts, one of which condemned him to a short prison term for libel. But where they agreed, Collenuccio's polemic against Rome became the centerpiece of a strident Neapolitan historiographical chestnut, an anti-Roman brief embellished with Costo's and Mazzella's chronicles, lists, descriptions, and vitae of an independent state founded before Rome.

The first edition of an eschatological, turn-of-the-century, Counter-Reformation history of the three principal cities in the world—Jerusalem, Rome, and Naples—published in Naples in 1598 by Michele Zappullo, brings together Naples's classical inheritance (founded 408 years before Romulus's Rome) and its Christian faith (founded before Rome in 44 c.e. by St. Peter, whose staff is kept in the cathedral) into the common tradition of progressive epochs succeeding one another.[64] Zappullo recounts world history as a progression of ages in the fulfillment of God's plan for mankind. According to Zappullo, whereas the Jews of Jerusalem remained God's chosen people until their rejection of Christ and the destruction of the temple by Titus, Rome was the seat of a Gentile empire whose cults of false gods and idols ruled there until Constantine accepted Christianity publicly in 325. Naples, on the other hand, proved to be the first city of Europe converted to Christianity and the refuge of Christianity during the persecution of the primitive church, and since then it has remained steadfast in its ancient faith with "more holy places than any other city in the world" and "the most devout of every other part of Italy" in order that the "intercession of the just and their good works" might placate the wrath of God. Naples was the New Jerusalem, a religious center with priority and fidelity in the West before Rome.

Such local historiographical investigations culminated in 1601–2 in the first two volumes of Giovan Antonio Summonte's definitive 1,143-page *Dell' Historia della Città e Regno di Napoli*. Summonte narrated the city's foundation up to the mid-fifteenth-century Aragonese conquest. He was an admirer of Mazzella, who had given Summonte an ancient inscription gratefully acknowledged in volume 1.[65] The last two volumes of Summonte, another 1,037 pages, which continues his history from the Aragonese conquest of the kingdom in 1443 through Philip II's reign to 1590 (including a narrative of the Starace riot, with an appended list of the condemned by their form of punishment), appeared much later, posthumously in 1640 and 1643.[66]

Among the Neapolitan historians, Summonte is the most meticulous in chronicling all available sources. In his long chapter 2 on "The building of the City of Cuma and the origins of the City of Naples," Summonte cites ancient sources (Strabo, Livy, Servius, Pliny, Solino, Eustatius, Dionysius Atro, Alexander of Alexandria, Statius, Apollodoro, and Iginio) and modern authors (Falco Beneventano, Giovanni Pontano, Marino Frezza, and Giustino Politano) in order to verify the name and identity of Partenope, not as the *favolosa* Siren or maligned prostitute, but to state the truth as he saw it.[67] Beyond discerning true from false and fable from history, the Neapolitan historians are interested in interpreting the myth of the origin of their city as a moral lesson, which, after all, is what a fable is meant to be. Summonte promotes *napolitanità*—the distinctiveness, priority, and preeminence of Naples. He records that the sources agree: "Following many, they say that the City of Naples was built by the Cumaeans who came from the island of Euboea, now called Negroponte, as much as 170 years after the fall of Troy, 260 years before Rome was built, 4,213 or (following another correcting opinion) 4,036 years after the creation of the world, and 1,168 years before the birth of Our Lord Jesus Christ."[68] Above all, Summonte's narrative history aims at establishing the political independence of Naples from Rome, both in the ancient past and more importantly in the present relationship between its Spanish absentee-king and nominal papal suzerain lord.

In 1602, the year of Summonte's first volumes of his history of Naples and Costo's book on the secretary, the fifty-year-old Giulio Cesare Capaccio received recognition for his already distinguished career in literary studies and local historical-archaeological erudition with his appointment as secretary of the city of Naples.[69] A Capaccio letter had been included in the appendix to Costo's 1582 edition of Tasso; and in 1589, a dozen years before Costo, Capaccio had also written a treatise on the secretary, which was republished four times in Venice.[70] In 1613 Capaccio attended the court of the Prince of Urbino and in 1623 the court of Urban VIII. Costo's and Capaccio's contemporary careers are not just parallel but deeply intertwined and nowhere more so than in their aristocratic sympathies, political opinions, and historical studies, which conferred a conservative, ruling-class interpretation on the Neapolitan past. In the tradition of city chancellors and secretaries drawn from provincial roots, such as the Florentine chancellor Leonardo Bruni Aretino, who became passionate propagandists for their adopted capital city,[71] Capaccio was born in Campagna d'Eboli in the modern province of Salerno (the place where, according to Carlo Levi, "Christ stopped"). As city secretary, Capaccio produced an authoritative two-volume Latin history of his adoptive city in 1607, and the much more accessible vernacular version with the posthumous publication of *Il Forastiero* many years later in 1634, which should be seen as the culmination of the literary-historiographical culture of some thirty years before.[72]

Capaccio's Foreigner-Citizen Dialogue

Il Forastiero's description of the wonders of the marvelous city of Naples recounts persons, places, and actions in the dominant Baroque aesthetic of awe and admiration associated with the literary style of the great Neapolitan poet and courtier, Giambattista Marino (1569–1625). The word *maraviglio* or its derivatives *maravigliosa* and *maravigliosissima* appear seven times in Capaccio's opening four-page dedication to his patron, Don Emmanuel de Zuñiga, Count of Monterey, viceroy of Naples (1631–37), and double brother-in-law of the Count-Duke Olivares (each having married the other's sister). Capaccio, in fact, makes explicit the symmetry between the city's gifts of nature (its serene air, tranquil sea, and sublime site) and its gifts of fortune (its foreign commerce, large population, and "the splendor of its ancient and powerful nobility") with the intellectual gifts of its viceroy, by nature (his sublime intelligence, divine judgment, and lively memory) and by fortune (his network of correspondents, universal praise and celebrity, and glorious family).[73] Although published a third of a century after Capaccio became city secretary, *Il Forastiero* reflects the conservative politico-religious program put in play in Naples in the 1590s that sees the double blessing of nature and fortune as marks of true nobility, and the viceroy's virtues as the mirror image of the city's glories. *Il Forastiero* should be understood as the fruition of that formative moment in the establishment of a Counter-Reformation *paideia* for the Neapolitan nobility and the epitome of Capaccio's lifetime of service to the Spanish government of Naples. Capaccio's dialogue on the city of Naples is thus a handbook for civilizing its court-society nobility. In full Baroque fashion, Capaccio uses the conceit between a foreigner-stranger newly arrived by ship in Naples and a native Neapolitan citizen-guide to mimic the untutored-uncivilized meets the cultured-civilized dynamic.

Capaccio considers that the dialogue form with its introductory frame of praise for the contemporary city and its many luminaries, the disputations, and numerous digressions of a Neapolitan insider and foreign outsider is better than narrative history, because traditional history does not provide a sufficient style to relate the marvels of Naples. Things Neapolitan are only too magnificent in their "universal variety of descriptions, reports, unexpected Royal events, governments, wars, memories of ancient things, the succession of states, encomia of families and persons worthy of honor, and a thousand similar things which entertain a beautiful creativity to draw lessons, and which are useful for a variety of ways of knowing."[74] The dialogue's conversational exchange allows Capaccio "to explain his ideas" because it allows him "to offer such a great vastness of new thoughts and so many things that a curious man would judge worthy of taking account." His dialogue, then, can transcend history to become, in the best tradition of Renaissance humanism, philosophical disputation and moral instruction for the ruling class.

The authority of Capaccio's dialogical scene depends on his long lists and seemingly interminable details in a standard, late Renaissance rhetorical theory that derives from Giambattista Manso (ca. 1560–1645), the leader of the Neapolitan Accademia degli Oziosi. Manso's *Del dialogo: trattato del Marchese della Villa* (1628) pays lip service to their common mentor Tasso and his *Discourse on the Art of the Dialogue* (1585).[75] Like Manso, Capaccio downplays the delight and pleasure in the fictive conversation in order to emphasize the overriding purpose of a dialogue as effective, persuasive didacticism for a beneficial moral lesson. Capaccio's dialogue hides no heterodox opinions and harbors no comic irony, but instead relies on an expert, often esoteric, insider analysis through long discourses by the *Cittadino*. The *Forastiero*, a word that literally means someone from the wilds of the woods rather than the civilization of the city, is hardly a rustic interlocutor but is, in fact, such an erudite literati that he presents himself as "traveling around the world for curiosity to learn many things that not everyone has a taste for." Yet the foreigner is merely a stage prop who asks leading questions and responds in knowing assent to the Citizen-Capaccio, who is if not "un virtuoso da tutte le discipline," what we would call a Renaissance man, then "at least applies himself to being very well informed about his *patria*."[76] In *Il Forastiero*, Capaccio bows in imitation of Tasso's own voice as the Forestiero Napolitano in many of Tasso's dialogues—for example, in *Il Malpiglio overo de la corte* (1585), where Tasso employs a Forestiero Napolitano as the chief interlocutor on court life by explaining to Vincenzo and Giovanlorenzo Malpiglio, father and son in the court of Ferrara, "how to win grace from princes and avoid the envy and ill will of courtiers."[77] Back in Capaccio's scene in Naples, the tables are turned as a visiting Forastiero meets the Cittadino Napolitano, but the knowledgeable and polished Neapolitan courtier at home is still the center of attention as he explains things to his dialogic partner.

Beyond literary form, late sixteenth-century local Neapolitan antiquarian studies and historical writings established a necessary context for Capaccio's Foreigner-Citizen dialogue. What makes this half-forgotten dialogic history important, however, is not only its creation of a "national" history for the city and Kingdom of Naples but also its attempt to resolve the Renaissance debate on the problem of good government and the anti-Machiavel literature on *ragion di stato*.[78] The political-philosophical debate on the nature of the state eulogizes the

Counter-Reformation Neapolitan historians in the Catholic anti-Machiavel camp, in both their rethinking of the origins of ancient Italy and their use of examples for contemporary Naples circa 1600. Prioritizing Naples raises it above its suzerain lord in Rome, which in turn, changes the lord-vassal relationship between the papal prince and the King of Naples, who is at one and the same time the Spanish monarch required to present the annual tribute of a white horse, the *chinea*, to his papal lord.

The Neapolitan historiographical tradition from Collenuccio to Costo, the Costo polemic against frauds and lies in the controversy with Mazzella and Summonte, and Capaccio's own antiquarian studies shaped his whole argument in the ten books on the ten-day visit of *Il Forastiero*. Days 1 and 2 develop an interpretation of the origins and foundation of Naples and of its ancient religion and wars that established the nobles' pretensions to their freedom and their service to the state and to the church. For Capaccio's Citizen, the myth of the foundation of the city—the old story claiming independent foundation before Rome by Greek settlers from Cuma—became part of an elaborate Counter-Reformation revival of the city nobility's prerogatives. The Citizen argues that in ancient Greek times when superstition ruled and the Sirens dominated the region, all the gods worshiped there as a holy place.[79] The emblem of the ancient Greek republic was the owl (*la civetta* or *la nottola*) because, even though it is mute, the most eloquent man in the world is the one who knows how to observe silence when necessary.[80] But that ancient Greek liberty was lost in Naples in the year 1130 with the crowning of the Norman king Roger II and his monarchical claims over a unified kingdom joining the mainland and the island of Sicily—in Capaccio's words, "a thing to marvel at since the city of Naples, which after the time of the Roman Empire could never be conquered by arms, was finally subjugated with only one word."[81] Reading *Il Forastiero* requires an understanding of the overtones from Capaccio's study of emblems and fables that resonate through the historical narrative, the exposition of institutions, the description of customs, and the discussion of political theory in order to teach the princely virtues through his insider-outsider interrogation.[82]

In day 2, Capaccio links his foundation-myth moral of Partenope with *buon governo*. As "the first founder of this City" and one of the three Sirens, Partenope was a half-female and half-bird-legged creature, who accompanied her sister Sirens' song on her lyre. These two distinctive attributes—her lyre and her bird's legs—point to the good government of Naples under Spanish rule and the Catholic faith. Capaccio uses the first image of the lyre as a metaphor of harmony for international politics and internal policies. The second image of the half-bird

Siren emphasizes the Neapolitans' faithful, willing service to the Spanish monarchy and their eagerness to fly with the wings of heaven to spread its greatness and superiority.

The first image of Partenope's lyre becomes a symbol of faith and trust in international affairs, where the government of the Kingdom of Spain is a new foundation goddess whose lyre has drawn together various dominions from around the world in consonance and perfect harmony: "The lyre was the clear symbol of the consonance of all things that could be imagined in this City such as the government with so much order that has acquired its perfection in these times under the perfect harmony of the Kingdom of Spain." And in civic politics, in imitation of international affairs, Capaccio's Citizen claims that the Neapolitans have been "willing vassals who have united the different states of plebs, *popolo*, and nobility in concord to serve their lord, just as the different strings of the lyre have come together from their diversity to make a most perfect union of faith."[83] Earlier in his *Delle Imprese*, Capaccio had identified the lyre with Concordia, and its six strings represented the union of the city's six *seggi*, the five noble districts and the one of the *popolo*, into one city government.[84] But the primary sources for the six-stringed lyre as a metaphor for the republic can be found in Andrea Alciato's emblem 10 ("Foedera") and its translation in Capaccio's *Il Principe* ("Triegua" ["Alliances"]).[85] The pleasure of the lyre's song comes from the harmonizing of its strings, just as the peace of Italy comes from the concords of its princes. The lyre's various voices, "distinct and dissimilar," forming one harmony, provide the etymology for *Concordia* and thus become the metaphor for the republic. Within his state, the prince has no better guide than love to govern his subjects, who owe him constant peace, unquestioned faith, and prompt obedience.[86] And the underlying rationale that both international treaties and civic polities hold is the solidarity of signatories and citizens who trust one another. The Spartan king Agesilaus explains in answer to a series of questions: "Why does Sparta have no walls? Because the Citizens united with concord formed the best presidio to defend the City. And how could the Prince feel secure without outside allies? Because he commanded his people like a father over his children."[87] Citizens who are united together in concord and ruled paternally as sons to their father the prince provide a better defense of a city than their city walls. But what causes Plutarch's praise for this "stable union of Citizens" that Capaccio adds immediately after the example of Agesilaus?[88] Is it the glue of mutual interdependence? Love or fear as analyzed by Machiavelli? Why have the citizens come together in concord to trust one another?

Before answering this question, we need to look at the second image of the

Siren Partenope's essence as a bird to understand her true nature. Capaccio extends his lyrical metaphor, "To also have the nature of a bird, signifies none other than the happiness of the ingenious Neapolitans, eager to disperse in the service of their Kings, most eager to acquire all their greatness, and to fly with contemplation to the heavens to fuse with the new Christian Religion to become superior to every nation."[89] Harmony results in the total commitment of the subject Neapolitans to their kings, which allows them to soar with them and the church to the front rank of states with priority over all others.

Thus, Partenope is illustrated in Capaccio's *Delle Imprese* (1592) as a winged half-woman and half-bird figure with a lyre at her feet. And despite her mythical ("fraudolenta" and "inganna") existence, the Siren founder of Naples is a symbol of the city's sensual delights and its nurturing strength. By expressing milk from her naked breasts, the goddess has the power to dampen the fires of the quaking volcano of Vesuvius and as a muse to inspire the musical harmony of the city.[90] A few years earlier in 1586, Mazzella's frontispiece in *Descrittione del Regno di Napoli* reproduced a similarly winged Partenope, with a female upper torso and a birdlike lower torso, but that more regal Siren is there crowned and holding the escutcheons of the city of Naples and province of Calabria with the city and Bay of Naples in the background. These two book illustrations of Partenope were not inventions of the humanist historical writers. Rather, this iconography was unmistakably modeled on a sixteenth-century marble fountain outside the Church of Santa Caterina Spinacorona where Partenope stands in the crater of Vesuvius, a lyre lying on the fiery mountain to her left and water flowing from her breasts (fig. 1.1).[91]

Santa Caterina Spinacorona, which is near the Seggio di Portanova on the main street just west toward the Seggio di Porto (with the church and fountain plainly visible on the 1629 and 1670 Baratta maps), was formerly called Santa Caterina de' Trinettari, after the lace merchants whose shops lined the street.[92] The fountain, attributed to the sculptor Giovanni da Nola, likely commemorates the triumphal entry of Charles V on 25 November 1535, the feast of St. Catherine of Alexandria. In addition to the clearly visible imperial coat of arms on the statue, one tradition identifies Giovanni da Nola as the designer of the allegorical *apparati* in the triumphal entry program. Along the parade route stood giant statues that included the Siren Partenope and the river god of Naples, Sebeto, as well as a representation of Charles's victorious conquest of Tunis with battle scenes in the nearby piazza and street of the Sellaria, featuring the mythological "Battle of the Giants" against Zeus, who fires thunderbolts overseen by the imperial eagle onto a great mountain in flames.[93] Further tradition links the Church of

Figure 1.1. Giovanni da Nola, Partenope statue in the fountain at Santa Caterina Spinacorona. © Archivio dell'Arte / Luciano Pedicini, Naples.

Santa Caterina with the special patronage of Viceroy Pedro de Toledo about this time. Certain Jews turned New Christians around 1535 were said to have provided for twenty-five orphan girls of impoverished noble families in keeping with St. Catherine's patronage of young virgins. At Pedro de Toledo's order in 1546, the twenty-five orphans were transferred to a new conservatory built at S. Eligio, but the custom of naming the orphans daughters of St. Catherine continued in their new location.[94]

In *Il Forastiero*, the seductress Siren, even in defeat and death, has founded a city of harmony and continues to protect its subjects through all misfortunes. The Citizen-Capaccio confirms, "This goddess [Partenope] holds first place among the Neapolitans."[95] Citizen-Capaccio, however, immediately explains that the major god of ancient Naples was not the Siren Partenope, but the sun god, called Hebone.[96] In his detailed examination of the cult of Hebone, Pasquale

Novellino emphasizes the importance of Capaccio's encyclopedic curiosity or his "varietà del sapere" as the starting point for a comparative method contrasting ancient wisdom and practices with today.[97] The whole point of excavating the ruins of the ancient Republic of Naples and its ancient religion is to learn what it tells the reader about himself and his time.[98] The ancient republic provides the key and continuity to the present. Hebone was the multiform, polyvalent hieroglyphic of "infinite caprice" represented, among other things, as an ox, bull, rooster, snake, and bee; as Mercury, Bacchus, Mithra, Serapis, and Esculapio; as fertility, astrology, and the harmonious government of the prince.[99] For among Hebone's symbols is a lyre, which, like the Sun, moderates the harmony of the celestial spheres.[100]

And with the introduction of the sun god Hebone, Capaccio's Foreigner begins to learn the answer to the question of why citizens would trust one another in Naples. We are in the world of Machiavelli, but with a prince who is the complete opposite of Machiavelli's prince. Capaccio's Citizen-guide to Naples thus attempts to achieve the goal of a balanced harmony by exalting the prince and by redefining the city and its citizens from the top down. In Capaccio's *Il Principe*, a book of 200 emblems without illustrations, according to its subtitle, "per l'ottima eruditione di Costumi, Economia, e Governo di Stati," another figure, half human and half beast, appears in emblem 139, "Teachers of Princes. Chiron."[101] This emblem of the centaur-teacher is taken directly from Alciato's emblem 146, "Consiliarij Principum," which is one of his six emblems on princes. Taught by such a half man and half horse, the prince would be subject to the worst counselors of tyrants and a clone of Machiavellian dissimulation—false to friend and foe, far from God, and feigner of piety. In *The Prince*, chapter 18, Machiavelli had turned the traditional interpretation of Chiron as the model of humanist education on its head by emphasizing the bestial nature of the centaur and, thus, permitting the prince to be like his teacher, half man and half beast when need be, with the cunning of a fox or the force of a lion.[102] Unlike "The Counselors of the Good Prince" in the preceding emblem, Alciato's emblem 147, "In Senatum boni Principis," where the counselors who constitute the Senate are depicted as seated "because they should be grave judges of calm demeanor and not frivolous spirits" and without hands "so that they should take no gifts," and the prince himself is blind "because without emotion, with his ears alone he listens and executes what the Senate with its laws embraces,"[103] these "bad teachers in the end are the Machiavellis," who are like "Chiron Centaurs, bestial men, who make themselves impediments and opponents like a cloud over the Sun."[104] Capaccio's good prince is his answer to the question of solidarity and trust, as we have already seen in the image of the half-bird and half-woman Siren Partenope and as we shall see in the wise and just prince who will act as a good father to his people.

Capaccio follows his discussion of the ancient foundations of Naples with a review of its political history and government by dynasties, from the Norman, Hohenstaufen, and Angevin kings (day 3), the Aragonese kings (day 4), and the Habsburgs kings (day 5). Day 6 surveys the Neapolitan viceroys, and day 7 the governmental system of justice and administration by tribunals and councils. Day 8 describes the city's inhabitants—natives (the nobility in their residential wards or *seggi*, the nobility outside the *seggi*, the *popolo*, the plebs) and foreign residents. Day 9 describes the "The City's Body," that is, the corporate society of the Old Regime, its buildings and monuments made by human hands. Then day 10 concludes with a return to the city's site, its attributes and beauties made by nature. The *laudatio* of Naples is framed by virtue of nature and fortune, just as the virtue of its noble ruling class is fired by blood and deeds. An eighty-six-page addendum dialogue between the Foreigner and the Citizen expounds upon the Incendio di Vesuvio as a metaphor for the history and tradition of Naples and the Campania. A discussion of the causes and consequences of the "violent fires" from mythology, geology, and history begins with the stupefying power of Vesuvius upon the most courageous men of the world, such that it reduces the Foreigner to believe that its volcanic eruption will mark the end of the world. The dialogue ends with the Citizen's affirmation that Vesuvius provides perpetual illumination for the glory of the church, the Spanish Habsburgs, the Holy Roman Empire, and "the most faithful City of Naples, which always erupts in flames of Charity, Love, and Devotion, which are the true revolution of the planets."[105]

Violence and instability (for in the seventeenth century, "revolution" meant a short-term, sudden change in fortune or disorder and is not yet, "exclusively, in the political order of states")[106] are the keys to understanding Capaccio's hard-line descriptions of Neapolitan society and his reactionary ire against the plebs. In day 6, Rome again provides the basis for comparison in understanding the question of the divisions in society between nobles (who demonstrate their worth through virtuous actions), the *popolo* (who distinguish themselves as landlords, civil magistrates, and merchants), and the plebs (a marginalized underclass of vile, seditious rabble).[107] Disorder and disparity in the times mark the difference between past and present when it comes to the *popolo*. Placing *Il Forastiero* in the wider context of late sixteenth-century historiography shaped by the riot of 9 May 1585 around the murder and dragging through the streets of the *eletto del popolo* Giovan Vincenzo Starace helps to explain Capaccio's vituperative condemnation of the growing divisions in Neapolitan society between nobles and commoners.[108] Citizen-Capaccio describes the scene. The plebs, "like rabid dogs and wild beasts," dragged Starace's corpse throughout the whole city, sprinkling the blood of the murdered *eletto* everywhere, and "reduced the cadaver to such an end that one could not find either flesh, skin, or bone, nor could one bury it, for we could say that it was buried throughout the whole city of Naples." With such fear and tumult, the crowd's cries in front of the viceroy's palace of "Viva il Re, e mora il mal governo" rang hollow as those assembled then marched to sack the dead *eletto*'s house. The Citizen's narrative of events concludes with a verbal picture of the terrifying public monument and its niches displaying the heads and hands of the executed in order to visualize the punishment doled out to the condemned rioters. Capaccio describes the site of the complicit *popolo* leader Giovan Leonardo Pisano's razed house, where salt had been sown by order of the good government of the viceroy Duke of Osuna and a marble stone erected with a Latin epitaph identifying Pisano as "an enemy of the fatherland." In response, the Foreigner quakes in expressing Capaccio's rage and judgment, "I tremble to hear these words of just vendetta, so appropriate and meaningful."[109]

Capaccio's Digression on Reason of State

The Citizen-guide's long, introductory digression on "Ragion di Stato" in day 7 ("Del governo di Tribunali regii, e publico") of *Il Forastiero* clarifies the problem of violence and vendetta, justice and judgment. This excursus aims at orienting the day's itinerary through the political organization and bureaucratic administration of the government's councils, courts, and offices in order to correct the false notion of Reason of State—"modi fantastichi di governi"—that the state should be ruled by the will of its lords rather than reason: "And for this reason we will today discover the two true modes of government that establish the grandeur of the King and the needs of vassals in a city such as Naples."[110] Those "two true modes of government" are the application of Roman law in the king's tribunals without sophistries, and civil procedures in the public assemblies of the city's *seggi* based on statutes and rules drawn from these same laws.[111] The Citizen's exposition on Reason of State develops Capaccio's anti-Machiavellian political theory for the Counter-Reformation prince.

Capaccio contrasts the "true" practice of Reason of State in Spanish Naples to "an impure Machiavelli and his followers, pests of the world, built upon the instability of Heresy," in order to establish the philosophical core of his apology for the dogmas of the Roman, Apostolic Church and the benevolence of Spanish imperial rule and to insert his polemic against the vile and seditious *popolo* and plebs.[112] This impure Machiavelli invokes Capaccio's thoughts on Alciato's emblem 6, "Ficta Religio," which he translates as "Finta Religione," with an emphasis on his added subtitle "the seven-headed beast," the frightening animal ridden by the common apocalyptic figure from the Middle Ages, the whore of Babylon, with whose cup of false wisdom "the impure Machiavellis" tempt the princes of the world.[113] Heresy and ignorance are the two dangers to "Christian Politics" from the bad intent and malpractice of Reason of State; and thus, because it is founded on the rock of Peter, the Church can be the only guide to a "vera ragion di Stato."[114] For, as Aristotle says in the *Politics*, religion is the basis of good government because it teaches the people to fear God.[115] Machiavelli, so purified from his emphasis on the need for the people to fear the prince, leads to an understanding that the true religion of the Church is the foundation of the state and that obedience to the Church is true Reason of State.[116]

Halfway through this digression on Ragion di Stato, the Foreigner-visitor to Naples interjects an anecdote from his own experience in antiphonal response to the Citizen-*cicerone*'s previous praise for the Duke of Urbino, Francesco Maria II della Rovere, Capaccio's patron after his exile from Naples to reside at the duke's court in Pesaro in 1613.[117] The Foreigner's fond recollection restates the thesis of this whole section by recalling two *imprese*, "one is a bird's nest above a sea rock, the other a warrior's helmet filled with the honeybees' hive; both of which signify the model of a true Prince, who knows, with true reason of state, how to maintain the state."[118]

Alciato's order places the latter bees' honeycombed helmet first at emblem 178, "Ex bello pax" (After War Peace) and the former seabird's rocky nest second at emblem 179, "Ex pace ubertas" (After Peace Abundance).[119] In Capaccio's retelling, honey replaces war's bloodstains on the helmet of peace, because "Peace ought always to be desired and procured." And the example of the halcyon, the kingfisher seabird, who feathers its nest and nurtures its young on craggy rocks in the midst of the sea, shows how plenty comes from peace: "The true establishment of peace with the *popolo* is food provisioning, which is in every way the duty of the Prince . . . for nothing differentiates the good Prince from the good father."[120] Peace and prosperity are linked to the good government of the people's prince-father.

Alciato's emblem 177, "Pax," which pictures an elephant having recognized concord among nations now bearing the burdens of peace, precedes these two emblems on the consequences of peace; and Capaccio's commentary emphasizes the importance of maintaining the peace in a discussion of the causes of a just war.[121] The three emblems on peace form a response to the previous five emblems on just vendettas, Alciato's emblems 172–76, which in Capaccio's retelling also all emphasize the folly of vengeance; for the one seeking punishment upon another often has it applied to himself.[122] Whether the Cyclops Polyphemus, the crow and the scorpion, an army's trumpeter, a dog's chewing a stone, or mad Ajax's slaying pigs, the problem of the vendetta is that everyone loses. While the root cause of every vendetta is the insult to one's honor, the reason for its violence and feud is the absence of civil society and of the trust in government's just redress.

Thus, in closing his explication of the last emblem on the halcyon days of peace and tranquility in this series, Capaccio finds the trustless, fickle plebs to be at fault. Capaccio goes beyond repeating the commentary on Alciato's emblem attributed to the first-century C.E. Greek rhetorician and philosopher Dio Chrysostom on the ship of state. Capaccio affirms the truth of this cautionary aphorism, that while the ship's passengers sleep, play, and eat, the captain remains vigilant.[123] But then he adds a gloss of his own: despite the good government of the prince, one day, for want of food, the plebs will knock the head off the statue of the good emperor Antoninus Pius.[124] Such a sardonic observation is meant to resonate with vivid memories of the *popolo*'s notorious murder of their *eletto* Giovan Vincenzo Starace and their lack of bonds with the polity. For Capaccio in the previous day 6's discussion of the Starace episode, the vile plebs were the ungrateful enemy.[125]

The Citizen will lament later in day 8 the changes in the relationship between the nobility and the *popolo*, "to the great damage of the city and the perpetuation of disorder and disparity." The Citizen returns to the metaphor of the lyre, now out of tune, with high and low strings sounding discordant tones, because the *popolo* makes as if they are equal to the nobility: he notes that "from disparity is born that civil discord which erects various walls, because in the negotiations between them, each group affects superiority, whence the Lyre sounds dissonant."[126] Commenting on the virtue of hope in the context of his annotations on good government in Alciato's emblems, Capaccio's *Il Principe* had earlier made clear that the best form of government was that of the aristocratic Venetian Republic, which had no truck with the base plebs.[127]

To conclude his discourse on Ragion di Stato at the beginning of day 7, then, the Citizen-Capaccio returns to the "chimeras" of Machiavelli and recounts a short history lesson from the teachings of Collenuccio to the Foreigner: "In history, the disorders that this Reason of State has caused date from the fifteenth-century" divisions between states and the church, all to the detriment of poor Italy.[128] The Citizen identifies five examples of the incorrect intentions of the statists' theory of Reason of State:

1. Guardians rule: only elite guardians with great intellect, prudence, and experience understand the art of governing.
2. Moral and civil laws do not apply: political decisions should not follow moral or civil laws, because governors who abide by the laws do not follow Reason of State.
3. Situational ethics rule: the prince should apply the law as circumstances dictate.
4. Only grave issues of state apply: only the gravest, most important affairs of the prince—not little questions—apply.
5. Whatever means necessary must be employed to conserve prince and state: in order to conserve the prince and his state, governors should rule by extraordinary means, do whatever is necessary, and are not obliged to observe divine or human laws.[129]

The Foreigner has learned the lesson well and understands that such Ragion di Stato does not keep faith, destroys honesty, transgresses justice, causes the Prince "to be a tyrant with men and with God," and makes one's tongue rather than intellect rule.[130]

In Alciato's emblem 11 on Silence, the poem reminds us of the fool's indiscretions of the tongue—"Both tongue and voice are the index of his folly"—and Capaccio's annotations of the emblem in his *Il Principe* reinforce the point.[131] Capaccio finds the brief speeches of Menelaus and the cleverness of Ulysses, who thinks before he speaks, exemplary. Zeno's etiology of human physiognomy explains that two ears for listening lead to prudent judgment, while one mouth limits speech to keep counsel. Talkativeness is a sign of madness and the opposite of silence and wisdom, as "loquaciousness" is a "great sign of madness," whereas "silence is the grand prize." The dumb man is not crazy, but trustworthy; his silence is wisdom. And thus, Capaccio has returned full circle to the sun god. Harpocrates, a form of the Egyptian sun god Horus, is the visual representation of the emblem in the shape of a young boy seated at a writing desk with a finger over his lips to signify the need to keep confidences and not betray one's trust.[132] Silence is not just golden; it is, as we have already seen, the distinctive attribute of the owl, the emblem of the ancient Greek republic.

For Capaccio's courtier, Counter-Reformation political theory is the standard, conservative rationale for Spanish rule in Naples and princely rule in general. Vertical association (hierarchical authority) does not deny the necessary exercise of ancient and contemporary horizontal bonds of assent and association among equal, contracting parties that make the state what it is, but rather vertical association blesses the present political structure as the natural order of things and enshrines "Christian Politics" as the moral centerpiece of community and human action, with the Roman church as the spiritual guide and Spanish government as its temporal guardian. Both theory and practice reflect and reenact covenants of consent and virtues of compliance that are commemorated and celebrated by Capaccio in seven separate festival-book descriptions of the annual feast of San Giovanni in Naples, which marked the covenant between the absentee king's alter-ego viceroy and the Neapolitan *popolo*.[133] For learned men of the sixteenth and seventeenth centuries such as Capaccio, despite however much their erudition exacerbated the tension between esoteric knowledge for the initiated few and plain images accessible to all, studying the past meant engagement with their present.

In the city and the kingdom, then, the Neapolitan nobility was born to rule— from antiquity, from past service in battle, from religious fidelity, and from moral rectitude. Near the end of book 7's review of the workings of Neapolitan government in the parallel offices and administration of kingdom and city, Capaccio's Citizen identifies the Neapolitan Parlamento Generale as the lone deputation combining men from both the city and the baronage.[134] In reality, a vestigial institution without any real power that met biennially until it was curtailed less than a decade later in 1642, the Neapolitan parliament's main charge was to vote monetary aids (*donativi*) in exchange for listing grievances or petitions for redress (*grazie*).[135] The viceroy inaugurated parliament with a letter written by the city secretary (another opportunity for Capaccio to display his humanist rhetorical skills) and concluded it with receipt of the *donativi*. And a procession led by the *seggio* representative, who had precedence at that time as *sindaco* (mayor), began and ended the parliamentary term.

From the arrival of the Aragonese in 1442, parliament met in the former refectory of the convent (a large hall measuring forty by ten meters) adjacent to the Church of S. Lorenzo Maggiore in the center of the old city. Its vault, decorated under Philip III and the viceroy Count of Lemos in 1600, joined together the ideas of good government on heaven and earth, a program of virtues that restated visually the humanist education program that the Neapolitan historians advocated for its best citizens, both the urban and feudal nobility. Seven primary virtues, who were flanked by four attendant, subsidiary virtues, all represented on the ceiling, presided over representations of the twelve provinces of the kingdom in the lunettes.[136] Entering from the convent cloister into the hall dedicated to the public business of the kingdom, the parliamentary representatives would walk under a vault of virtues leading from Gravitas up to Royal Authority and her four attendant moral virtues:

> Gravitas attended by Maturity, Constancy, Firmness, and Perseverance
> Affability attended by Grace, Benignity, Courtesy, and Gratitude
> Clemency attended by Mercy, Piety, Peace, and Meekness
> Magnificence attended by Liberality, Felicity, Glory, and Honor
> Magnanimity attended by Valor, Order, Victory, and Nobility
> Providence attended by Vigilance, Hope, Counsel, and Good Fortune
> Royal Authority attended by Justice, Temperance, Fortitude, and Prudence

These thirty-five virtues provided the parliamentarians of the kingdom models of behavior to reflect upon during their debates and deliberations over issues affecting the twelve provinces. The moral life defined the public life for the ideal noble in Counter-Reformation Naples. To be old nobility of blood was to be a nobleman of virtue.

A large group of Neapolitan imprints on local history and geography linked Counter-Reformation spirituality with the ancient history of the city in order to emphasize the distinctiveness of its noble citizens' contributions and continuing commitment to the church and the crown. Thus, Capaccio's *cicerone* for the Foreigner was really a humanist primer for the Noble Citizen. Excluded from such a noble citizen's consciousness were both *popolo* and plebs, who would soon rise up against their lords, both monarch and nobles, in the nine-month revolt from 7 July 1647 to 6 April 1648, only to find themselves all the more repressed by the moral imperatives of that same "virtuous" nobility. The other in Spanish Naples was not so much the lying, foreign historian or the curious foreign visitor out to see the world, but rather the resident commoners—the *popolo* and plebs—whose "unfaithfulness" and "un-reason" challenged noble governance and authority.

The question of disorder and disparity or of harmony and solidarity in southern Italy may revolve around how we measure or understand the crisis of Italian liberty in the wake of the Spanish conquest of Naples and the rise of the early modern bureaucratic state. In Spanish Naples, late sixteenth- and early seventeenth-century historians mined classical sources to trace the origins of the city, rationalize Spanish rule, and promote *napolitanità*—the distinctiveness, priority, and preeminence of Naples—in order to link the ancient republic to the present under Spanish Habsburg rule.[137] Two reconstructed models of that ancient republic arose: an oligarchic republic similar to Venice presided over by ministers such as Carlo Tapia and championed by the apologists for the status quo in what

Vittor Ivo Comparato calls the "fiscal-provisioning state"; and a republic of the *popolo* forwarded by Camillo Tutini in what Giuseppe Galasso identifies as a new oligarchic-bourgeois "historical block."[138]

To whom does history belong, and for whom will the story of the past become a part of their present? History does not belong to the actors who make it but rather to those who write it. In the Renaissance commonplace, fame yields to time, and thus Achilles gives way to Homer, who memorializes the warrior's deeds. But when foreigners write the history of a place or a people not their own, whose truth do they tell? Are they subject to distortions and lies, ruled by their passions or prejudices rather than reason? On the other hand, what authorizes the native, rather than the other, to tell the truth? Likewise, whose story is it, the winners or the losers?

The facts and fictions of Capaccio's dialogue in 1634, like those of Basile's 1634–36 fairy tales, do the same thing in the Italian vernacular and Neapolitan dialect as the Latin humanists did in their histories and panegyrics. The emergent new Baroque aesthetic that was to develop from the late sixteenth century emphasized sharp and sudden insight, an overwhelming stupor created by the sublime and all-powerful—in short, the faith and commitment to God and king that reflected and reinforced the program of post-Tridentine politico-religious spirituality and stability. These emotive and expressive literary exaggerations and elaborations found enthusiastic proponents such as Basile and Capaccio in narrative and dialogic form. They infused the new style with the color of local religiosity and the content of Counter-Reformation reform, while underlining the importance of aristocratic society and noble decorum as the dominant influence on Neapolitan learning and literature, in order to glorify the Spanish victory in Italy and their project of restoring the lost, ancient imperium. Empire restored, not republicanism lost; universal faith, not *cuius regio, eius religio*, is the story. While Basile says that there is nothing more enticing than hearing a good story, it is a story that even the conservative propagandist Capaccio understood was always at risk. But it was essentially the same story—the myth of *buon governo* as the history of triumphant nobility, possessive of its privileges, wedded to the Spanish monarchy and the church, antagonistic to the *popolo*, and disdainful of the plebs.

CHAPTER TWO

Ritual Time and Ritual Space

Nature's Time: The Agricultural Cycle

Rituals, both religious and civic, are slow to change. In Spanish Naples, as in early modern Europe in general, rituals were closely tied to the primary mode of production, agriculture, which grounded material life in the climatic cycles of winter rain and summer sun, the alternating labor of planting and harvest, and the consequent limits of feast and famine. This biannual oscillation, which marked the change of seasons and defined the material world, structured urban life in large cities as much as rural life in the countryside with a repetitive regularity and recurrence. Seasonal rhythms defined both the tempo and duration of every aspect of urban life from the kind and quantity of foodstuffs, the supply of raw materials, and the influx of unskilled labor in the dominant textile trades to folkways and folk wisdom in the public square in a seamless continuum between city and countryside, nature and culture.

This seasonal structuring has persisted both in the reckoning of time and in the traditional festival foods even in contemporary industrial and postindustrial societies. Vestigial practices such as the academic calendar's autumnal beginning of the school year, for example, continue even though few students still labor in the fields for the annual harvest. Likewise, not in conformity with the calendar year, the U.S. governmental budget year shifts the financial year to another season in response to the problem of protracted negotiations during legislative holidays or summer recess, as does the fiscal year for many retail businesses on the logic of distorted December inventories from holiday shoppers. Similarly, holidays still feed memories full of Lenten or Ramadan fasting and subsequent feasting. Special holiday foods such as Christmas ham, Easter lamb, Passover Seder, and Purim hamantaschen are filled with symbolic meaning and nostalgic yearning. Early modern urban populations organized daily life around the seasonal variations of climate and production such that it was taken for granted as the natural order of things, just as schoolchildren and their teachers today assume that summer vacation is their natural right and that Hanukkah and Christmas bring them gifts and presents, or financial advisers make decisions based on seasonal variation and the April taxman. One cannot overemphasize the permanence and perseverance of the mental habits organizing premodern time to begin a new year with the end of summer in early September—fifteenth-century Neapolitan documents still used the medieval, indiction-cycle dating system with its new year beginning on 1 September. Artisans' and women's work was structured days and weeks before major holidays with the physical labor of endless hours making and repairing costumes and *apparati* or in specialty food preparation; and anxious anticipation in children of all ages sparked timeless memories as "visions of sugar-plums danced in their heads." Festivals live beyond the moment to order daily life, control labor as much as leisure, and feed dreams.

The Neapolitan hinterland's natural abundance of fruits and vegetables and its consequent license lie at the core of Capaccio's 1634 description of immigrants from the Neapolitan provinces, who, he estimates, made up "almost one-third" of the city's population. When he praises these folk from all over the kingdom—Calabresi, Pugliesi, and Abruzzesi and the closer Costaioli and Cavaioli—for "ennobling" the city as "it seems they are reborn, change customs, and their hometown coarseness becomes civility and a liberty proper to Naples," he goes on to explain what he means is that the city's plenty had changed these former peasants' diet from subsistence to surplus. "They have a taste and wish for bread at a better price, both whiter [bread] and bigger [loaves], they no longer remember barley bread or millet that they used to eat before. These are the proper greatness and allures of this Siren."[1] For Capaccio, the true charms of the Siren's call to Naples were this breaking of the cycle of hunger through the agricultural abundance flowing into the city.

While the annual grain harvest of mid-July to mid-August was being completed by the summer fair, *ferragosto*, fruit and vegetable produce from the nearby Neapolitan countryside that could not be transported long distances was being sold in the city's markets. A Parisian visitor to Naples in 1632, Jean-Jacques Bouchard, chronicled the end-of-summer harvest of fruits and vegetables at the conclusion of his diary account of his Neapolitan travels in order to praise the abundance of nature in the *Campania Felice*. Grapes were first on Bouchard's list of the bountiful harvest; for, as he recounted it, the vindemia in the Kingdom of Naples turned into an unusual bacchic festival of free-flowing wine that loosened tongues in uninhibited and uncensored speech. "The two months of September and October, and even into November, allowed for a strange sort of license, as a result of the vindemia, during which the grape pickers are permitted to say all sorts of insults, even the most atrocious and villainous, to all kinds of people whatever their station, without even exempting princes or viceroys."[2] The linkage between food, drink, sex, and violence as expressed in licentious speech—per Bouchard's short digression on the carry-over of the vindemia celebration into the city and the etymology of the epithet, *un Napolitano cornuto* (a Neapolitan cuckold)—pertains to all festivals, not only to the world of Carnival so well documented for early modern Europe.[3] Bouchard finds that the unrest from affronts to honor over such sexual insults "reigned generally in all Italy, but particularly in the Kingdom of Naples," and could lead to its well-known political instability and riots, as evidenced by the Sicilian Vespers, which Bouchard attributes to "their jealousy which could not suffer the liberty and insolence of the French toward their women."[4] Festivals create a special time outside of time that permits inversion, which in turn reinforces the social order but also provides the language and practices for resistance that can sometimes be used to challenge that order.[5]

Bouchard identifies thirteen varietal wines from the native grapes around Naples and gives a catalog of eight varieties of grapes that began to be harvested at the end of July and continued through August, September, and October, with even four late varieties able to be preserved until Easter. There follows the seasonal calendar of fruits and vegetables beginning with April (strawberries), May (cherries), June (apricots, plums, figs, pears), July (peaches, melons, cucumbers, squash, broccolis), and August (apples)—all of which "are very excellent, as are all the other vegetables, and generally all the fruits, of which Naples abounds more than any other Italian and perhaps even European city."[6]

In early modern Naples, as in the early modern Mediterranean world, a common genealogy with deep roots as much in history and culture as in nature and its bounty had codified, rationalized, and unified beliefs and practices over the years through language, religion, and law, so that recurrent, annual remembrances and rituals had become second nature. In the legislative decrees "On Holidays" of the Neapolitan Collateral Council, such feasts and festivals (Lat. *feriae publicae*) were divided into the same three categories as those of ancient Greco-Roman classical civilizations: immovable or fixed holidays in the calendar year; movable feasts set by the lunar calendar; and extraordinary events that became special occasions to petition for deliverance from natural disaster, famine, disease, war, and death.[7] This tripartite classification of holidays followed the same seasonal calendar and carried the same structural associations with the natural world over millennia and across civilizations.

The Mediterranean climatic zone of hot, dry summers and cool, wet winters established the agricultural calendar of Naples,[8] which neatly divided the calendar year into two seasons, fall-winter and spring-summer, not the temperate zone's four seasons. Giuseppe Galasso underlines this seasonal dualism of the agricultural cycle in Naples as being its "natural foundation and objective climate," which even Neapolitan dialect recognizes with "only two seasons, *vierne* and *staggione*, 'winter' and the 'season par excellence,' or the 'good season,'" and upon which the liturgical year's Advent-Nativity-Lent-Resurrection and Resurrection-Ascension-Pentecost-Assumption cycles are grafted. Winter was the ritual season of "reflection, piety, preparation, and waiting"; summer was the festival season of "actual celebration, exultation, glorification, realization, and harvest."[9] We shall see that the fall-winter season in Naples coincides with the autumnal equinox and thus begins with the feast of Piedigrotta (the Nativity of the Blessed Virgin Mary) on 8 September and is punctuated at midwinter at the winter solstice by Christmas on 25 December; while the spring-summer season in Naples coincides with the vernal equinox that begins with the feast of the Annunciation on 25 March and celebrates midsummer at the summer equinox on 24 June with St. John the Baptist's Day. What is important in the duality of the two seasons is the presence at one and the same time of cyclical repetition as well as the sharp, roller-coaster alternation of polar opposites.

The repetitive redress of the ambiguity and uncertainty of the transitions from plenty to dearth and dearth to plenty were conceived not only in terms of recurrent cycles but also as extreme discontinuities, such as night and day, drought and flood, age and youth, birth and death, work and leisure. The playing out of winter's relative inactivity and summer's productivity in festival performances functioned not only to order time but also to establish the dynamic of time that distinguished the here and now from the there and then, while simultaneously linking past, present, and future through ritual.[10] Ritual time was not just a "time out of time" or connection to "the myth of the eternal return" but was literally the reincarnation of the founding act establishing time itself, an act of death that gave birth and made reversible the irreversibility of life and death. Seasonal dualism was easily translated into ritual transcendence and millenarian visions, both readily baptized by Christianity.

Carlo Celano's definitive 1692 guidebook explains in its history of the religion of Naples that in the ancient Italo-Greek city all its rites were those practiced in ancient Athens. Only traces of the temples of false gods have survived, but games, festivals, and sacrifices dedicated to them were appropriated by the Romans in their theaters, gymnasiums, baths, and streets.[11] In turn, syncretism employed by Christianization of pagan feasts retained much of the content and practice of earlier myths and rituals, albeit in a new form and inventive elaboration derived from the logic of Christian doctrine and liturgy.[12] The fixed date of the midwinter nativity of Christ on 25 December and the analogous midsummer nativity of John the Baptist on 24 June continued ancient, pagan agrarian rites marking the winter and summer solstice low and high point of the solar and agricultural year with overtones of fertility and fecundity, regeneration and baptism, and omens and signs in an eschatological present. Lupercalia, the festival of light, became Candlemas (the Purification of the Virgin Mary on 2 February), which was set forty days after Christmas and continued the purification of candles through the following day's feast of St. Blaise (3 February); similarly, Ascension Thursday followed forty days after Easter to celebrate the risen Christ's ascension into heaven. The festival of the agrarian god Martinis Marvos was transformed into St. Joseph's Day on 19 March; and summer's *ferragosto* displaced the harvest festival of the goddess Diana (13 August) with the Assumption of the Virgin (15 August).[13] The *translatio* of San Gennaro (I Preti Inghirlandati [The Garlanding of the Priests]), set as the Saturday before the first Sunday of May, sanctified the old pagan Mayday fertility rites of the agricultural calendar at the beginning of summer to ward off the dead and evil spirits, just as six months later All Saints and All Souls Days (1 and 2 November) likewise commemorated the communion of saints by crossing over the boundary between the living and the dead. Such parallel celebrations in the two seasons are neither accidental nor artificial but are the conscious creation of an agrarian society in tune with nature and its rhythms.

The sheer number and distinctive features of these feasts in Naples were the subject of reflection by local citizens and foreign visitors alike. Our reliable foreign witness, Bouchard, the Parisian visitor to Naples in 1632, was taken by what was unique to Naples, the fact that its feasts were "more solemn and even better than at Rome, primarily for the practices, where they are much more beautiful in their mystery."[14] Moreover, Bouchard found Neapolitan festivals proverbially continuous, with the solemnity and magnificence of its processions due not only to the quantity of relics in the city but especially to two striking marks of religiosity. First and foremost, the Neapolitan devotion to the liquefaction of saints' blood made it the *urbs sanguinum*, the city at the center of the cult of blood devotion; and also its mourning rituals and obsequies, with widows cutting their hair and throwing it on their deceased husbands, were described as a lugubrious affair bearing a strong flavor of antiquity.[15]

The Neapolitan citizen Michele Zappullo, writing a third of a century earlier in 1598, however, explains this unique Neapolitan religiosity as fulfilling the biblical injunction of Ecclesiastes 3 to do "everything in its proper season, for there is a time to every purpose under heaven." For Zappullo, his interpretation of Ecclesiastes 3 extends the dichotomies of the scripture verse to emphasize a time for leisure (*otio*) and a time for its negation, work (*negotio*): "Thus, the more devout the Kingdom of Naples is than any other part of Italy, the less it becomes miserable and unhappy, and in this is verified in what the Sage in Ecclesiastes 3 says, 'I have seen the travail, which God hath given to the sons of men to be exercised in it. He hath made every *thing* beautiful in his time: also he hath set the world in their heart, so that no man can find out the work that God maketh from the beginning to the end.' "[16] Zappullo then goes on to enumerate the extraordinary quantity of Neapolitan feasts: 83 from the government pragmatics on public holidays closing business, plus another 52 for Sundays, 7 more for mobile feasts (Ascension, the two days after Pentecost Sunday, Corpus Christi and its octave, and the Saturday before the first Sunday of May [the second feast of San Gennaro], 30 other religious holidays (Christmas, Easter, and other days in honor of God), 6 days for Carnival, 2 months for the summer holiday when only Thursdays are workdays, not to mention on special 3-day holidays for royal life-cycle events (births, marriages, and deaths), the one-half day closures on holiday vigils when workers did not return after the midday meal, or other special events. In sum, Zappullo's list adds up to 230 days or 63 percent of the year! And even if we do not count the two-month summer holiday in July and August, Zappullo's number is still high at 178 holidays, some 49 percent of the year. His count of one-half to two-thirds of the days of the year as holidays does not confirm Prince Hal's famous words written by Shakespeare only a year before Zappullo's text:

> If all the year were playing holidays,
> To sport would be as tedious as to work;
> But when they seldom come, they wish'd for come,
> And nothing pleaseth but rare accidents.   (*Henry IV, Part I*, 1.2.74–77)

No, for Zappullo having numerous holidays was not tedious or excessive; rather, the number of holidays answers the question posed in Ecclesiastes 3:10, "What profit hath he that worketh in that wherein he laboreth?" In other words, Ecclesiastes 11–12 quoted by Zappullo means that the Neapolitan's extreme religiosity is the right answer to God's having made men work (*negotium*); for, by finding the negation of work (*otio*) in religious holidays, both work and leisure become "beautiful" as man's God-given task. All time past, present, and future is one and the same in God. For Zappullo, the Neapolitans could not have too many holidays to praise God.

The Festive Occasion

The noble *eletti* took turns as the city's *sindaco* (mayor) according to a predetermined rotation, with representatives of the five noble *seggi* (Capuana, Montagna, Nido, Porto, and Portanova) following one another in turn. According to the town council's records of *seggi* precedence (*Praecedentiarum*), the city *sindaco* presided over public ceremonies some eighty times during the Spanish viceroyalty's first half-century rule between 1504 and 1556.[17] Ceremonial occasions can be separated into six general types:

1. Biennial parliaments
2. Receptions and entries of new viceroys, other commanding officers, royals, and other dignitaries
3. Commemorations of the life-cycle events of members of the royal family and political landmarks of state
4. Politico-religious occasions for other rulers
5. Crises and extraordinary emergencies
6. Religious holidays[18]

During this fifty-three-year period, such ceremonies had an irregular frequency of about 1.5 per year. But long periods could go by with no public ceremonies of this kind, such as the five and a half years between the 17 September 1520 closing of parliament and the 16 March 1526 welcoming of a new viceroy, or the three years before the next viceroy reception ceremony on 25 April 1529. On the other hand, a full week could be given over to festivities, such as the four ceremonies involving four different *sindaci* held between 28 July and 5 August 1535 in celebration of Charles V's military victory at Tunis. Given the sporadic call for the *sindaco*'s ceremonial performance, the large number of noble families represented in the list of *sindaci* is not surprising, although the importance within their own *seggi* of a few families, such as the Gennaro of Porto and the Mormile of Portanova in these smaller *seggi*, is shown by their frequency in the office.

In the seven extant books of the *Praecedentiarum* (1554–1642),[19] formal designation of the *sindaco* for cavalcades over this eighty-eight-year period is documented 1.2 times per year,[20] beginning on 31 October 1554 with the entrance of the Marquis of Pescara as proxy for Philip II's swearing in and extending to the last Neapolitan parliament of 1642.[21] Assignment of *sindaco* precedence for the religious cavalcades followed the immovable and movable feast days of the saints' and liturgical calendar. The five other established festival occasions, however, do not fit neatly into this movable/immovable distinction and can be more appropriately described as part of court ceremonial.[22] Here a binary division between the religious calendar and civil occasions seems more appropriate, even though in the celebrations themselves one should not deny the "sacred" character of ritual time in both the religious and civil festivals, nor can one separate the overlapping and commingling connections to both the religious and civil spheres.[23] Such an undifferentiated, politico-religious category, nevertheless, can be applied to two types of more political, public ceremonies not linked to the church calendar. One kind of normal celebration of these occasional, nonpredictable, recurring events, which were celebrated regularly but with no fixed date or even seasonal timetable, concerns governance and lordship, such as the biennial meetings of parliament (opening and closing ceremonies and the presentation of *donativi* [monetary aids] and *grazie* [petitions]);[24] the comings and goings of viceroys (arrival, entry, *possesso* [inauguration]), their substitutes when the viceroys were called off to war or papal conclaves, or other VIP visits;[25] royal family life-cycle commemorations (pledging of homage and fealty upon accessions, coronations, royal marriages, births of royal children, deaths of members of the royal family, or their recovery from illness);[26] and similar commemorations for other rulers.[27] A second kind of politico-religious occasion applies to the extraordinary celebrations held in thanksgiving for military or political victories (victorious battles, alliances, peace treaties)[28] and in petitioning for divine intercession in times of emergency (for rain in the drought of 1605 or for deliverance from the volcanic eruption of 16 December 1631).[29] These civic or politico-religious festivals, nevertheless, constituted an ambiguous category, as witnessed by the viceroy's participation.

Two masters of ceremonies at the viceregal court of Naples from the 1580s to 1630s have left written accounts of the viceroy's ceremonial responsibilities in civic and religious festivals, which followed Burgundian etiquette and local custom. Miguel Diéz de Aux, at the center of the court of Naples for almost forty years from the 1580s to 1622, was master of ceremonies and governor of Pozzuoli under two viceroys, Juan Alonso Pimentel de Herrera, Count of Benavente (1603–10), and Pedro Fernández de Castro, Count of Lemos (1610–16).[30] Diéz de Aux describes both civic ceremonies (convening of the Neapolitan parliament, the viceroy's *possesso*, visits by other dignitaries, royal births, royal deaths, and a papal election) and religious festivals (Holy Week and Easter, Corpus Christi, S. Giovanni, and S. Gennaro), as well as the summer holidays spent at Posillipo. Diéz de Aux's unpublished manuscript not only records the funeral obsequies for Philip II and Philip III held during his tenure in Naples but, more tellingly for continuity and tradition in court etiquette and protocol, also details the royal obsequies for Charles V at Brussels, which make up the single, longest entry with some twenty-three folios in his manuscript.[31]

José Raneo, a *portero de camera* of His Excellency the viceroy and the master of ceremonies for fourteen years during the seven-year terms of two viceroys, Antonio Álvarez de Toledo, Duke of Alba (1622–29), and Manuel de Zuñiga y Fonseca, Count of Monterrey (1631–37), documented the etiquette for the Neapolitan court in 1634.[32] Raneo summarized the occasions on which the viceroy rode in the ceremonial cavalcades and participated in the city's public festivals with the *sindaco* and *eletti* of the city. The viceroy annually attended fifty-six feasts (fifty-two immovable and four movable), plus Septuagesima (the Sundays between Epiphany and Lent) and the five Sundays of Lent. Of the fifty-six festivals with viceregal participation, not counting the pre-Lenten and Lenten Sundays, fifty-three were religious feast days and three were extraordinary days of political thanksgiving and remembrance that had been institutionalized as permanent, fixed holidays: 7 September for the victory of the Cardinal-Infante Ferdinand at the Battle of Nördlingen in1634 during the Thirty Years' War; 7 October (Our Lady of Victory, later Our Lady of the Rosary) for the victory of Don Juan of Austria at the Battle of Lepanto in 1571 against the Turks; and 16 December (the third feast of San Gennaro) for intercession during the volcanic eruption of Vesuvius in 1631. Many of these festivals had a political significance beyond the religious feast day, such as Saturday before the first Sunday of May (the *translatio* of San Gennaro, the so-called Garlanding of the Priests) when the liquefaction of San Gennaro's blood was the occasion for all the clergy in the city to pledge their allegiance to the archbishop; 23 June (St. John's Day Eve) for its association with the *popolo;* and the numerous city patron saints' days for their association with particular churches, religious orders, foreign resident communities, guild members, and citizen neighborhoods.

In her analysis of the two religious processions of San Gennaro and Corpus Christi, Maria Antonietta Visceglia argues that, as these politico-religious celebrations reflected Naples's increasing dependence on Spain and the complex process of the capital's growth in the sixteenth and seventeenth centuries, they created an ambiguous model of the Neapolitan political festival.[33] No Neapolitan political ceremonies were only civic or exclusively celebratory of the monarchy; yet all religious rituals were deeply imbued with political meaning. Visceglia concludes that public rituals betrayed the underlying political-social instability of the city, as urban political institutions became sacralized in the language of religious celebrations. Thus, in the ongoing competition and conflict among social groups and civic entities in Naples, the religious component of festivals eventually overwhelmed and subordinated the secular and political profile of Neapolitan public rituals in the second half of the seventeenth century.

Parliamentary Ceremonies

Raneo provides short descriptions of the protocol or summaries of specific occasions for the five types of these politico-religious festivals. Parliamentary ceremonies began with the viceroy's participation in the procession to S. Lorenzo for the opening session, continued for the reception of the *donativi* contributions and the list of *grazie* requests, and ended with the closing ceremonies.[34] Carlos Hernando has analyzed how the Neapolitan parliament was appropriated as a "theater of power" by Charles V in 1535–36 during his winter sojourn in Naples as a means of consolidating the Neapolitan kingdom into the larger structure and design of his empire.[35] The parliamentary ceremonial thus highlighted two forms of "representation": the viceroy as *pro rex*, the absentee king; and the deputies of the feudal nobility and the urban patriciate. At the same time, Hernando argues that parliament became the "arena of factions," where nobles jockeyed in opposition or support of viceregal policies, the king's increasing monetary demands for *donativi*, and the baronage's defense of feudal privileges. The rivalry between noble clans and the dynamic between monarchic centralization and local power played out in the symbolic and ceremonial display of parliament, with the institution itself declining in importance until its eventual extinction in 1642.

The Possesso: Swearing in Kings and Vice-Kings

A second festive occasion for the viceroy was his *possesso*, his official taking "possession" of the kingdom upon formal entry, which was a ceremony of welcome and inauguration that emphasized the swearing in of the surrogate king to uphold the laws and rights of the kingdom. After the long tenure of Pedro de Toledo (1532–53), sixteenth- and seventeenth-century Spanish viceroys in Naples normally served a three-year term that could often be renewed for a total of six years; thus, the *possesso* became a regular feature of the city's public ritual. The viceroy's *possesso* replicated the ceremonies for the royal entry of the king throughout the Spanish monarchy and had resonances with the *possesso* of the pope in his inaugural march along the *via papalis* in Rome.[36] As the king's proxy, the viceroy was fêted as the king himself, and his *possesso* in Naples should be seen, above all, as a triumphant royal entry with the conferring of the church's legitimacy by the archbishop at the cathedral swearing in. When a king took possession of the kingdom upon his inauguration, there was a dual swearing-in ceremony in which the king (or his proxy, as in the case of the Marquis of Pescara for Philip II in 1554) pledged to protect the laws and privileges of his subjects and the citizens pledged their fidelity to the king.

The iconic example of the Neapolitan *possesso* took place upon the arrival of Charles V in 1535 flush from his victory in Tunis. His entry and four-month winter sojourn received a full twelve-page description in the printed transcription of the Raneo text, the longest chronicled event in his ceremonial book. Charles's triumphal entrance in 1535 had been modeled on an earlier festival in Naples in his honor sixteen years before, upon his election as emperor in the summer of 1519, as described by Girolamo Britonio, court poet of Ferrante Francesco d'Avolos, Marquis of Pescara, and his wife Vittoria Colonna.[37] Britonio's conceit personified Naples as the dependent bride in an amorous marriage.[38] Sumptuous celebrations circulated around the whole kingdom, and the city of Naples became a theater for six days of processions and six nights of fireworks. The final *festa da ballo* for all the noble citizens at the Castel Nuovo was followed by a mock naval battle visible from the balcony windows as it was fought below in the Bay of Naples. The dance was held in the Sala dei Baroni, whose walls boasted rich silk tapestries depicting the Last Judgment, the seven deadly sins, and the Nativity with numerous horses and other animals in attendance at the Christ Child's birth. A square wooden stage with arches of garlanded myrtle dedicated to Aphrodite and the imperial coat of arms triumphantly set amid the arbors was constructed in the center of the room, and on its eastern side music worthy of the Elysian Fields filled the room from two orchestra pits. Isabella d'Aragona, the daughter of Alfonso II and the widowed Duchess of Milan, could be seen in a balcony above part of the southern side of the stage, from which hung a tapestry of the flight of Daedalus and Icarus. The viceroy Ramón de Cardona (r. 1509–22) presided. Emphasized even more than the elegant vestments, ephemeral architecture, and mythical images in Britonio's account were the sounds of heavenly music and the bombardment bursts as the fierce, reenacted sea battle dominated the panorama with flashes of light and thunderous explosions. The *naumachia* turned the castle guests into the onlooking audience of the simulated, dramatic battle as the stage shifted outside among the ships and galleys on the bay and exploited the landscape of Naples to extend the stage of the festivities beyond the sacred ground within the boundaries of the city walls to the sky above and the sea beyond.

A typical, sixteenth-century viceroy *possesso* filled with sound and fury was described in 1586 with all the nobility and *popolo* of the city of Naples receiving the new viceroy Juan de Zuñiga, Count of Miranda (r. 1586–95), "with the greatest happiness and honor." As he disembarked from his galley, the sound of cannon saluting from the numerous other ships in the harbor and reverberating delightfully in response from the nearby Castel Nuovo and Castel dell'Ovo, and from Castel S. Elmo high above the city commanding the bay, "although festive and in high exaltation, made Naples seem to be trying to defend itself from the assault of enemy squadrons." The city itself, "illuminated by flashing fusillades, could well be said to be another Troy, or Rome set ablaze by Nero." These sounds and sights of 1586 chronicled by the Neapolitan diarist Scipione Guerra led him to conclude his description of the much anticipated new viceroy's reception at the port in exclamation: "In truth, these were things not done for many years before. Thus, if the person of the King Our Lord Philip II himself were to arrive here, they would not be able to make more superb and sumptuous demonstrations of rejoicing [*allegrezza*] and obsequiousness."[39] With Naples the site of Virgil's tomb, one might well see artillery-lit Spanish Naples as the new imperial successor to fiery Troy and burning Rome, and the new viceroy, who was assuming the persona of the absent king, as accepting the festive joy and fawning obedience of the Spanish Empire's "most faithful" city.

As the bombardment ended, the new viceroy mounted a beautiful horse all covered in a gold and silver train led by all the lords of the kingdom and the holders of the major offices. Language fails our chronicler in his hyperbole and enthusiasm:

> And there was so great a multitude of horses, coaches, and citizens with the multitude of the *popolo* that one cannot narrate it all with words. I do not believe that in the memory of man one could remember so great a multitude of people. They were in so great number that the halberdiers with their singular impertinence alone could make way for His Excellency and his entourage to pass through with their horses and coaches. Finally, he was accompanied to the Royal Palace with the greatest applause and jubilation; the company that accompanied him was about six hundred.

Despite Guerra's rather repetitive diction, his account sparkles with aural and visual metaphors to convey the ecstatic welcome for the Count of Miranda by the Neapolitans, who "did not cease to demonstrate with a thousand signs how great was their satisfaction and joyfulness [*allegrezza*] now having been liberated from the long and fierce tyranny" of the odious previous viceroy, Pedro Téllez Girón, Duke of Osuna (r. 1582–86).

Triumphant entrances to Naples came by land through the Capuana Gate, as did Charles V, or, more typically for new viceroys, by sea, by way of their earlier arrival in nearby Pozzuoli or Procida, to the port at the foot of the Castel Nuovo, and proceeded with a cavalcade around the city. The new viceroy's preferred entry by ship featured a richly decorated, cloth-covered gangway (*ponte*), whose functional purpose of providing a landing ramp to shore took on symbolic meaning in its ritual pillage, as described in the entries of Cardinal Granvelle (1571), the Duke of Osuna (1582), and the counts of Miranda (1586), Olivares (1595), and Lemos (1599).[40] Giuliana Vitale has documented the explosion of ritual violence and the sacking of the ruler's goods and property or ephemeral objects from the death of Ferdinand II (Ferrandino) in 1496 and the royal entry of Ferdinand the Catholic in 1506.[41] The sack of *castellane* (colossal wooden funerary structures to hold corpses), *ponte* or *tabernacolo* (galleries, passageways, or gangways), and *pallio* (special vestments) used in liminal contexts of arrivals and departures (literal entries and exits, successions of kingship, or death and burial), she argues, should be seen not only as signs of grief, anxiety, or fear over the uncertainty caused by the sovereign's absence, interregnum, or suspension of the laws. The acquisition of "sacred" objects in such ritual violence was a desire not for monetary gain but rather for the spiritual and thaumaturgic properties that turn normal objects of saints and kings into holy relics because of their proximity to the royal or saintly body. The short sentence describing the *ponte* sack for the arrival of Cardinal Granvelle in 1571 offers an alternative, utilitarian explanation, that "the order was sent that the *ponte* should be sacked to avoid the inconvenience and dangers that used to occur" and, as such, could be understood as a form of the king's largesse and magnanimity, such as the distribution of bread or throwing of coins during processions.[42] The ceremony welcoming the new viceroy the Count of Miranda in 1586 may have been exceptionally joyful because of the departure of his hated predecessor; but, as Scipione Guerra's chronicle reports, even if the person of the king himself had been present, it could not have been any better. Philip II, however, never did visit his Neapolitan kingdom or its capital, his empire's largest city. One of Philip's dying injunctions to his son and heir Philip III cautioned against leaving Spain and even "excessive traveling" about it.[43]

Philip II, nevertheless, alone after his father Charles V was the sixteenth-century's most traveled monarch, with two extended trips outside Spain for a total of eight years.[44] The twenty-one-year-old prince Philip journeyed from October 1548 to July 1551 via Barcelona, Genoa, Milan, Mantua, Trent, Innsbruck, Munich, and Heidelberg, to Brussels and the Low Countries, where "the cities of Flanders and Brabant, especially Antwerp, and the sumptuous magnificence of the old Burgundian court" made a "lasting impact on him." Again later, as he was to become "king consort" of Mary Tudor, he sailed in July 1554 from La Coruña for England, where he would stay some thirteen months. On 24 July 1554, the day before the marriage ceremony, in order to have equal title with his queen bride, Philip accepted the first of his father's great gifts, a wedding present of formal investiture as King of Naples and Duke of Milan, whence Philip styled himself "king-prince" (*el rey príncipe*).[45] He crossed over to Brussels, where he received his father's other realms and titles in formal investiture after Charles's abdication on 25 October 1555. From Brussels, Philip administered affairs and eventually "combined the roles of commander in chief and paymaster general" in the war against France, traveled to Cambrai near the front, toured Saint-Quentin three days after the Spanish victory of 10 August 1557, and led a countercharge two weeks later to retake Saint-Quentin after it had fallen briefly back into French hands. He presided over the making of the peace, mourned at the funeral obsequies for his father Charles V in Brussels on 28 November 1558, and remained after the signing of the Treaty of Cateau-Cambrésis on 3 April 1559 until his departure for Spain in August 1559. In Naples and throughout most of his vast empire, however, Philip ruled as an absentee king, in the person of a "substitute," "surrogate," or vice-king.

Thus, in the 1554 "swearing in and homage" given to Philip as King of Naples, of Jerusalem, and Duke of Milan with presentation before the *sindaco*, *seggi* representatives, and barons for their oath of allegiance at S. Lorenzo and on to the Neapolitan archbishop's palace for his own swearing in, Ferrante Francesco d'Avolos, marchese di Pescara, stood in Philip's stead. Son of Alfonso, marchese del Vasto, the young marchese di Pescara was the royal procurator, had accompanied Philip to England for his marriage to Mary Tudor on 25 July 1554, and returned to Naples for the *possesso*. The viceroy Cardinal Pietro Pacheco, surrounded by fifty halberdiers, led the procession with the marchese di Pescara on his right and the *sindaco*, Pietro Antonio Sanseverino, Prince of Bisignano, on his left. In the customary "sign of liberality and joyfulness," the kingdom's treasurer, Alonzo Sanchez, rode in the cavalcade carrying two large sacks of gold and silver coins, from which he threw fistfuls of money as they crossed through the nobles' *seggi* and other places along the parade route.[46] In the description of the swearing-in ceremony for the absentee king, a twelve-page printed book dated 26 November 1554 expresses hopes for a coming golden age and for the new king's actual coming, the "Real presenza" of Philip in the future.[47] The most interesting reference in the document is not this pun on royal/real or the presence of the king/Eucharist; but the dedication letter to Sempronio Romulo, the name of the imaginary Roman citizen to whom the description of Charles V's 1535 entrance nineteen years earlier had been addressed.[48] Philip's *possesso*, even in absentia, is in the same tradition of the ancient imperial triumph that predates the papacy (and its claim of suzerainty over Naples), and further it invokes the ruling class's claim of the most faithful, "repubblica partenopea" in accord with the victorious Caesar in triumph from Tunis, so that, in the words of Tobia Toscano, "the triumph of Charles V should also be the triumph of Naples."[49]

The relationship between the king or the viceroy and the papacy or the archbishop of Naples is a key component of the *possesso*. Sabina de Cavi has exploited the diary of the cathedral of Naples and other sources to construct two different narratives of the *possesso* from the perspective of the monarchy and the church, and to place the Neapolitan *possesso* in the broad context of imperial Spain.[50] De Cavi argues that the "exchange of courtesies between the viceroy and the archbishop of Naples" is one of the central acts of the ceremony. Examining the *possesso* from these two different points of view reveals how much the codified etiquette was played out as a positive or negative negotiation between the secular and religious powers, as the viceroy's cavalcade circumscribed the city to legitimate Spanish political power at the time that each new viceroy assumed authority.

Other Visitors and Entries

The subcategory of other visitors comprises the largest number of Raneo's short chapters, and for good reason. Because the viceroy's master of ceremonies was involved in overseeing protocol for the viceroy and his court, such frequent state visits were part of the routine communication and general services network of Spanish rule in Italy. Whether for the Sicilian viceroy, the Roman ambassador, Spanish visitors-general, church officials, or foreign dignitaries, the port of Naples remained a gateway to and from Spanish Italy. In addition to generic visitors discussed by their office, Diéz de Aux described the visit of the Prince of Savoy, Filiberto Emanuel, while Raneo identified specific visitors such as the Prince of Poland, the Duke of Lorraine, the Duke of Mantua, and numerous Spaniards. Their visits provided opportunities to offer hospitality and engage in entertainments and diversions for the Neapolitan nobility. No visitor during this period received more attention or stayed longer than Maria Anna d'Austria, sister of Philip IV, Queen of Bohemia and Hungary, on her way from Spain to Austria to join her Habsburg cousin, the emperor Ferdinand II's son and future Ferdinand III, whom she had married by proxy the year before in 1629.[51]

Life-Cycle Events of Royals

Festivals for the life-cycle events of the Spanish royal family were grafted onto the normal affairs of state. During Maria d'Austria's visit, for example, the king's birthday on 17 October 1630 was celebrated in Naples with the first performance of one of the first musical dramas in Naples, Giambattista Basile's court masque, *Monte Parnaso. Mascarata da Cavalieri Napoletani*. The praise of Capaccio's Foreigner gives some sense of the masque's reception: "I do not know what greater work could be compared for its grace, splendor, delight, and variety among those to be found in the treasury of poetry."[52] The setting and story of Mount Parnassus, home of Apollo and the Muses, reinforce the Neapolitan self-image of a city blessed for its arts and learning. In Fellecchia's panegyric to summarize the brilliance of Naples and its entertainments during the queen Maria d'Austria's visit, he introduces the Basile masque with a set of sustained astronomical metaphors to praise Naples: "Her Majesty stayed in the famous city of Naples, which is the most ancient and noble Mother of Heroes, Arsenal of arms, and guardrail of Mars; that Naples, whose ordering resembles a beautiful Sky, whose prime mover is the nobility, whose North Pole is science, whose South Pole is magnanimity, whose base is faith, whose Zones are the senses, whose circles are the powers, whose motions are thoughts, whose stars are the virtues, [and] whose signs are its merits, provided hospitality for her Highness the Queen."[53] Naples itself is clearly another Mount Parnassus.

The masque, set to music by Giacinto Lambardo, has no real plot but unfolds in a series of scenes centered on five ballets. In the palace theater against a sylvan-scene backdrop crowned with the Habsburg coat of arms in the middle of the two pillars of Hercules of the royal *impresa*, "Plus ultra," a temple with two lively statues of Honor and Glory stood center stage. A chorus sings verses in praise of the queen to introduce the first scene between Night, who enters from the sky on an azure chariot studded with stars, and Fame, who emerges from the temple, to join in song in praise of the queen. From an ivy-covered cave on the side, a river brings six white swans to dance the first ballet. The scene shifts to the summit of Mount Parnassus where Apollo with quiver and lyre and the nine Muses with their iconographic attributes preside in similar songs of praise. The second ballet is danced by eight graceful nymphs in a delightful garden. The third ballet in pastoral mode is danced by four bacchant nymphs and four satyrs. A cavernous underground forge appears for the fourth ballet with three Cyclops of Vulcan and three diminutive and haggard dwarves. Mount Parnassus and the Muses disappear to be replaced by the Elysian Fields, where the final ballet with forty-eight noblemen, the Cavalieri Napolitani of Basile's subtitle, is danced to six stanzas, all ending with the same refrain couplet in praise of the visiting queen to end the masque:

> Celebre or chi farà
> Il tuo valor la tua beltà?
> Who will make famous now
> Your valor and your beauty?

Immediately following Basile's text of the masque, the names of the participating noblemen are given "with the precedence of their place" and the nephew of the Duke of Alba, Marquis di Villa Nova del Rio, at the head of the list. The critical question of priority of place was not a curiosity or affectation of court life, but central to the nobility's persona or mask worn on the court stage. Drama and performance with its singing and dancing were not ornaments of ritual play but were competitive tests of skill in the one-upmanship of gaining and maintaining status and honor at court. Court celebrations emphasized agonistic play in theatrical performance, tournaments, and games to reinforce the hierarchical social structure of the absolutist monarchies.

Court rituals also were used to help return to "normalcy" after extraordinary times. Thus, Viceroy Iñigo Velez de Guevara, Count of Oñate (r. 1648–53), whose *possesso* as viceroy on 2 March 1648 allowed him to preside over the final phases of the pacification of the 1647 revolt, slowly began to reestablish festivals, first court and then public, in order to reinforce the restoration of Spanish rule. In 1648, for the marriage of Philip IV with his niece Marianna d'Austria, who was traveling from Austria to Spain, the drama *Trionfo di Partenope Liberata* was put on in the Royal Palace in Naples for the "gentlemen of the Court" by the viceroy on the occasion of "the happy arrival in Milan of the Royal Spouse" of Philip IV "with the assistance of Cardinal Filomarino and the most important Ladies and Knights of the Kingdom."[54] On 6 April 1649, Oñate celebrated the one-year anniversary of the end of the revolt of 1647; in 1652 he sponsored a festival for the capture of Barcelona during the Catalan revolt and, in that same year, restored the masquerade of Carnival, albeit with heavy restrictions. He is also credited with restoring "the use of comedy in music in the city."[55]

Like the civic celebrations of parliaments, viceroys' *possessos*, and the visits of dignitaries, the occasional festivals for royal births, marriages, sicknesses, and deaths reinforced the remembrance of the life-cycle events that structured the birth-to-death Christological and Marian devotions of the religious calendar and connected the life-cycle events of the ordinary citizen to the essential mystery of divine and royal incarnation through ritual practice. Such holidays became occasions for the collective celebration not only of the royal holiday but, inasmuch as their ruler embodied the state, of all subjects of every rank and station, who were celebrating the royal milestone as their own.

Raneo described obsequies for four deaths and provided a generic description for royal births in his ceremonial protocols.[56] The first royal death, Philip II's in 1598, became the prototype for royal obsequies in Naples with its tripartite combination of mourning for the deceased, exaltation of his great deeds and virtues, and glorification of his beatification and succession. Such obsequies became a live enactment of a *momento mori*, whose meditation on the king's life served as a model for his subjects. The funeral ceremonies for the viceroy Count of Lemos in 1600 and the commemoration in honor of Philip III's queen, Margherita of Austria, in 1612 and Philip IV's brother Don Carlos in 1630 all followed the same model set by the obsequies for Philip II. The royal births, on the other hand, allowed for carnivalesque celebrations of life and rebirth, with prognostications of dynastic fluorescence through rejoicing at tournaments, comedies, and masked balls with fireworks and *luminaries*, art and *apparati*, music and dance. Such life-cycle festivities were forms of prayer that joined the dynastic occasion of mourning or celebration in praise, propitiation, thanksgiving, and petition. The future weighs as heavily as the present and past in the festival's stopping of time and in tying the ephemeral moment to the timeless eternal and universal meaning of the event.

Political Landmarks, Politico-Religious Occasions for Other Rulers, Crises, and Emergencies

Political and military victories and the political-religious occasions of other rulers were civic festivals related to foreign policy. What connected them to the extraordinary processions in momentary crises and emergencies was the impact that they may sometimes have exerted on society to become institutionalized as annual rather than one-time celebrations. As we have already seen, the Holy League's victory against the Turks at Lepanto (7 October 1571) became the annual feast of Our Lady of Victory, later Our Lady of the Rosary; and the Catholic Imperial army's victory over the Protestant forces at the Battle of Nördlingen (7 September 1634), which commemorated the decisive defeat of the Swedes to end the third phase of the Thirty Years' War, became a fixture of the Neapolitan calendar, even though the fourth phase of the war led to eventual Spanish defeat. Parallel coincidences in these two Spanish victories help explain why they became institutionalized holidays rather than merely ephemeral events. The victorious royal heroes, Don Juan of Austria (half brother of Philip II) and Cardinal-Infante Ferdinand (brother of Philip IV), both followed their momentous victories with continued military command in the breakaway Low Countries. Don Juan, as governor general of the Low Countries, and Cardinal-Infante Ferdinand, as governor general of the Spanish Netherlands, both died of illness during military campaigns seven years after their great victories at Lepanto and Nördlingen at the young age of thirty-one and thirty-two, respectively. Just as commemoration of the U.S. Civil War dead established in 1868 as Decoration Day became the national holiday of Memorial Day, and the end of World War I's Armistice Day became Veterans Day, Lepanto and Nördlingen Victory Days memorialized the young chivalric heroes who had led Spanish forces to victories that celebrated national honor and pride. These two holidays also reinforced the religious mission of the Spanish monarchy against the infidel Turks and heretical Protestants to show that God was indeed on their side. Remembrance found its place in both the spiritual and secular world, as in the case of the Lepanto victory, when the rosary would become the popular religious tool for ensuring reciprocal exchange with the Virgin. Rituals, however, were only a small part of the multimedia explosion of activity surrounding emergencies. Tommaso Costo's 1573 epic poem, *La rotta di Lepanto*, which was revised and amplified in 1582 as *La vittoria della Lega*, was modeled in *ottava rime* on Ariosto and Tasso and is a perfect example of how a momentary event could be transformed into high art with the hope of creating a literary classic.[57]

For the city of Naples, the eruption of Vesuvius (16 December 1631) was the most important of these ephemeral events turned into annual holidays as it became the third feast of the city's most important patron saint, S. Gennaro. Here, too, a multimedia response exploded with some fifty books published in Naples between 1631 and 1633 on the Vesuvius eruption.[58] Two different processions petitioning the intercession of saints were depicted in the paintings of Domenico Gargiulo (Micco Spadaro) and Scipione Compagno preserved in the Museo di San Martino.[59] Gargiulo's famous painting of the *Eruption of Vesuvius* presents the circular march of the nobility and clergy carrying the reliquaries of the city's eleven secondary patron saints ahead of the canopied monstrance with the Eucharist and the reliquary of its primary patron S. Gennaro, followed by the archbishop Cardinal Boncompagni and the viceroy Count of Monterrey in the piazza outside the Porta Capuana. S. Gennaro and a half-dozen *putti* fly above the scene on a cloud with the city patron saint's hands upraised to stop the lava and plumes of ash from reaching the city. Compagno's *Eruption of Vesuvius in 1631* is set a few

days later on Friday, 19 December, and records the procession carrying the body
of Blessed Giacomo della Marca, made city patron in 1626 and saint in 1726,
from the Church of S. Maria la Nova to his chapel at the Ponte della Maddalena
outside the city on the road to Vesuvius. Processions and patron saints were part
of the normal response to natural disasters and disease throughout the early
modern world from S. Rocco's intercession during the 1576 plague in Venice to
S. Rosalia's during the 1624 plague in Palermo. Cities invoked supernatural intercession and aid through propitiation during the crisis and created new patron
saints in thanksgiving afterward. This kind of cult of remembrance mirrored the
prayers for the dead, because of the common belief in the timeless immanence
of the supernatural to affect the natural world. The 1656 plague in Naples created a similar response, with the procession and veneration at the Church of
S. Maria di Costantinopli at the center of plague prevention. An ex voto of the
Madonna of Costantinopli painted by Mattia Preti for installation in the Church
of S. Maria della Verità (S. Agostino degli Scalzi), commissioned by the Schipani
family in 1657, depicts the enthroned Virgin and Child crowning S. Rosalia and
surrounded by saints Gennaro, Rocco, Joseph, and Nicasio.[60] S. Maria di Costantinopli had already been venerated at the center of the city patrons in a print by
Giovanni Orlandi representing her intercession in the 1631 eruption of Vesuvius.[61] This image of the Virgin flanked by a dozen of the city patrons had been
used previously by Orlandi in city maps in 1611 and 1626 and was elaborated by
Pierre Miotte in his well-known city map indicating the events of the revolt of
1647 (fig. I.2).[62] The Virgin on a cloud similarly appears in Gargiulo's painting
of *Largo Mercatello during the Plague of 1656*, with the Virgin beseeching Christ to
allay the angel's sword and save the city, and again in Gragiulo's *Thanksgiving after
the Plague of 1656* where she receives the Carthusian petition while she floats up
to intercede with Christ (fig. 2.1).[63]

Many Neapolitans not only invoked ritual processions and patrons to preserve
the city from the plague but also blamed the erosion of ritual practice as the cause
of the plague in the first place. Parrino reports that, with his arrival in November
1654, the new viceroy Garcia di Avellaneda y Haro, Count of Castrillo, understood
that rendering justice to his subjects was most important for "good administration," and he considered how the judicial system could be improved through the
expeditious resolution of legal disputes, which had multiplied because of the
cunning of litigants, the lack of care by state officials, and "above all by too great
a number of festival days, which had become a little less than infinite."[64] He determined to raise the probity of judges and to reform the state's festival calendar
by canceling civic or "court" holidays, while still keeping both those traditionally

Figure 2.1. Domenico Gargiulo, *Thanksgiving after the Plague of 1656.* Soprintendenza per i Beni Architettonici e Paesaggistici e per il Patrimonio Storici, Artistici ed Etnoantropologici per Napoli e Provincia, Naples.

required and those ordered by the church. In fact, the viceroy's 1656 order kept only those holidays which were required, and the lawcourts continued to work even on former holidays such as the feast of St. Mark on 25 April. Among the judiciary, opposition voices argued that God had mandated these holidays and that "the violation of the feast days" had a dangerous precedent in the untimely death that came to those counselors of Ferrante I who had induced him to suppress court holidays during his reign. As the plague spread in May, especially in the *popolo* quarters, popular opinion began to grow that the "divine vendetta" had not been unleashed against the people of Naples but was a result of the elimination of feast days. With mortality mounting— by the end of the year 1656 mortality is conservatively estimated at almost 300,000 inhabitants, about two-thirds of the city population—the viceroy rescinded his order to reform the state's holiday calendar; and prayers and processions to thaumaturgic saints increased.[65]

Extra Holidays and the Summer Break

The viceroy's master of ceremonies, Raneo, also lists government holidays when the Collateral Council and lawcourts did not meet: fifteen religious holidays, all Fridays in March, all Saturdays during the year, and long breaks around the major feasts of Christmas, Carnival, and Easter.[66] Because of the heat in the "Dog Days" of summer (Caniculares), Raneo includes the closure of government councils and courts from the Friday before 15 July to 8 September, while the added holiday list of 1555 in the formal edicts of the Neapolitan councils gives the summer holiday for the harvest and vindemia from 14 July to 4 October.[67] The French visitor Bouchard identifies these summer holidays as extending from the first Sunday after St. John's Day on 24 June to 8 September.[68] Despite some variation defining the beginning and end of the summer season, July and August marked the time for the leisure pursuits of the Neapolitan nobles in their *passeggio* or *spassi di Posillipo* (diversions of Posillipo). The summer ex-urban exodus of nobles to nearby Posillipo just to the west of the city and the hot-weather pleasures of this long noblemen's holiday roughly parallel winter's Carnival from St. Anthony Abbot on 17 January to Ash Wednesday (the movable feast from 4 February to 14 March). Whereas Carnival expresses the last gasp of plenty and pleasure before Lent, the *spassi di Posillipo* basked in the indulgence of the harvest abundance. The summer holiday season's conclusion on 8 September, the Feast of Piedigrotta and the Nativity of the Virgin, is also the beginning of the festival new year in the fall, which confirms the urban festival calendar's conformity with the agricultural calendar.

The Religious Calendar

As traditional as rituals remained, the more they changed through invention and elaboration. Two religious ritual calendars from the provincial hinterland around the Neapolitan capital that regularized festivals after the Council of Trent provide a baseline measure to allow us to move from the simple to the more complex forms of religious practice (see table A.1 in the appendix). By comparing these two provincial ritual calendars with the ritual calendar of Naples in the sixteenth and seventeenth centuries, we can understand both the structure and change of ritual time in Spanish Naples. Religious feast days were celebrated according to four principal categories:

1. The Christological, liturgical year (Christmas and Easter cycles), which combined fixed dates from the solar calendar with the movable feasts of the lunar calendar
2. The calendar of saints, especially biblical and early Christian or medieval saints
3. Local saint cults, which augmented the canon of saints
4. The Marian cult, whose many manifestations punctuated the saints' calendar

Religious ritual time thus follows the two overlapping temporal cycles of the seasonal and calendar year simultaneously, with special emphasis on local supernatural commemorations and, above all, the intercession of the Virgin, whose fixed feast days of the Nativity (Piedigrotta) on 8 September and the Annunciation on 25 March, not by chance, marked the beginning of the fall-winter and spring-summer seasons.

Two Provincial Religious Calendars

The archbishop of Conza (Conza della Campania), a remote town on the southeast border of Principato Ultra with Basilicata, presided over a metropolitan see that comprised five dioceses (Muro, Cangiano, Monteverde, Cedonia, and Sant'Angelo dei Lombardi-Bisaccia) and included some twenty-four towns.[69] The five bishopric seats were typical agro-towns with concentrated populations engaged primarily in the agricultural production of cereals, legumes, wine, chestnuts, and fruits. According to the 1595 hearth count, none of the diocesan seats had populations greater than 2,500 inhabitants, while Conza itself numbered only 136 hearths or approximately 680 inhabitants.[70] Scipione Gesualdo, archbishop of Conza (1584–1608), published a 213-page book of the "Constitutions and decrees" from the diocesan synod of 19 October 1597, which includes a ritual calendar of thirty-one immovable and five movable feast days (not counting Sundays), for a total of thirty-six feast days.[71] Religious feast days occur on traditional dates and can be divided into the four main types of celebrations:

1. Nine feasts that follow the Christological liturgy from Christmas, Circumcision, and Epiphany to Holy Thursday, Easter, Ascension, and Pentecost with Corpus Christi and the Invention of the Holy Cross
2. Eighteen feasts that follow the calendar of saints in two groups: twelve biblical saints of angels, apostles, and evangelists (St. Matthias, St. Mark, Sts. Philip and James, St. John the Baptist, St. James, St. Bartholomew, St.

Matthew, St. Michael the Archangel, Sts. Simon and Jude, St. Andrew, St. Thomas, St. John the Evangelist) and six early church or medieval saints (St. Lawrence, All Saints, St. Martin, St. Catherine, St. Lucy, St. Stephen)

3. Three feasts that commemorate the local saint S. Erberto (a medieval archbishop of Conza) and two saints associated with the capital of Naples (St. Thomas Aquinas and S. Gennaro)

4. Six feasts that honor the Marian cult (Purification, Annunciation, Visitation, Assumption, Nativity of the Virgin, and Immaculate Conception)

This template of thirty-six feast days reduces local cults to a bare minimum, with only three local feasts observed—the medieval bishop of Conza and two saints especially venerated in the Neapolitan capital. There is a concentration of five movable feasts in the two months between Holy Thursday and Corpus Christi in the spring, but otherwise only eleven holidays averaging less than two per month were celebrated in the six and a half months before the summer harvest beginning in mid-July. The concentration of twenty immovable feasts in the second half of the calendar year reflects the decreased need for agricultural labor in the rural world after the grain harvest.

In the same spirit of Tridentine reform, Giulio Rossini from Macerata, the archbishop of Amalfi, published the "Constitutions and decrees" of his diocesan synod of January 1594 with a fifty-six-date ritual calendar (excluding Sundays).[72] Amalfi, which had been a great medieval trading city rivaling Venice, Genoa, and Pisa, was reduced to 463 hearths or about 2,315 inhabitants in the 1595 hearth census and was a metropolitan see that encompassed four dioceses (Lettere, Capri, Minori, and Scala).[73] Because agricultural production there was limited to wine and fruit growing, less labor was needed overall than in regions of extensive wheat, mixed grain and orchard cultivation, especially during harvest season.[74] Consequently, its fifty-six feast days were more evenly distributed across the year than Conza's and averaged a little more than one per week, with an even 50 percent of its holidays (twenty-eight feasts) celebrated by the 2 July Visitation of the Virgin Mary, a full month and a half before Conza's midpoint of feasts. Amalfi's ritual calendar included thirty-five of the thirty-six feasts in Conza (excluding only the feast of the local Conza archbishop S. Erberto), and added twenty-one more feasts:

1. Six additional local saint holidays (St. Anthony Abbot, St. Macarius of Egypt, S. Francesco di Paola, Translation of St. Andrew, Translation of St. Macarius of Egypt, Miracle of St. Andrew)

2. Thirteen other saints' dates: twelve saints from the early church and Ro-

man martyrology, apostles, and evangelists (St. Fabian, St. Gregory, St. Barnabus, SS. Vito and Modesto, Sts. Peter and Paul, St. Mary Magdalene, St. Augustine, St. Jerome, St. Luke, St. Ambrose, the Holy Innocents, St. Sylvester) and only one medieval Italian saint day (St. Anthony of Padua)

3. One new Marian holiday (St. Mary of the Snows commemorating the Miracle of S. Maria Maggiore in Rome in 385)

4. One additional Christological feast (Transfiguration)

Thus, Amalfi's ritual calendar reinforces what we have seen in the devotions at Conza. Annual ritual holidays were built upon the same four types of public feasts: the liturgical year following the life of Christ; the calendar of the saints, especially the early Christian saints of the New Testament (apostles, evangelists, and witnesses), the old Roman martyrology, the fathers and doctors of the Church, and medieval devotional favorites; an infusion of local saints' cults; and the recurrent reinforcement of devotion to Marian cults.

The Festival Calendar of the City of Naples

Ritual tradition in the Neapolitan capital itself, given its population, steady immigration from the countryside, numerous competing religious orders, and fertile ground for local cults, was extensive. In its pragmatics "De Feriis," the Neapolitan Collateral Council oversaw feast days by reducing their number to seventy-two designated legal holidays (sixty-eight immovable and four movable) in the decade before Trent in a pragmatic of 1555–56 (see table A.2 in the appendix).[75] On feast days, lawyers and prosecutors were forbidden to try cases; tribunals and royal judges did not meet. The 1555–56 legal holiday list included forty-four of the fifty-six feasts in Amalfi. Later in the sixteenth century, six new feasts were added (S. Francesco di Paola, St. Mary Magdalene, St. Stephen, St. John the Evangelist, the Holy Innocents, and St. Sylvester), and six other local Amalfitano feasts were not on the Neapolitan calendar (St. Macarius of Egypt, Translation of St. Andrew, Translation of St. Macarius of Egypt, Sts. Vitus and Modestus, Miracle of St. Andrew, and Holy Thursday). The twenty-eight different feasts celebrated in Naples in 1555–56 reflected its local patron saints and favored cults not found in the countryside: the original six city patrons beyond S. Gennaro (S. Severo, S. Eufebio, S. Atanasio, S. Aspreno, S. Agrippino, and S. Agnello); six other local cults (S. Restituta, the original patron of the duomo, and five saints who would become city patrons later [St. Dominic in 1640, St. Nicholas in 1675, St. Blaise and St. Peter Martyr in 1690, St. Francis of Assisi in 1691]); nine popular saint cults not particular to Naples (St. Agatha, St. Joseph, St. Benedict, St. George, St. Anne, St. Martha, St. Peter in Chains, St. Bernard, S. Leonardo); and seven days commemorating saints, Marian feasts, or special observances (Conversion of St. Paul, Apparition of St. Michael, S. Maria del Carmine, Beheading of St. John the Baptist, Triumph of the Holy Cross, All Souls Day, Presentation of the Virgin). As in the countryside, the majority of the seventy-two holidays in Naples came in the second half of the calendar year, with only thirty-two (44 percent) before the harvest in mid-July. August logged the most holidays with eleven feasts plus two successive days of celebration following the Assumption, whereas the months of November and December together counted fifteen feasts.

Summer harvest created peak demand for agricultural labor, and the days from mid-July were the subject of an earlier 1534 pragmatic that freed debtor prisoners in the Vicaria and Admiralty jails according to ancient custom, "with the pledge to satisfy their debts or to return to prison in a certain term."[76] And similarly in a 1587 pragmatic, imprisoned debtors were released during the concentration of holidays in the hot days of August as well as around Christmas and at Carnival, in order "to satisfy their creditors and rehabilitate themselves during the holidays."[77] The long period of harvest and vindemia from 14 July to 4 October was codified as an extended holiday, as already noted, in an appendix to the 1555–56 pragmatic.[78]

This appended list to the 1555–56 holidays pragmatic gives forty-seven immovable holidays and adds two more movable feasts. Naples added ten feasts for saints who would become new city patrons (S. Andrea Avellino [1625], S. Patrizia, Blessed Giacomo della Marca, and S. Francesco di Paola [1626], St. Teresa of Avila [1664], St. Philip Neri [1667], Blessed Gaetano da Thiene [1671], St. Francis Xavier [1691], St. Francis Borgia [1695], and St. Mary Magdelene [1705]). Six feasts were added for local relics and cults (S. Maria del Principio after a painting of the Virgin said to have been painted by St. Luke and kept in the Church of S. Aspreno, the Translation of St. Thomas Aquinas, the Translation of S. Gennaro, St. Ivo of Helory [patron of judges, lawyers, and notaries], St. Dominic of Sora, and S. Sossio). Spanish religiosity brought a range of new Iberian cults to Naples in addition to the aforementioned saints who became city patrons (Teresa of Avila, Francis Xavier, and Francis Borgia). Spanish saints and cults included twelve medieval favorites and Counter-Reformation models: St. Raymond of Peñafort, St. Peter Nolasco, St. Frances of Rome (canonized in 1608), St. Isidore, St. Ferdinand III of Castile, St. Ignatius, the Portiuncula Chapel of St. Francis of Assisi, the plague saints S. Rocco and S. Rosalia, St. Peter of Alcantara, and St. Charles Borromeo, as well as Philip II's favorite, S. Diego di Alcalá,[79] whose intercession was believed to have cured the king's son and heir Don Carlos of a head injury. And seven traditional feasts were added: Sts. Cosmas and Damian, Guardian Angel, St. Barbara, St. Stephen, St. John the Evangelist, the Holy Innocents, and St. Sylvester. Three special occasions also were incorporated into the Neapolitan calendar: 7 September commemorated the victory of the Cardinal-Infante Ferdinand at the Battle of Nördlingen in 1634 during the Thirty Years' War, 7 October continued to celebrate the victory over the Turks at Lepanto in 1571, and 16 December became the third annual feast of S. Gennaro for his intercession in calming the eruption of Vesuvius in 1631. The addendum calendar also established a number of related holidays (four days before Epiphany, six days before Ash Wednesday, seven days before and after Easter, the Octave of S. Lorenzo).

In the short-lived pragmatic in the plague year of 1656, as we have already seen, the old and new feasts were again reduced and stabilized at seventy-eight immovable and movable feasts.[80] Of the original seventy-two feasts from the 1555–56 holiday list, forty-five continued through a century later to 1656, while twenty-seven had been suppressed. Only nineteen feasts that were found in both Neapolitan legal holiday lists were also celebrated in the provincial diocesan calendar of Amalfi in 1594. In the century from the beginning of Philip II's reign to near the end of that of his grandson Philip IV, more than one-third (37.5 percent) of the legal holidays in Naples had changed, while only one-quarter (26.4 percent) had been continuously celebrated in both the capital and the provinces. The plague year 1656, however, was an unusual year for public gatherings in Naples because of the massive mortality and fear of contagion. A better measure of ritual change over time and the permanence of the core ritual celebrations in Naples comes from a comparison of the 1555–56 holiday list with the viceroy's ritual calendar from 1634.

While the ritual calendars recorded in the pragmatics "De Feriis" listed legal holidays for the city's lawcourts and offices, master of ceremonies José Raneo compiled his ritual calendar for the etiquette of the Spanish viceroy and his court in Naples in 1634.[81] Raneo's Neapolitan ritual calendar identified those feasts in which the viceroy participated and listed where the celebrations were held. Only five of these fifty-six feasts are not recorded in the calendars of legal holidays: Our Lady of the Afflicted at S. Giovanni a Carbonara in June, the Eve of St. John's Day on 23 June, St. Ursula on 20 October, St. Ursula and the 11,000 Virgins on 21 October, and the Novena of Our Lady of the Angels at the end of December. Of the seventy-two legal holidays in 1555–56, the viceroy continued to participate in thirty-four of them in 1634; and of the seventy-eight legal holidays recognized in 1656, the viceroy had participated in thirty-four of them twenty years earlier in 1634.

The Principal Feasts of Naples

Viceregal patronage and local practice elevated some feasts above the rest of the innumerable holidays in Naples. A short, anonymous note circa 1600 appended to a larger, unrelated anonymous description of the city of Naples circa 1607–8 identifies twelve principal feasts celebrated every year, four of which receive a short line of their own (S. Gennaro, Corpus Christi, St. John the Baptist, and St. Mary Magdalene) and the remaining eight merely listed consecutively (St. Anthony Abbot, S. Chiara, S. Maria la Nova, Annunciation, S. Giovanni a Carbonara, Piedigrotta [Nativity of the Blessed Virgin Mary], St. Paul, S. Gennaro [19 September]).[82] During his almost nine-month visit to Naples from 17 March to 6 November 1632, Bouchard saw the feasts of the Annunciation (25 March) and St. John the Baptist (24 June)—which correspond to the vernal equinox and summer solstice in the spring-summer calendar—as the two most celebrated holidays among those with the largest cavalcades making a city circuit at public ceremonies in which the viceroy participated.[83] One should note that Bouchard did not winter in Naples and thus did not witness Carnival and its opening festivities on 17 January. The mid-nineteenth-century editor of Celano's *Notize del bello*, Giovanni Battista Chiarini, provides in his footnote commentary two lists of feast days, one sanctioned by papal decrees (1818–49) and the other "Neapolitan popular feasts."[84] His lists are in chronological order, with the high church holidays numbering six Christological, six Marian, and eight saints' feasts, and the popular feasts comprising six Christological holidays followed by two saints' days, one Marian feast, and an additional five highlighted Christological devotions noted for their "pomp and richness." Comparing these four lists of principal feasts from the early seventeenth and nineteenth centuries (see table 2.1), we can identify feasts that gained or lost their importance (winners such as the Christological feasts of the liturgical year and losers such as the saint days of John the Baptist and Mary Magdalene), as well as three major constellations of feasts that maintained their centrality in Neapolitan ritual: the spring-summer feasts of S. Gennaro, Corpus Christi, and St. John the Baptist; the start of Carnival on St. Anthony Abbot; and the beginning of the new year's winter and summer season with the Marian holidays of Piedigrotta and the Annunciation.[85]

Naples's three most important religious feast days[86]—S. Gennaro (Saturday

TABLE 2.1.
The Principal Feasts of Naples

Anonymous (1607–8)	Bouchard (1632)	Chiarini (1818–49)	Chiarini (1860)
S. Gennaro (Inghirlandati)	Annunciation	Circumcision	Christmas
Corpus Christi	St. John the Baptist	Easter	Epiphany
St. John the Baptist		Purification	Ascension
St. Mary Magdalene		Annunciation	Pentecost
St. Anthony Abbot		St. Joseph	Corpus Christi
S. Chiara		Ascension	Corpus Christi Octave
S. Maria de la Nova		Corpus Christi	St. Anthony Abbot
Annunciation		St. John the Baptist	Piedigrotta (Nativity of the Blessed Virgin)
S. Giovanni a Carbonara		Sts. Peter and Paul	S. Gennaro (Inghirlandati)
Piedigrotta (Nativity of the Blessed Virgin)		Assumption	Christmas*
St. Paul		Piedigrotta (Nativity of the Blessed Virgin)	Holy Week*
S. Gennaro (19 September)		All Saints	Holy Cross*
		Immaculate Conception	Forty Hours*
		Christmas	Pentecost & Monday After*
		Madonna della Grazie	
		St. Michael	
		S. Gennaro	
		St. Anthony of Padova	
		St. Anne	
		Presentation of the Blessed Virgin	

Sources: Archivio storico per le province napoletane 7 (1882): 797; Bouchard, *Voyage dans le Royaume de Naples*, 266; Celano, *Notize*, 1: 345–47, 349.
    *Special pomp and richness.

before the first Sunday of May), Corpus Christi (within the month 24 May to 24 June according to the Easter calendar), and S. Giovanni (on 23–24 June)—formed a political-religious unit that came to play a central role in the ritual life of Naples because of the way they linked the religious holidays that had appropriated the traditional agrarian and astrological calendar with the rising star of Spanish government and the viceroy's secular rule in Naples. These three feasts took their

modern form under Spanish political rule as a way of restoring the disrupted order after the French invasions of 1494. In 1456 Alfonso of Aragón, the Aragonese
dynasty's conquering founder in Naples, had abolished the *seggio del popolo* at
S. Agostino, which reinforced the pretensions of the nobles in the five noble *seggi*
to be the only true citizens of the city. In 1494 the French conqueror of Naples,
Charles VIII, reinstated the *popolo* district in an attempt to broaden support for
his short-lived rule. Upon the French king's departure in 1495, the Aragonese returned to power and were constrained to retain the *popolo seggio* with its restored
rights in city government.[87] Under the newly ascended Aragonese king Frederick
(1496–1501), the translation of S. Gennaro's body to the city in 1497 caused the
saint's traditional spring feast day on Passion Sunday (two weeks before Easter)
to be moved to the Saturday before the first Sunday of May.[88] Like the feast of
the leading city patron S. Gennaro, Corpus Christi in Naples owes its definitive
structure to a 1497 reform, which reorganized this medieval celebration of the
Eucharist to give precedence to the *popolo* and its *eletto*.[89] Thus, Frederick's two
1497 feasts pandered to *popolo* pretensions to citizenship by incorporating commoner participation in the newly stabilized May S. Gennaro and seasonal May-
June Corpus Christi rituals.

With the Spanish invasion and conquest of Naples complete at the end of December 1503, Ferdinand the Catholic and his successors emphasized the legitimacy of the Spanish monarchy as heirs to their Aragonese ancestors and forged
a strategic political-economic and ceremonial alliance near their core stronghold
with their Genoese financiers.[90] In 1507 the *seggio del popolo* received concessions
from the new Spanish king, and St. John's Day assumed direct political significance with the municipal statutes of 1522, which indicate the election of the Santissima Annunziata officers and investiture of the *eletto del popolo* on the feast.[91]
With his participation in these three feasts, the Spanish surrogate king or viceroy
took his place in the ritual life of the city and fostered group solidarity among
the *popolo*, who reasserted long-eroded rights and privileges, as the new Spanish
government consciously attempted to divide and dominate native groups one
from another within its newly acquired kingdom.

Céline Dauverd shows how the Eucharistic feast of Corpus Christi is linked
to Holy Week with the Holy Thursday procession of the Genoese, the feast of
S. Gennaro, and the reinstitution of the procession of the Quattro Altari on the
octave of Corpus Domini by Viceroy Pedro de Toledo through the Genoese-
Spanish alliance in Naples.[92] Soon after the Spanish conquest, the Genoese were
able to commission a new national church financed around 1525 by the Genoese
Galeazzo Giustiniano at S. Giorgio dei Genovesi, a few blocks closer to the central

Spanish religious foundation of S. Giacomo degli Spagnuoli than their medieval storehouse and ceremonial center at S. Maria la Nova. The new Genoese church was completed by about 1560, and the transfer of rites celebrated on 1 November 1587.[93]

After the Council of Trent and its reaffirmation of the doctrine of the Eucharist, Corpus Christi took on added significance; and in late seventeenth-century Naples the clergy used the procession of this Eucharistic feast through the *popolo* quarter to assimilate and eliminate the vestigial pagan practices of the most ancient of this holiday triad, St. John the Baptist Day.[94] Similarly, the feast of La Maddalena (St. Mary Magdalene) on 22 July fell out of popular favor over time. The feast had been introduced into Angevin Naples in the early fourteenth century by the end of the reign of Charles II (1285–1309).[95] The Dominicans spread the cult as an antidote to prostitution, which had increased with urbanization and the marginalization of the poor. As a devotional story for impoverished women, it was a form of social control that aimed as much at assistance and recovery of penitents as prevention. The religious model of early modern Catholic spirituality promoted centralization in the hands of hierarchical authority and the elimination of the excesses of popular piety. This anti-*popolo* offensive joined clergy and nobility with the viceregal government and extended to other constellations of popular feasts, such as the St. Anthony Abbot Day opening of the Carnival season and the two Marian feasts of spring and fall. With a similar strategy for pacification and co-option of the nobility, viceregal government promoted the celebration of the life-cycle events of the Spanish royal family in order to integrate the local nobility into the larger Spanish world and subordinate the nobles' provincial and familial interests to those of the monarchy. Thus, we can see that, while celebrating together, clergy, nobility, and commoners vied among one another in defining the occasion and meaning of feasts. These destabilizing rivalries provided the monarchy and its viceregal government the rationale to intervene on one side or another to reorganize and redirect ritual practice in order to centralize power, bolster social control, and foster dependence on vertical rather than horizontal bonds of sociability.

The Threat of Violence

The viceroy, however, had always to be on guard for manifestations of discontent, because public festivities could easily turn from celebration to conflict. Soon after the notorious riot, murder, and ritual cannibalism of the *eletto del popolo* Giovan Vincenzo Starace on 9 May 1585, posters appeared calling for a resumption of rebellion, with one explicitly linking revolt to the upcoming holidays, "Oh heedless people, you have not finished what you have begun! On Corpus Christi let every man prepare; on St. John's day let every man leave his bread and take up arms!"[96] Scipione Guerra's chronicle in 1585 thus notes that the viceroy participated in both the Corpus Christi and San Giovanni processions with a heavily armed escort.[97] Almost twenty years later during the San Giovanni procession in 1601, while stopping along the parade route in the *popolo* quarter to read the sonnets praising him, the viceroy Count of Lemos heard a great commotion. Lemos saw a crowd of nobles with unsheathed swords surrounding a deadly duel between two nobles in which one was killed; "much displeased with that unhappy event," Lemos had the victor jailed.[98] With more momentous consequences in 1647, weeks before the feast of the Carmine on 16 July and the outbreak of the revolt on 7 July that would last for nine months, the viceroy overheard the *popolo* murmuring under their breathe. Also, placards calling for the *popolo* "to make a great tumult on the feast of San Giovanni" were posted around the city because of the mounting grievances over reduction of the regulated weight of a loaf of bread and the imposition of new gabelles at a time of famine, especially the gabelle on fruit. For fear of what a large gathering of the *popolo* might do, the viceroy suspended the San Giovanni feast.[99] After the revolt ended in April 1648, although the Spanish had regained control of the city for more than two-and-one-half months, the June feast of San Giovanni was again canceled because "the city [was] almost ruined from the recent turbulence."[100] Such incidents were not isolated examples.

In this cautionary vein, Juan de Garnica, a Spanish doctor of law at Rome in 1595 and formerly in Salamanca and Naples, offered advice on the Neapolitan court ceremonial to a possible future viceroy, Gonzalo Fernández de Córdoba, Duke of Sessa and presently the Spanish ambassador in Rome, who had aspired unsuccessfully to become viceroy in Naples after Juan de Zuñiga, Count of Miranda (r. 1586–95).[101] After a section of the text explaining "the disorder caused by carriages" in the courtyard of the viceroy's palace where so much noise is produced that it "makes such a racket that the site seems a chaotic Babel," Garnica follows with a section title warning, "Of the Procession That the Spaniards Hold in Naples on the Night of Good Friday and the Risks Involved in It."[102] The Spanish had introduced their traditional Good Friday devotion as a new ceremony to Naples, a candlelight procession that began two hours after sunset. "A great multitude of soldiers and other Spaniards, who flagellate themselves, wear habits, and carry torches," march "with great devotion, silence, and order." Just outside the viceroy's place when the procession crosses the Via Toledo, which is so clogged with carriages on both sides of the street that no one can pass except between the rows of carriages, "if for some reason a carriage gets disturbed due to some violent movement, all the others get out of order and the procession is disrupted and wrecked so that it does not return to its proper place or it stops altogether without returning to the church whence it had come." And Garnica continues by explaining that the consequences of this conditional disruption of the procession can be much more dire than merely disordering or stopping the procession.

> All this happened last year. As the procession was walking through with its devotion and fervor, a carriage was suddenly stirred, exiting furiously. A great uproar followed, and all those around it started to shout. Because of these shouts and voices, many began to turn to their swords, not knowing what had happened, or what to do. The rumor started that Naples was in revolt. This commotion caused so much fear that some people in the palace began to flee in great fright through the Park surrounding the Castel Nuovo. Finally, miraculously through one man's diligence, it was known that nothing had happened, that it had been just a carriage, and so everything turned quiet and back to normal. But in any case, it was a bad experience for suspecting minds.

Garnica's point was not simply "that it is a very great inconvenience to have carriages participate in the procession in any shape or form." Rather, he argued that, "although this procession is of great devotion and importance, it still carries with it a very great and hidden risk and danger," because "the Spaniards on Good Friday, be it because they are flagellants or because they accompany the flagellants and the procession, not only do they not carry weapons nor are near an area where they could be gotten, but they are covered, head and body, with their habits so that even before they could respond to an attack their throats and bodies would be cut to pieces on any occasion that would arise." The threat of violence in 1595 was real, as was well known because the local grievances from the famine of 1585 had already erupted in the riot and murder of the *eletto del popolo* Starace. While the subsequent repression and harsh punishment had quelled the disturbances with brutal force, the underlying causes—grain shortages, increased population pressure, gabelles and imposts on commodities, unequal representation in the city council, and the billeting of Spanish troops—had not been addressed, and famine and economic crisis continued in the 1590s.[103]

Garnica's reasoning provides a critical insight into Spanish suspicions of revolt and the fears of murder in the streets. While the Spanish remained at risk if the procession were not discontinued, on the other hand, if it were discontinued, the native Neapolitans might take it as an even greater insult impugning their loyalty and undermining trust.

> May God guard us, even from a band of outlaws or other scorned and bold people. It appears that, were this procession to be eliminated, this would cause a furor. And if the cause of the decision were to be made public, it would cause suspicion in our friends, who would think that the King does not trust them, or doubts their loyalty, which would be a great insult. And, as the Holy Scripture says, if our enemies must not be affronted, our friends should be treated very gracefully, so as not to cause them to be suspicious and result in an affront. On the other hand, if this procession is allowed to continue, there is much risk involved, endangering the lives of so many and noble Spanish people. The patrimony of the King our lord is in danger and the Holy Church and universal Christendom would lose a great leader, and the wings of its heart would fall. I ask, what is more important, the procession or what I have just said? The Holy Spirit says that man was not created for love of the temple, but the temple was created for the love of man. So it is more just for the temple to die that man can be free.[104]

In his advice to the aspirant viceroy, Garnica makes it clear that Spanish rule in the city of Naples is a precarious enterprise, not only fraught with the actual, physical danger of revolt but also requiring a diplomatic awareness of local sensibilities to perceived insults. In his summary words on the meaning of a "true" church in the Christian tradition of "true" spirituality, Garnica explains that "the above-mentioned procession is not of such importance when compared with the risks involved in holding it."[105] For Garnica, true Christianity was about internal belief, not external actions; and the ritual trappings of religious practice were subordinate to true spirituality. He constantly justifies practical actions with scripturally based reasoning, in order to reinforce the spiritual purity of Spanish secular rule and afford the office of the viceroy with the widest possible latitude in adapting policy to local Neapolitan conditions.

Viceroys themselves were often rivals in the larger game of court favoritism among the Spanish ruling class in Madrid, which could play out in Naples between incoming and outgoing viceroys, with ramifications for their relationship with the Neapolitans, both nobles and commoners. In 1630 Philip IV commissioned the Duke of Alba, less than a year after his departure as viceroy of Naples, and the cardinal of Seville to escort the newlywed queen Maria d'Austria on her trip from Madrid to Austria, which detoured south at Genoa from the usual itinerary across northern Italy because of plague in Lombardy. Chroniclers

emphasize that this diversion to Naples was not unplanned, because the entourage's leader, the Duke of Alba, had desired "to return to Naples in order with his
presence to obscure the authority of the viceroy, for whom he had little love."[106]
Maria d'Austria arrived at Procida and transferred to Posillipo before her formal
entrance into Naples, where she remained for four months from 8 August to
16 December 1630. Her prolonged royal visit revealed much about the rivalries
within the Spanish court in Madrid and the limits of power and comportment
within the viceroy's court in Naples. At the end of her stay, she crossed inland
along the grain road to Foggia, then north through Capitanata and the Abruzzi
on pilgrimage to Loreto before embarking on Venetian galleys from Ancona to
Trieste.[107] The aged Giulio Cesare Capaccio published a panegyric in praise of the
Spanish princess, which shows how Naples had seen in her "one of the blood
of our most serene Padroni, and a Queen of such grandeur, such that nothing
greater had been seen for such a long time"[108] As with all true nobility, it was not
blood alone that made her exceptional, such that Capaccio catalogs the ancient
virtues of wisdom, religiosity, modesty, gravitas, long-suffering, piety, counsel—
in sum, all the virtues that were epitomized in her.[109]

The visit of Maria d'Austria conformed to the outward form of the celebrations
of a royal visit in its ceremonies emphasizing royal virtue; but, in actual practice,
the contested jockeying for position among the nobility exasperated their rivalries and the instability in their world of hierarchical titles and privileges. From
the timing of the queen's arrival to coincide with the nobility's summer season
of leisure holidays in the "terrestrial paradise" of Posillipo, with songs sung as
part of a mock "battle of love" among the noble ladies, to the disputes over precedence in processions and the hierarchical protocol demanded by the queen
with regard to her interaction with Neapolitan noblewomen, the viceroy Duke of
Alcalá (1629–31) found his authority challenged and his position threatened. He
was put on the defensive in terms of finding the money to support the extravagant expectations of the festivities and preserving local noble privileges. When
the *sindaco* Hettore Capecelatro from the *seggio* of Capuana, who had spent 8,000
ducats—an amount almost equivalent to the viceroy's 10,000-ducat annual government stipend—found himself barred from the *sindaco*'s privileged position at
the royal visitor's side in the welcoming procession ceremonies, not only did he
withdraw along with the *seggi eletti* and the Seven Great Officers, but the noble
elite petitioned the king in Madrid for redress.[110] The *popolo* were also deprived
of their usual ritual pillage of the expensive gangway (*ponte*), the most sumptuous heretofore created,[111] when the queen ordered that it not be sacked but given
to charity instead. Even the titled noblewomen of Naples, twenty-eight of whom

were profiled in Alessandro Fellecchia's apologist account of the visit during the festivities at Posillipo, were insulted by the queen, who would allow only five of their number to receive her seated on cushions, as the rest were disdained as too lowborn and had to sit on a carpet on the floor.[112] The Duke of Alba, who embarrassed the viceroy by receiving public applause and adulation from the crowds as he passed through the streets—albeit bought and paid for by "his confidants and friends"—manipulated the whole visit to denigrate his rival and successor viceroy, the Duke of Alcalá, and successfully maneuvered to have him recalled to Madrid less than six months later.[113]

Nature's Order: The Precedence of Honor

Because festival life was a marker of one's place in the social structure, ritual practice cannot be understood without an examination of ritual space and hierarchical order or honorific precedence. The *sindaco*'s chief responsibility as the rotating delegate of the noble *seggi* at the head of city affairs was purely ceremonial and honorific. He represented the city of Naples in public ceremonies (civic and religious cavalcades and processions) and served as president of general parliament sessions. The *sindaco* had precedence over all other Neapolitans—the holders of the Seven Great Offices in the kingdom (once the most important vassals and counselors to the king but, under Spanish rule, performing only vestigial and honorary functions),[114] titled nobility, and representatives to the general parliament. As personification of the corporate entity of the city, the *sindaco* walked on equal footing with the king, viceroy, and all other secular or ecclesiastical rulers during processions in the city. This dignity equally shared and jealously guarded by the noble *seggi* lay at the heart of the numerous disputes over precedence.

The sequence of *seggi* turns or the order of precedence—Capuana, Montagna, Nido, Porto, Portanova—reflected the itinerary followed in the geographically determined processional route from the land entry to Naples at Porta Capuana on the east of the old city, where previously Charles VIII in 1495, the Great Captain Gonzalo Fernández de Córdoba in 1503, and the viceroy Pedro de Toledo in 1532 had entered. When visitors entered the city from the sea, they disembarked at the Molo Grande near the Castel Nuovo and followed this same itinerary in reverse order, as with the royal entrances of Alfonso I the Magnanimous in 1443, Alfonso II in 1494, and Ferdinand the Catholic in 1506, as well as the *possesso* of many viceroys.[115]

The traditional land-entry route (fig. 2.2), which can be traced by following the numbers in the legend at the bottom of the Du Pérac map printed by Lafreri in

1566, is well documented in the numerous accounts of the iconic, 25 November 1535 royal entrance of the Habsburg emperor Charles V at the beginning of his four-month winter sojourn in Naples after his great victory over the Turks in Tunis earlier that summer.[116] The *sindaco*, Ferrante Sanseverino, Prince of Salerno, led an entourage of twelve *portieri* (six nobles and six commoners), twelve trumpeters, thirty-six noblemen of the *seggi*, and ten *popolo consoltori* with the twenty-nine captains of the *ottine* from the Tribunal of San Lorenzo to meet the triumphant emperor outside the Porta Capuana. The emperor entered the old city with them at the Porta Capuana (5), where ephemeral statues of the mythical city founders, the siren Partenope and the river god Sebeto, stood guard outside the city gate. Charles passed through an elaborately decorated triumphal arch with four colossal statues of ancient conquering generals on one side (Scipio Africanus, Julius Caesar, Alexander the Great, and Hannibal) and four colossals of ancestral Habsburg emperors on the other (Frederick, Maximilian, Philip, and Ferdinand).[117] Constructed for the occasion, this three-bayed, ephemeral arch (100 × 90 × 50 *palmi*) was covered with fifty-two paintings. On the facade with the conquerors, one painting on the base of each of the colossal statues complemented a painting of the Victory at Tunis; on the facade with the emperors, paintings at the base of each statue highlighted a painting of the Victories in Hungary and Vienna; and forty-two emblematic paintings praised the emperor's virtues, attributes, and deeds, with twenty-one appearing on each side of the arch. Laurel arches that celebrated the emperor's triumphant victory in Hungary and Africa were also erected in each of the noble and the *popolo seggi* visited by the processing royal entry. Inside the Porta Capuana, mirroring the two mythological figures on the outside, stood statues of two of the city's patron saints and protectors, S. Agnello and S. Gennaro.

From the Castel Capuana (47), Charles, the *sindaco*, and city *eletti* proceeded west along the *decumanus major* through the *seggio* of Capuano (42), where statues of a nude Jove brandishing a lightning bolt with an eagle at his feet and Minerva, goddess of wisdom, awaited. The procession stopped at the Duomo (17) for double oaths, Charles's confirmation of privileges and the Neapolitans' swearing of fealty; continued past San Lorenzo (18) and its two statues of a white-clad Faith and winged Victory crowned with a laurel wreath; and on to the *seggio* of Montagna (43) with its statues of Atlas shouldering the heavens and Hercules bearing the two columns, together symbols of the emperor's *imprese* "Plus ultra." The procession turned south to pass through the *seggio* of Nido (44) to see a nude Mars stripped of his arms of war, which were given to the emperor along with "the oriental spoils of Turkey," and a winged Fame all tongues, eyes, and mouths

42 seggio di Capuana
43 seggio di Montagna
44 seggio di Nido
45 seggio di Porto
46 seggio di Portanova
46a seggio del popolo
63 Piazza della Sellaria

Figure 2.2. The Royal Way: Procession route through the noble *seggi*, detail Du Pérac (1566). Soprintendenza per i Beni Architettonici e Paesaggistici e per il Patrimonio Storici, Artistici ed Etnoantropologici per Napoli e Provincia, Naples.

allowing her to gather all the news and spread it with her horn. The royal parade then marched east along the *decumanus inferior* and down to the *seggio del popolo* at Sant'Agostino (46a), where the largest statue of all awaited, a gigantic Abundance with a cornucopia in her left hand and a rudder in her right guaranteeing the fidelity of the *popolo*. Written above the door to the *seggio del popolo*'s meeting hall was the motto, "Quivi è il simulacro de la Fede," and above it the imperial arms and insignia with the motto, "Lo popolo partenopeo a la fedeltà cesarea è ligato con amore, verità et onore" (The partenopean commons is bound to imperial fidelity with love, truth, and honor). Turning back west, the procession continued through the *popolo* stronghold at Piazza della Selleria (63), where a spectacular display of Giants thrown down from their assault on Mount Olympus by Jove all burst into flames from a fiery Eagle. Like the contemporaneous Giulio Romano painting of the *Fall of the Giants* (1531–36) at the Palazzo Te for the Duke of Mantua, Federico II Gonzaga, this Neapolitan reenactment of the throwing down of the rebellious children of Gaia by the Olympian gods aided by Hercules takes on added meaning, as the rebels are crushed beneath the rocks and rubble of volcanic activity (here at Naples in the shadow of Vesuvius, literally readily at hand) that allegorizes Charles V's victory over his enemies and the unfaithful in his election to the imperial crown, the victory of his troops at Pavia, the Sack of Rome, and now the triumph in Tunis and Hungary.[118] The march turned west through the *seggio* of Portanova (46) with statues of Janus clutching two keys and a club standing guard over a closed temple, which symbolized the emperor holding the power for peace or war, and of Fury above a cloud of arms "signifying the fury of unfaithful peoples." Finally, from the *seggio* of Porto (45) with two statues, one of the ancient Roman port-god Portunus holding an anchor and a marine horn to lead (in the manner of the emperor) everyone back to port and the other of Fortuna holding in her hands winged boots and a winged club head in an offering to the emperor for whom no gift could be worthy of his great honor, the procession went on through great throngs along the strada della Incoronata to the Castel Nuovo ablaze with fireworks and artillery salutes.

The ideological program of the *renovatio imperii* had been imprinted on the political seats of the Neapolitan nobility throughout the city. The sumptuous display along the route of march was matched by the elegant uniforms, robes, hats, and boots worn by the ranks on parade before the triumphant Charles V. The right of precedence in public ritual defined the city's ideal order and the noble *seggi*'s picture of themselves. A procession of friars and priests holding their crosses high led the way. Then came the nobility arranged according to precedence—barons, counts, marquises, dukes, princes, and the seven *eletti* representatives of the city *seggi*, who were dressed in the formal robes of the town priors. Behind them marching side by side were the young Carafa, Prince of Stigliano, on the right and Felipe de Lannoy, Prince of Sulmona (son of the former viceroy), on the left. Three of the Kingdom's Seven Great Officers followed: the Great Protonotary (Ferrante Spinello, Duke of Castrovillari); the Great Admiral (Ferrante di Cardona, Duke of Somma); and the Great Constable (Ascanio Colonna, Duke of Tagliacozzo and Paliano). Next on horseback, escorted by twenty-five standard-bearers, came Ferrante Sanseverino, Prince of Salerno, the *eletto* from Nido, whose turn it was to be the *sindaco* of the city. Nido later commemorated its role in the event with a now lost fresco by Bellisario Corenzio (1623–90), which once decorated a wall of its *seggio* church S. Angelo a Nilo.[119] A row of three followed, from left to right: the viceroy Pedro de Toledo; Pier Luigi Farnese, Prince of Parma and Piacenza (natural son of Paul III); and Ferrante de Aragón, Duke of Montalto (natural son of Ferrante I). Behind them and immediately preceding the emperor, marched the Great Chamberlain of the kingdom (Alfonso d'Avalos, Marquis of Vasto). Two heralds in livery then walked a little in front of the emperor Charles V, the most honored visitor. The emperor himself rode on horseback under an elaborately brocaded baldachin, which was carried by nobles on foot, who represented each *seggio*. Finally, a guard of some two hundred cavalry and infantry closed the ranks, marching before, on both sides, and behind the emperor.

Horses both demonstrated and symbolized noble power in the city. Not only were horses represented in *seggi* coats of arms as bridled and unbridled steeds rearing up on their hind legs, but they presented the nobility with an unparalleled weapon of domination and intimidation in the narrow city streets as much as on the fields of battle. Just as mounted police still are used in crowd control, mounted and armed nobles could command obedience, respect, and fear in the Neapolitan streets to lead parades or quell riots. In the vast southern countryside, donkeys and mules did the work of plowing and hauling; horses remained a nobleman's luxury commodity that required extraordinary wealth for care and feeding. Federico Grisone, a Neapolitan gentleman, wrote a book on the rules of horse riding with numerous woodcuts of horse bits, *Ordini di cavalcare* (1551), one of the most influential and oft-translated sixteenth-century works on horses and horsemanship. In 1602 Pirro Antonio Ferraro, stablemaster of the Real Cavallarizza di Napoli located just outside the Porta del Carmine before the Ponte della Maddalena, authored *Cavallo Frenato*. Divided in four books, Ferraro summarized the work of his father on breeding, training, and caring for horses. The Royal Stables were part of the royal patrimony (a line item in the Neapolitan state budgets) and provided horses for the Spanish cavalry as well as the annual white horse (the *chinea*) given to the pope as part of the feudal dues paid by the King of Spain because, as King of Naples, he was the pope's vassal.[120] The importance of horses cannot be overemphasized in any portrait of the city and its nobility.[121]

The nobles marching to the sound of Charles V's drummers had distinguished themselves as military allies and members of the Spanish party during the previous forty years of war. With the last serious French threat to the Kingdom of Naples removed by the failure of Lautrec's 35,000-troop invasion in 1528, a new era of Spanish consolidation began. In 1530 titles, lands, and offices of the pro-French Neapolitans were confiscated and redistributed to loyal pro-Spanish vassals and subjects in reward for their faithful service and deeds.[122] It was also the moment when the Genoese began to enter the kingdom in force.[123] Andrea Doria, whose transfer of loyalties and his fleet to the Spanish cause had turned the tide of the military struggle in favor of Charles received the largest feudal state in the kingdom, with the title of Prince of Melfi in 1531. It was taken from the pro-French prince, Giovanni Caracciolo, who had fled into French exile.

Visual evidence of Naples on parade also shows the ideal order of march in the city. A 1629 view of the "most noble city" by Alessandro Baratta, one of four versions of a large map measuring 920 × 2,475 centimeters, places Naples under the watchful patronage of the Virgin and Child and above the pageantry of civic life[124] (fig. 2.3). On a separate frieze below the map's legend and unrelated to the city view is a cavalcade marching from west to east, as the caption reads: "True design of the Most Noble Cavalcade done only in this Most Faithful City of Naples, such as it is upon the entrance of each Viceroy, as on all other occasions of the offering of parliamentary aides to His Royal Catholic Majesty or of other joyful and particular occasions that demonstrate the Fidelity and Magnificence of the whole kingdom."[125] Twenty-two individuals or groups are identified in the cavalcade with the viceroy and *sindaco* riding side by side at position 15, followed by the member of the ruling councils and judges of the courts. Another 1632 Baratta map commemorating the Neapolitan entry of Maria d'Austria, Queen of Hungary, on 8 August 1630 with the cavalcade marching east to west against a panoramic profile of Naples was reprinted almost exactly in 1680 with a new title for the royal marriage of Charles II of Spain to Queen Maria Luisa of Bourbon.[126] The shore and cityscape with only the spires, facades, and cupolas of larger buildings rise low in the background. Interestingly, no clerics appear among the noble and civic ranks in either of the two Baratta designs. In the latter designs with the cavalcade portrayed against the city perspective, a few additional marchers are identified: cavalry, barons, the postmaster, and commoner accountants (*razionali*) in the city administration, as well as Queen Maria d'Austria, her ladies in waiting, and her entourage in the 1632 exemplar.

Two engravings of later cavalcades also visualize the order of precedence. An engraving of the cavalcade held at Naples on 21 May 1690 for the marriage of Charles II to Maria Anna of the Palatinate-Neuburg shows the procession climbing through an imaginary city landscape from the royal palace near the port to the Archbishop's Palace in the center of the old city (fig. 2.4).[127] The cavalcade had been delayed twice because of bad weather in April, and in this representation of the Sunday 21 May parade after the afternoon meal, we can see a number of citizens viewing the event from the windows of their palaces lining the steep route of march. Another cavalcade engraving, commemorating the royal entrance of Philip V into Naples on 20 May 1702, shows the marchers alone without any city or topographical features save a freestanding Porta Capuana as the goal of the parade, and with their procession going out of rather than into the city.[128] This

Figure 2.3. Alessandro Baratta, *Fidelissimae Urbis Neapolitanae* (1629), detail of the city. © Archivio dell'Arte / Luciano Pedicini, Naples.

Figure 2.4. Cavalcade for the Marriage of Charles II (1690). Soprintendenza per i Beni Architettonici e Paesaggistici e per il Patrimonio Storici, Artistici ed Etnoantropologici per Napoli e Provincia, Naples.

"order of march" was dedicated to the Most Illustrious Signor Don Francesco d'Anna, Duke of Castel Grandine and *eletto del popolo*,[129] which may explain the unusual fact that this parade had the people marching in mass behind the dignitaries: males and females, with two doffed and waving hats just visible before the marchers dissolve into the background.

Parrino's order of precedence provided in his *Teatro eroico* corresponds to the visual representation in the three earlier Baratta engravings of 1627, 1629, and 1632 and the three later engravings of 1680, 1690, and 1702.[130] First came a contingent of troops. The lieutenant general and his adjutants with their cavalry company and its trumpeters led the way, followed by trumpeters of the city and the king, the captains of justice and jailers. Next was a series of conveyances—carriages, sedan chairs, and horses out of respect for the dignity of the chief participants (viceroy, *sindaco*, or distinguished visitors). The Neapolitan nobility followed, grouped by title (dukes, princes, counts, marquises, and barons) but in mixed order so that there would be no contestations of precedence within each rank. Next came administrative officials (*portieri* and others) with their master of ceremonies. There followed the *eletti* of the city's *seggi*. After them came the officers of the royal palace (*portieri di camera* of the viceroy) and the master of ceremonies of the palace. The Seven Great Officers of the kingdom, each with their special dignity and insignia came next. Then, the central players marched side by side, the viceroy with the *sindaco* on his left hand. (In 1535 and 1702, when the king himself was present, the viceroy marched ahead with the Seven Great Officers. In 1535 the *sindaco* marched alone, ahead of the king and emperor Charles V; but in 1702, next to king Philip V in a special place of honor, the city *sindaco* rode on a horse at the left hand of the king, both under a canopy held by noblemen of the *seggi*.) If clerics were included in the procession, they (cardinals, bishops, and archbishops) would join the ranks of royal ministers in the kingdom's various tribunals and complete the order of dignitaries. (In the 1702 cavalcade, for example, the archbishop and all the clergy of Naples did not process with the noble city cavalcade but waited outside the Porta Capuana to receive the king.) Closing the ranks were other carriages for the viceroy, others in his household, and a final contingent of lancers and cavalry.

In both the verbal and visual evidence of noble cavalcades, the ideal order of rank is clear. After the honor guard came the captains of justice, the Neapolitan baronage in hierarchical order (first undifferentiated barons and nobles and then titled nobility), followed by the city-district representatives and the officers of the kingdom, who preceded the viceroy and the city *sindaco*. It is important to note that the king or his proxy viceroy always appeared in a position of equilibrium with the city *sindaco*. (In 1535 the *sindaco* marched alone as the emperor himself did, surrounded by a bodyguard; in 1702 he marched next to the king.) The Spanish viceroy, for his part, not only acted as administrator of the kingdom for the absentee king, but he literally stood "in the place of" the king as his charge was to honor the king's formal relationship with his subjects, who retained the appearance of city rule under the city council *seggi eletti* and their rotating member as *sindaco*.

Political theory did not, however, prevent a viceroy like Pedro de Toledo from personally appropriating the symbols of power in art, if not in fact. A splendid bas-relief sculpture of Charles V's entrance in 1535 adorns the tomb of the viceroy Pedro de Toledo in the Church of S. Giacomo degli Spagnuoli, now part of the present-day town hall of Naples (fig. 2.5). In that scene, set outside the Porta Capuana, Pedro de Toledo awaits the emperor and his troop at the head of the whole city. But, in actual fact, the viceroy was not the city representative and thus not qualified to greet the entering emperor for the city. Because the viceroy was the absentee king's alter ego or proxy persona, he could not very well officially greet "himself." Only the city fathers could do that. The honor of presenting the emperor with the key to the city, as well as speaking to confirm the city's chapters and privileges, was reserved for the city representatives, the noble *eletti*, in the person of their rotating *sindaco*, and the archbishop who administered the oath.

As much as Charles V's 1535 royal entrance proved iconic for the presence of the king (or his proxy) in Neapolitan royal ceremonial under Spanish rule, the ceremonies for his obsequies in Brussels after his death on 21 September 1558 at the remote retreat of the Hieronymite monastery at Yuste proved equally determinative for his permanent absence from this world, as symbolic funeral rituals confirmed the transition of power throughout the royal realms according to the political theology of the king's two bodies.[131] In Naples Summonte later recorded that the Brussels "obsequies caused the greatest astonishment, [for] never before were similar ones celebrated for another Prince."[132] Obsequies commemorating the emperor's death numbered more than three thousand funeral ceremonies throughout his worldwide empire,[133] and the ceremonies at Brussels became a formative model for future royal obsequies not only in Naples but throughout Europe.[134]

The deceased emperor had borrowed from Burgundian court ritual and the church's Latin rite to introduce a new funeral ceremony into the Spanish monarchy's traditional funeral rituals.[135] For Charles V's royal funerary honors, churches were turned into elaborate mourning chapels full of symbolism with black draperies covering the external entrance, nave, and transept, with coats of

Figure 2.5. Entrance of Charles V in Naples in 1535, bas-relief in San Giacomo delgi Spagnuoli. Soprintendenza per i Beni Architettonici e Paesaggistici e per il Patrimonio Storici, Artistici ed Etnoantropologici per Napoli e Provincia, Naples.

arms, flags, emblems, *imprese*, statues of the virtues, and narrative paintings of the ruler's deeds strategically placed for viewing by the procession of hierarchically ordered nobility and clergy entering the church, with the focal point a catafalque alit with candles, the *chapelle ardente* (flaming chapel)—an architecturally elaborate columned and arched construction (Sp. *túmulo*; It. *apparato*)—at the transept, and with the centerpiece under the catafalque's arch a sepulchral slab displaying the crown, sword, scepter, and orb symbols of royal authority.[136]

One spectacular mobile *apparato* for the Brussels obsequies was an allegorical, eagle-prowed, three-masted ship named Victory that was pulled by two marine monsters and followed by two other marine monsters drawing the Pillars of Hercules rising out of two rocks and adorned with the imperial crowns atop—all sitting upon a flat slab of sea waves. This victory ship had a crew of the three theological virtues Faith, Hope, and Charity, flew sixteen flags with the coats of arms of Charles V's kingdoms, and had twelve narrative paintings of his victorious deeds displayed on its sides and stern.[137] Each side of the forecastle had a motto and narrative painting of Italian victories (the acquisition of Milan and the liberation of Genoa). The port and starboard of the hull each had four mottoes and paintings portraying the victories in the New World (Navigation to Peru and Christianity to the Indies) and against the Turks (Suleiman Fleeing Vienna, Tremisseno or Mauritania, Mediterranean Pirates Pacified, Capture of Goleta and

Tunis, Capture of the Ottoman Morea) with a lone image of the wars in Germany. The narrative cycle was completed on the stern with two mottoes and paintings of reception in the Low Countries and Libyan coastal towns in North Africa. In addition, Charles had one enduring and universal *impresa*, Plus ultra,[138] with the motto displayed on the ship's poop deck ahead of the two columns of Hercules drawn behind. Both the emperor's deeds and his virtues became part of his persona and, consequently, part of all the obsequies in his honor.

In Naples the obsequies for Charles V were held on his birth date, the feast of the twelfth apostle St. Matthias (24 February), which was one day before the one-year anniversary of the death of his elder sister, Eleanor of Austria, Queen of France, and three days before the obsequies for Philip II's wife and Queen of England, Mary Tudor.[139] The ceremonies commemorating Charles's death began on the feast's vigil with a procession from S. Chiara to the cathedral led by all the city's religious orders accompanied by all the titled nobility, royal officials, and city magistrates. The cathedral was lit by torches and draped in black cloth covered with the imperial insignia and verse, and prose *imprese* and triumphs of Charles were displayed on a black, Persian silk centerpiece. Inside the cathedral two funeral constructions filled the sanctuary: a great *apparato* with the emperor's motto "Plus ultra" that extended from the entrance of the choir to the high altar; and a tall *túmulo* covered by a celestial globe with the twelve signs of the zodiac upon which a very large, two-headed imperial eagle stood guard. The ten inscriptions alluding to Charles's deeds presented by Summonte compare generally with the twelve narrative paintings from the Brussels obsequies, but they are words, not pictures. The first three inscriptions offer two generic statements on the emperor's virtues (Charles's virtues and Charles on earth and in heaven) with the third on his conquest of Naples from the French. The last seven inscriptions all refer to deeds represented in the Brussels paintings: the New World, Italy Secured (rather than the sea), Suleiman Defeated in Hungary, Tunis Captured, the Low Countries, the Morea Liberated, and Victories against Rebels in Germany. Charles V's deeds and victories in the New World, Mediterranean, and German theaters were well known and reflected his virtues, both princely and personal. Only the reference to Italy, especially the conquest of Naples from the French, is unique to the Neapolitan obsequies for its local interest.

City Itineraries

Six main ritual itineraries were etched into the city streets. The principal civic itinerary was the royal way between the Porta Capuana and the Royal Palace that passed through the five noble and one *popolo seggi*. It connected all formal political bases of the monarchy, nobility, and *popolo* together. Next, the viceroy, as described by Raneo, was constantly in formal procession from the Royal Palace to individual churches and monasteries to celebrate the many feast days on his calendar. Although not a single itinerary, the viceroy's constant, formal movements constituted a second map of the city that we might call the viceregal way. The third way is the religious way from the Archbishop's Palace in a circuit through the six *seggi* from Capuana to the *popolo*, Portanova, Porto, Nido, and Montagna, back to the cathedral. The religious way was established in the processions of S. Gennaro and Corpus Christi. The fourth itinerary takes us through the streets of the *popolo* quarter from the *largo del Castello* through the guild neighborhoods between the *seggi* and the sea, on the way to the *seggio del popolo*, Piazza della Sellaria, and the Piazza del Mercato. This *popolo* way is examined during the analysis of the procession on the vigil of St. John's Day in chapter 5. In all four of these itineraries—royal, viceregal, religious, and *popolo*—formal processions marked the way.

The two other itineraries are "celebrations" of a different kind but followed ways of march just as well demarcated and ritualistic. The fifth itinerary is the way of the condemned, the march made by condemned prisoners on the way to their execution.[140] Guido Panico has counted 1,377 condemned prisoners, or about 32 executions per year between 1556 and 1599. This high-water mark of more than one hanging every other week during the "peaceful" reign of Philip II declined in the seventeenth century through the reign of Philip IV until 1660 to about 20 to 25 executions per year. The rite of capital punishment was a spectacle with a cortege that passed from the place of the condemned's incarceration (typically the Vicaria jail) through the dense *popolo* quarter on "the way of the cross" to the place of execution in Piazza del Mercato, where the gallows were permanently erected and prominently displayed in most city maps. This ancient ceremony of state violence lasted about two hours and was designed to engage a large audience of spectators to witness the cruelty and horror of the execution. With the hanging complete and the crowd's emotions spent, the ceremony concluded by exposing the corpse as a final sign of the justice of the state.

The sixth itinerary was a spontaneous and frenetic, if not jubilant outpouring of pent up emotion often at a time of social inversion, which might be called the way of the *charivari*.[141] Its emotive content, from playful joy and taunting to macabre and ferocious violence, could be seen most dramatically in 1585 at the forced march of the *eletto* Starace (and his corpse) from S. Maria de la Nova to the *seggio del popolo* and back to the Royal Palace; or, again, in the eruption of violence at the murder of Don Giuseppe Carafa in the streets during the early stages of the revolt of 1647. Panico quotes the impassioned injunctions to the crowd as reported by chroniclers to give a sense of the ritualistic character of the crowd's actions. During the Starace march, someone in the crowd cried, "Guardano, guardano, camminate signori, camminiamo"; and on 7 July 1647 in Piazza del Mercato, Masaniello shouted, "Allegrezza, allegrezza, compagni e fratelli miei, sono finite le nostre miserie."[142] Later, as part of the crowd's fury in 1647, a map can also be drawn of the festive marches to the houses of targeted nobles and tax farmers, where the people sacked and lit their houses on fire.[143] Panico reconstructs sixteen documented cases of people being hunted down in this kind of ritual murder. Desecration of their corpses sometimes included dragging their bodies through the streets, decapitation, triumphal exposition of the corpse, mutilation of the corpse, disposing of it without burial, and in two cases even cannibalism.[144]

Rituals could also take crowds on itineraries outside the city. The feast of the Nativity of the Blessed Virgin Mary at Piedigrotta, which marked the beginning of the autumn festival calendar on 8 September, was just to the west of the city. And following soon after Piedigrotta on September 19, the feast of S. Gennaro was celebrated outside the walls at the city's northern gate at the site of the patron saint's martyrdom and tomb. The festivals of Madonna dell'Arco some eleven kilometers outside the southeast gate of the Carmine was a pilgrimage site for votive requests of healing celebrated on Easter Monday and throughout the season of Pentecost. To the west from Mergellina and south along Posillipo, often meeting in boats or on constructed platforms in the bay, the Neapolitan nobility celebrated the summer festival of Posillipo in July and August. Processions and pilgrimages marked this traffic in and out of the city—north, south (onto the bay of Naples), east, and west.

Madonna dell'Arco, some eleven kilometers on the road to the north side of Vesuvius, is described in a 1608 chronicle as drawing a great number of pilgrims, both nobles and commoners, from the *casali* around Naples and the towns around Vesuvius, but the largest numbers came from Naples itself: "So great was the multitude of nobility and *popolo*, of carriages, coaches, and horses that left from Naples that for many and many days from the Carmine Gate up to Madonna Santissima dell'Arco for four miles and more it was difficult to be able to pass and walk forward or back."[145] The first miracle at the site dated from the mid-fifteenth-century when a croquet-like ball or stones thrown by an irate loser at an Easter Monday game of *palla e maglio* (Pall Mall) struck the virgin's image, which caused it to bleed from the cheek.[146] A small, two-room chapel was built, but only developed into a large sanctuary constructed by the Dominicans between 1593/94 and 1610 after a second miracle in 1589/90 gained credence among the faithful.

Finally, one external itinerary was an imaginary one of significant import, not for the citizens of Naples but for the viceroy and his army of occupation. On the interior apse over the main gate of the Castel Nuovo where the main contingent of Spanish troops was garrisoned, a fresco of the Plaza Mayor of Madrid was painted between 1648 and 1653 by Domenico Gargiulo and Viviano Codazzi.[147] After the violence of the revolt of 1647, soldiers leaving the safety of the Castel Nuovo would be able to contemplate home and hearth in Madrid as they entered the piazze and streets of Naples. Both soldiers and the viceroy himself might be reminded that S. Giovanni was also the patron of Madrid, as they attempted to pacify Naples recently in revolt.

Time, Space, and Power in Naples

The verbal and visual representations of how Neapolitans interacted suggest something far more nuanced than the orthodox explanation of colonial exploitation of a degenerate oligarchic political culture caught in the debilitating downward spiral of a backward economy. Instead, the contestations of early modern Naples appear to have been the product of a conscious policy pursued by the Spanish occupation to incorporate Naples into its imperial system as the centerpiece of its Mediterranean policy. After restoration of the *seggio del popolo* in 1494, the manipulation of the conflict between nobility and *popolo* became the cornerstone of a foreign hegemony created by playing off native power against itself. The Spaniards promoted a juridical elite of robed nobility to institutionalize a kind of suspended animation in which constant conflict brought no change at all. This dialectic without synthesis, I would argue, formed the essence of early modern absolutist rule in Naples—the ability of superior military force and centralized bureaucratic institutions to exert control by manipulating traditional local antagonisms between indigenous vying parties. Nobles and *popolo* still retained more than the illusion of self-governance in city affairs through the familial-neighborhood *seggi*. But the asymmetrical social relationships of noble patrons, commoner clients, and the poor added up to reinforced Spanish control of power, because the monarchy's "good arms" held the status quo in check.[148]

Early modern Naples did, however, have a middle-class citizenry of merchants, professionals, bureaucrats, and guildsmen. Fernand Braudel describes its huge population at the end of the sixteenth century as having "no equivalent in Christendom":

> The size of the population was one reason why so many luxury goods were produced there. Neapolitan goods in the sixteenth century were what would be called fancy goods today: lace, braids, frills, trimmings, silks, light fabrics (taffetas), silken knots and cockades of all colors, and fine linens. These goods traveled as far as Cologne in large quantities. . . . There were many other industries either already established in the city or which the vast labour force could have attracted there.[149]

Some eighty-eight guilds existed during the Spanish period.[150] Undoubtedly weakened by Spanish fiscal exactions, and the economic crises of the seventeenth century, the Neapolitan *popolo* could nonetheless, in 1644, still be displayed as the most important city component of Tutini's tract on the *seggi*.[151] In 1647 a whole range of guildsmen appeared as active participants in the revolt.[152] Even after the revolt, according to the 1671 edition of Bacco's guide to Naples, non-noble citizens had sufficient wealth to continue to support some ninety-seven charitable institutions that provided dowries to poor girls.[153] Almost 34,000 ducats annually funded 665 such charitable gifts. Further, when compared with a population larger than any other city of Italy through the early modern period, the relative number of Neapolitan clergymen, nobles, and unemployed does not seem to be disproportionately large. In 1600 Naples's clergy numbered 2 to 3 percent of the total population, roughly equivalent to the clerical population in other Italian cities.[154] Similarly, about 1600 the great Republic of Venice, still Italy's richest and most economically productive city, counted about 2,150 male nobles (1.4 percent of total population) and had 77 percent of its population not in the work force, whereas Napoli Gentile, still strongly dominated by its feudal nobility, claimed approximately 3,225 total noblemen (1.2 percent) and about 83 percent of its population not in the work force.[155] Naples, like each of Italy's cities, was unique, but far less different than is generally believed.

The surface area of Naples was not, however, the expansive space one found in sparsely inhabited Rome, or smaller Florence, which, with about 60,000 inhabitants in the sixteenth century, had only about one-half its late medieval population. Rural migrants fleeing from distress kept crowding into Naples, straining its already overburdened services. By 1600 its population was about twice the size of Venice, although its 600-hectare area (including the newly assimilated Spanish Quarter and Via Toledo) was only one-third as large. Population density in Naples was about 430 per hectare, as opposed to 340 per hectare in Venice, and

about 300 per hectare in Florence. And while Venetian and Florentine population remained relatively static in the seventeenth century, more arrivals in Naples
had further increased population density to about 580 per hectare by 1650.[156] Its
total population ranked Naples with the more dynamic capitals of London and
Paris, both of which surpassed it in size only by the mid-seventeenth century.

In 1471, before the French invasions and the Spanish conquest at the end of
the century, Loise de Rosa had praised his native Naples with sunny optimism as
the most beautiful city in the world. He used thirteen criteria to rank cities and
found Naples lacking in only one of them, far outstripping all the other cities he
surveyed.[157] Naples was best in its well-placed site, for proximity to sea, mountains, plains, and water; best in its access to the four elements of water, air, fire
and earth; and best in streets, houses, churches, and newly built fountains. Pre-
sciently, he found Renaissance Naples, before the Spanish occupation, deficient
only in walls, which made the city vulnerable to foreign invasion and conquest.
The newly victorious Spanish conquerors thus gave Naples walls—the most sacred perimeter of a city. These Spanish works were not walls of beauty, but defensive walls designed to keep out enemies, initially the French from returning
(having departed in 1495) and the Ottoman Turks from attacking (because they
had occupied Otranto, the southeastern-most town on the heel of Italy for a full
year in 1480–81). When Lautrec's French expeditionary forces proved to be the
last to threaten Naples and the Turks never came, the walls stood on guard to
keep the population itself enclosed and disciplined.

Circumscribed space was a function of Spanish control. Its advantages were
manifest to the Spanish occupiers in the aftermath of the Masaniello revolt. Pedro
de Toledo's military defense projects a century earlier had provided the strategic
means for the Spanish to retake the city, and Naples had become an armed camp,
billeted with foreign troops in their own residential quarter. Such social control,
because it created a zero-sum game for limited space, also had disadvantages. It
increased competition between native groups, heightened urban violence, and
inhibited private architectural development. The crowded space also limited the
possibilities of employment. Cheap labor abounded, provisioning was precarious, and dependence, destitution, and despair became the legacy of the urban
plebs. With the economic crisis of the 1610s and 1620s devastating the wool and
silk industries, the working class, which was concentrated in the old city, threatened to become a permanent underclass.[158] When the economic situation of the
late seventeenth century improved, little viable infrastructure still remained to
respond to new opportunities. Rich and poor had grown farther apart as they
lived closer together in their overlapping domains.

In such a city—a world unto itself—conflict and contention were as normal as bargaining in the streets and markets; face-to-face interchange held things together. And in the midst of this solidarity through exchange, all kinds of institutions—both lay and ecclesiastical, from noble *seggi* and the dowry fund of the twenty-nine Caracciolo families to the *popolo*'s twenty-nine *ottine* and the dowry fund of the master tailors—kept the city going. Neither bad government nor changed dynasties defined *Napoli nobilissima*. In fact, *Napoli nobilissima* was itself the faded dream of a nostalgic nobility, a dream not open to the middling orders. A truer Naples was the turbulent one masquerading as *fedelissima* (the most faithful city), an ambiguous appellation claimed by the people in the excluded middle, who were held in check by Spanish arms, noble *seggi* exclusion, and their own accommodation.[159]

PART TWO

CITY SOLIDARITIES AND
NODES OF POWER

CHAPTER THREE

Patronage

The Church and the Heavenly City

The Three Faces of Patronage

When one tries to assess power and influence in the city, simple models assist in defining the problem. Binary models of vertical and horizontal networks help focus on the bonds of affiliation, whether hierarchical or among equals; but one begins to see how quickly networks multiply among kin, neighbors, and friends with both overlapping and conflicting associations at the same time among an individual's political ward, parish, confraternity, and guild. In the corporate society of the Old Regime, the central question is how to measure an individual's fidelity to any one entity—from family and clan to corporation or institution. All operative relationships oscillate on a continuum between integration, representation, and resistance. We can thus see in the political sphere how associational bonds create integration and inclusion through the formal and informal power of administrative bureaucracies and court societies; how power is represented in the logic of exchange and compromise between groups; and how resistance to that power is possible by negotiating conflict or in open rebellion.[1]

The method of interactive exchange hypothesized and practiced by actors of unequal power in early modern Italy was patronage.[2] Patronage follows a model derived from the relationship of God and the saints in the supernatural world with human beings in the natural world, *patronato* or the prayers offered to and intercession received from the deity or a patron saint. In the natural world, patronage, whether *mecenatismo* (support and financing of the arts through commissions and largesse) or *clientelismo* (patron-client relations based upon reciprocity of protection and support), is closely related in the crisscrossing of interests and intents in favoring people and things in exchange for some quid pro quo. Hierarchy, exchange, and fidelity create the ties that bind, and we can see these three aspects of patronage in the importance of saints' lives in Neapolitan culture, in the ideology of Naples as the New Jerusalem portrayed in the sacristy of the Certosa di San Martino, and in the obsequies of Philip II attended by the Neapolitan nobility.

Hagiography and Patron Saints in Neapolitan Spirituality

S. Agnello (d. 625), one of the seven original patron saints of the city of Naples, was known as much for his just punishment to those inattentive to his cult as for his innumerable curative miracles for the faithful. His traditional hagiography includes the story of a pregnant woman, who did not honor the saint's feast day, but worked instead, cutting a piece of wood with a knife, only to have her son born without an arm.[3] Paolo Regio concludes with complete conviction in his 1593 revised version of S. Agnello's life that such stories were not ancient legends, because only a few years before in 1590, the same kind of deformed child was born as the result of similar disrespect to S. Agnello by the pregnant wife of Giovan Paolo Maioni from Terra di Somma, one of the communes around Vesuvius.[4] Such a homologous, newly appended example of the immanence of the supernatural and the power of miracles, even as the learned Bishop Regio wrote his lives of the saints of Naples, verified how the belief in the past structured the understanding of the present.

Direct, physical punishment for blasphemous disregard of the cult of the saints was not an isolated anecdote limited to the veneration of S. Agnello. A similar story circulated in that same year, 1590, at the most popular pilgrimage site around Naples, Madonna dell'Arco, also on the road to Vesuvius, which dated from the mid-fifteenth-century miracle of the statue's bleeding from the cheek after an angry loser at an Easter Monday game of *palla e maglio* (an early ball-and-mallet game like croquet) struck the image with a ball or stones. On the shrine's Easter Monday feast day in 1589, then, one Aurelia Del Prete reluctantly agreed to walk with her husband to the shrine to deposit an ex-voto for him. In the crush of pilgrims near the shrine, she lost a piglet she was carrying and, in anger, threw her husband's votive to the ground, cursed the Madonna, the painter of her image, and all who venerated it. In the night between Easter and Easter Monday 1590 on the anniversary of her previous blasphemies, it is recorded that both of her feet fall off. And they can be seen still today on display in a small iron cage in the church's sacristy![5] As in the S. Agnello story, cause-and-effect rules the patron-client relationship between the natural and supernatural worlds. Blasphemy and disrespect for the saints bring proportional punishment and disaster, whereas veneration and prayer bring protection and blessing.

In Paolo Regio's encyclopedia of Neapolitan spirituality, his monumental, two-volume, 1,838-page compendium of Neapolitan saints' lives, *Dell'Opere spirituali*, "in which is contained the lives of those Blessed Apostles and other Saints and Holy Martyrs of God who either were venerated [in Naples] for their religious life or were born in the Kingdom of Naples," history becomes theology in order to rationalize belief and exhort emulation of the moral life in the telling of such stories as those about S. Agnello and the Madonna dell'Arco devotion. Regio compiles and supplements his collection of fifty saints' lives with "many notable facts, which occurred in diverse Regions beyond their histories, whence one can learn the disdain for the vanity of the World, and the examples and the teachings of the servants of Christ."[6] Twenty-two of these fifty lives had been previously published over the past twenty years in the ten books in seventeen editions that had already made Regio, the bishop of Vico Equense, near Sorrento on the southern rim of the Bay of Naples, the single most prolific author in sixteenth-century Neapolitan publishing history.[7]

On first turning to the print culture of post-Tridentine Naples and encountering the quantity of vernacular religious literature composed by Paolo Regio, some twenty-two titles in thirty-four editions published during his lifetime (table 3.1), one might marvel at his productivity, relegate him to the rank of a hack historian or anecdotal popularizer, and not recognize his stature within the literary culture of late sixteenth-century Naples, where the theologian Telesio, the poet Tasso, and the scientist-dramatist Giambattista della Porta held sway.[8] The noble bishop, born of the Venetian family of the Orseoli in Naples in 1545, was an honored member of the Neapolitan Accademia degli Svegliati, in which his name among the "Wide-Awake Ones" was Solitario, for his preference of the contemplative life.[9] Far from passively withdrawing from society, however, he published at least some twenty-two sonnets, poems, elegies, songs, or letters in books other than his own between 1572 and his death in 1607.[10] His works were well known in Rome to Cesare Baronio, with whom he corresponded,[11] and continued to be reprinted in Naples through the seventeenth century, with Nicolò Toppi's standard 1678 reference book on illustrious Neapolitan writers "not wishing to speak of him because so much praise due him could not be contained in so small a space."[12]

Regio came to both his clerical and literary vocation after marriage and a child. Married at age seventeen in 1562 and finding himself a widower with a baby son after his wife's death two years later in 1564, he only then began to dedicate himself to religious pursuits. At twenty-four in 1569, he had published his first literary efforts, *Siracusa: Pescatoria*, poetry inspired by Sanazzaro; and, at twenty-eight in 1573, his first foray into hagiography, *Vite dei sette santi protettori di Napoli*.

TABLE 3.I.
Paolo Regio's Bibliography

1569	*Siracusa: Pescatoria* (Giovanni de Boy)
1572	*Lucrezia*, 2nd ed.
1573	*Vita dei sette santi protettore di Napoli* (Cacchii), later editions: 1579, 1623, 1673
1576	*Discorsi intorno le virtu morali* (Salviani)
1578	*Vita e miracoli di S. Francesco da Paolo* (Salviani), later editions: 1581, 1581, 1587, 1605
1580	*La Vita dell'Angelico Dottor S. Tomaso d'Aquino* (Salviani)
1581	*La Vita di S. Pietro Celestino* (Cappelli)
1582	*La Vita del Santo Padre Antonino Abbate* (Cappelli)
1584	*Le Vite de i tre Santissimi Vescovi Vitaliano, Ireneo, et Fortunato* (Salviani and Cesari)
1584	*Le Vite del Santo Padre Guglielmo fondator...di Monte Vergine e di S Amato suo discepolo* (Cacchii), later edition: 1593
1586–87	*Delle vite dei santi*, 2 vols. (Cacchii), 2nd ed.: 1588–87 *Della historia Catholica*, 2 vols.
1588	*La Vita del B. Jacopo della Marcha* (Cacchii), 2nd ed.: 1589
1590	*La Vita di S. Patricia vegine sacra* (Cacchii), later editions: 1633, 1642
1591	*Dialoghi intorno la felicità, et la miseria, et la fragilità della vita humana* (Cacchii)
1592–93	*Delle opere spirituale*, 2 vols. (Cacchii)
1595	*Sermoni intorno le tre virtù teologiche* (Stigliola)
1597	*Delle osservanze Catholica. Dialoghi sette. Prima parte degli Opusculi Morali* (Carlino and Pace)
1597	*Della felicità e della miseria. Dialoghi sette. Seconda parte degli Opusculi Morali* (Carlino and Pace)
1598	*Della consolatione e del consiglio. Dialoghi sette. Terza parte degli Opuscoli Morali* (Carlino and Pace)
1598	*Vita di S. Potito martire* (Carlino and Pace), later edition: 1673
1601	*Vita di S. Honofrio heremita* (Carlino), 2nd ed.: 1604
1603	*Sirenide: Poema Spirituali* (Pace), 2nd ed.: 1604
1612	(posthumous) *Vita di S. Panfilo vescovo e confessore* (Chieti, Isidoro Facii)

From 1576 to 1581, he oversaw the index of prohibited books and the press in Naples, both local and imported books. By 1580 he had become a professor of sacred theology, and in 1583, bishop of Vico Equense, which served as his base of operations and seat of the press of Giuseppe Cacchii, with whom he published exclusively for the next ten years. All through the 1570s and 1580s, Regio dedicated himself to his hagiographic vocation, and its quantity easily explains why that writing has dominated our view of Regio's place in the Neapolitan literary scene. His theological writing, some six books on the theological and moral virtues, five of which were written in the 1590s, provides the key, however, to Regio's magisterial hagiographic project and his importance in the making of citizen identity in Naples.

The first of these theological books, *Discorsi del Regio intorno le virtu morali*, appears early in Regio's literary career in 1576, only three years after his first hagiography on the Neapolitan saints had appeared. These four discourses on justice, prudence, temperance, and fortitude demonstrate how the four moral virtues are necessary for the formation of the soul and its governance. Hardly original, Regio traces the standard medieval argument in his *proemio*—after God's creation of the world and man, original sin weakened man's will so that it became subject to desire. The moral virtues, thus, provide the antidote to the crippled intellect to recover its preeminence in moral decision making. With special attention to the problem of the Prince and the Republic, the four moral virtues in this Counter-Reformation "Mirror-for-Princes" context are the Christian's means to combat and conquer fortune.

After fifteen years of concerted hagiographic effort, Regio turned his energies to direct spiritual consolation in the 1590s. Still proposing a conventional Counter-Reformation spirituality in his three dialogues of 1591, *Dialoghi intorno la felicità, et la miseria, et la fragilità della vita humana*, Regio, however, does bring a distinctive Neapolitan perspective to the biblical commonplace on *vanitas vanitatem*. One easily recognizes these first three dialogues as a book of preliminary exercises in this new genre, as these 186 pages of dialogue were more than doubled in the 1597–98 *Opusculi Morali*'s second volume of 403 pages in seven dialogues. How this early 1591 experiment in dialogue was expanded in the final three-volume version of 1,252 pages a half dozen years later tells us much about Regio's orientation and understanding of his mission.

The small format (135 × 80 millimeters) of the 1591 dialogues, "Happiness, Misery, and the Fragility of Human Life," between three speakers were less true exchanges between equals than a platform for Solitario (Bishop Regio's Accademia degli Svegliati voice) to respond to questions posed by two interlocutors, Montinio and Portenio. The first dialogue is grounded in moral principles and examines vanity's false pleasure in the world, the virtues that bring true happiness, and how we ought not to fear death because the living of virtuous lives brings true happiness.[13]

> Virtue separates the nobles from those ignoble, slaves
> from freemen. Virtue is the death of concupiscence.
> Virtue is the best and the most certain of all the other
> arts. Virtue conquers all adversity.[14]

Arguments are based on the "imperatives of Nature," with Christian acceptance of the laws of the natural world as the means to trample vanity under foot and find truth in religion.

The second dialogue applies these precepts to the lessons of Neapolitan history in the details of dynastic fall and familial extinction. "The unhappy events experienced by many Kings, Princes, and nobles of the Kingdom of Naples," who were all "subject to human miseries,"[15] turns local history into moral message. Violent death and loss of their temporal goods in the infinite mutations witnessed through Neapolitan history draw attention to the local manifestations of human frailty in Naples's monarchs and ruling class, which underlines the fruitlessness of human actions in the secular sphere. Regio begins with the Normans and the Hohenstaufen kings, who were the first rulers of Naples to lose their kingdom "through civil war and violent deaths."[16] While ten days, as opposed to the lone fictional day of each dialogue, would not be sufficient to remember this whole history, Regio elides the story of Naples's medieval forebears to be able to expand upon the tribulations of its Aragonese conquerors from the irony of Alfonso's triumphal entry in 1442, through the tumults of endemic civil war under Ferrante, to their ignominious exile after the French Invasions of 1494 and Spanish Conquest of 1503. No record of royal deeds memorializes human frailty better than the wooden coffins of the Aragonese royal family, which before the 1593–94 royal pantheon intervention by Philip II, sat abandoned and disordered on the floor of the sacristy in S. Domenico Maggiore. Nothing remains "save the inscriptions of their names."[17]

Citing the standard chroniclers and historians of Naples from Pontano to Giovio and Guicciardini,[18] Regio moves to the noble antagonists, pro-Aragonese and pro-Angevin, whose great deeds and personal sacrifices were now forgotten, their families defunct or impoverished. "Today one sees many in Naples whose ancestors were very rich or were high officials, but whose palaces are inhabited by their former friends and servants while they live in poverty and misery."[19] Above all, Regio continually reminds his readers of the ephemeral character of human accomplishments: "Such happiness as this is similar to a lamp, which, as soon as it is lighted, is extinguished."[20] Regio reiterates the biblical promise of inversion, the last shall be first and the first, last: "In Antonello Petrucci," who rose from a mere notary's adopted son to King Ferrante's secretary before falling from power in the second baronial conspiracy of 1485 and whom Regio singles out as one of the principle subjects of his argument, Regio asks his readers rhetorically to consider "what is greater, his misery or his happiness, his low birth or his high estate; certainly each one of [the changes of fortune] is equal to the other, [the rise] from low birth to noble office, and [the fall] from his high place to the most miserable debasement."[21] Such juxtapositions were commonplace in late sixteenth-century Naples, where the parallels between the frequent noble cavalcades in religious or secular procession and the omnipresent criminal parades to the hangman along the same city route, or between the conservation of saints' heads as relics in churches and the posting of criminals' heads in the streets, constantly reminded the city's inhabitants of the porous boundaries between good and evil, the haves and the have-nots, the living and the dead.

The third dialogue generalizes upon the examples of Neapolitan history by reviewing the wisdom of ancient philosophers and sacred scripture on mankind's true end, the end of the world, the immortality of the soul, and the transitory nature of earthly existence. "Our life is similar to a sailor's" on a tempestuous sea.[22] Yet life has meaning as long as one remembers the true goal of life everlasting.

A 1595 collection of Regio's sermons on the three theological virtues, faith, hope, and charity, *Sermoni intorno le tre virtù teologiche*, points us further in the direction of Bishop Regio's operative rationale, the centerpiece of a Christian's life in action. The first ten sermons on faith have a strong, Tridentine, anti-evangelical ring, with emphasis on the importance of the church, its clergy, and the Eucharist, all as manifestations of the good Christian's works. The ten sermons on hope emphasize prayer as the exercise of spiritual work, whereas the ten sermons on charity underline the meaning of love and friendship in the visible expression of one's deeds. In charity especially, through both the corporal and spiritual works of mercy, a good Counter-Reformation Catholic can demonstrate how Christian doctrine is observed.[23]

The three-volume *Opusculi Morali* maintained the small format (135 × 75 millimeters) and the principle speaker, Regio's persona as Solitario.[24] But a number of new speakers are added: in volume 1, "On Catholic Observance," Fanello, who stands for the Benedictine monk Prospero Fanele; in volume 3, "On Consolation and Counsel," Melibeo, who signifies temporal matters in the voice of a rich nobleman, and Gratiano, a doctor of law. Each volume is dedicated to a different cardinal: volume 1, to Cardinal Baronio; volume 2, to Cardinal Antonio Carafa, the protector of Regio's only son and the dedicatee of the 1591 preliminary dialogues; and volume 3, to Cardinal Montelparo, to whom the 1595 sermons had also been dedicated. Not only is Regio moving in higher ecclesiastical circles, but his argument has also taken on a higher intellectual tone and more complex philosophical epistemology in these 1579–98 dialogues on the moral life.

The first volume immediately introduces the reader to the more profound philosophical discourse by focusing its argument around the human body, its senses, thoughts, and deeds. Volume 2, then, continues the argument on desire in relationship to the human quest for happiness, but it finds only misery in the natural world. And volume 3 delves beyond the appearance or manifestation of the body's miseries, natural disasters, and war by probing into the causes of such things. The philosophical principle behind Regio's spiritual writing is that of Bernardino Telesio (1509–88), a Benedictine monk like Fanello, the interlocutor in volume 1; Telesio was the subject of an unpublished, no-longer-extant biography by Regio, the master of the lives of the saints genre.[25]

Telesio had published the first two books of his *De natura juxta propria principia* in 1565, not coincidentally at the beginning of Regio's studies. Telesio's speculations, made in Naples and Cosenza, inspired a generation of students striving to rethink the teaching of Aristotle by relying upon sensory evidence drawn from the natural world. With the appearance in 1586 of the complete edition of the *Rerum natura*, Sertorio Quattromani's short and accessible Italian translation of Telesio's ideas available only three years later in 1589,[26] and Tommaso Campanella's 500-page defense of Telesio, *Ordinis praedicatorum philosophia*, published in 1591, Telesio's teachings on the existence of two elements (heaven and earth), rather than four, and their parallel hot and cold forces at war became local Neapolitan orthodoxy as much as the new sensory-based, empirical method.[27] Even though Telesio's works were placed on the index in 1596 "pending correction," Regio seems to have been appropriating and applying Telesio's ideas to mainstream theological topics in order to demonstrate their utility and orthodoxy.

Book 1's argument follows the method of Telesio quite explicitly. Seven days of dialogue correspond to the seven predicaments or "observances" faced by Catholics. The seven dialogues focus respectively on seeing, hearing, thinking, praying, speaking, going or comporting oneself, and acting—that is, on good works, especially the theological virtues of faith, hope, and charity (as he had already argued in the 1595 *Sermoni*). In dialogue 2, Fanello asks Solitario directly how to observe.[28] Solitario's long explanation is a kind of catechism on observance, which requires mastery of the liberal arts. Each of the learned disciplines corresponds to a practical field of activity, and all of this advice, Solitario assures his interlocutor, was learned "in my days at the university of Naples in S. Domenico,"[29] that is, the same environment in the same years that had spawned Giordano Bruno between 1565 and 1576 and later Campanella after 1589.[30]

Did the good orthodox bishop Regio also share in the revolutionary and visionary spirit of his two more famous Dominican fellow students? In Regio's two dedications to the newly elected Pope Clement VIII and the order in which the lives of the saints are presented in each volume of the *Dell'Opere spirituale*, we have some clues to his ideas about the kind of spiritual and political renewal of the church that Regio commended. Volume 1 does not begin with the life of S. Gennaro or one of the other popular patron saints of Naples, nor do its opening lives fit the chronological or hierarchical plan of the rest of the volume. Rather, the lives of St. Clement and St. Luke lead the way to the lives of four apostles—Sts. Andrew, Matthew, Bartholomew, and Thomas—before the early church martyrs, including S. Gennaro, with St. Stephen at their head. It is not just the onomastic of Clement that Regio is using to put himself in good stead with the pope. Sts. Clement and Luke come first because their relics are preserved in Naples, with both their heads in the Church of S. Agostino. Regio's attachment to Telesio and the naturalist circle in Naples may well have spilled over into practical politics in such a preference for the Augustinians, whose church as the seat of the Neapolitan *seggio del popolo* was the center of commoner political activity in late sixteenth-century Naples.

Similarly, volume 2 focuses on patron saints in the city, with entries two through six portraits of five of Naples's original patrons, and then moves to saints around the kingdom with such provincial patrons as St. Nicolas of Bari. The text begins, however, with the life of Pope Celestine V, the holy monk who abdicated the papacy in favor of Boniface VIII in 1294, and whom Dante placed in the antechamber of hell where he resided with the uncommitted for his cowardly abdication (*Inferno*, Canto 3). Pope St. Celestine occupies pride of place according to Regio's introduction because his personal sanctity and commitment to spiritual matters above political faction make him a model worthy of Pope Clement's emulation in the Counter-Reformation program to restore the papacy as the cornerstone of Christian right thinking.[31] Bishop Regio's vision of reform demanded individual, spiritual renewal through imitation of the saints—even for the pope.

Not surprisingly, the culmination of Regio's publication career came in a highly literary work, *La Sirenide. Poema Spirituali* of 1603, which was a mixed genre of prose and poetry aimed as a guide for meditation. According to its dedication, its distinctive poetic form had long been in the making, albeit its argument recapitulates Regio's consistent rationale to give up vanity and search for wisdom, for the soul needs virtue, both the moral and theological virtues, to keep it on the right path and avoid vice and misery.

Veneration of the saints in early modern Naples was not simply a functional "form of shamanism with the miracle a variety of a symbolic cure,"[32] or a devotional strategy designed for popular reinforcement of Counter-Reformation spirituality, but was rather an activity central to the spiritual works and moral obligations of the Neapolitan faithful, as they understood the reciprocity between patrons and clients in becoming citizens of heaven while on earth in their native city. Hagiographical and prayer books are the material remains of a spiritual exercise, whose object was to make saints. Few examples can explain how this process of spiritual patronage worked better than the notorious case of the false saint Suor Giulia de Marco and her carnal spirituality.

Making and Unmaking a Living Saint: The Beata Suor Giulia de Marco

The Roman diarist Giacinto Gigli wrote a long entry for Sunday 12 July 1615 in describing the abjuration of three heretics at the Church of S. Maria Sopra Minerva.[33] He recorded a "thing that it is incredible to recount," that drew a large crowd of the *popolo*, and that was delayed almost five hours while the crowd waited for all the cardinals to assemble. The "feigned sanctity" of the "wolf in sheep's clothing . . . a demon in the form of a Saint," the so-called *beata*, Suor Giulia de Marco, had beguiled "a great number of people, especially women and virgins, as well as the elite" of Naples, by her claim to divine revelations. She had purported to receive visions from God "that He had forgiven her sins and assured her that she would be saved, and therefore, that in the future He would give her freedom of conscience, and beyond that that God had made her know how much He wished to fill up the Seats of Paradise; whence therefore it was necessary to multiply, for which God permitted her to have carnal relations with how many ever and whatever kind of persons she wished."

In Naples the chronicle of Tommaso Costo recorded that "the proceedings were read solemnly in the cathedral in front of the cardinal archbishop and all the prelates in the city on 9 August.[34] Costo also recorded that one year earlier on 23 August 1614 "a certain Giuseppe de Vicariis and a little later a certain Suor Giulia not professed in orders and esteemed by the crowd as a *santa viva* were jailed by order of Rome and the Holy Office." The Neapolitan chronicler Scipione Guerra likewise inserted the story of "the infamous nun Suor Giulia de Marco, her confessor Father Aniello Arciero of the Order of the Regular Clerics of the Ministers of the Sick (Ordo Clericorum Regularium Ministrantium Infirmis or Camillians), Giuseppe de Vicariis, and other accomplices" in his account of the rule of the viceroy Pedro Fernández de Castro y Andrade, Count of Lemos (r. 13 July 1610–8 July 1616).[35] His wife, Caterina Gómez de Sandoval y Rojas, sister of the Duke of Lerma, Philip III's favorite, had frequented Suor Giulia because the vicereine was childless and hoped that the prayers of the *santa viva* would intercede on her behalf.

But when a young female supporter sought a Theatine confessor to seek absolution over the scruples she felt from resisting Suor Giulia's unwelcome sexual counsel, the three principals were arrested and the vicereine's honor was saved from the false *beata*. Although the viceroy and Cardinal Decio Carafa of Naples had defended Suor Giulia from the beginning, the fact that the viceroy's brother, Francisco Domingo Ruiz de Castro, formerly viceroy for two years from 1601 upon the death of their father, Fernández Ruiz de Castro, the former viceroy Count of Lemos (r. 1599–1601), had been Spanish ambassador in Rome since 1609 and close to Pope Paul V (r. 1605–21) prevented any hint of scandal filtering out to the Spanish ruling class.

The broad outlines of this notorious case as recorded by the chroniclers make it clear that it reached into the highest ranks of Neapolitan society and Spanish viceregal government, that the sexual promiscuity at the center of the abjurations raised questions of heresy beyond the overt sinful adulterous acts themselves, and that special attention is due the salvific role assigned to the Theatines— who at the same time had their own *santa viva*, Orsola Benincasa, the venerated founder of the female branch of their order in residence in Castel S. Elmo above Naples since 1581, when she had been cleared by the Roman Inquisition.[36] Yet, not by accident, no record of Suor Giulia is preserved in the Spanish archives in Simancas, in neither *Estado Napoles* nor *Estado Roma*.[37] Likewise, the Jesuit chroniclers of this period leave no trace of the case, despite the fact that the Jesuits were Suor Giulia's primary proponents in their attempt to establish a spiritual rival to Orsola Benincasa in their struggle with the Theatines to dominate the spiritual life of Naples.[38]

In English, Anne Jacobson Schutte captures the essence of the case and follows the standard interpretation of Suor Giulia, "by far the most complex instance of pretense of holiness in Naples . . . the bizarre amalgam of spirituality and sexual libertinism."[39] Schutte places Suor Giulia in the company of three contemporary Neapolitan cases of presumed sanctity to conclude that "the local tribunal of the Inquisition was less than confident in handling pretense of holiness" and preferred transferring such cases to Rome. Her main source is Jean-Michel Sallmann's study of Baroque saints in Naples and the text of the abjuration itself as published by Amabile in the late nineteenth century.[40]

The full text of the three abjurations, in which an anonymous "Historia e processo delle eresie di Suor Giulia de Marco e de' suoi seguaci" places the condemned in the context of Neapolitan spiritualism and Lutheran heresy, exists in an oft-copied manuscript probably written by the Theatine Valerio Pagano.[41] The prurient elements of the story are highlighted: group sex with as many as ten males and ten females pairing up in couples in noble palaces with copulation the height of their spiritual communion as "carnal charity." Orgasm became mystical ecstasy, with ejaculation received by Suor Giulia in pious refrain, "Gesù, Maria; Gesù, Maria." Suor Giulia confessed to having five or six abortions. Her confessor Arciero revealed that following their separation in 1607, he began homosexual relations with a fellow priest in Rome. The lawyer de Vicariis explained that Suor Giulia "assured [them] that their carnal acts were not sins, but new virtues infused by the Holy Spirit."[42] Until recently, these bare facts were about all we knew.

Elisa Novi Chavarria, however, has uncovered new documentation in the Biblioteca Nazionale di Napoli, the Vatican Library, and the Congregazione della Dottrina della Fede.[43] My summary and analysis follows Novi's lead in presenting a new understanding of the social group that constituted Suor Giulia's followers and supporters to reexamine patronage from the upper echelons of Neapolitan society and Spanish viceregal rule, Jesuit patronage and Theatine opposition, and the complex theological controversy on grace that lie behind the whole affair. Feigned sanctity it may have been, but more complicated problems of female infertility and charismatic spirituality, rivalry between new Counter-Reformation religious orders, and contested politics in state and church rather than titillating sexual promiscuity were at stake.

When the initial damaging denunciation of 31 July 1614 opened the investigation by the local Neapolitan inquisition that led to her arrest and conviction, Suor Giulia stood at the height of her influence. In order to identify the nodes of power coalescing around her in the summer of 1614, we should first establish her itinerary in time and space around Naples in the previous decade, which can be divided into three periods. We shall see that her star shone for only ten years and her personal charisma in Naples was most dominant for about two to three years, from 1611/12 to 1614.

Giulia was born in 1574 or 1575 in the province of Molise in the small 2,000-inhabitant town of Sepino near Campobasso on one of the four principal sheep-walks to Foggia, where an ancient Roman arch commemorating the ancient system of transhumance still stands. Her father was an agricultural laborer and her mother the daughter of a similar agricultural laborer and a converted Turkish slave. She herself became a domestic servant, followed her sister to Naples, and had a son that she turned over to the foundling hospital of Santissima Annunziata. Inheriting property upon her mistress's death, she became a Franciscan tertiary.

In her first period of public notice, Suor Giulia began to gain some notoriety in Naples as a holy woman after 1604 when the Jesuit priest Girolamo Gesio became her confessor. In 1605 Aniello Arciero, superior of the Neapolitan convent of the Ministers of the Sick, became her spiritual director and their liaison attracted an investigation by the Neapolitan inquisitor, the bishop of Caserta, Deodato Gentile, in 1607–8. In order to dampen popular interest in Suor Giulia, her confessor Arciero was transferred to his order's mother house of S. Maria Maddalena in Rome and forbidden to return to Naples, while Suor Giulia was moved to the Franciscan convent of S. Antonio di Padova in Naples later in 1608 and given a new spiritual director, Ludovico Antinoro, a Theatine from S. Paolo Maggiore. Her growing cult following led Bishop Gentile to transfer her to the convent of S. Maria Madre di Cristo in Cerreto Sannita northeast of Caserta, a few days' journey from the Neapolitan capital.[44] This first period of about three to four years of public fame centered on her ecstasies and visions but ended with questions about her "affected sanctity" and concerns about her role as the "Spiritual Mother" of a developing cult.

The second period of about three to four years saw Suor Giulia physically absent from Naples in Cerreto and then in 1611 transferred closer to Naples by a new Inquisition examiner, the bishop of Nocera, Stefano de Vicariis, a relative of her devoted lawyer follower Giuseppe de Vicariis. Giulia was brought to the Franciscan convent of S. Chiara in Nocera, east of Pompei on the road halfway to Salerno, under the observation of the inquisitor and remained there for eight months before being allowed to return to Naples itself in 1611–12.

The third period, extending from her arrival in Naples in 1611–12 until the serious accusation of 31 July 1614 that led to her arrest three weeks later on 24 August, saw the forging of powerful patronage networks as she took residence in the prestigious Neapolitan noblewomen's convent of S. Maria Donna Regina. In this Franciscan convent, she often received the inquisitor Bishop Stefano de Vicariis and the vicereine, the Countess of Lemos, who had special permission from the Neapolitan archbishop Decio Carafa to enter cloistered convents twice a month with twelve ladies of her court. Eventually Suor Giulia was allowed to leave the circumscribed life of the cloister in order to have closer contact with her spiritual children by taking up residence in the home of the regent of the Collateral Council Alfonso Suarez, a key figure in the power clique supporting the viceroy. It was during this third period that she met the Theatine *beata* Orsola Benincasa face-to-face in the convent of S. Maria della Concezione.[45]

The first question concerning Giulia de Marco's reception focuses on her religious program and its appeal.[46] Why did she attract such attention and protection from the highest circles within the Spanish and Neapolitan elites? Novi's analysis is drawn from the letters of Suor Giulia's spiritual "children" and the list of her correspondents and followers in reconstructing the *beata*'s persona and theology. What emerges is Suor Giulia's strong charismatic presence that gripped and galvanized her "children" in a Lutheran-like theology of Christian freedom with her "interior light" and a priesthood of all believers that "denied ecclesiastical authority and the mediation of the clergy in the rapport with the sacred."[47] Not addressed by Novi, however, is what led the followers to engage in their "carnal charity," a kind of communal sex. The answer can be found in the infertility of the vicereine Countess of Lemos and in the role Suor Giulia played as what we might call today a "fertility counselor" or "sex therapist." In Rudolph Bell's study of Renaissance "how to do it" books for good living, his chapter on advice for conception discusses both male impotence and infertility in women. In addition to the physical and biological remedies, Bell points out that "at least a few authors should be noted for their understanding that infertility among wives might be a complex problem, one requiring attention to emotional needs no less than to purely physical matters."[48] Herein lies the key to the scandal, because the personal and societal imperative for children and heirs found a religious remedy in Suor Giulia's sponsorship of a controlled environment for evenings dedicated to "religious" intercourse among partners desiring conception. These clandestine soirees are described as individual couples pairing off in a communal, sanctified space—not really group sex at all but more like infertile couples having intercourse in church in order to receive God's blessing to promote conception.

The social geography of Suor Giulia's movements in and around Naples helps explain the large following she would gain among the foreign and Neapolitan nobility as well as the bureaucratic elite. In the first period of activity, Suor Giulia developed her mystical persona under the guidance of her spiritual adviser, Father Aniello Arciero, the superior of the seventy-member Ministers of the Sick congregation in Naples, and began to make important contacts with influential spiritual authorities.[49] In 1607 the Ministers of the Sick's founder Camillo de Lellis wrote her to thank her for her prayers for him and the order.[50] And again in 1607 correspondence with Cardinal Federico Borromeo of Milan led to his sending her some relics of his saintly uncle Carlo Borromeo.[51] While still establishing herself in the city, she was placed in a Franciscan convent for closer scrutiny after the first Inquisition investigation of 1607–8; Bishop Gentile chose St. Anthony of Padua at Port'Alba at a western gate of the city, the second smallest of the city's Franciscan convents with forty members in 1607–8.[52]

All of Suor Giulia's four convent placements—S. Antonio in Naples, S. Maria Madre di Cristo in Cerreto, S. Chiara in Nocera, and again in Naples at S. Maria

Donna Regina—were in Franciscan houses in keeping with her statues as a Franciscan tertiary. In 1607–8 the nine Franciscan convents in Naples counted 806 nuns, 31 percent of the city's total of twenty-nine convents and 41 percent of its 1,972 nuns.[53] Most important, upon her return to Naples in 1611–12, Suor Giulia was placed in S. Maria Donna Regina, the second largest house with 86 members, located in the heart of the old city's *seggio* of Capuana across the street from the Archbishop's Palace. In the list of her followers, 178 nuns were named: 19 from her sojourn at S. Chiara in Nocera; in Naples 112 nuns from the 86-member convent of S. Maria Donna Regina (perhaps counting nuns from S. Antonio), 13 of the 100 Benedictine nuns at S. Gregorio Armeno, but only 1 out of 50 nuns at the Theatine convent of S. Andrea.[54] Among the clergy, Suor Giulia's spiritual children also included five cardinals, seven bishops, sixty-one members of religious orders, eight priests, and twenty-five others who had corresponded with her. The vectors of support from those in religious orders—especially Franciscan and Benedictine nuns, and the reform Frati Zoccolanti Franciscan, Jesuit, Carthusian, and Ministers of the Sick male religious[55]—helped to legitimate her spirituality and create a wider network of followers. What emerges from this profile of clerical and religious support for the *beata* Suor Giulia is the cleavage between a Jesuit-Franciscan spirituality and apostolate in Naples and a Theatine-Dominican one.

Suor Giulia's lay following among the rich and powerful ruling elite in Naples cut across the normal divisions between nobles of all levels and distinctions and between Neapolitan and foreign nobility.[56] Both male and female nobles, both titled nobles (heads of households, their wives, and families) and female relatives (aunts, sisters, and daughters) in convents counted among Suor Giulia's followers. The two largest clans among the old nobility in the city, the rival Caracciolo in the *seggio* of Capuana and the Carafa in the *seggio* of Nido were exemplary of Suor Giulia's followers: the Caracciolo included the Duke of Acerenza and his wife, the abbess of S. Maria Donna Regina Suor Olimpia Caracciolo and nine other nuns from the family; the Carafa included the prince of Stigliano and his wife, the Duke of Nocera, the Princess of Sansevero, the marchesa d'Anzi, the Duchess of Andria, and two Carafa nuns at S. Maria Donna Regina. Foreign nobles new to Naples also frequented Suor Giulia: the Centurione, Grimaldo, Spinola, de Marini, Gentile, Lomellino, and nine male and eight female Doria from Genoa; six Crescenzi from Rome; and sixty-nine Spaniards (sixteen men and fifty-three women) in addition to the thirty-three Spanish women in the Concezione convent. Pious children of Suor Giulia, active in charitable fraternities or placed in convents, formed a who's who among the highest nobility and chief government officials in Naples. The important linkage between all these diverse groups was their connection to the political-administrative structure of Spanish government, as we have already seen, from the viceroy and vicereine down to the secretary of the viceroy, the Collateral Council regent Suarez, five members of the Sacred Royal Council, two presidents of the exchequer's council of the Sommaria, and four judges of the Vicaria Court. The spiritual message of Suor Giulia coincided with the political and cultural reform program of the viceroy Count of Lemos and the larger policy of the Duke of Lerma for "self-representation," "reinforcement of royal preeminence over ecclesiastical power," and "an increase of the social base of government."[57]

The Theatines of S. Paolo Maggiore, however, sought to undermine their rival Jesuit's growing cult among the city's rich and powerful. The chief Theatine antagonist was Father Benedetto Mandina, who had one of his penitents, the holy woman Francesca Jencara, infiltrate Suor Giulia's confidence. Suor Francesca Jencara reported that Suor Giulia counseled her children not to listen to their confessors but to their own consciences. Father Mandina along with two other Theatines, Father Andrea Castaldo and Father Marco Palescandolo, conspired to solicit information in the secret of the confessional from other followers of Suor Giulia. Two male children, Roberto de Robertis and Vincenzo Negri, confessed that Suor Giulia claimed "to possess the gift of interior charity" that allowed her "to have sexual relations with the lawyer de Vicariis and others without any taint of sin."[58] On 31 July 1614, the Theatine accusations, which broke the seal of confession, were made to the Inquisition delegate, Bishop Stefano de Vicariis of Nocera, whom we have already seen was related to the lawyer accomplice of Suor Giulia and was himself one of her followers. In her defense, they orchestrated support from the Jesuits and the viceroy to defame the Theatines for calumny. Amid such reciprocal inflammatory charges, the *eletto del popolo*, the *popolo*'s city council representative, feared for an urban revolt. On 15 August the Theatines sidestepped normal judicial protocol and forwarded written proof of their accusations to Cardinal Aldobrandini, secretary of the Roman Inquisition, and to the Neapolitan archbishop Decio Carafa. Two days before, the three main accusers, who were joined by a fourth, Beatrice Urbano, arrived at the Holy Office in Rome.

Rome was interested in the case because the theological question at stake in Suor Giulia's claim to special status in possessing "the grace of interior chastity"[59] related directly to the bitter controversy over "efficacious grace" (what "help" grace affords) and the long deliberations of the Congregation de Auxiliis on the writing of the Spanish Jesuit Luis de Molina (d. 1600) and his Dominican opponent,

Domingo Bañez (d. 1604).[60] The dispute dated back to 1581 and proceeded from a scholastic university debate at Louvain, to Spain and Portugal with Molina's 1588 book, *Concordia liberi arbitriis cum gratiae donis*, and finally to Rome. Clement VIII Aldobrandini (1592–1605) actively tried to defuse the polemics: he solicited a dozen scholarly opinions on the problem between 1594 and 1597; he set aside two condemnations of Molina's book made by his commission in 1598 as being too hasty; he ordered a series of conferences before the commission led by the Dominican and Jesuit generals and their theologians; and he personally attended sixty-eight sessions of debates between 1602 and 1605. Paul V Borghese, who had assisted at the earlier debates, took up the complex theological dispute and personally attended seventeen more debates between 1605 and 1607, when he decreed in September a modus vivendi—both Dominicans and Jesuits could teach their interpretation of grace while refraining from attacking the other position until a final papal decision was made. A moratorium on further publication on the subject of efficacious grace was issued in December 1611 and remained in effect through most of the century.

The problem centered on grace and free will, predestination and eternal punishment. The Dominicans taught God's "predetermination" in the giving of grace, whereas the Jesuits explained a middle way of God's foreknowledge of an individual's possible actions. The Dominicans, as masters of Thomistic theology, resented the upstart Jesuits' entry into their traditional theological domain and accused them of granting too much to free will per the Pelagian heresy. The Jesuits retorted that the Dominicans did not value free will highly enough and were guilty of teaching Calvinist predestination. In Naples, where St. Thomas Aquinas, scion of an old noble family, had recently in 1605 been made a new eighth patron of the city,[61] Jesuits' meddling in such theological matters suggested a personal agenda to appropriate the Dominican saint for themselves.

Moving from fact to fiction, we should remember that the city of Naples also serves as the setting for the opening scene in the first dramatic incarnation of the much better-known story of Don Juan, *El burlador de Sevilla y convidado de piedra*. "The Burlador or Trickster of Seville and the Statue of Stone" was first published in 1630 but probably written by Tirso de Molina sometime after 1616, with one of its earliest documented performances in 1625 in Naples under the title of Don Juan's motto, *Tan largo me lo fiáis* (Plenty of time for me to pay that debt).[62] After the initial double deception of the Duchess Isabel and the audience by "a man without a name" and the succeeding double deception of the King of Naples and Isabel's innocent lover Duke Octavio by the arresting officer—who with dizzying improbability happens to be, at one and the same time, the Spanish ambassador, the Neapolitan king's trusted counselor, and Don Juan's uncle—all further action, the *burlas*, that is, the other deceptions, tricks, dissimulations, and seductions, takes place in Spain.[63] The playwright's choice to begin his plot in Naples, of course, had nothing to do with the location of one its earliest recorded performances; but neither was the Neapolitan setting accidental. Naples was a literary topos in Spanish Golden Age literature, with numerous references in Cervantes and Lope de Vega, for example, depicting Naples as a paradise of love and seduction, deceit and pleasure, "the most vice-ridden city in the whole universe."[64] It should be remembered that the Count of Lemos was a famous literary patron (and writer himself): Lope de Vega (his secretary in 1598), Quevedo, Góngora, and Cervantes all dedicated works to him; the Aragonese poet Lupercio Leonardo de Argensola was nominated as the viceroy's secretary; and Giovan Battista Manso honored him as the founding patron for his Accademia degli Oziosi in Naples in 1611.[65] What is significant here, however, is that dishonorable sexuality underlines what contemporaries considered to be wrong with Don Juan's behavior, that is, not his illicit loves per se, but his seductions, his breaking of reputations by his broken oaths. Justice and condemnation, deception and credit or trust, are the central themes of the original Don Juan story. Don Juan's paying of his debt to the statue-come-to-life is not an extraneous moral tag to redeem the audience's salacious interest or please a court or episcopal censor. Rather, it is the essential argument of Tirso de Molina's play—why critics place it in the context of the contemporary debates between Jesuit Molinists and Dominican Bañezians over predestination versus free will, the theological controversy and real currency of the Suor Giulia de Marco affair.

Back in Rome on 20 August 1514, the Roman Inquisition substituted the bishop of Calvi, Fabio Maranta, for Bishop de Vicariis of Nocera and four days later Suor Giulia and the lawyer Vicariis were jailed. The viceroy intervened to influence Bishop Maranta's minimalist judicial inquiry, while the Theatines and Archbishop Carafa applied unusual extralegal pressure on the Holy Office in Rome. Between 14 and 27 September, the case was reassigned to the apostolic nuncio of Naples, Deodato Gentile, who had been Suor Giulia's inquisitor back in March 1609, and matters changed dramatically. The lawyer de Vicarris was shipped in chains to Rome by boat; Father Arciero was found and imprisoned in Rome; and Suor Giulia was taken "at midnight under heavy armed guard in a six-horse carriage so that at dawn they were well past Capua, where an armed twelve-man cavalry unit escorted her day and night, stopping not at inns along the way but only in open and secure country to rest the horses, until they reached the Holy Office in Rome."[66] At the news, Naples was in an uproar. Further arrests were made that included the son of the *eletto del popolo*. Meanwhile, the three principles—Suor Giulia, Father Arciero, and the lawyer de Vicarris—were tortured and the whole story spilled out as they confessed "all their errors and abominations."

Novi asks if their torture induced true confessions, but our information is insufficient to say if they actually committed the crimes or if they were trumped-up charges to save face and secure a life sentence. From the perspective of the twenty-first century, their acts sound more like a religious cult practicing a kind of sexual therapy—long before modern methods of in vitro fertilization—in order to employ religious belief to assist infertile couples among the nobility to conceive heirs.

What we do know is the extraordinary judicial irregularities of undue influence and behind the scenes manipulation, the circumvention of normal procedures, the abnormal changing of inquisitors, and the breaking of the seal of confession. The case was not forwarded to Rome because of local reluctance to decide accusations of "feigned sanctity"; the charge itself seems almost to be beside the point in the rivalry for thaumaturgic living saints between Jesuits and Theatines,[67] the controversy on grace between Jesuits and Dominicans, viceregal pressure and Spanish support, noble and government officer implication in the case, and popular enthusiasm threatening riot. Such tensions are not exaggerated, for in Naples the initial accuser, the Theatine spy Suor Francesca Jencara, who seems to have needed placement in a witness protection program, was struck in the head by a thrown rock while she was walking along a city street, and she hovered near death in August. Later, on 20 February 1615, the apostolic nuncio, Bishop Deodato Gentile of Caserta, the first and also final inquisitor of Suor Giulia, wrote in a letter to Rome without mentioning her by name that the real problem was "the number of *beati*" identified by the Jesuits and represented in paintings in churches throughout the city now for many years, "almost all with signs of blessedness and sanctity such as halos, royalty, insignia of martyrdom, of raptures, and miracles."[68] The Jesuits found and promoted what they were looking for. The truth of the story, however, is far from straightforward; and the Jesuits expunged it from their memory.

The controversy between religious orders over the sanctity of Suor Giulia de Marco was clearly an extreme example of the competition in the colonization of Naples by new, Counter-Reformation religious orders such as the Jesuits, Theatines, Discalced Carmelites, Oratorians, and Ministers of the Sick, as well as reformed, older communities of Benedictines, Franciscans, and Carthusians. More typical were the campaigns among competing groups, whether noble families or religious orders, to promote their particular patron saint to the status of a city patron. Between the 1605 elevation of St. Thomas Aquinas as a city patron and the end of Spanish rule, twenty-five new patron saints were added to the original city patrons. From seven original patron saints, five new protectors were added between 1605 and 1630, seven more between 1640 and 1675, thirteen more in the decade 1688–99, and finally three more by 1731, for a total of thirty-five city patron saints in all.[69] Equally common were disputes between religious orders over urban space, as Helen Hills describes in the long-running real estate rivalry between the Jesuit College and Gesù Vecchio and the Benedictine convent of SS. Marcellino e Festo beginning in 1557 and extending into the 1720s.[70] Not only architectural additions but above all control of communications through the streets were at issue: "The Jesuits were well aware that urban dominance was achieved not simply by out-building one's immediate neighbors in height, but by achieving greater urban command through street layout."[71] Omnipresent in seventeenth-century Naples were active, competitive religious orders in both the spiritual and physical realm that vied for patronage among the wealthy and influential elites.

Church Patronage for the New Jerusalem

The construction of churches and the support of religious orders was the most visible expenditure of the material resources of patrons for a spiritual good. The nobility's patronage (*mecenatismo*) of the Carthusian monastery, the Certosa di San Martino, overlooking the city of Naples maintained a daily reminder of the monks' constant prayer and protection of the city, whether such advocacy had come during the 1656 plague or in better days. In a survey of Naples's ninety-two monasteries and convents by the city's archbishop between 1580 and 1585, the Certosa di San Martino, with its twenty-five cloistered monks and forty brothers praying above the city of Naples, ranked first in wealth, with an 18,000-ducat annual income.[72] About that time, Severo Turbolo, the Tuscan prior of San Martino from 1581 to 1597, initiated the Certosa's reconstruction as part of a monumental Counter-Reformation rebuilding campaign already beginning to revitalize other Neapolitan religious foundations—the Theatines at S. Paolo Maggiore after 1583; the Jesuits at Gesù Nuovo after 1584; the Dominicans at the Church of the Sanità, designed in 1588; and the Oratorians at the Church of the Girolamini from 1590.[73] In the rebuilding of the Certosa, which was initiated because of fire damage caused by the lightning strike of December 1587 and extended from 1591 to 1656, individual architectural and artistic elements fused Carthusian eschatological spirituality with High Renaissance architectural theory on the ideal city to make the Counter-Reformation Certosa the site of the New Jerusalem.[74] Not only was the monastery itself an apocalyptic city "on the threshold of Paradise," but Counter-Reformation Naples itself, with its teeming mass of some 250,000 Neapolitans below, was also seen as the New Jerusalem, watched over and prayed for by the monks' vigilance.

The key to the whole monastery's Baroque architectural program can be found in the Certosa's newly decorated sacristy (figs. 3.1–3.3), especially in the fifty-four intarsia scenes on the *armadios* (wardrobes) where the monks vested for liturgical services.[75] Two intarsia artists from the Spanish Netherlands, the Flemish Lorenzo Ducha and the Frisian Teodoro de Voghel, executed the commission documented in payments from 1587 and 1588.[76] They modeled their wood inlay panels on engravings taken from two northern European sources, the illustrated German Bible of the Swiss painter-designer Tobias Stimmer, *Neue künstliche Figuren Biblischer Historien,* published in Basel in 1576,[77] and a 1560s collection of architectural views, *Scenographiae sive perspectivae,* by the "Flemish Vitruvius," the Friesland-born, German Dutch artist Jan Vredeman de Vries.[78] The intarsia artists employed both their Netherlandish craft and northern designs in what appear to be stylistic anachronisms in contrast to the overarching new design.

The thirteen colored wood inlay panels from the Old Testament along the north *armadio* combined monastic and Counter-Reformation spirituality to emphasize the figural nature of Old Testament prophecy of the promised Messiah and His Church (table 3.2). For example, in panel 2, Noah prays to God as the animals are loaded onto the ark two-by-two; in panel 3, Melchizedek gives bread to Abraham; in panel 5, a cup is found in Benjamin's baggage; and in panel 7, Joshua and his army are shown before the walls of Jericho (fig. 3.4).[79] In panel 2, a hilltop Certosa intercedes between the praying Noah and an approving God above the clouds that conventionally separate the natural from the supernatural world, and similarly in panel 3, three large hills, each dotted with monastic foundations, loom behind the high priest Melchizedek's head. In fact, representations of the Cathusians' Certosa can be found in the background landscapes of twelve of the thirteen Old Testament narrative scenes that begin the sacristy program.[80] Three other Counter-Reformation themes of the Old Testament intarsia are especially relevant: first, the figural Resurrection of Christ (panel 4: The Triumph of Joseph, and panel 10: Jonah in the Whale, as well as panel 13: Daniel in the Lion's Den); second, the allegorical punishment to be inflicted upon the sacrilegious and blasphemous Protestant world (panel 1: Heliodorus Beaten by Angels; panel 6: Man Stoned before Moses and Aaron in the Desert; panel 8: Samson Pulls

Figure 3.1. Sacristy of the Certosa di San Martino, west view to choir. © Archivio dell'Arte / Luciano Pedicini, Naples.

down the Philistine Temple; and panel 11: Joab Spears Absalom); and third, distinctively Catholic beliefs and practices (panel 9: David Plays the Harp for Saul, and panel 12: Tobias Burying the Dead).

The Old Testament prefiguration of Christ's passion finds fulfillment in the nineteen wall and ceiling frescoes of 1596–97 by Lazzaro Tavarone and Giuseppe Cesari (Cavalier d'Arpino), two painters brought from Rome by the Certosa's first head architect, Giovanni Antonio Dosio.[81] There, Christ's First Coming on the ceiling and walls is linked to the hoped for Second Coming in the Apocalypse cycle depicted in more or less narrative order along the south and west wardrobe panels (table 3.3). Two representative scenes illustrate how the intarsia Apocalypse

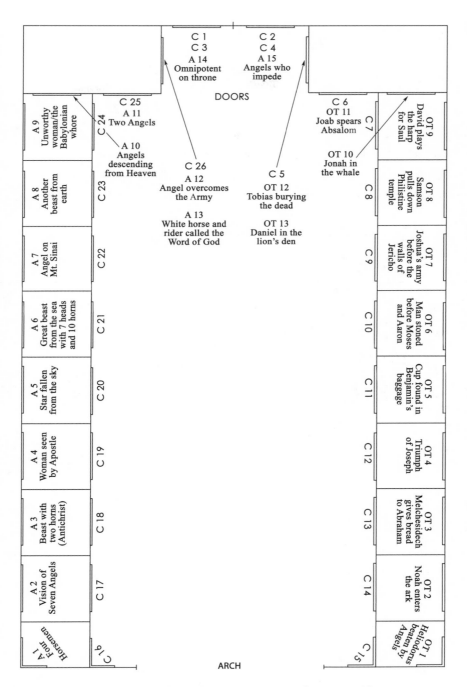

C 1
C 3
A 14
Omnipotent
on throne

C 2
C 4
A 15
Angels who
impede

DOORS

C 25
A 11
Two Angels

C 24

A 10
Angels
descending
from Heaven

A 9
Unworthy
woman/the
Babylonian
whore

C 26
A 12
Angel overcomes
the Army

A 13
White horse and
rider called the
Word of God

C 6
OT 11
Joab spears
Absalom

C 7

OT 9
David plays
the harp
for Saul

OT 10
Jonah in
the whale

C 5
OT 12
Tobias burying
the dead

OT 13
Daniel in the
lion's den

A 8
Another
beast from
earth

C 23

C 22

A 7
Angel on
Mt. Sinai

OT 8
Samson
pulls down
Philistine
temple

C 8

OT 7
Joshua's army
before the
walls of
Jericho

C 9

A 6
Great beast
from the sea
with 7 heads
and 10 horns

C 21

OT 6
Man stoned
before Moses
and Aaron

C 10

A 5
Star fallen
from the sky

C 20

OT 5
Cup found in
Benjamin's
baggage

C 11

A 4
Woman seen
by Apostle

C 19

OT 4
Triumph
of Joseph

C 12

A 3
Beast with
two horns
(Antichrist)

C 18

OT 3
Melchesidech
gives bread
to Abraham

C 13

A 2
Vision of
Seven Angels

C 17

OT 2
Noah enters
the ark

C 14

A 1
Four
Horsemen

C 16

OT 1
Heliodorus
beaten by
Angels

C 15

ARCH

Figure 3.2. Sacristy of Certosa di San Martino: Marquetry panels, upper and lower registers.
Design by Michele Greenstein.

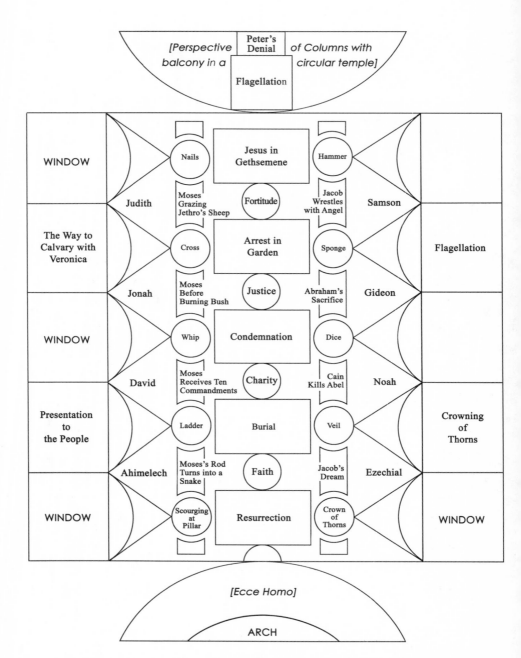

Figure 3.3. Sacristy of Certosa di San Martino: Vault and walls. Design by Michele Greenstein.

TABLE 3.2.
Sacristy of the Certosa di San Martino: The Old Testament Key

PROMISE OF THE MESSIAH AND THE CHURCH

Wood Cabinets, Upper Register, North Wall (13 Old Testament wood inlay panels)
Giovanni Battista Vigilante and Nunzio Ferraro (Neapolitan wood carvers)
Lorenzo Ducha (Frisian) and Teodoro de Voghel (Flemish) (wood inlay artists)
Enrico d'Utrecht (metalworker)
Source: Tobias Stimmer, *Neue künstliche Figuren Biblischer Historien*
 1. Heliodorus beaten by Angels (2 Macc. 3:22–30)
 2. Noah enters the ark (Gen. 6:7–9)
 3. Melkesidek gives bread to Abraham (Gen. 14:18–19)
 4. Triumph of Joseph (Gen. 41:42–43)
 5. Cup found in Benjamin's baggage (Gen. 44:12)
 6. Man stoned before Moses and Aaron (Lev. 24:10–23; Num. 15:32–36)
 7. Gideon's army before the walls of Jericho (Judg. 7:15–22)
 8. Samson pulls down Philistine temple (Judg. 16:26–30)
 9. David plays the harp for Saul (1 Sam. 16:14–23)
 10. Jonah in the whale (Jon. 1:17–2:10)
 11. Joab spears Absalom (2 Sam. 18:14–16)
 12. Tobias burying the dead (Tob. 1:17–18)
 13. Daniel in the lion's den (Dan. 6:1–17)

Vault Paintings (Giuseppe Cesari [Cavaliere d'Arpino])
Side Rectangles (4 Genesis and 4 Exodus landscape paintings)
 North Wall
  1. Jacob wrestles with the Angel (Gen. 32:24–30)
  2. Abraham's sacrifice (Gen. 22:1–18)
  3. Cain kills Abel (Gen. 4:8)
  4. Jacob's dream (Gen. 28:1–10)
 South Wall
  5. Moses grazing Jethro's sheep (Exod. 3:1)
  6. Moses prostrate before the burning bush (Exod. 3:2–6)
  7. Moses receives the Ten Commandments (Exod. 26:1–17)
  8. Moses's rod turns into a snake (Exod. 4:1–5)

Triangles
 1. Samson
 2. Noah
 3. Gideon
 4. Ezekiel
 5. Ahimelek
 6. Judith
 7. Jonah
 8. David

Lunettes (10 paintings of sibyls and prophets)

program derives from the Stimmer source, which in turn is modeled on Dürer's more famous 1498 woodcuts.[82] Scene 4, The Apocalyptic Woman Clothed with the Sun and the Seven-Headed Dragon (Rev. 12:1–9), reproduces one of the most ubiquitous images of Counter-Reformation culture. This woman, long identified with both the church and the Virgin as the Immaculate Conception, had long received special devotion from the Dominicans; and this devotion was taken up

Figure 3.4. An Old Testament scene: Joshua's Army before the Walls of Jericho (Joshua 6). © Archivio dell'Arte / Luciano Pedicini, Naples.

by the Jesuits, who were strong supporters of the cloistered Carthusians and had dedicated their new church in Naples, Gesù Nuovo, to the Immaculate Conception after its acquisition in 1584.[83] Her image "clothed with the sun, with the moon under her feet, and on her head a crown of twelve stars," was widely diffused, although not, as uniquely shown here, with a certosa in her aura in the lower right corner.[84] Similarly, scene 6, The Great Beast from the Sea and the Land (Rev. 13:1–18), in San Martino dramatically introduces a set of dominating pyramid-like hills, reminiscent of the Melchizedek panel, with an unmistakable certosa in the center background. (fig. 3.5)

The intarsia apocalypse concludes its representations on the paneled entrance doors with two scenes taken out of narrative order from the earliest illustrations in the Stimmer Bible—Apocalypse panel 14: the "Maiestas Domini" (Rev. 4:2–5:14), most often found as a single scene representation of the Apocalypse from late antiquity;[85] and Apocalypse panel 15: The Four Angels Holding Back the Four Winds (Rev. 7:1–12). In both intarsia scenes, the Omnipotent with the Lamb on

TABLE 3.3.
Sacristy of the Certosa di San Martino: The New Testament Key

THE PASSION NARRATIVE

Walls (4 paintings by Giuseppe Cesari [Cavaliere d'Arpino])
1. Flagellation
2. Crowning of Thorns
3. Presentation to the People
4. The Way to Calvary

Vault (5 paintings by Giuseppe Cesari [Cavaliere d'Arpino])
1. Jesus in Gethsemene
2. Arrest in the Garden
3. Condemnation
4. Burial
5. Resurrection
   (10 circular *putti* with instruments of the passion)

Arches
   Massimo Stanzione, *Ecce Homo* (1644)
   Luca Cambiaso, *Flagellation* substituted in 1631 by Giuseppe Cesari, *Crucifixion*
   Caravaggio, *Peter's Denial* later substituted by one by Master of Judgment of Solomon
   Perspective of Columns with balcony in a circular temple

THE APOCALYPSE CYCLE

Wood Cabinets, Upper Register, South Wall and Doors (15 wood inlay panels from Revelations)
   Giovanni Battista Vigilante and Nunzio Ferraro (Neapolitan wood carvers)
   Lorenzo Ducha (Frisian) and Teodoro de Voghel (Flemish) (wood inlay artists)
   Enrico d'Utrecht (metalworker)
   Source: Tobias Stimmer, *Neue künstliche Figuren Biblischer Historien*
1. The Four Horsemen (Rev. 6:1–8)
2. Vision of the Son of Man among Seven Angels (Rev. 8:1–5)
3. The Beast from the Bottomless Pit (Antichrist) (Rev. 11:7–13)
4. Woman Clothed with the Sun (Rev. 12: 1–5)
5. Star fallen from the Sky (Rev. 9:1–6)
6. Great Beast from the Sea and from the Land (Rev. 13:1–18)
7. Lamb of Mount Zion (Rev. 14:1–12)
8. The Seven Vials (Rev. 15:1–16:21)
9. The Babylonian Whore (Rev. 17:1–18)
10. Angel descending from Heaven (Rev. 10:1–11)
11. The Harvest of God's Wrath (Rev. 14:14–20)
12. Dirge over the Fallen City (Rev. 18:1–24)
13. White Horse and Rider called the Word of God (Rev. 19:11–21)
14. Omnipotent on Throne (Rev. 4:2–5:14)
15. Four Angels holding back the Four Winds (Rev. 7:1–12)

Wood Cabinets, Lower Register, North and South Cabinets and Doors (26 wood inlay panels)
   City Views and Architectural Perspectives: The Heavenly City of the New Jerusalem
Source: Vredeman de Vries, *Scenographiae*

Figure 3.5. Apocalypse cycle: The Great Beast from the Sea and the Land (Rev. 13:1–18). ©
Archivio dell'Arte / Luciano Pedicini, Naples.

the Throne dominates the image with a conspicuous representation of a Carthusian monastery center stage. A large cloister occupies the left foreground of
marquetry 14 and a characteristic monastic building complex stands alone in the
center below the throne in marquetry 15. Vesting monks able to view the upper
door panels with a sideways glance could, no doubt, almost hear the Lord's voice
from the throne saying: "Behold, the dwelling of God is with man" (Rev. 21:3).
What appears missing is the heavenly city; but it is not lost, because it is found all
around the viewer in the twenty-six panels of the wardrobes' lower register on all
sides of the room. Some scenes depict architectural interiors; others, perspectival
views of exteriors.

   All of the twenty-six intarsia city views are modeled directly on designs of Jan
Vredeman de Vries's early work, *Scenographiae sive perspectivae*, which appeared
in at least three editions at Antwerp between 1560 and 1562 (fig. 3.6).[86] Moving
from the Catholic world of the Spanish Low Countries to sympathize with the
Dutch rebels, Vredeman de Vries might not be expected to be found in Spanish
Naples in the late sixteenth century. While San Martino's Netherlandish intarsia

Figure 3.6. Cityscape panel with Certosa in bottom left foreground. © Archivio dell'Arte / Luciano Pedicini, Naples.

artists may have imported their Vredeman de Vries with them, more than likely they could have found his engravings already in Naples in the library brought there by Cardinal Granvelle, Antoine Perrenot, the Spanish viceroy to Naples (1571–75), to whom the *Scenographiae* had been originally dedicated when he was chief counselor (1559–64) to Margaret of Parma, regent of the Low Countries (1559–67).[87]

Like the Stimmer biblical models, the Vredeman de Vries perspectival models were copied exactly, with minor alterations in details. The copying process caused the intarsia images to be transposed, and the colored wood inlay panels include clouds or flying birds, center views to fit the panel size or format, and elements to increase the perspectival effect. Here again an obviously inserted certosa can be found in the cityscape panels, so that one would naturally begin to view the cityscapes not at but really as the culmination of the Apocalypse cycle. Above all, these small modifications aimed at highlighting symmetry and order in the creation of ever more perfect visions of the Heavenly Jerusalem.

Most of the scholarly interest in apocalyptic visions in Naples circa 1600 heretofore has centered on the political implications of the twin Dominican students and residents of S. Domenico Maggiore, Giordano Bruno (resident, 1565–76) and Tommaso Campanella (resident, first in 1589).[88] Among Bruno's Italian dialogues, only *La cabala del cavallo pegaseo* (written in these same years, 1584–85) mentions the "celestial" or "triumphant" city of Jerusalem, which is coterminous with the *anima mundi*—a cyclical conception of the cosmos, where at the end of the cycle there is a kind of rebirth (*restitutio*).[89] Likewise, at the heart of Campanella's 1602 utopian dialogue, *La Città del Sole*, the Solarian capital is named in direct contrast to Thomas More's Utopian capital of Amaurote (city of darkness). In *The City of the Sun*, from calculations Campanella made during his first stay in Naples in 1589, one finds an astrological convergence believed to bring about political and religious renewal: "[The Solarians] admit that the ages of the world succeed one another according to the order of the planets, and they believe that changes in their apsides [orbits] every thousand years or every thousand six hundred years produce great changes in the world."[90] One does not have to check the calendar to know that, in Campanella's reckoning, the beginning of the seventeenth century would be the beginning of the first "great change in the world" since the birth of Christ.

Both Bruno and Campanella were influenced by Giambattista della Porta's naturalist circle.[91] Della Porta's *Natural Magic* (first published in four books in 1558 and in a second Neapolitan edition in twenty books in 1589) and his *De humana Physiognomonia* (published in 1586 in four books and in 1599 in six) lie behind much of the hermetic and Neoplatonic thinking. One example of Della Porta's millennial allusions, a reference to the Four Horsemen from his 1601 play *Gli duoi fratelli rivali* must suffice:

> Hunger was a live person, lean and thin, who
> barely had bones and skin; and she used to go
> about with famine, plague, and war,
> and she killed more people than the swords did.[92]

The social and political threats manifested in the very real famines and crises after 1585,[93] however, were not the only sources for apocalyptic thought available to inspire the monks and artists collaborating in the San Martino sacristy. An inward, spiritual interpretation of the book of Revelation written by the Spanish biblical scholar Benito Aries Montano was published by Christophe Plantin in Antwerp in 1588.[94] Montano, who served as royal chaplain and librarian of the Escorial from early 1577, published in Antwerp because he had spent seven years abroad actively involved with Plantin's Polyglot Bible project. Montano's mystical interpretation of Revelation owes much to his reading between 1583 and 1586 in French or Latin translation of the Dutch spiritual writer Hendrik Jansen van Barrefelt, called Hiël. The apocalyptic ideas of Montano via Hiël are important for a rethinking of Netherlandish artists working in a Carthusian monastery in Spanish Naples because they point to a confluence of Protestant and Catholic thought in the Low Countries of the 1570s and 1580s, in the context of northern European reaction to Luther on the importance of the spirit over the letter of scriptures. Thus, the Hiël-Montano exegesis reinforces older Carthusian spiritualist readings of Revelation on the ladder of mystical ascent and the astrological symbolism of the Neapolitan naturalist circle as he emphasizes a series of mystical progressions toward the union of the human heart or soul with God, with no reference to a church, visible or invisible.

If we return to the visual representations before us, the traditions of intarsia subject matter will lead us to this same confluence of spirit-ideal and letter-material in late sixteenth-century Italy. Wood inlay panels and perspectival representations were intertwined from the first Renaissance intarsia executed more than a century earlier in the cathedral at Modena (1461–65), the sacristy of the duomo in Florence (1463), and the choir stalls in Padova (1462–69)—all in turn probably inspired by architectural motifs developed in Florence in the 1440s as part of the envisioned architecture of humanism from Alberti's circle.[95] Early Neapolitan examples of intarsia date from what André Chastel calls "the golden age of Italian marquetry in the half-century between 1470 and 1520," with the 1510 architectural views by Fra Giovanni da Verona in Monteoliveto and the 1520s views of the Certosa itself by Giovan Francesco d'Arezzo in the old choir and now in its Choir of the Conversi.[96] Such intarsia perspectival representations are similar to the famous 1470s panels in Urbino, Baltimore, and Berlin because both wood inlay and painted panels "draw on the same legacy of humanist architecture," which long predates the theatrical scenery of the Comic and Tragic Scene in Serlio's architecture, according to Krautheimer's correction of his earlier opinion.[97] What remains important for our purposes is how the "consistent use of perspective," again according to Krautheimer, "conjure[s] up an artificial world into which the spectator is forcefully drawn, a world beyond the reality of everyday life." In keeping with the original purpose of such architectural perspectives to represent a history or tell a story, the S. Martino Old Testament and Apocalypse intarsia narrate a *storia*, as do the bare, seemingly unrelated perspectival views that complete it as the Heavenly Jerusalem. By the late sixteenth century, the visual representation of fifteenth-century humanist architecture and the humanists' verbal description of the ideal city had been fused with the prophecies of the Second Coming.[98]

Precedents for the identification of individual Renaissance Italian cities and the New Jerusalem abound.[99] A quick tour of Italy's New Jerusalems in Venice, Milan, Florence, Rome, and even Naples easily demonstrates what scholars have come to identify as the variants of humanism and how the idea of the New Jerusalem was adapted to each city's particular civic image.[100] Venice's multilayered myth—as equal to and independent from pope and emperor, as direct heir of Constantinople, as the defender of Christianity, as the "most serene" city ruled by unanimity—informed its formal and symbolic urban character and fueled its historic mission.[101] Venice assumed the role of the Heavenly Jerusalem as its doge replaced the crumbling Byzantine centers with his private chapel as a dazzling basilica at the apex of a monumental piazza. The Venetian cult and procession of the True Cross is eloquent testimony that Venice saw itself as inheriting the mantle of Christian leadership as the New Jerusalem. Milan also possessed a historical and cosmic myth as the New Jerusalem that was grounded in the congruence of its organization and urban form with that of the Heavenly City—that is, circular walls, twelve principle gates, and the bodies of the twelve patron saints associated with them. Humanist panegyrics also connected Milan, like Venice, with Greek Byzantine traditions and made much of Milan's centrality in the fecund Lombard plain. Filarete's ideal city of Sforzinda partakes of this local Milanese mystique and the cosmic symbolism of the Heavenly Jerusalem in the book of Revelation. In Florence, the importance of the Baptistery of San Giovanni in the formation of the Christian life for its inhabitants cannot be overemphasized. In the fifteenth century, the 1439 council on church reunification legitimized Florence's role as mediator and the center of a new beginning for Christianity, as did Savonarola's prophecies that saw Florence at the head of a new age after 1494. Rome, of course, as the seat of the papacy was by definition the Christian mirror of Jerusalem. Renaissance urban projects dating from Nicholas V aimed at restoring and rationalizing the haphazard medieval urban development of the city to conform to classical and ideal plans. All these cities, as the capitals of independent states, saw themselves at the center of a political universe of national and international consequence and attempted to assert their dominance in both physical space and symbolic scope.

Naples was no stranger to this myth of the New Jerusalem that began to take root in fifteenth-century humanist circles. From the triumphal entrance after the Aragonese conquest of the kingdom in 1442 and its glorification in the Castel Nuovo arch and relief, Alfonso the Magnanimous and his humanist court wished not only to represent and immortalize the Aragonese victory but also to re-create Naples as the New Rome of a Mediterranean empire under Alfonso as father and savior.[102] Aragonese architectural patronage continued in a Vitruvian-Albertian mode in a direct line from Alfonso I to his grandson Alfonso II in an attempt to supersede the monuments of the classical tradition by restoring the city of Naples through ideal design and planning.[103] Vitruvians such as Francesco Patrizi of Siena, bishop of Gaeta (in Naples from 1462 to 1492) and Francesco di Giorgio Martini and Fra Giovanni Giocondo (both counselors in the employ of the young Alfonso, Duke of Calabria, in the 1490s) applied their study of classical antiquity to the reconstruction of the city. Notable Aragonese urban projects included defensive works: the restructuring of castles, the building up of the city's east wall, urban rationalization projects, and the opening of an internal road to the east away from the coastal route from the port to the market in the popular quarter.

Such humanist inspired architectural activity, we should not forget, was much influenced by the ancient center of Naples, which continued to be marked with classical monuments. The decumanus major one block west of the cardo crossing next to the forum of the ancient Neapolis, for example, was dwarfed by the temple of the Dioscuri, which was built in the first century c.e. and remained relatively intact through the Middle Ages, as shown in a design by Francisco de Holando in 1540, which dates only two years after the eighth-century medieval church had been transferred to the Theatines.[104] In the same years as the reconstruction of S. Martino, Francesco Grimaldi's radical restructuring (1583–1603) incorporated the ancient facade of the Dioscuri temple in the Theatine Church of S. Paolo Maggiore, as can be seen in a painting by Antonio Joli (1700–1777) and in the 1773 project for the facade by Giuseppe Astarita. The classical orders represented in the New Jerusalem intarsia in the San Martino sacristy were clearly not Vitruvian fancy alone, nor was the city of Naples the modern Babylon depicted in Spanish Golden Age literature; rather, ancient realities were reincorporated with apocalyptic visions into the rebuilding of Naples as the renewed Counter-Reformation city.

The first edition of a turn-of-the-century, Counter-Reformation history of the three principle cities in the world—Jerusalem, Rome, and Naples—published in Naples in 1598 by Michele Zappullo, brings together Naples's classical inheritance and the common view of successive epochs.[105] Zappullo recounts world history as a succession of ages in the light of God's intervention into human affairs. According to Zappullo, whereas Jerusalem was sacred to the Jews, who remained God's chosen people until their rejection of Christ and the destruction of the temple by Titus, Rome was the seat of a Gentile empire whose cults of false gods and idols ruled there until Constantine accepted Christianity publicly in 325. Naples, on the other hand, proved to be the first city of Europe converted to Christianity and the refuge of Christianity during the persecution of the primitive church, and since then it has remained steadfast in its ancient faith. Zappullo includes a catalog of natural disasters—such as earthquakes, storms, and fires, including the lightning strike of 13 December 1587, which saw rocks thrown down from the Castel S. Elmo on the whole city to everyone's incredulous amazement and whose fire damage to the neighboring Certosa, which precipitated its massive rebuilding—as "manifest signs of God's wrath against us who are justifiably unworthy through our sins."[106] But mankind is spared only because of "the intercession of the just and their good works, which here [in Naples] the religious monasteries countenance more than in any other city in the world." Such was the eternal mission of the cloistered Carthusians, expecting and interceding with their prayers for the New Jerusalem at S. Martino. And with the passing of 1600 without an end to the world, Zappullo's subsequent editions were able to expand his argument to the spread of Christianity to the Venetians and to the peoples of the New World.

As monks vested in the sacristy to enter the sacred space in the choir around the high altar, they could meditate upon the shift from secular space to ideal space and from secular time to Christian time. The San Martino Apocalypse expressed both a Counter-Reformation religio-political message of reform and renewal and a cloistered monastic one of prayer and intercession. The sacristy resonated with the religious fervor of Old Testament *figura* common in Counter-Reformation Spanish Naples, with devotion to the Apocalypse from Carthusian spirituality, with the "ideal city" of High Renaissance culture, with the scientific and political ideas percolating around Giambattista della Porta's naturalist circle, and with millennial images drawn from the confrontation between Catholics and Protestants in the Spanish Netherlands that corresponded to Bruno's and Campanella's critique of the Roman Church and the Spanish Empire. The ideal cityscapes represented in the San Martino intarsia evoked tragic stage sets to tell a *storia* (narrative history) that recounts to the deeper realities beyond the sacristy that were visible from the monastery's perch atop the Vomero overlooking the New Jerusalem of Counter-Reformation Naples. Just as a century and a half earlier the Aragonese arch in the Castel Nuovo in its commemoration of the royal entrance of Alfonso the Magnanimous turned Naples into the New Rome, the San Martino Apocalypse, as it stands above the Aragonese monument to complete Naples's dorsal spine, commemorates the Second Coming and the Carthusians place as intermediaries ushering in the New Jerusalem. For 1590s Counter-Reformation Naples, the end of the world was imminent, and the New Jerusalem was present in the city's reform and rebuilding, participated in and prayed for by the Certosa's Carthusians. The death of Philip II in 1598 marked the end of his forty-four-year reign in Naples, an age of tightening bonds with Spain for the city nobility and the routinization of its patron-client relationship with the crown mediated by the church. It was one more sign of the changing, uncertain times.

Patron-Clients in Ritual Practice: The Obsequies for Philip II

News of the death of Philip II on Sunday, 13 September 1598, reached Naples one month later on Sunday, 11 October, in a letter from his son, the new king Philip III, to the Neapolitan town council, the *eletti* representatives of the city *seggi* or districts. Noting the coincidence of the king's death on another Sunday a month earlier, a noble cavalcade immediately took to the streets and began to march along the city's traditional processional route around the five noble and one *popolo seggi* to mourn the king's death and to announce the accession of Philip III with joyous shouts (*allegrissima grida*).[107] The city went into three days of mourning: the viceroy would receive no one except in the Royal Chapel, where mass was said every day for the dead king; all the viceroyalty's lawcourts remained closed; and all titled nobility and royal officials wore brown for an additional nine days as a sign of their public and common sorrow. During that novena of mourning, requiem masses in almost all the city's churches expressed the public sorrow and prayers in ceremonies of great solemnity, with the cathedral exceeding all others in pomp and circumstance.[108]

The outpouring of spontaneous grief for the seventy-one-year-old Philip and the end of his long reign that had begun as a wedding gift upon his marriage to Mary Tudor in 1554 is all quite understandable, and the immediate response as well as its duration not unusual. The most spectacular public celebration in the city during Philip's reign had lasted seven days after the most glorious victory twenty-seven years earlier in 1571, when news of Lepanto reached Naples.[109] In both cases, sudden, unexpected news from Lepanto on the Holy League's victory and from the Escorial on Philip II's death led to spontaneous and unplanned expressions of joy or grief.

Other more organized memorials were forthcoming in the months after the king's death: in Capua, an Italian oration was delivered in its duomo on 9 November 1598,[110] and a Latin oration was delivered to the local Capua Senate.[111] In the duomo in Naples on 31 January 1599, an elaborate commemorative funeral was staged more than three months after the arrival of the news of the king's death, and a detailed description and interpretation of all the decoration went to the press immediately thereafter on 26 February 1599.[112] An ornate Latin oration delivered on that occasion[113] and five other orations (two in Latin,[114] two in Italian,[115] and one in Spanish)[116] with references to the *apparati* prepared for the cathedral obsequies all went to press in that same time frame between late January and March 1599. In addition, in Naples in April 1599 a small book of Latin poems and epigrams (in addition to the numerous incidental poems adorning the other publications) went to the printers.[117] None of these works was the result of the spontaneous outpouring of emotion, and the commemorative funeral especially took time to plan and its ornate artistic program months to build.

An examination of the obsequies reveals how the powers and prelates in the Neapolitan capital wanted to remember their absentee king and use his death as an example for the living left behind. Such didacticism was the goal of funerary oratory and funerary pageantry in the Renaissance and early modern period, and what the long life and eventful reign of Philip meant for his Neapolitan kingdom was no exception.[118] The king's virtues were proved by his deeds; and the glory of his empire, the fame of his reign, and the examples of his personal life—with Philip now in heaven—would last forever.

The obsequies presented a mausoleum centerpiece designed by Domenico Fontana, who had been working in Naples since 1592 and in the duomo for Cardinal Gesualdo, the archbishop of Naples, since 1597.[119] Ottavio Caputi of Cosenza, the author of the 147-page source on the obsequies, which were dedicated to Diomede Carafa, Duke of Cerce and Treasurer General of the Kingdom of Naples, designed the sculpture and other *apparati*, as he did again later in the 1612 obsequies for Philip III's queen, Margherita of Austria.[120] Caputi gives due credit to others for particular items; for example, to Cavalier Sereno, for assistance in designing the sculpture; to Francesco Como, for an emblem of a bird with a broken wing to symbolize the happy death of the king; and to Giovan Vincenzo della Porta (the elder of the della Porta brothers), for twenty-eight Latin epitaphs associated with the twenty-eight paintings of the king's deeds; but, above all, to the Jesuits in Naples for their extraordinary ingenuity in conceiving dozens of epigrams and emblems, the iconography for the twenty-eight paintings, and innumerable other pomp and poetry. On the last day of January, the 500-horse cavalcade made its way to the duomo to participate in the obsequies and to hear the bishop of Ascoli, Ferdinando Davila, deliver his funeral oration.[121] The procession was ordered in rank by the master of ceremonies: eight trumpeters, the minor ministers of all the Tribunals, the secretary and other officials of the city, the captains of the city streets, the guards of the king, the Neapolitan nobility in the city (including the counts, marquises, dukes, and princes), the general of the army and four *portieri*, the Prince of Montesarchi and the Marquis of Grottola (who were carrying the king's sword and scepter as representatives of the Collateral or council of state), the Duke of Bovino as the Great Seneschal and the Prince of Conca as the Great Admiral (who were carrying the king's orb and crown as representatives of the Seven Great Offices), the elected representatives of the city council, the viceroy and the syndic of the city council, other state councilors, the regents of the Cancellaria, and other state officers.[122] The dignitaries entered a sumptuous setting prepared to instruct those assembled on the meaning of the king's reign and life as an inspiration for their own office and a model for their own life.

In the middle of the sanctuary stood a mausoleum, forty *palmi* square, with decorations emphasizing the king's virtues and crowned with a cupola studded with dozens of burning candles (fig. 3.7). Each of its four facades displayed four statues of virtues (sixteen in all), six *imprese* or emblems (twenty-four in all), and an epitaph (four in all), which hung above the arch opening to the effigy sarcophagus, where the sword, scepter, orb, and crown were placed.[123] The lower level of statues, one statue in a niche on each side of the arch, viewed counterclockwise from the left niche as seen by the congregation in the central nave, represented Christian Religion, the four cardinal or moral virtues (justice, temperance, fortitude, and prudence), and the three theological virtues (faith, hope, and charity). On pediments attached to the railing at the top of each facade were eight other virtues associated with the rule of the ideal prince: magnanimity, liberality, meekness, vigilance, mercy, peace, maturity, and wisdom. Angels sounding their trumpets and animals symbolizing the king's attributes also adorned each facade. (The bear and oxen depicted in Caputi's design do not correspond to his verbal description of the facade; other facade animals indicated are the eagle, lion, lamb, and rooster.) Finally, in the center above each arch, an epitaph commemorated each of the important themes of the whole project: Philip and his deeds, Philip and his virtues, Philip and his titles, and Philip and Christianity.

counter-clockwise from bottom left

Interior Niches

1 Africa
2 America
3 Asia
4 Europa

Exterior Niches

A Christian Religion
B Justice
C Fortitude
D Temperance
E Prudence
F Faith
G Christian Charity
H Speranza

Cupola Balustrade Statues

a Magnanimity
b Liberality
c Vigilance
d Meekness
e Mercy
f Peace
g Wisdom
h Maturity

Figure 3.7. Domenico Fontana, *Mausolaei Typus Neapoli in Funere Philippi II*. Bibliothèque nationale de France.

The program of twenty-four emblems (three on each side of the arch on each of the four facades) was an important Jesuit addition, because only five emblems had been previously associated with Philip during his long forty-two-year reign. Earlier during the long forty-year reign of his father, Charles V (1516–56), only one *impresa* (fig. 3.7) had been used, the "famous device of the two columns with the motto 'Plus ultra,' [which was] praised above all others and routinely mentioned as perfect by later authors on *imprese*."[124] Charles's *impresa* was invented in the Burgundian court in 1516 as he came to the Spanish throne and means "Further beyond" the columns of Hercules, in a geographic sense to expand his rule beyond the boundaries of the Spanish inheritance. The *impresa* or device, which developed from the mid-fifteenth century in the tradition of court culture as the expression of a prince's purpose or undertaking, preceded the invention of the genre of the emblem by Andrea Alciato in his publications of 1531 and 1534. The liturgical rituals at Spanish Naples for the royal obsequies of Philip II as recorded in the festival book by Ottavio Caputi reveal an explosion in the number of *imprese* associated with Philip's life and deeds, with fifty-two new royal emblems on display.

The facade facing the central nave reproduced by Caputi allows us to see the only visual evidence of any of the twenty-four mausoleum emblems and to correlate each of these six *imprese* with the ekphrasis in his text (fig. 3.8).[125] Their moral message is quite clear. Reading Caputi's verbal order, which does not correspond to the design, we see the five traditional devices previously associated with Philip during his life. First, Hercules carrying the world on his shoulders was already seen in Antwerp at Philip's 1549 entry, and both motif and motto, "Ut quiescat Atlas" (So that Atlas rests), derive from a commemorative medal struck in 1555 upon the abdication of Charles V, who, like the fatigued Atlas, had the weight of the world put on his son Philip II, the new Hercules.[126] The second *impresa* shows Phoebus Apollo guiding his sun chariot, a device that was conceived at the beginning of Philip's reign in the hope that his virtue would not be in vain; for, just as the Sun and Night illuminated the world below, so too Philip's virtues were to do the same: "Iam illustrabit omnia" (Henceforth he shall illuminate everything).[127] On the opposite side of the arch, the *impresa* of the Scales signify the constancy and greatness of spirit of the king, who never changed with either prosperity or unhappiness, not from despair or fear. The motto "Nec spe, necu metu" (Not out of hope, not out of fear) is taken from an oration of Cicero and was inscribed on the facade of the tower of the Schepenhuis (Aldermen's House) of Aalst, where Philip had been made earl in 1555.[128] The next *impresa* with a palfrey rampant and exercising in a circle, which according to Caputi should be read as an imperial sign, means that just as such a horse wants to break out of its circle, the greatness of the king's spirit (like that of Alexander the Great) is greater than the world alone. The motto "Non sufficit orbis" (The world is not enough) appeared on a 1583 medal and had been incorporated into the royal arms of Spain by 1586.[129] Finally, the last traditional *impresa* displays the Gordian Knot with the motto, "Tanto monta, monta tanto" (One is worth as much as the other), as was used by Philip's ancestor Ferdinand the Catholic (Charles V's maternal grandfather) when he took Granada; and it also appeared on coins of Ferdinand and Isabella, of Juana and her son Charles, and in England of Mary Tudor and Philip II to denote joint kingship. Its invention is credited to the Spanish humanist Antonio de Lebrija, and the motto was reappropriated by Philip in his Portuguese enterprise of 1580. Just as Alexander in obeying the oracle could not untie the knot peacefully but had to use a sword to cut through it, so, too, Philip had to use force to resolve the impasse and make good his claim to the Portuguese crown. The only completely new *impresa* not previously Philip's in this facade was invented by the Jesuits and has a compass with one of its feet pinned down in the center ("Circuit immotus" [Going around unmoved]) in Caputi's text, but "Arbore et constant" (A tree and constant) in the visual design. It signifies that, if even in life Philip stayed in Spain, his high and generous thought circumscribed the world and his undefeatable power circled the earth. Overall, these six emblems speak to the same imperial images of Philip and his deeds—as a "Cavalier Sereno," a serene knight whose duty, brilliance, prudence, virtue, and decisiveness fulfilled the hopes and aspirations of his dynasty and his own life.[130]

The mausoleum's remaining eighteen newly invented Jesuit emblems addressed similar themes, with each of the three facades carrying a particular message. The right face compared Philip to the sun with images of the Eighth Sphere, a Serene Heaven, a Falling Star, Lightning, a tree with a dead bird, and the balsam tree with a motto from Horace (Ode 4:59–60): "Ab ipso ducit opes" (From it he derives strength). Philip's virtues brought peace and tranquillity to earth. The facade facing the main altar again invoked solar images, for example, the sun setting in the west, to symbolize how one cannot see the sun directly with one's eye, but now in death, in sunset, we can see Philip's virtues. Similarly, are pictured images of the bird of paradise, a bird with a broken wing, scales with one paten toward heaven the other toward earth, refined pure gold above a fiery furnace, and a vine inside a large ditch in need of pruning. With the separation of body and soul, death brings Philip fame forever. The final facade to the left invokes a series of images—the sun near sunset leaving another reflection in the center of the sky, a small phoenix, an eaglet just ready to fly, an old fallen oak tree

Figure 3.8. Detail of Philip II Mausoleum with six *imprese*. Bibliothèque nationale de France.

giving rise to new sprouts, part of the zodiac with the sign of a lion, and an aged lion saved by a generous young cub fighting off a dragon, which all offer direct messages on the passing of the kingdom to his son Philip III—the king is dead, long live the king; or, as one motto from Virgil (*Aeneid* 6:142) offers, "Non deficit alter" (When one is torn away, another succeeds). Whether the often esoteric meanings of the *imprese* could have been read without Caputi's explication is an open question; once explained, however, their meanings appear transparent in a new and often unexpected light as a Baroque surprise.

Inside the mausoleum visible in the center of the arch sits a crown and sword on a half throne. At its corners, four niches shelter statues of the four continents of Philip's empire—Europe, Asia, Africa, and America. Each niche bears a Latin epigram above it pronouncing Philip a citizen in heaven who wears a crown of glory for his praiseworthy deeds (Europe); all his kingdoms having been unable to fill up his great soul, Philip now can enjoy the true gifts and goods of heaven (Asia); Philip in his virtue gives honor and glory to the House of Habsburg (Africa); and this monument constructed in Naples, as magnificent as it is, can only pale in comparison to Philip's merits (America).[131]

The mausoleum stood in front and apart from the congregation, but further extensive decoration of the whole church turned the cathedral itself into a giant mausoleum with statues, coats of arms, paintings, emblems, and writings arranged in chronological order to be read counterclockwise from the front left pillar in the central nave to the back of the nave, across the main portal, back up the pillars on the right along the central nave, and following around the transept on the right, along the apse, and around the left arm of the transept back to the starting point on the left front pillar (figs. 3.8–3.9). Two sight lines defined the field of decoration: first, the area above and between the arches up to the cornice contained alternating images of coats of arms of the king and his kingdoms (the first, peninsular Spain) and twenty-eight large narrative paintings of his deeds, measuring 13 × 16 *palmi*; below them, a wooden corridor was created by temporarily filling in the arches from the tops of the pillars to the top of each arch, and on the black silk-covered wood panels hung another forty-one coats of arms of king and kingdoms alternating with thirty-three emblems and mottoes (the imbalance between coats of arms and emblems defined by the architectural constraints of the duomo's walls).

On the lower level of festooned black silk, the newly invented emblems carried much the same message as those on the mausoleum. *Imprese* (images and mottoes) with the sun and the moon, fire, lightning, high mountains, ships on tranquil seas, rocks in tempestuous oceans, a pepper tree, an open pomegranate, lions, and eagles all point to Philip's virtues and accomplishments. A classical reference from Virgil (*Aeneid* 1:400), "Aut tenet, aut plenis subit" (Either has or will enter in full), for example, accompanies a ship in full sail with a favorable wind on a tranquil sea already entering a secure port, which Caputi writes "demonstrates that King Philip, having passed this sea of mortal life very tranquilly, and having the wind of favorable divine grace, entered the most happy port of Heaven." But this invocation of *Aeneid* 1:393–400 does much more than extol the king's passing safely to heaven; for it is filled with book 1's augury as Aeneas lands in Carthage and his mother Venus explains that the twelve swans, which have escaped the attack of an eagle, foreshadow that his ships, thought lost, are either safe in port or approaching port in full sail—a safe landing following Jupiter's prophecy to Venus of the coming greatness of the new Trojan Caesar.[132] How the erudite Jesuits combine literary allusion with royal beatification and mythical prophecy with funerary pomp goes far in illustrating how such emblems were supposed to work in multiple registers on their audience. In an appendix, sixteen of twenty-eight Jesuit-composed poems for twenty-eight miscellaneous *imprese* and emblems highlight the most common metaphor, the two animals

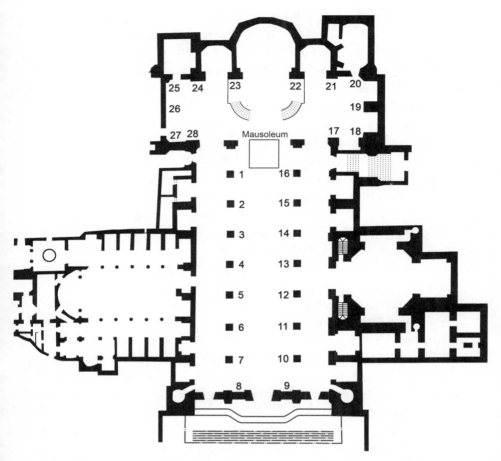

Figure 3.9. Plan of Naples Duomo with narrative paintings for Philip II obsequies. Design by Michele Greenstein.

that symbolize the king's lordship on earth and in the heavens—the lion and the eagle.[133]

The proof of whom Philip II was and why he is to be remembered with such pomp and circumstance, however, moves from his attributes to his deeds. The dominance of the twenty-eight narrative paintings (*storie*) between the nave's arches tell the history of his long reign and why he was so important to his subjects. Caputi gives an ekphrasis of each painting—title, short historical reprise of the circumstances surrounding the action depicted, and description of each painting's contents.[134] Even if we cannot see these paintings, Caputi allows us to visualize them and understand their importance in the victories against the

French at and after Saint-Quentin (six paintings); against the corsairs in North Africa and the Turks in the Mediterranean (four paintings); against the Portuguese in Portugal, the Azores, and India and Asia, especially in the Philippines (four paintings); against the Dutch rebels in Flanders (six paintings); and against the French Huguenots and other rebels in Granada, Genoa, and Aragón (five paintings). The picture of an ever-expanding Spanish Empire in defense of the Faith, led by victorious conquerors and advancing armies, is clearly portrayed.

Let us review them one by one, beginning with the seven *storie* hung along the left wall of the main nave. The first two paintings recount scenes from the Spanish victory at the Battle of Saint-Quentin in 1557, which ended the long Habsburg-Valois Wars that had traumatized Italy and western Europe for a half century. The first narrative painting is a battle scene with the king surrounded by one hundred of his guard waiting to assist in the battle below if needed. The second storia is another battle scene of the taking of the town Saint-Quentin after the French rout. The third scene is also a battle from 1557 and represents the taking of the fortress of Civitella, depicted on its hill, with French troops in flight below. The fourth narrative is the capture of the French general, Paul de la Barthe, maréchal de Thermes at Gravelines in Flanders in 1558. The fifth painting shows Philip II's triumphant entrance into France. The sixth recounts the definitive peace made with Henry II at Cateau-Cambrésis in dramatic fashion: Philip II stands at his throne receiving in submission Cardinal de Guise. The final painting along the left nave is a naval scene depicting aid to Oran in Algeria with an armada entering the North African port against the Turks.

Four statues, one on the first and last pillar on each side of the nave, separate the history paintings in the nave into three groups: the seven paintings on the left between the first and second statue, two narratives on the back wall above the main portal between statues 2 and 3, and seven paintings on the right row of pillars between statues 3 and 4. The first statue depicts a female figure identified as Virtue, with her head crowned with laurel, her breast emblazoned with the sun, and a horn of plenty at her feet; the second, a male figure of Valor, depicts a king with his scepter, garlands, and lions; the third, a female with a garland and a shaft of wheat on her head, is Abundance; and the fourth, a female statue of Victory with an eagle. The four statues of Virtue, Valor, Abundance, and Victory thus provide a shorthand summary of Philip's attributes strategically placed at the four corners of the chronological narrative of his deeds.

To return to the twenty-eight *storia*, we were on the back wall at paintings 8 and 9, both naval battle scenes. Painting 8, the taking of Fort Pignone, which was a nest of corsairs in Algeria in 1564, shows the assault on an impregnable fort.

Narrative 9 depicts the defense of Malta in 1565, with a map of the island and its parts as the Spanish fleet arrives and the Turkish fleet is put to flight.

The nave's right arches display the next seven paintings, numbers 10 through 16. In the tenth narrative, the putting down of the Granada rebellion of 1568 is shown in another battle scene, the Spanish fighting and the Berbers in flight. In the eleventh, the great victory of Don Juan of Austria, Philip's half brother, over the Turks at Lepanto is called the victory at the island of Cocciolare, and the Turkish fleet is seen scattering in all directions. The twelfth narrative recounts the Genoese embassy in a diplomatic scene set in the Genoese meeting hall. The thirteenth shows victory against the French Huguenots, who are depicted as heretics in the camp. Two scenes from the Revolt of the Netherlands appear in narratives 14 and 15. Surely these ephemeral victories should have appeared to be ironic claims by the king's death in 1598. Nevertheless, Philip's defense of the faith in the War of Flanders seems not to lose its luster as told from the Spanish Neapolitan point of view. In narrative 14, the great army of Flanders is seen in formation, and in narrative 15, the duke of Parma captures Antwerp in 1585 as shown by the citizens coming out of the city of Antwerp to surrender. Narrative 16 is the first of three histories of the conquest of Portugal and its empire. First the Duke of Alba conquers Portugal, and a surrender scene depicts victory with Portuguese nobles presenting the keys of the port to Philip II with galleys under the city walls.

As we move into the right transept for six scenes, two battle scenes of victory in the Portuguese overseas empire continue the narrative of the conquest of Portugal. Narrative 17 is the naval Battle of Ponta Delgada in 1582 in the Azores at the island of Terceira, and 18 shows the naval entry with a naval battle in progress as the Spanish reconquer the island of Terceira in 1583. Narrative 20 returns to the War in Flanders and pushes ahead to 1590 with the relief of Paris against Henry of Navarre, as the Duke of Parma valorously enters Paris as a conquering captain. Note no reference to the Armada expedition, not to mention its defeat and great losses of life and material in 1588. Such defeat cannot be properly presented in visual narrative and must wait to be set as appropriate lessons in the orations. One cannot help but ask how difficult it may have been to fill the twenty-eight architectural spaces with sufficient moments of Spanish glory and victory in light of the ambiguous record during Philip's reign.

The instability of Spanish rule becomes even clearer with the last two narratives in the right transept. History number 21 depicts the revolt of Aragón in 1591; in the countryside outside the city, a captain beheads one seditionist. History 22 shows the taking of Ulst in Flanders in 1596. When a Spanish force seems ready to retreat, another contingent climbs up a tower to save the day. Underlying resistance to Spanish rule—whether in the open rebellion of Flanders or local uprisings in Aragón, or even in Naples itself with the murder of the *eletto* Starace in 1585[135]—was always met with swift and uncompromising repression. The kind of social control exercised by Spanish administration in the day-to-day running of its empire was always backed up by the threat of harsh justice and military might.

The left transept concludes the history of Philip's deeds with three last triumphant entries of the previous two years as three more general invocations of Spanish power. The three entries are portrayed in different manners. The taking of Cambrai in 1596 shows the Count of Fuentes entering the city in the company of two citizens, with the Spanish infantry in front and cavalry in the rear; the acquisition of Calais in 1595 depicts the archduke entering the city; and the taking of Amiens in Picardy in 1597 has soldiers entering with swords drawn. The picture of an ever-expanding Spanish Empire, led by victorious conquerors and advancing armies is clearly portrayed. Religion and peace seal the Spanish conquests to confirm the new order imposed on subject cities in the final three history paintings. The Church of S. Lorenzo in the Escorial is painted from a design model and the *storia* thus ends where it began, when S. Lorenzo, whose intercession on his feast day provided for the defeat of the French at the Battle of Saint-Quentin, now is given due thanks in the dedication and naming of the king's retreat-residence church. Likewise, the penultimate history depicts the ceremony in St. John Lateran with the pope and cardinals present in sumptuous ritual for the canonization of S. Diego di Alcalá, whose curative powers were seen to have intervened in saving Philip's son, the young Prince Carlos, from death in 1561.[136] The last *storia* renders a picture of "All Italy as it is." A map of Italy now overcome by Peace, which is personified as a woman riding a horse and carrying an olive branch, renders the innumerable previous battle scenes subordinate to the divine purpose of Spanish rule in the establishment and maintenance of God's peaceful kingdom on earth.

The six orations delivered around the cathedral decorations make the link between Philip's virtues and deeds even more explicit. Philip is variously praised as a second King David by Davila; Hercules and Hannibal by Capaccio; Mattathias the father of Judas Maccabeus, St. Louis, Gideon, Pompey the Great, Hannibal, Perseus, and Abraham by Caracciolo; similar to Theodosius and Trajan in justice, to Ladislas king of Hungary in clemency, to Ptolemy II Philadelphus and Solomon in liberality, again to Solomon in prudence, to Leonidas king of Sparta in magnanimity, to Socrates, Gaius Lelius, and Alfonso Tarracone king of Sicily in constancy—all according to Filante; and Alexander in valor, Aristotle in justice, Socrates in temperance, Cato in common sense, Numa Pompilius in religion, and Samson in strength according to Turamini. Leaving all his other virtues aside "in his zeal for justice and religion," Turamini further declares that "he governed so many kingdoms" like another David.[137] And Philip's good government was matched by his defense of the faith—"against the cursed heretic Luther," in "the warlike country of Germany," and in Flanders against "the pestilence introduced by that insolent Calvin"—all deeds that made him another Catholic King like his great-grandfather Ferdinand the Catholic. His public career in government and defense of religion reflected his personal virtues in private to make him an ideal prince and an ideal model for emulation. The orations celebrated not only his life and deeds linked to his virtues but also his actions at death, his textbook preparation for "good dying" that made his death a saintly example.[138] As for Partenope, the Siren Naples who is "left almost a widow, disconsolate dressed in mourning," Caracciolo turns praise into prayer to invoke the aid of the new "St. Philip" to look over and not forget his people in Naples.[139]

For the literate audience hearing (or reading) the orations and seeing the ornate funeral decorations in praise of Philip II, this unanimous summary judgment of the king's life reinforced the sense of their own place in history at the heart of a great empire in defense of the one, true faith. It is that sense of continuity with tradition and the fulfillment of God's plan that turns the funeral orations and obsequies in Naples from ephemeral grief into a theological understanding of the meaning of life and death.

Much of this royal "theology" had already been established in the obsequies for Philip's father Charles V. In the famous Brussels obsequies, as we have seen, a number of similar items stand out: the sword, scepter, orb, and crown placed on a catafalque at the center of a quadruple crown scaffold with innumerable candles, mottoes, inscriptions, the coats of arms of his dominions, scenes of his triumphant deeds, and statues of the virtues.[140] The virtues, in fact, had become associated with the dynasty and House of Habsburg itself, which was the theme of a dynastic genealogy printed in Naples in 1599 by the local historian, Cornelio Vitignano.[141] An earlier 1595 chronicle of the kingdom had won Vitignano the praise of Philip II; and the 1599 book manuscript must have been sent to Spain for royal approval by Philip before publication, because a 29 September 1598 letter of Philip III—only sixteen days after the old king's death and twelve days before the news reached Naples—praised Vitignano's work.[142] Vitignano, for his part, traced the Habsburg House of Austria back to Aeneas and praised its well-known grandeur, religion, valor, and antiquity.[143]

What then did the nobles and state officials attending Philip II's Neapolitan obsequies see? They saw the deeds and virtues of the king in narrative paintings of victories over enemies and rebels and in the symbolic and secret language of the *imprese* with their esoteric iconography, cryptic poetry, and erudite knowledge. What was the relationship between secret knowledge and public spectacle? Who authored these *imprese*—words and image? What were their contents? What models or references stood behind them? What message did they convey? Who was the intended audience? What did the audience understand upon seeing these often enigmatic emblems? Was there a change in authorship, content, or construction of the royal obsequy emblem as its invention moved from the court to the Jesuits and members of academies? We want to know how these esoteric symbols functioned in state funerary spectacles and how to read their arcane images and cryptic language of binary oppositions between religious/state, clergy/laity, royals/nobles, elite/*popolo*, public/private, and male/female identities and interests.

As a group, the Jesuits provided the most influential intervention in the invention of emblems. In the definitive third edition of the *Ratio studiorum*, the Jesuits' curriculum and administrative plan for their fast-expanding colleges, first published in Naples in 1598 and promulgated in 1599, three references to the teaching of emblems explain how they were taught.[144] In the "Rules of the Teacher of Rhetoric," rule 12 specifies that "the class content or exercise" was to include, in a list of some dozen practices, "interpreting hieroglyphics and Pythagorean symbols, maxims, proverbs, emblems, riddles, delivering declamations, and other similar exercises at the teacher's pleasure." Further, in rule 15, "on the weekly holidays in place of the historical work, for the sake of erudition, other and more recondite subjects may be introduced, for examples, hieroglyphics, emblems," and other genres and topics. And in the "Rules of the Prefect of Lower Studies," rule 3 states that these "emblematic compositions and poems which are to be displayed on the greater feast days were to be read by two judges appointed by the rector, and they were to select the best." Thus, the Jesuits were not only masters of emblematic inventions themselves but also teachers of emblematic invention to their students, who were instructed to devise emblems on holidays for judged competitions. At the turn of the seventeenth century, we are at the beginning not only of an explosion of emblematic invention but also of the creation of an audience trained to both understand and appreciate the intricacies of the genre.

Jan David's *Veridicus Christianus* (The True Christian), published in Antwerp in 1601, was the first Jesuit emblem book. It explains how the combination of image and word worked together to create the desired interior effect to move the soul.[145] Jesuit emblem theory emphasized two traditions: the medieval rhetorical tradition of literary exegesis, that is, the movement from the literal sense to the spiritual interpretation of an allegorical, tropologoical, or anagogical meaning; and the Ignatian ideas on meditation, as in the *Spiritual Exercises*, whereby contemplation prepared one for the interior effect of enlightened transcendence. In the triparitite fusion of motto, *pictura*, and epigram and/or commentary, it is most often the words of the commentary that reorient and reveal the deeper meaning of the commonplace object, scene, or symbol. Interpretation is the key to understanding the hidden, mystical meaning of the emblem.

Not only Jesuit rhetoric and spirituality but also emblem theory informed the Neapolitan inventions. The Caputi emblems of Philip II are copied and explained in detail within the framework outlined earlier by Giulio Cesare Capaccio, the erudite writer of local Neapolitan lore, a founding member of the Accademia degli Oziosi, and later city secretary after 1602, in his *Delle imprese* of 1592. For Capaccio, "any object that can be represented to the intellect can be the matter for *imprese*."[146] Capaccio's inclusion of everything obscure, mystical, imaginary, and similtudinous corresponds to the three kinds of mental vision—corporal, spiritual, and intellectual. His Neoplatonic vision acquires knowledge by a kind of sight reading, such "that an *impresa* should be understood through intuition rather than discursive reason" and should be drawn "from an innate store of ideas." And he makes a sharp distinction between *imprese* and emblems. Whereas *imprese* express ideas in "the mind, the inferior emblem deals with moral precepts."

Modern commentators on Renaissance and Baroque emblems as symbol theory emphasize the difficulty for the observer of interpreting the image as a puzzle that is "anti-mimetic"; in other words, "poetic, moralistic, or doctrinal motives" often worked against the grain of imitation.[147] Thus, the familiar was presented in a new way, in a veiled allegorical language, "concealing esoteric wisdom from the vulgar" by emphasizing poetic language as the only way to "behold the dazzling ray of divine truth" in order to foster belief more completely in a flash of all comprehending lightning.[148] The commonplace became vessels of hidden meaning, profound truth, and inexplicable beauty; the emblematic puzzle revealed a kind of Baroque *Sileni Alcibiades*, where delight was mixed with knowledge upon the intuitive grasping of the hidden meaning.

As a control, we might take a brief look at the collection of another ninety-five royal *imprese* not only recorded but also reproduced by our same witness, Ottavio Caputi, in his festival book thirteen years later on the Neapolitan obsequies of the Spanish queen and wife of Philip III, Margherita d'Austria (d. 1612). What we see over and over again is how gender determined the emblem's content, message, and audience. The queen's holiness, virtues, and fecundity are represented in allegories drawn from countless natural objects, here, for example, the unopened oyster with its hidden pearl, the evening star emerging at the setting of the sun, the prickly pear in abundant bloom, and the dove building its nest for its young.[149] Humdrum domestic allegories turn our thoughts to praise of the queen at the same time that they act as moral injunctions for their audience.

What we have learned from the obsequies for Philip II in Naples is the esteem that the Neapolitan ruling class held for him and for themselves. The *imprese* portray royal power and moral virtue through mythological, astronomical, geographic, and animal iconography. Typologies of the emblematic images reveal the rules of ideology as much as the ideology of rule. Cracking the code of this emblemology helps explain how these secret meanings in motto and image became mannered manipulations of royal propaganda for the ruling class in its close identification with Spanish rule and its moral imperative to lead dutiful, virtuous lives. The language of the elites is reflected in a hall of mirrors of royal and aristocratic views on good government and a good death. The authoritative teachers drawing out these visual and verbal lessons from Philip's life were the Jesuits in Naples, whose message of the staunch Counter-Reformation offensive against Protestantism and proponents of the worldwide Spanish imperium in Europe, Asia, Africa, and America was the subject of the twenty-eight history paintings that reinforced their own special ministry to the local elites as it did the life of the dead king. What is especially poignant about this message, however, is the fact that most viewers probably could not understand the message at the time of the spectacle, because as *imprese* or narrative paintings without commentary, their interpretation awaited exegesis. The festival book thus became much more than a record or memento of the event, but rather its narrative function as a *memento mori* was to re-create the church spectacle so that readers could relive it in light of the new understanding of its hidden meaning and deeper significance. The result was a virtual, armchair spectacle with all the secrets revealed and all bonds of fidelity reaffirmed.

CHAPTER FOUR

The Rule of the Games

Playing Court

The Game of Games

Michel de Certeau's evocation of the old Game of Goose as a metaphor for culture itself in his 1972 book, *Culture in the Plural*, provides us with an excellent point of departure to understand much more than the meaning of a game's rules.

> If in every society, games make clear the formality of its practices for the reason that, outside of the conflicts of everyday life, it no longer has to be concealed, then the old Game of Goose becomes a kind of map in which, on a series of places and according to a sum of rules, a social *art* unfolds a field of play in order to create itineraries, and to make use of the surprises that lie ahead. It is a scale model, a theoretical fiction. In effect, culture can be compared to this art, conditioned by places, rules, and givens; it is a proliferation of inventions in limited spaces.[1]

Certeau argues for the possibility of using the rules of games to reveal the governing principles, the underlying contradictions, and the quotidian creativity of individuals in society. In the context of the rarified world of the early modern European court, in a very literal sense, games ruled court society; for the real business of the court was simply to play court. The purpose of this chapter, following Certeau, is to examine the rationale behind the playing of games at court. We begin with an analysis of the sixty-two games cited in the first printed collection of European fairy tales, Giambattista Basile's 1634–36 *Lo Cunto de li cunti* (*The Tale of Tales; or, Entertainment for Little Ones*), the so-called *Pentamerone*, as an introduction to the complex performances staged in the viceroy's court to commemorate such events as a royal recovery of health and the birth of heirs. Such festive occasions were essentially the prerogative of the nobility to reinforce the structure of hierarchy and reassert the logic of its rule.

Certeau's reference to the Game of Goose was not a chance example, for Goose

is generally considered to be among those games that introduced a modern period of board gaming with illustrative and thematic elements to replace earlier
symbolic and mathematical ones. Essentially a lottery entirely determined by the
chance roll of two dice with not the least bit of skill or player interaction, it was a
high stakes gambling game for the nobility in which twelve counters were moved
around spaces numbered 1 to 63. The game is thought to have originated in Florence, based upon a reference in a 1617 Italian book on the game of chess that
reports Francesco I de' Medici (1574–87) sent the Royal Game of Goose (Gioca
dell'Oca) as a gift to Philip II of Spain.[2] The game was widely diffused from the
last quarter of the sixteenth century: in addition to the gift from the Grand Duke
of Tuscany to the Spanish king, a 1589 German exemplar (except for the center
figure of the goose replaced by Fortuna) is in the collection of the Graz Museum,
a 1597 London game was registered at Stationers Hall, and in France a 1601 Ly-
ons edition and a 1612 diary entry by Louis XIII's doctor are recorded. The rules
of the Game of Goose were invariable across countries and traditionally specified
in twelve numbered paragraphs so well known that, as the game began to trickle
down from royalty and the aristocracy, its boards often just reproduced pictures
without the verbal instructions. A couplet from Oliver Goldsmith's 1770 *Deserted
Village* provides a perfect example:

> The pictures plac'd for ornament and use,
> The Twelve good rules, the Royal Game of Goose.

In addition, the game's wide diffusion allowed it to be appropriated for political
propaganda and popular consumption, as in the French Revolutionary "Le Jeu
de la Révolution française," a board game of Goose whose squares reproduced
topical revolutionary images such as the storming of the Bastille, the women's
march on Versailles, and the suppression of the religious orders.[3]

By the late eighteenth century, more all-consuming state lotteries undermined
such board-gambling games, and Goose began to migrate from an adult game
of chance to a childhood game played with counters. Early modern states came
to employ the lottery as a source of conflict-free revenues, because such betting
was a "voluntary" tax paid on the hope of some gain. Between the seventeenth
and eighteenth centuries, a Genoese and a Dutch model of the lottery spread
throughout Europe on the basis of a cultural habit of speculative passion for bid-
ding on products, saving in tontines, and playing games of chance. Paolo Macry's
study of the social, cultural, and institutional history of the lottery in eighteenth-
and nineteenth-century Naples demonstrates both how life in Naples is a game
and, conversely, how the game in Naples (the classic lottery of ninety numbers)

is life. Macry exposes the expected world of corruption, crime, and fraud; parasitism, favoritism, nepotism, and *clientelismo*. At the same time, he engages readers in the unexpected by facing the problem of anomalies, probabilities, risk, and uncertainty, while grappling with fortune, futurology, and divination. The lottery in Naples has mythologized and domesticated the wheel of fortune, as its workings call into question the rules of the game—rationality and causality in both material culture and ideology.[4]

These preliminary findings on the distinction between adult games and children's games, the courtly etiology of games, games' dependence on Fate and Fortune, the popularity of high-stakes betting games, and the dissemination of games down the social ladder over time allow us to begin with some working hypotheses as we examine the place of games in the culture of the Neapolitan nobility. Basile's new literary genre of *The Pentamerone* is exemplary of the kind of literary production coursing through the Neapolitan public sphere. In this kingdom's capital without a king or a royal court, the circulation of ideas, news, and commodities found its locus in innumerable noble courts, the hundreds of offices in the viceregal bureaucracy, and the various academies created around them.

Not only did every literary work have its noble patron praised profusely in dedications, but specially educated, humanist-trained literati worked directly as secretaries in noble houses and state offices. Tommaso Costo (1545?–1612) and Basile (1566?–1632), for example, spent their professional lives in the employ of various Neapolitan noble families; Giulio Cesare Capaccio (1552–1634), in civic office, with his exile from Naples as librarian, ambassador, and orator for the court of the Duke of Urbino, Francesco Maria II della Rovere, proves the rule.[5] Costo served as secretary to the marchese di San Lucido, Ferrante Carafa, and his son Frederico; to Giovanni d'Avalos and his wife, Maria Orsini (1577–1581/82); to the marchese di Lauro, Scipione Pignatelli, and his son (1581/82–1599); and to the Grand Court of the Admiralty under the Prince of Conca, Matteo di Capua, Great Admiral of Naples (from 1599). Basile was associated with the courts of the Prince of Stigliano, Luigi Carafa, and of the Duke of Mantua, Vincenzo Gonzaga (1608–15); served as governor of Montenaro (1615); and served in the courts of the marchese di Trevico, Cocco di Loffredo (1617), of the Prince of Avellino, Marino Caracciolo (1618–22), and of the Spanish viceroy of Naples, the Duke of Alba, Antonio Álvarez de Toledo (1622–29). Capaccio was a professor of sacred theology (1587), *provveditori di grani e degli ogli* (1592–1602), secretary of the city of Naples (1602–13), in the employ of the Duke of Urbino (1616–23), and *maestro di scuola* back in Naples (from 1623). Although early modern Naples was a capital city without a resident royal court, noble courts proliferated and the ruling-class propaganda of their secretary-humanists created a lively proving ground for debates on noble virtue, gentility, and the place of the burgeoning bourgeoisie in a city that was growing from more than 250,000 inhabitants around 1600 to 360,000 by the mid-seventeenth century, before the devastation of the 1656 plague.

The urban history of Naples reveals growing caste and class conflicts during the process of rapid population growth in the face of blocked inclusion of foreign nobles, some local noble families, nobles of the robe, and wealthy commoners into the city's ruling noble *seggi*. An examination of the transformation of literary genres and the transposition of the norms of religious discourse into civic concerns critical of the traditional local nobility can be traced in seventeenth-century Naples, just as similar "popular" literature has been studied for seventeenth-century Paris.[6] Such a history of storytelling in art and literature provides an alternative model for the process of societal transformation in early modern Europe. This Neapolitan model gives due regard to the political economic basis of conflict as it integrates the role of pervasive and persistent cultural values—here, namely, the old humanist debate on the need for a nobility of virtue—in the story of the creation of a bourgeois public sphere of civil society quite different from that found in the world of the Parisian salon, the London coffeehouse, or the Dutch and German Protestant ethic.

These first fairy tales, which appeared in Naples sixty years before that other Game of Goose, Charles Perrault's *Mother Goose* of 1697, were transcribed conversations, repertories of proverbs, and compendia of literary allusions compiled for the same audience in the same venues as Basile's other literary works—madrigals, celebratory songs, comedies, dance texts, and masques, that is, entertainments or games to be enjoyed at court.[7] The tales were diversions to be read aloud at academy banquets or small noble and ecclesiastical courts at the end of the meal while the table was being cleared and the main entertainment prepared. Called *trattenemienti* or pastimes, Basile's fairy tales were typical of the game of games and jokes upon jokes created for the complex play and clever repartee of stylized court conversation propagated by Castiglione's model of court society a century earlier. Because the tales underline the paradoxical relationship between fact and fantasy in storytelling and attempt to reinforce societal values through wit and humor, not surprisingly they tell us more about erudite courtly literary production and elite comportment than about popular attitudes in Naples in the first half of the seventeenth century.

Basile's plots entertain and please as they confirm, criticize, and often contradict norms of courtesy and ethical conduct. The destabilizing nature of the jokes and incongruities also undermines those norms and countenances a rethinking and reordering of the social hierarchy.[8] The opening of ethical discourse to satirical derision thus creates unintended consequences for the local culture of aristocratic Naples and its set of distinctive values in the Counter-Reformation city. Such late sixteenth- and early seventeenth-century vernacular and, in this case, dialect writing aimed at claiming the city for the virtuous noble gentleman— what we might call "civic humanism in late Renaissance Naples"; but it also becomes the vehicle for those not in this caste to resist its pretensions and construct a hierarchy based on virtue rather than birth.

Basile's classical source brings with it this same two-edged sword of ambiguous meanings, whose plasticity allows for later bourgeois purposes.[9] As is well known, Ovid's *Metamorphoses* is the closest literary and philosophical model for the unexpected, theatrical turns of fortune of Basile's fifty stories. Thus, as we have come to expect in fairy tales, the core of each story treats of a change in status from low to high, from poverty to wealth, from childhood to adulthood, from innocence to experience, from danger and sorrow to happiness ever after.[10] But at the same time, despite the deceptive happy endings that present a central resolution to the instability of the world, plots fraught with trials and dangers of the conflict between chaos and harmony give voice to an unsettling anxiety about human striving, a gnawing uncertainty over the priority of *fortuna* or *virtù*, and an ambiguous questioning of the order of the universe—all likewise dilemmas of Renaissance humanist thought. We should not be surprised to find that games function in much the same way as the tales themselves in passing the time and relieving boredom, in their close linkage with *fortuna* and *virtù*, and in their social control of rivalries, violence, and aggression by transforming them into more constructive civilizing activities.

If such functional purposes of the rule of order imposed on courts by games can be so readily established, can a study of the rules of court games further reveal court society's concealed tensions and lay bare its deeper meaning? How does the act of playing games reinforce social relationships, set manners, and structure interactions that hold the whole fabric of society together in the midst of contestation and competition?[11]

In Basile, games enter the text often and in three distinct ways. First, games punctuate individual tales as references, similes, and sources of doggerel rhyme. Second, lists of games are presented seriatim in three of the five introductions to each day's storytelling. Third, the Boccaccesque form of serial storytelling around a frame is a game of games such as we find in Castiglione's *The Book of the Court-*

ier. The focus of this chapter is not to explore the playful genre of serial storytelling, as important as it is in Basile's following of Boccaccio's *Decameron* model, but rather to tighten our lens on the much smaller internal references to games in order to get at the much bigger question of the rules of the games.

We must, nevertheless, take a parenthetical glance at the game of games in Castiglione. There to pass the evening at court in Urbino the duchess-moderator decrees "that each propose some game after his own liking that we have never played," which leads to seven conversation proposals, with the adoption of the last generating the brilliant conversation on the formation of the perfect courtier.[12] Just as Castiglione's four-day conversation topic allows for a consideration of standard Renaissance topoi on the question of nobility, on arms versus letters, on the language question of Tuscan versus court patois, on the merits of painting versus sculpture, and on a host of other problems similarly framed in binary oppositions,[13] Basile's five days of storytelling also explore the range of court dilemmas from the individual to society, and back again.

Basile's games are cited in his fairy tales as simple references. Tale 1.10, "La Vecchia Scortecata" (The Old Woman Who Was Skinned), for example, embeds seven games in three typical modes.[14] In the first instance, the words and rhymes of children's games are directly quoted. "Apre le porte a povero farcone! famme la 'nferta si me la vuoi fare!" (Open the doors to the poor falcon! Give me a present if you will) runs together two different games' ditties. The former reference is to the last of the thirty-one games cataloged in the introduction to day 2, in which a child shut in the middle of a hand-holding circle (like a bird [the falcon] in a cage) tries to get out by escaping under the clasped arms, and the second is to the New Year's Day game in which children scurry around the house looking for gifts. Similarly, "Vienela, vienela" (Come forth, come forth) are the words used in the game of Hide and Seek ("cuccipannella," a variation of "covalèra" ["The Brooding Hen"]) in both the compendium and the introduction to day 2, and again, "Viata te co la catena" (Lucky you with the chain) is from a game mentioned by Basile in his Neapolitan *Lettere.* In other cases, games can simply be named. Triumph and Bankrupt are two card games of trump, previously mentioned in tale 1.2, and later also among the card games used in the bantering game in the introduction to day 5. And sometimes the rules or results of games are used as metaphors. "You're mad yourself; you don't know your good fortune: if it turns out even" (i.e., if it turns out that I win) is taken from the game of Odds and Evens (Paro o sparo), listed in the day 4 introduction.[15] Similarly, in tale 5.1, Basile draws a metaphor from the game of billiards: "In spite of their wretched life there was no danger that the ball of necessity hitting against that of honor would knock it away."[16] A fourth kind of reference appears in tale 1.2, when the citation of two children's games is used as a double-entendre for two sexual games: "Clinging to her like an octopus, he began to play at 'dumb sparrow' [la passara muta] and 'stone in the apron' [a preta 'nsino]."[17] At a first literal level, then, games are jewels studded inside the larger game of storytelling.

A second level of gaming references are made in the form of long lists. The introduction to day 2 lists thirty-one games, that to day 4 lists fourteen games, while the introduction to day 5 plays a game of penalty in which each lady must wittily explain why she does not wish to play the card game presented to her—with ten card games offered before a loser is penalized—that is, fifty-six games listed in all (31 + 14 + 1 + 10). I have found another six games not in these three lists for a total of sixty-two games in Basile's text (see Table A.4).

Such catalogs of games were a common Renaissance trope. In 1534 Rabelais listed Gargantua's 217 children's games of cards, dice, and board games as part of the elder giant's early education (bk. 1, chap. 22), all played to "shorten the time." After Gargantua had thus enjoyed his games and "thoroughly sifted, winnowed, and dispensed his time"[18]—in other words, after he played the games to pass the time—he took a drink and fell asleep for a two- or three-hour nap. Later after supper, he might choose to play a board game (three more new games are named) "to shorten the time" or he might choose alternative entertainment seeing and supping with the local girls.

Similarly, Bruegel's 1560 painting *Children's Games* references forty-six games, and interpretations of the painting require an understanding of "sixteenth-century attitudes toward children, the Renaissance fascination with plural meanings, and the conflicts of Bruegel's cultural moment."[19] Interpretations of Bruegel's representations and of lists of games in general fall into two major camps: literalists, who see in these lists nothing more than a catalog of children's games full of innocence and free of care; and iconographers, who find disguised moral meanings in games that symbolize human folly and satirize the world upside down.

There should, however, be no question in interpreting such catalogs of games. Because Gargantua's games are identified as part of his childhood education, the humanist educational project and its ethical imperatives are readily apparent in the parody that makes the innocent follies of children serious truth. Such encyclopedic lists and visual cornucopia of games revel in contradictions and juxtapositions, play with indeterminacy and ambiguity, glorify chaos, and establish antistructure only to reinforce order and structure in its denial.[20] Play, in Gargantua's education, Bruegel's children, and Basile's games at court, thus is what makes us all who we are, what allows us to discern between the real and the make-believe, and what teaches us that rules always define or give meaning to our actions.

The third kind of gaming references in Basile derives from the structural placement of the lists in his narrative order.[21] *When* games are played is important for the mimetic repetition of the frame story introducing day 1, the serial storytelling to follow, and the interruption of that order. The frame begins with a short paragraph jumble of proverbs, references to Firenzuola's *Consigli degli animali* and Pulci's *Morgante*, and a reference to the children's game of "La Rota de li cauce" (The Wheel of Kicks, second game day 2 introduction) in which a child tries to break through and get inside a circle of joined hands by warding off the kicks of the members of the circle who are trying to keep him or her out—this game is the same, but opposite action of the previously cited "Apre le porte a povero farcone" when someone tries to break out of—rather than into—the circle. Proverbial wisdom, the two fanciful texts by Firenzuola and Pulci, and children's games are equally weighted as typical courtly pastimes.

Immediately follows Basile's frame story, "Once upon a time" a king tried to dispel his daughter's melancholy by making her laugh.[22] Some fourteen remedies are listed before the tale is told of the princess's cure, but subsequent trials—her curse, pilgrimage, sleep, and betrayal that will generate the rest of the fifty tales to entertain the pregnant wife of the princess's longed-for prince. At the end of the frame story, ten women are selected to tell one story per day and a pattern that conforms to a typical day at court is decreed for the rest of their meetings. They were to meet at the same place in the garden of the palace, eat a big meal, tell their stories, and the day's activities would end with the servants reciting an eclogue. Thus, the centerpiece of each day's program was the telling of the ten stories in a great game of entertainment to pass the time for the waiting, pregnant wife of the prince.

The programmatic order of the day's activities helps us understand their function: where games fit in the daily routine and what they mean as they interrupt the prescribed schedule. In three of the days, playing the list of games passes the time waiting for dinner by amusing the company of storytellers and the prince's entourage. The only exception is day 3, when the pastime between morning and dinner is happily spent with music in dance ("passare allegramente . . . ecommenzaro co gusto granne ad abballare").[23] Similarly in days 4 and 5, music and singing replaced game playing. In day 4, the prince is wearied by so many games that he orders music and singing. In day 5, the penalty for losing in the card-game repartee is for the loser to sing a Neapolitan song. Telling stories, dancing, singing, and playing games were functional equivalents at court. Such activity passed the time, amused, and entertained in order to relieve the boredom.

One of the card games in the day 5 introduction makes the tedious lot of the courtier explicit. The steward prompts,

> "Let us spend a couple of hours at Discontented."
>
> "Excuse me, that is a game for courtiers," answers one of the ladies.
>
> "She has hit the nail on the head, for that is a class of person who is never content," says the prince.

The witty steward in this game of verbal puns, however, had introduced his game of games by explaining that games were more than mere amusements to pass the time and fill the space in the court's daily program:

> It has always been considered, ladies and gentlemen, that a pleasure was insipid if it had in it no element of utility, and that amusements and evening entertainments were not devised simply for useless pleasure, but also for enjoyable profit. In this kind of game, one does not only pass the time, but one makes the mind apt and quick in solving problems and answering questions.[24]

Basile is not only reminding us of classical aesthetic theory that demands that art instruct, move, and delight its audience. He is also preparing us for the game of games itself, which lists both money (coins or quantities used in betting) and the ten card games (structured plays of chance with calculable odds). The steward's game of games requires knowledge of the rules of the card games to create another game of witty rejoinders. In other words, to speak in social conversation without paying a penalty, each woman must know how to speak without stopping to think and without hesitation. Such verbal acuity requires that she has mastered the rules of myriad other games according to the instructions set down for "a game of solitude, by which [the speakers] form a portrait of the *vita solitaria*," in Stefano Guazzo's *La civil conversatione*, the dialogue on conversation that, following its publication in 1573, became the late Renaissance handbook on conversation in society.[25]

This particular game of games is a game of proposals and counterproposals, verification of the true and the false, a debate between the affirmative and the negative—above all, a test not of wills but of wits.[26] Its goal is not to reward the winner by identifying the single best wit but rather it is a "game of blunders" to eliminate the loser and to keep everyone else playing and speaking faster than thinking. It is a game of sociability and socialization. By being singled out, each loser in turn would have to debase herself before the group in a kind of hazing ritual of reinitiation. The humiliated court lady becomes smaller than the group and subordinates herself to reenter it—not unlike the children's game of breaking into or out of the circle of joined hands.[27] The loser in Basile's game can regain entry into the charmed circle only after paying the penalty; here by singing a Neapolitan *villanelle*, a song to instruct, move, and delight the company. The song itself is a mishmash of proverbs explaining how a former lover, as love wanes, no longer is blinded by the lover's wiles. Paradoxically, the song smacks of defiance and of thoughtful, clear-sighted verbal facility. The argument is parallel to the plight of the "punished" courtier in the game of games, singled out for not knowing the rules of the game, but now seeing through the game's facade. The conundrum for the courtier (or court lady) is, however, not a game; the courtier must maintain one's individuality amid conformity and must assert one's place in the hierarchy or demonstrate one's superiority amid the fictive equality of those subordinate to one's prince.

The penalty, payment, or play of the game of games is the song, the conversation, or the story; and at this point, we should listen to one exemplary, relatively obscure story among Basile's fifty tales—rather than a famous one such as Cinderella or Sleeping Beauty—which can serve to reveal the same kind of problematic, emotive set of contradictions as it confronts the rarified rules of court life, the uneasy tensions between high and low, and the duplicity of the ruling caste. The fifth tale of day 3, "Lo scarafone, lo sorece e lo grillo" (The Cockroach, the Mouse, and the Cricket) plays with two folkloric motifs—the gifts of three magical animals and the challenge to make a king's melancholic daughter laugh. I have chosen this tale of Basile's not only because its 1634 publication date coincides with Capaccio's *Il Forastiero* and it is important to my argument about a growing public sphere of identity formation in Naples, but above all because its plot recapitulates the frame story about making a melancholy princess laugh. Not by chance, the structure of Basile's collection of tales gives added importance to this tale. Placed as tale 3.5, this tale comes at the exact midpoint of the fifty tales with the frame story of the princess who cannot laugh divided in half at the beginning and end of the tales: ½ + 24 + 1 + 24 + ½. Thus, form reinforces not only this tale's meaning but Basile's meaning for the whole work.

The tale of "The Cockroach, the Mouse, and the Cricket" addresses much more than what appears on the entertaining surface—namely, the oft examined and much more serious question of a nobility of virtue, not birth, in the context of the classical debate over the private versus the public life. It is unfortunate that we cannot hear the tale in its original Neapolitan dialect because there the tale's language itself exaggerates the contrast between the base, ribald plot and its high-minded theme, between the practical wisdom of daily life and the simulated morality of courtly manners, between the naive spontaneity of a gullible commoner and the sophisticated sensibilities of the nobility at court. Here let us at least introduce the problem of such contradictions by following the narrative for a moment in a literal translation, which allows us to hear the repetitions, the proverbs, and the direct discourse of conversation.[28]

> Once upon a time on the Vomero[29] there lived a very rich farmer named Miccone, who had a son, Nardiello, who was the most near-do-well dunderhead that could ever be found among the world's ship of fools; so much so that the poor father became embittered and despairing for he did not know by what mode or manner to guide his son to do any worthwhile or useful thing.
>
> If he went to the tavern to gorge himself with his companions, these no-accounts cheated him. If he consorted with prostitutes, he chose the worst meat and paid way too much. If he frequented gambling dens, they flattened him like a pizza between them and beat him to a pulp, so that in one way or another he had squandered half of his father's fortune.
>
> For this reason, Miccone was always up in arms, yelling, threatening, and saying: "What do you think you are going to do, spendthrift? Don't you see that all I have is slipping away like water at low tide? Leave these cursed taverns . . . leave this condemnable gaming . . . leave the damnable whoring. . . . Remove yourself from the occasions of sin and you will eliminate your vices, as they say: removing the cause removes the effect. Listen, take these one hundred ducats, go to the fair of Salerno and buy some calves so that in three or four years they will become oxen. Once they are oxen, we'll set them to work the fields. Once the fields are worked, we'll be grain merchants; and if we're blessed with a good famine, we'll count ducats by the bushel. Then if nothing else happens, I'll buy you a noble title on some friend's fief and you too will become titled like so many others. So pay attention, my son, everything has a beginning, but he who does not begin does not get on."

Let us pause here at the beginning of a fantastic scatological story to listen to the advice of a very rich father, Miccone, who alerts us to the underlying importance of material life, economic logic, and the agricultural realities of early modern European culture even—or, I should emphasize, especially—for large city populations such as that in Naples, where civic harmony depended upon sufficient bread to feed the people.[30] Miccone's paternal injunctions play upon three important themes in the history of agriculture and the relationship between city and countryside. First, with his clear control of the practice of agriculture—how the calves mature in three or four years and how the oxen plow the fields to prepare them for the cash-cropping of wheat—the father is speaking of the principles of agronomy. The technical aspects of cultivation, the crops, and the animals form the first level of agricultural history, something that every well-informed farmer had to know. Second, father Miccone also understands the principle, perhaps only imperfectly, of supply and demand because he hopes for "a good famine" in order to make his son's fortune. From the relationship between buyers and sellers comes an understanding of the market price of commodities and, ultimately, of another of the great themes of agricultural history, the development of the market and the transition from feudalism to capitalism. And, finally, our father from the Vomero obviously understands the fruits of this labor. It is not money itself but, more important for his pathetic son, what money can buy—landed property and the venality of offices and titles—that provides social mobility to become someone important. Such possibilities initiate us into the third theme of material life: social stratification, coercion and cohesion, and the antagonisms leading to revolt or pacification in the countryside. In sum, from production to the market to social structure, we can move from fact to theory. Such theory is not the fantasy of social mobility, how the three animals purchased by Nardiello will make the fortune of the spendthrift plebeian, but rather, in the satire of this would-be *bourgeois gentilhomme*, how pervasive are the ideology of agrarian culture and the relationship between production, distribution, and consumption to the development of urban society and values.

What may be most important for my argument about the assertion of the noble ideology of virtue is the use of folkloric culture to transform high and low, for this tale is essentially a stinging criticism of noble prevarication and pretension. Basile employs scatology to attack his readers' taboos with the most shocking—here outrageously humorous—assault on decorum.[31] Contrasting court conceits and commoners' sense, the details of Basile's plot in the rest of the folktale are thus extremely relevant to the inversion of a hierarchical order of blood and the creation of a social order defined by deeds, not birth.

The fairy tale's plot develops around a triad of typical triplications. First, Nardiello takes one hundred ducats from his father three different times and, before even reaching the Salerno fair, squanders it each time on a bizarre purchase of a guitar-playing cockroach, a dancing mouse, and a singing cricket. Then, Nardiello escapes from his father's predictable wrath and takes the three magical animals to Lombardy where they make a king's daughter, who had not smiled in seven years, laugh. The king, however, breaks his promise of his daughter's hand by drugging Nardiello three evenings in a row at the wedding feast in order to prevent the marriage's consummation. Thrown into a lions' den, Nardiello frees the three magical animals, who in gratitude save him from the lions and further offer their services to help him achieve his heart's desire, the beautiful princess, who in the meantime has been betrothed to a German nobleman now that her melancholic spell has been broken. Finally, this time it is the animals who intervene on three successive evenings to prevent the consummation of the princess's marriage.

This concluding set of episodes helps us discern the way Basile's inversions work to make his case. On the first night, the three animals hide in the newly-weds' bedroom where the German bridegroom, drunk from the wedding feast, falls asleep as soon as he lies down on the marriage bed. The cockroach then crawls up into the bed, under the covers, and up the groom's anus where (in the exact words of the narrative):

> it acts like a suppository to pierce his body in such a way that one could say with Petrarch
>
> "Love draws from it a subtle liquid."[32]
>
> And the bride, hearing the rumbling of this dysentery [our author again quoting Petrarch]
>
> "The breath and the fragrance and the coolness and the shade,"[33]
>
> wakes her husband, who, seeing with what perfume he had incensed his idol, would die with shame and burst with anger.

On the second night, the German groom's servants swathe him in a cloth diaper to prevent some new embarrassing excretion. But the mouse eats his way through the binding to make way for the cockroach and his medicinal cure that precipitates a topaz sea and such foul scents that the bride awakens nauseated and runs from their room holding her nose.

On the third night to save his family honor, the noble bridegroom vows to remain awake, has his artillery man insert a wooden plug in his anus as they might stop up a cannon, and dares not touch his bride for fear of dislodging it. This time the cockroach finds the groom awake, so the cricket sings him to sleep. When the cockroach finds the path blocked, the mouse lades his tail with mustard and sticks it up the German's nose with the result that he sneezes so violently that the cork pops like a projectile, striking the bride with such force in the breast nearly to kill her. Her screams rouse her father, who, finding such stench and filth, learns that this was the third liquefaction of this kind. Dare we think this fecal liquefaction is a sacrilegious antithesis to that of S. Gennaro and the other saintly blood liquefactions that made Naples the *urbs sanguinum*? The outraged king kicks the German prince out and laments that cruelty to Nardiello had led to this state of affairs.

Finally, informed by the cricket that Nardiello is, in fact, still alive, the king welcomes him back, gives him his daughter, calls Nardiello's father from the Vomero and

> everyone lives happily ever after, proving that after a thousand troubles and a thousand tears, *More happens in an hour than in a hundred years.*

Because we are focused on Neapolitans rather than Germans, and Alan Dundes has already published the fruit of his psychoanalytic interpretation of the anal erotic national character of Germans in German folklore, I happily do not feel compelled to explore the psychoanalytically incisive juxtaposition of sexuality and defecation.[34] But the lines of such an inquiry in terms of a hostile infantile anality are forcefully outlined by Bruno Bettelheim, despite his anachronistic and ahistorical misunderstanding of how changing context changes meanings in fairy tales.[35]

For our purposes, it is enough to point out a number of the more obvious meanings in the social context of seventeenth-century Naples. The first point is that this Basile tale is a classic story of social class inversion in which one could not imagine a more negative portrait of Europe's Brahmin caste. Whatever role court manners played in the civilizing process, a melancholy princess who cannot even smile, a deceitful king who goes back on his word, and a noble bridegroom who proves that he cannot even keep his pants clean were far from Castiglione's ideal virtues of grace and *sprezzatura*.[36]

Second, on the question of Germans per se, it is noteworthy that in the 1714 Neapolitan edition "German" is changed to "English."[37] If later Neapolitans were sensitive to the overt insult to their new Austrian Habsburg sovereigns after the War of the Spanish Succession, we can be fairly certain that earlier Neapolitans at the time of the Thirty Years' War when the story was first published understood the reference as some stereotypical caricature of German national character or political affairs. Perhaps Basile wished to satirize the spit-and-polish officiousness of the militaristic German nobility, to indict the long history of imperial intervention in Italian affairs, or possibly even to chide the absentee Spanish Habsburg kings of Naples and Lombardy, who were the senior branch of the House of Austria. In point of fact, the viceroy's bodyguard was a German contingent and, like the pope's Swiss guard, was an elite, foreign presence in the viceroy's household.[38] It was a visible presence in the countless public processions and cavalcades made by the viceroy on holidays, his visits around the city, and his formal entrance and exit. More than likely, the viceroy's German bodyguard was the butt of Basile's joke.

Third, Mary Douglas's writing on purity and danger teaches us that such scatology defines the existence of systems of classification that delimit sets of binary categories, such as polite/impolite behavior or toilet training/incontinence, ultimately to arrive at good and evil; here, read virtue and vice.[39] Because Basile's narrative quite graphically plays upon the five senses, especially smell and sound, to create social embarrassment in order to turn the world upside down, lower bodily functions are employed to establish ideological belief in a hierarchy of virtue over one of breeding.

Fourth, compared to the helpful animals found in variants of this tale type (the golden goose in the Grimm brothers, the mouse, ape, and bear in the Kalmuck version, or dogs, cats, and snakes in Finnish, Kashmirian, and other Indian versions), the nature/culture dichotomy in Basile is extremely vivid.[40] The cockroach, mouse, and cricket are all found in close proximity to the household, but are considered repulsive or disruptive and excluded from civilized space.[41] Their power from nature, an untamable primitive, proximate nature that evokes the harsh realities of the physical world and material life, provides the ingenuous hero with a natural authenticity as he castigates the lying and filthy manners of an uncivilized nobleman not even housebroken. The concluding proverb sums up the moral quite well as the natural power of an instant over the inevitability expected by artificial, human affairs.

Can one derive from Miccone's story, the game of games in day 5, and the rules of the sixty other games in Basile some general principles or some manageable categories? We can identify about 90 percent of the games and can categorize them in terms already described: games of in and out ("Rota de li cauce" and "Aprite le porte a povero farcone"), games of hide and seek ("Covalera," "Vienela, vienela," and also "Auciello, auciello maneca de fierro"), games of guessing or choosing often used to determine precedence or one's turn like Odds or Evens ("Paro o sparo," "Capo o croce," "Morra," "Tuocco," "Anca Nicola," and "La lampa a la lampa"), card and dice games of chance (the ten card games in the day 5 introduction and also "Cucco o viento" and "Norchie" or dice games "sbaraglino" and "scarreca l'aseno"), and games of skill like billiards and skittles ("Sbriglie," "Campana," "Accosta palla," and "Palla"). In all these games, the métier of the courtier—chance and skill, *fortuna* and *virtù*—are in play. In some games, one could easily identify a teasing, tormenting dynamic probably attributable to gender, age, strength, or size differences.[42] Variants of games of It isolate players trying to get in or out of groups; or in games of penalty, isolation spotlights the individual and gives her or him the opportunity to stand out or show off. In "Li forasciute" (variants include Turks and Christians, Soldiers and Brigands, Cops and Robbers, Cowboys and Indians), an air of make-believe holds sway. And still in games such as "Salipendola," the seesaw or running in circles gives us chills and thrills by making us purposely giddy and dizzy.

Lying behind my categorization of Basile's games are four typologies theorized by Roger Caillois: games of competition (*agôn*), games of chance (*alea*), games of simulation (mimicry), and games of vertigo (*ilinx*).[43] For Caillois, these four "attitudes" are often joined in specific games with a fundamental relationship between competition and chance on the one hand and between mimicry and vertigo on the other. His goal is to sketch not only a sociology of games but a "sociology *derived from* games" in which he finds two types of societies. Merit and chance are contradictory yet complementary principles that resolve the opposition between wealth and poverty, glory and obscurity, power and dependence. They create a society of law; and they stress order, hierarchy, codification, and the ambiguity between worth and birth. Pantomime and ecstasy, for their part, when joined together, lead to the alienation of individuality and are associated with less complex societies where prestige and strength find their origin in trances, spasms, and states of possession based upon masks and magic. Caillois argues that games may be placed on a continuum of evolution from *paidia* (the active, tumultuous, exuberant, and spontaneous) to *ludus* (the calculated, contrived, and subordinated to rules). In games at court, one finds an almost perfect verification of Caillois's theories—calculation, rationalization, and civilization in games of competition or chance constantly attempt to discredit, discourage, control, or neutralize the dangerous and menacing power of the excesses and paroxysms of games of mimicry and vertigo. Thus, theater and dance, two transformative performances of simulation and vertigo par excellence, are formalized and ritualized at court. In Caillois's words, "games discipline instincts and institutionalize them."[44]

If Basile's court games fit Caillois's typology so well, is there anything peculiarly Neapolitan about them? Basile's games themselves often find a source or resonance in Tasso's dialogues on games and Tomaso Garzoni's description of "Game-Players" in his catalog of all the world's professions, both drawn from the 1580s Este court in Ferrara; for, if not borrowed directly from ancient Roman games, they shared a common court culture.[45] Thomas Greene has demonstrated how coronation ceremonies and parodies of crowning in Renaissance literature operate according to a pattern we might call the "ritual process" or the "civilizing process": ceremonial breakdown, displacement of one social organization for another, tension and anxiety, improvised solution ratified by improvised ceremony, ambiguity, and finally creativity in storytelling and making communal life.[46] Basile's seventeenth-century fairy tales similarly made their way to early modern France, Germany, and the contemporary world without a hint of their Neapolitan origins or context. Basile's court games and their function at court are part of a shared pan-Italian, pan-European court culture. As an aside, one should emphasize not the uniqueness of Naples but rather its centrality to European culture and society.

Basile's Neapolitan context further adds an important understanding of games at court. The leading figure in the most intellectual court and numerous academies in Naples, Giambattista della Porta, provides the key in one of his many scientific compendia, the *De Humana Physiognomia* of 1586.[47] Physiognomy uses the signs of the body to argue for the similarities between physical features and temperaments. The importance of laughter for deriving human comportment is further spelled out by another Neapolitan book, Prospero Aldorisio's *La Gelotoscopia* of 1611.[48] The shameless laugh, associated with the lungs and air expelled to form the verbal sound *a* and the refined laugh with the verbal sound *i* are examples of how externals reveal internals and how human features or comportment reveal hidden truths of customs and nature. At their most profound personal level, games can lead one to reveal oneself and even to know oneself.

Looking back at the rules of games played at court, then, we can see that games ruled because they set standards to measure one's actions and oneself. In other words, games governed with laws that bound society together. Further, games resolved the great predicament of Renaissance society—*fortuna* and *virtù*, human dignity yet human miseries, and worth versus birth. Games mediated these three disturbing contradictions, all permutations of the same underlying anxieties over hierarchy and equality. Such problems and debates were not just personal dilemmas but also broad-based societal concerns. Thus, at their most profound social level, games are rituals. They act as myths in action and as acted-out fairy tales would, with their own internal world of rules to provide the answers to resolve the indeterminate and ambiguous questions of self and society—even if only for the ephemeral, fleeting moment—by allowing its members to keep playing the game.

"Festa, riso, gioco, e gioia"

If we turn from the games chronicled in the tales told at court to the festivals celebrated in court, we find the same kind of underlying rules, structure, order, and hierarchy. Court festivities in 1620 exemplify how "celebration, laughter, play, and joy" reinforce the rules of the game.

On Quinquagesima (Carnival) Sunday, 1 March 1620, the viceregal court in Naples celebrated the return to health of their absentee king, Philip III. The forty-one-year-old king had fallen ill on his return in 1619 from a state visit to Lisbon, and "the present Feste in allegrezza of his recovery" was an added reason to make merry with special festivities at the end of the annual Carnival season. The multimedia spectacle, *Delizie di Posilipo Boscarecce e Maritime* (The Sylvan and Oceanic Delights of Posillipo) incorporated music, song, dance, stage decoration, and costume design in an elaborate *festa a ballo*. A festival book detailing the masque—texts with general information, lists of the principal artistic directors, names of the corps of twenty-four nobleman dancers, stage directions, and complete libretto; a musical section with the score, vocal, and instrumental pieces; and a dance section with diagrams of dance formations—has survived and a modern performance was recorded in 1988 by the New London Consort directed by Philip Pickett.[49]

The *festa a ballo* was a sixteenth- and seventeenth-century Italian court spectacle featuring the dance, similar to the French *ballet de cour* and the English masque. The Italian *festa a ballo* emphasized lavish visual scenery and costumes in support of its focus on dance; it differed from the contemporary developing genre of opera by the absence of dramatic continuity and vocal recitative.[50] Such court spectacles had three main elements: introductory musical numbers praising the reigning prince or patron and reflecting upon their connection to the present occasion or setting; the body of the entertainment by professional singers and dancers performing various loosely connected scenes; and a conclusion incorporating a great dance for the participating local aristocracy.

To give some idea of the scope of the original extravaganza, the modern recording employs six singers and forty-one musicians playing sixty-nine different instruments in a one-hour concert performance. One has to rely on one's imagination to visualize and hear the elaborate stage set (*l'inventione dell'apparato*)

> designed to reproduce the delightful mountain of Posillipo displaying with particular prominence the palace know as the Goletta, the residence of the said castellan in Posillipo, surrounded by its gardens, rocks, and grottoes. Behind and in front of it, is an enchanting sea-scape alive with darting fish, everything with the same beauty that can be enjoyed in Posillipo itself, with remarkable artifice just as in nature, and with a diversity of birdsong and the sweet sounds of instruments and of singing.[51]

On stage one would have seen the singers playing seventeen different parts: three nymphs and a shepherd appear on the threshold of the Goletta Palace in Posillipo; the goddesses Fortune, Time, Fame, and Envy enter in a boat; the three Sirens emerge respectively stage left and right from grottoes and center stage from the sea; the god Pan descends from the hills with three sylvan creatures (*silvani*), six satyrs (*selvaggi*), and six apes (*simie*); Venus rises from the sea in a shell drawn by eight swans with Cupid clasped in her arms. The six satyrs and six apes as well as the eight swans are all dancers, as are twenty-four knights wearing rustic, hunting costumes,

> all harmonious with swords lined with silver, embroidered in crimson and silver thread, and adorned with aquamarine stones which looked as if they were encrusted with jewels. They had small collars of gold plush simulating deer-skin, and beaver hats with thick gold cords, gems, and a quantity of plumes. They carried pistols at their sides, and the cut of the costume as a whole was suitable for country pursuits.[52]

Forty different instruments are scored for Pan's entrance piece and twenty-four musicians dressed as shepherds make up the string ensemble for the Dance of the Swans.

The original masque was performed in the Great Hall (Real Sala) of the viceregal palace in the presence of the soon-to-be-recalled viceroy Pedro Giron, Duke of Osuna, on the eve of his fall, with the replacement viceroy Cardinal Borgia arriving at the Castel Nuovo only three months later on 3 June 1620. The March masque's overall director was Alvaro di Mendozza, castellan of the Castel Nuovo and proprietor of the Goletta Palace. He participated in the noblemen ballet corps paired with his uncle Antonio di Mendozza, Count of Gambatesa, who was one of seven titled noblemen dancers. Stage sets were designed by Bartolomeo Cartaro, royal engineer of the kingdom's castles and son of the well-known royal engineer and cartographer of the kingdom, Mario Cartaro. Composing the songs were Giovanni Maria Trabaci, *maestro di cappella* to the viceroy; Francesco Lambardi, organist at the Royal Chapel; and Pietro Antonio Giramo, composer of the villanelle-like opening piece. Ballet music was composed by Giacomo Spiardo and Andrea Ansalone, from a family of local Neapolitan wind performers, with Spiardo also serving as choreographer. Such spectacle was exclusively by and for the court to celebrate the king's return to health and to praise his surrogate king, the viceroy Duke of Osuna.

The content of the script and the thrust of the libretto, not really a plot, thus bring together the Hispanofile nobility of Naples, the vice-king Osuna at the height of his power a few months before his recall to Spain, and all the elements of the myth of Naples from the river god Sebeto and the city's founding Sirens, the harmonious union of untamed nature's mountains, forests, and sea waves, to its fecundity and fortune under Spanish rule. Three nymphs and a shepherd greet the audience in the first song, a three-stanza *canzonetta* in which waves and mountains do not merely thrust aside worldly care, but are the embodiments of joy, as their charm and beauty go hand in hand with the creativity and fertility of the three Graces:

Festive, laughing, playing, and joyful	Festa, riso, gioco, e gioia
are these waves and this mountain.	Son quest'onde, a questo monte;
Everyone here has the Graces at hand;	Tutti han quì le Gratie pronte,
here is no sorrow, grief, or misfortune.	Nè v'è duol, mestitia, ò noia.
Here respounding from mountain to sea	Quì dal monte al mar sonoro
the birds make lasting song,	Fan gli augelli eterno canto,
to which at the same time dance	A cui van danzando intanto
the shadows, breezes, and sea among themselves.	L'ombre, e l'aure, e'l mar fra loro.
[All] delights and loves together	Le delizie, e in un gli Amori
have here their dear and joyful seats;	Seggi han quì giocondi, e cari;
here nature and heaven equally	Qui Natura, e'l Cielo al pari
have poured out all their treasures.	Versar tutti i lor tesori.[53]

Naples is invoked as the terrestrial paradise, an Arcadia with "no sorrow, grief, or misfortune," where "eternal song" and the dancing elements of light, wind, and water have established *seggi* (the same word as used for the city's ruling noble districts) of loves and delights to enjoy all of heaven and earth's treasures.

After the opening Song of the Nymphs and a Shepherd, a long discourse by Sebeto, a short Song of Fortune, Time, Fame, and Envy, and a Song of the Sirens provide dedicatory tribute to the viceroy Pedro Giron, Duke of Osuna, with fawning praise, mythical allusions, and punning on his family name Giron ("*giro*") as "circle" or "course." Sebeto, Naples's underground stream emptying into Lake Avernus at the entrance to the underworld identifies the mountain landscape as Atlas, with the viceroy as Hercules, bearing the weight of the sky, and his horse is Phoebus Apollo's winged Pegasus, whose flight carries him to Parnassus, where the Muses and the dulcet singing Sirens praise him. The stage's mythical landscape is really none other than the delights of Posillipo, which imprints its portrait on the surrounding waters "in perpetua primavera," as "a hospice of delights, beautiful mirror of Heaven, eternal garden of nature, paradise of joy, happy room of the Graces, pleasing seat of Love, *seggio* of the viceroy's empire, and temple of our Fame."[54] Sebeto continues lauding the viceroy, Famous and Heroic Prince, whose virtù from his face and strength from his beautiful eyes shine upon all the ladies present, while the singers and dancers perform in recompense for his esteem and affection. In praise of the healthy king, the Hispanic Jove, this Giron is a soaring eagle who can throw lightning bolts of wrath against enemies or spread his wings of security in most generous piety to friends, as he gives light to the sun in its great *giro*. Whence the mountains of Posillipo are warmed with the rays of immortal life by this Sun, who receives laurels and palms of victory as he is Phoebus who gives light and also Hercules who gives sustenance to his people. And so sing Fame, Time, Fortune, and Envy united together in chorus and individually in solo of Giron's subjugation of their powers which he does not fear. As twenty-four noblemen descend from the mountains, the dedications conclude with the Song of the three Sirens, the temptress founders of Naples, in praise of the Hero who is their lord—Sun, Neptune, Ulysses, Proteus, Phoebus Apollo, and Hercules.

Three more songs and four dances (song-dance, song-dance, dance, song-dance) make up the central action to underline the textual theme of unity, harmony, and health through love. The god Pan, accompanied by three wood nymphs, six apes, and six satyrs descends from the mountain, and twenty-four shepherds with string instruments enter from hidden grottoes, while Venus (with Cupid clasped in her arms) rises from the sea in a shell drawn by Swans. The Song of Venus is directed to the Ladies to delight in the Dance of the Swans, whose graceful circles (*giri*) explain the pride and glory in the ladies' eyes. The Song of Pan and the Wood Nymphs, the sole song in Spanish, follows with a refrain of the mountains singing the language of miracles and the surf singing the language of love, but inadequate to do justice in praise of the beauteous emeralds and pearls of the landscape of Pozzuoli, Baia, Ischia, and Cuma, for no language can match the visions of the Campi Flegrei. The Dance of the Satyrs and Apes is played by wind instruments with the dancers gesticulating according to their costumes in a "fantastic" (*stravagante*) dance. But then the two principal gods, the forest god Pan and the sea goddess Venus, dance together, joining the Sylvan and Oceanic delights, which is the highpoint of the feast "making it most worth seeing." In denouement, Cupid sings a short song to present the twenty-four noblemen—"merrymaking lovers [*amanti Festeggianti*], the sole foundation of his kingdom"—in a dance of artful formations to the Ladies. Love makes this world of sylvan and seaside folklore go round, a viceregal *giro* presided over by the city's mythic founders Sebeto and the Sirens to bring delight and pleasure to the Ladies and Gentlemen of court on this Sunday before Lent in thanksgiving for the new life given to their ailing, absentee king.

Coming on the last Sunday of Carnival, six months before the summer entertainments outside Naples at Posillipo, the 4 March 1620 celebration of Philip III's recovery from illness in the viceroy's palace suggests how much the end-of-Carnival feasting played upon the summer sights and sounds of sea and sylvan delights with the same kind of retreat and diversions reserved for the nobility's leisure flight there. In summer, the actual *spassi di Posillipo* replaced the palace stage sets with the real landscape. The setting itself, the Bay of Naples, stretched from the temple of Minerva on the Sorrentine Peninsula to the sepulcher of Misena, where Virgil's tomb was located at Cape Miseno, and was called in the Neapolitan dialect prose, the "Crater of the Siren," by Tommaso Costo's *Il Fuggilozio* in 1596 and almost ninety years later by Pompeo Sarnelli's "Scompetura de la Posilecheata overo festa de Posileco de li 26 de luglio1684" at the conclusion of his *Posilecheata*.[55] Posillipo, the most beautiful coastline along this "teacup" and sacred to the Siren Partenope, became the close-by destination in the heat of summer for the most beautiful Ladies and most noble Cavaliers to forget all the delights of Naples and to cover all past boredom with sweet oblivion.[56] As described by Sarnelli in 1684 and illustrated in an engraving published by Antonio Bulifon in 1685, here regattas of feluccas would meet for a great festival at the little harbor at Mergellina. Sarnelli recounts that, near the well-known palace of Donn'Anna, a golden triumphal carriage with four red wheels and pulled by two seemingly realistic sea horses bore the great silver, oyster-shell throne of Neptune and his wife. Triton, the Nereides, and other nymphs and water goddesses attended, playing and singing the most beautiful music. The seashore was lined with carriages filled with noblemen and women, who imbibed sweets and ices, songs and music, and the sights and sounds of the feast. All the houses and palaces of the Posillipo shore made a most beautiful theater with so many lights and bright torches "that the moon was ashamed to see its moonlight eclipsed by the earth's starlight"; and fireworks shot off fountains of flame everywhere to make one believe that another Vesuvius was born.[57] A year later, Bulifon's 1685 engraving identifies forty-four palaces of Neapolitan noble families along the Posillipo shore and depicts an artificial stage constructed on the water and surrounded by spectator boats and ships including twenty-three galleys watching a bull fight as part of the festivities celebrating the onomastico, St. Anne's day, 26 July, for the Queen of Spain.[58]

Royal Births: Spectacles of Fecundity and Succession

Similar festivities celebrated royal births three times during the reign of Philip IV. On the occasion of a royal birth in Spain—Balthasar Carlos (b. 17 October 1629), Maria Theresa (b. 20 September 1638), and Philip Prosper (b. 20 December 1657)—celebrations in Naples had both a public and private face. The public acts included lights and fireworks, cavalcades, singing of Te Deums, and the freeing of prisoners from the Vicaria jail. The viceroy orchestrated thanks for God's beneficence and responded in kind with his own largesse and patronage to the people of Naples. For the nobles, the celebrations went beyond festive exuberance and display in their cavalcades to concerted action in masques, formal balls, choreographed dances, comedies, tournaments, horse races, and jousts. Their play emphasized competition, whether of costume or skill, that was meant to reinforce solidarity as a ruling class loyal to the king, while asserting their individual differences in the hierarchical game of honor among themselves.

The celebration of the birth of Balthasar Carlos in 1629 fell under the aegis of the viceroy Fernando Afàn de Ribera, Duke of Alcalá. The viceroy manipulated the festivities for the birth of the Spanish infante to further his own family's dynastic pretensions by using the coincidence of the royal birth to co-celebrate the marriage festivities of his daughter to Luigi Guglielmo Moncada, Prince of Paternò from Sicily, firstborn son of Francesco Moncada, Duke of Moncada.[59] The festive ball in the viceroy's palace became a double cause for celebration; but when the viceroy placed his new son-in-law above the Seven Great Offices of the kingdom, the Chief Justice, the marchese di Fuscaldo was deeply insulted. Fuscaldo distanced himself from the viceroy, who had his revenge by confining Fuscaldo to his estates. The other noble *eletti* filed a notarial act of complaint to express their shared sense of dishonor, but they were constrained to participate in the ceremonies. The masked ball hosted thirty-six nobles in high fashion, including a costumed Neptune and Jupiter with the usual comedies following. Simone Vaaz, Count of Mola, one of the ten presidents of the Camera della Sommaria, financed the comedy, *La palabra cumplida, el amor mas que la sangre y la cara aventurosa*, and two of his sons were among the noblemen performing in it.[60] The celebrations ended with a noble tournament and a horse race.

For the nobles' entertainment celebrating the birth of the infanta Maria Theresa (the future first wife of Louis XIV in 1660), Antonio Bulifon's *Giornali di Napoli* records a celebration for her birth at the palace of the Duke of Gravina on Saturday, 5 November 1639.[61] That evening, "a celebrated company of Italian actors" performed a play, the *Rapimento d'Europa*, to the smiles and delight of the admiring audience, which also appreciated a masque by Andrea Cuccio, its author who played the part of Pulcinella. As part of the spectacle, a noble knightly ball included the finely costumed Ippolito di Costanzo of the *togati* dynasty, who later served as councilor on the Collateral Council (1645) and governor of the provinces of Terra d'Otranto (1645) and Calabria Ultra (1652).[62] A short time later, the Spanish viceroy, Ramiro Filippez de Guzmán, Duke of Medina de las Torres, hosted the play's performance at the viceroy's palace along with a masque danced by the vicereine Duchess Anna Carafa herself and twenty-three other distinguished ladies of court divided into four groups of six.[63]

The centerpiece of the 1639 court entertainment was the three-act *Rapimento d'Europa*, in which Pulcinella, the trickster of the Neapolitan *commedia dell'arte*, transformed into Jove. The usual three-act skeleton plots of the *commedia dell'arte* improvisational theater of Naples have been amplified in the 1639 festival book.[64] *Commedia dell'arte* plots typically satirized rivalries of marriage-family alliances versus romantic matches, old versus young lovers, or undesirable suitors versus the desired spouse. Pulcinella, the most popular mask of the Neapolitan tradition, was usually a stupid, good-natured simpleton who was one of the two servants moving the plot forward, variously aiding and subverting the resolution to the happy marriage. But here the protagonist god Jupiter is both the yearning lover, prancing and preening to have his way, and at the same time the object of scorn, ridiculed in all the jokes.

The subsequent metamorphoses of Jove into a dancing tiger, the seducing white bull, and eventually the imperial eagle (the totemic symbol of the House of Habsburg) that ravishes Europa also places the play in the genre of the *burla* (a practical joke or prank of slapstick humor, often cruel and painful), here "a pleasing subject of Love and an opportune stage for the ambiguity of appearances."[65] Jove is a *burlador* like Don Juan, whose well-known story, *El burlador de Sevilla y convidado de piedra*, as we have seen, had one of its earliest documented performances in 1625 in Naples. To think of Jove as Don Juan, whose first amour takes place in Naples at the opening of the Tirso de Molina play (act 1, scene 1), is to understand that the god of the heavens is someone whose sexual promiscuity makes and breaks fortune. He plays upon the Mediterranean values of honor and shame as he preys upon the objects of his desire and turns his sexual exploits into procreative acts of power and politics.[66] But rape and loss of honor are not without ambivalence, for there is always a loser for every winner; thus, the play alternates between rollicking ridicule and tear-jerking tension as it explores the multiple dimensions of the tragi-comedic myth.

The 1658 festival book for the birth of Philip IV's son, Philip Prosper, records a more extensive celebration that included all segments of the city population, high and low.[67] The *eletto del popolo*, for example, sponsored a masque with music and dancing. Noteworthy also in 1658 is the emphasis on the "infinite number of the *popolo*" that participated in what seemed to be their triumph over the 1656 plague and death.[68] The inclusion of the appointed head of the *popolo* quarter in the formal city celebrations and the emphasis on the return to normality in Naples after the devastating plague suggest a top-down attempt by the Spanish rulers to continue to control and co-opt *popolo* leaders.

In his description of the 1658 celebrations, Michele Rak follows the chronological organization of the festival book's thirty-six chapters to delineate twenty-four discrete "acts" in the celebration that he links to the twenty-four hours of the day.[69] The action moves from Te Deums at the viceroy's private chapel (the Capella Reale) to fireworks, floats, masques, and cavalcades through the streets to the city council's seat at the Church of San Lorenzo for Te Deums, on to freeing prisoners at the Vicaria and a march to the Piazza del Mercato for Te Deums at Santa Maria del Carmine, before returning to the viceroy's palace for private comedies, games, music, a bullfight in the Spanish style, masques, and tournaments. A tournament in the piazza of the viceroy's palace with a ceremonious entrance and circling of the temporary stage by four carriages in allegorical representation of the four continents (Europe, Africa, Asia, and America) encompassing Spanish imperial rule is described in twelve chapters, the culmination of the events and the book.[70] A number of the acts accommodated multiple activities so that Rak identifies a dozen kinds of celebrations in thirty-three "scenes." Ranked according to frequency, they suggest the ubiquity of certain actions throughout the festival and highlight the singular importance of others. Thus, six moments for dancing and diversion (*festino*) took place once the festivities returned to the privacy of the palace, while six masques and four fireworks displays punctuated the celebration throughout the day. Four times, floats (*carri*)—of musicians, of the flowers and fruits of Pomona in Abondanza, and of the four continents— paraded; three times Te Deums were sung; three plays were performed (two melodramas and a *comedia ridocola* in the genre of the *commedia dell'arte*); two cavalcades marched; and two tournaments were enacted. Only once were prisoners freed, a bullfight fought, and special games—a *festa a cavallo*, a *biscia con dardi*, and a *gioco dei caroselli*—played. The monumentality of the spectacle overwhelmed the audience with pomp and ostentation. Such noble entertainment by and for the lords and ladies of Naples and the viceroy's court put them all on stage as actors in the continuing drama of Spanish world-empire, with Naples as ancient Rome.

The structure of the celebrations can be divided into two phases aimed at two different audiences. Public festivities held outdoors for the people at large were similar to any major feast day. From the descriptions of 1629, 1639, and 1658, the public festivities included five celebratory actions in common:

1. Public offices and lawcourts were closed for three days.
2. Sound and light shows of cannon salutes, fireworks displays, and *luminaries* for three evenings made "Napoli la vera Città del Sole."[71]
3. Public Te Deums were sung by the kingdom's ministers and nobles in the Cappella Reale and the archbishop's cathedral and by the *popolo* in Piazza del Mercato and the Church of the Carmine.
4. A procession of the nobility cavalcading through the streets expressed the elite's congratulations to the royal family with extravagant expenditures in gratitude and vassalage to the delight of the city population.[72]
5. The viceroy released prisoners from the Vicaria jail.

In general, the people of Naples remained on the outside as spectators of pomp and circumstance, the recipients of charity and largesse, crowds to be awed by fireworks and fusillades. Private spectacles for the ruling elite, on the other hand, were held indoors in the noble courts of the palaces of the Neapolitan noble families and within the confines of the piazza, cortile, and halls of the viceroy's palace. The Neapolitan nobility and Spanish rulers in Naples experienced more complex and sustained entertainment—music and dance, masques and comedies, jousts and competitions—aimed at making them feel a part of the extended royal family and imperial rule.

Dancing, acting, and jousting should be understood as special kinds of court games that required both physical dexterity and strenuous practice. The goal was to appear natural (per the ideal of *sprezzatura*), while exerting oneself in athleticism or combat. Dancing, acting, and jousting, moreover, were contests that forced comparisons in the coordination or competition among dancers, actors, and combatants. The movements around the dance floor or the improvisational routines of this kind of comedic theater, like the armed battles of a joust, were uncertain; and this indeterminacy heightened the anxiety of expectation of the attending audience as much as the straining participants. In the *commedia dell'arte* tradition, for example, spontaneity and invention sparked crafted and signature comic routines (*lazzi*), both physical and verbal, and shone the spotlight on the creative challenges and dangerous improvisations of the actors.[73] Much more than the public parades through the streets for the crowds, the private entertainment for the nobles required a kind of concentration and exertion whereby the most insignificant error could lead to disaster or defeat. In making the performance, the nobles put all their skills to the test and their fortunes at risk. Such play was more than a court game for the celebration of a royal birth; it was an agonistic combat to maintain one's place at court.

This courtier high-wire act could not find a more perfect personification of the courtly ideal of dissimulation than Jove the *burlador*. Two years before Torquato Accetto's *Della dissimulazione onesta* was published in Naples in 1641 by the same Egidio Longo who had published the 1639 festival book,[74] the Neapolitan version of the myth of the Rape of Europa had raised questions central to the representation of reality and the limits of verisimilitude in fiction, as well as the role and place of dissimulating at court. But Jove's sexual *burla* was not honest dissimulation. Classical mythology reinforced the Mediterranean values of honor and shame, with power-broker patrons lording it over subservient vassals. Through his numerous disguises and identities from the trickster Pulcinella to the dancing tiger, the tame white bull, and the raping eagle, Jove exerted his superiority and authority over gods and men. As Lord of the Heavens, he reigned like the Planetary King, Philip IV, over a submissive, sublunary world, and the offspring of both god and king were born to rule heaven and earth in their name.

In 1639, on the very stage before the viceroy and his court where Jove himself is threatened with hanging, however, the noble god runs the gamut of emotions from fear to contrition to final vindication. Meanwhile, the audience rollicks in laughter as it identifies with the boisterous bravura, fawning flattery, humorous humiliation, and ecstatic exuberance of Jove. While the harsh gallows, symbol of the intransigence of Spanish rule, enforces discipline, the nobleman (like Jove), even caught in the act, will always find his way out of punishment. Instead of the gallows, he invokes the power of the native big man to be larger than the laws he makes and the rules he guards.

That paradox of good born out of evil is linked to the founding of the city of Naples by the Sirens in the ancient Greek past, centuries before Rome itself. It is this myth of Naples, with its wealth and abundance, its ancient founding, and its ambivalent nature that brings Europa, abducted and violated, back home as the fecund queen and mother of the god's sons, just as conquered Naples has become an indispensable cornerstone in Spain's imperial design, turned defeat into victory, and war (now in the midst of the Thirty Years' War) into hoped-for peace.

The End Game

With all the mythological images from Partenope and Sebeto to Jove and Europa floating about in festival garb, it would be easy to dismiss them as no more than disembodied spirits of no relevance other than the allegorical conventions of Baroque classical reference. If we are to take the religious spirits such as S. Gennaro and S. Giovanni seriously, however, we need to rethink the allusions and appearance of Naples's ancient mythical founders just as seriously. They were constantly represented in all the arts—word and music as much as statues and paintings—not only in ephemeral form on holidays but in marble and stone throughout the city. We have already seen the statue of Partenope dousing the flames of Vesuvius in front of the Church of S. Caterina Spinacorona between the Seggio di Portanova and the Seggio di Porto. Similarly, her gigantic presence could be found to the west of the Piazza del Mercato outside the main door to the Church of S. Eligio. There the head of a colossal marble statue said to be of Partenope and called the "capo-di-Napoli" stood on a pedestal with an inscription dated 1594.[75] Celano's editor Chiarini describes how the statue's nose had been defaced during the Spanish reprisals after the revolt of 1647, albeit a few years later restored with a "big false nose" (*nasone posticcio*). The restoration of the colossal Partenope's nose in the game of harsh rule's give-and-take may be a good way to summarize the nobility's way of playing the game. The Neapolitan nobility had tied its fate to the Spanish crown against the *popolo*, and nothing demonstrated the nobles' commitments on a daily basis more than their participation in the continual round of city myths and rituals.

The theory of games published by Tasso in "Il Gonzago secondo overo del giuoco" in 1582 helps explain the centrality of game playing in the court culture of the nobility that was shared as much in Naples as in Ferrara. Tasso found the origins of games among the ancients in funerary rituals that attempted "to temper sorrow with pleasure." Thus, in ancient Greece, "the Olympic games were made in honor of Jove by the death of Pelops; the Nemean games were sacred to Neptune for Archemorus; likewise the Isthmian games were consecrated because of Melicartes [Palaemon, whom the Romans called Portunus]; and the Pythian games to Apollo for the glory of the slain dragon."[76] The religious rituals commemorating the death of Philip II in obsequies found across the Spanish Empire and, as we have seen, in Naples in 1599 follow this same understanding of the purpose of public spectacle. The king's obsequies were grounded in religious ritual practice, as they reinforced the hierarchy established by patronage, but also created solidarity through leisure among the participants in the rituals. For Tasso, games alleviated the fatigue caused by the constant demands of the active and the contemplative life. They were a necessary relief or recreation, a *trattenimento* (an entertainment, diversion, or pastime).[77] This same word *trattenemiento* is used in Neapolitan by Basile for his tales, in the long tradition where literature itself is a game or pastime.[78] Most important, Tasso goes on to explain the goal of games is the pleasure derived from victory, which comes in their imitation or replication of reality under controlled conditions in order to test the gameplayer's skill. Caught in the predicament of the Renaissance, the tension between *fortuna* and *virtù*, courtiers played games to prepare themselves for action and decision making by showing how their skill could overcome luck. Even in games of chance, it is the skillful player who can make the most out of the circumstances; and this mastery of *fortuna* by *virtù* lies at the heart of the nobleman's ethic.

What is most striking about games at court and the rules of court society they enforce is that given such well-defined rules, games allowed players to be ambiguous. If we follow Brian Sutton-Smith's analysis of the diverse "rhetorics" of play with prominence given to the rhetoric of fate (chance vs. skill), power (equality vs. hierarchy), identity (self vs. society), and frivolity (foolishness vs. seriousness) in these premodern games, understanding games as a form of communication heightens the essential ambiguity in games themselves.[79] Like a language, games recreate a world of their own in the rarified culture of the court with the ambiguity of *sprezzatura* (in Castiglione's classic formulation, "that art is true art which does not seem to be art"), such that artifice masks and mimics nature so that seeming appears to be being. The plasticity of the players reflects the kind of oppositions and antitheses already emphasized in Caillois's study, with oscillation between poles of luck and learning, competition and cooperation, imitation and originality, safety and danger. The civilizing process of the court rewards the winners of games with wealth, glory, and power, while it challenges and threatens the central principle of noble identity that worth and birth are one. The mannered rituals of court, especially the staged celebrations in theater and dance, substitute playacting and practiced performance for authentic action and emotion, as the rules of the game allow the participants to lose themselves in perpetual play and alienate themselves from the wider world of truth and reality. It is a world where the court jester can be the most serious player and the wisest counselor, and where the wise counselor must often play the fool. The primary goal played for by the nobles at court rituals was to excel in rituals' performative medium and negotiations among themselves in order to increase their own status and power in the pecking order among their peers.[80]

CHAPTER FIVE

Allegrezza

The City Rules

Looking for the *Popolo*

In the procession on the vigil of St. John the Baptist's Day in Naples on 23 June 1629, the three bare-breasted, musical mermaid representations of the islands in the Bay of Naples (Capri playing a seven-string lute, Ischia playing a *lirone da gamba*, and Procida playing a *cornetto*) and the Siren founder of Naples (Partenope playing a *lira da braccio*) with a bramble-crowned male seated on the hills overlooking the sea (Posillipo holding a songbook and beating time) at the Rua Francesca–Rua Campana stop on the procession route were illustrated in Francesco Orilia's unusual festival book, *Lo Zodiaco, over, idea di perfettione di prencipi.*[1] Because of the 143 engravings and 72 emblems reproduced in this extraordinary tome, ephemeral art has been given continued life to explore the intersection of politics, society, and culture in Naples. These 1629 images of the goddesses of the Bay of Naples should make us pause as we explore the problem of the *popolo*'s participation and representation in rituals. Buxom beauties are not what one might expect to see in a religious procession to commemorate S. Giovanni, the precursor of Christ. Peter Burke has prepared us to see the ubiquitous presence of food, sex, and violence in the popular culture of Carnival and other early modern rituals, so we should not be surprised to recognize the syncretism of pagan and Christian rites and the conflation of religious, civic, and popular festivals in the celebration of St. John's Day at Naples. The festivities around the saint's day near the summer equinox made it much more than a religious event. Moreover, the particularity of Neapolitan religiosity and its unique approach to the sacred provide a window onto commoner involvement and reception of the ceremonial city. Because of the century-long rise and decline of the feast of S. Giovanni—which, although considered Naples's third most important festival after S. Gennaro and Corpus Christi around 1600,[2] had disappeared by the

1690s—we have a unique perspective on the festival's ideological intent together with its material practice over time.

In the local customs on St. John's vigil in Naples, three practices stand out as unusual yet long-lived ancient traditions. First was the betrothal rites for young Neapolitan maidens on 23–24 June in late medieval Naples, documented from a 1448 anecdote, which emphasized the customs and superstitions surrounding marriage. John the Baptist's condemnation of Herod's marriage made him a patron saint for securing a good marriage, and the Church of S. Giovanni a Mare provided a dozen dowries for poor young girls. The second practice involved the naked *il ballo di San Giovanni* (St. John's dance), which recalled Salome's dance for King Herod, and the bonfires along the shore during the night of the vigil, both of which attracted young Neapolitan women from their homes. The third was the Neapolitan custom of naked bathing of both males and females in the sea during the night of the St. John's vigil as a full immersion rebaptism in the Bay of Naples for the cure of spiritual and physical pains. Here the fertilizing power of water, the chief attribute associated with John the Baptist, was associated with his thaumaturgic patronage. The clergy did not participate in the St. John's Day rituals or march in the vigil's procession; and popular practices such as the naked "rebaptism" and naked St. John's dance with their biblical references to John the Baptist help explain the church's strong opposition to the peculiarities of the local celebration.

An unusual confluence of political crises and publishing crescendo during the second and third quarters of the seventeenth century has preserved fourteen detailed descriptions of the religio-civic feast of St. John the Baptist in the city of Naples that provide an exceptional portrait, beyond the ideology of the ruling elite and its public indoctrination on Spanish "good government," of the *popolo ottine* and their guilds in civic ritual.[3] During the early stages of the Thirty Years' War, Naples itself was buffeted by a series of destabilizing political changes at the head of state. On 4 June 1620 the Spanish viceroy Pedro Téllez Girón, the Duke of Osuna (r. 1616–20), who was accused of attempting to forge a special relationship with the Neapolitan *popolo* in order to create an independent state for himself, was recalled and dismissed. He was followed by two short-term caretaker viceroys: Cardinal Borgia (Gaspar de Borja y Velasco), who arrived from his post as ambassador to Rome on 3 June and returned to Rome six months later on 14 December 1620; and Cardinal Zapata (Antonio Zapata y Cisneros), who arrived at Pozzuoli on 10 November 1620 and entered Naples for his *possesso* over a month later on 16 December to carry out restructuring of a centralized administration totally dependent upon himself until his departure two years later on 26

December 1622. With the death of Philip III on 31 March 1621, the influence of the king's favorite, the Duke of Lerma, declined, and a consequent reshuffling of advisers and noble factions occurred with the ascent of Philip IV. The new viceroy, Antonio Álvarez de Toledo, Duke of Alba, arrived on 24 December 1622 to a future that was far from certain, but he ruled for six years eight months until his departure on 16 August 1629. The eight S. Giovanni festival books from 1623 to 1631 shed light on the stabilization of the festival under Alba's tenure in Naples during the 1620s; and coupled with Andrea Rubino's six detailed diary entries of the S. Giovanni procession between 1649 and 1668, we can see the disruption and reconfiguration of the practices and meaning of the feast during the difficult twenty years following the 1647 revolt of Naples and the horrific plague of 1656.[4] This unique information from fourteen celebrations of the feast in the mid-seventeenth century (eight before and six after the revolt) on the decoration of the parade route for the vigil of S. Giovanni in Naples allows us to analyze more than a snapshot of a one-time event.

The Trajectory of the Feast of San Giovanni in Naples

As political-religious events freighted with political and religious symbols and significance, the social and spatial context of rituals and their complex iconography connected the participants in a symbolic geography to particular places and a polemical history. The winning parties in the family rivalries of the city and the dynastic wars for the Kingdom of Naples from the end of the fifteenth century shared that history and shaped it. The Neapolitan feast that had been co-opted most directly to confirm Spanish viceregal rule was the feast of S. Giovanni. On the vigil of the feast (23 June), an elaborate procession led by the *eletto del popolo* wended its way through the streets of the densely populated working-class quarter of Naples rather than through the center of noble citizens' power in their *seggi*. These public manifestations and representations of Spanish government had an elaborate development and eventual decline over the two centuries of Spanish rule from about 1500 to 1700, as the ceremonies and decorations of Neapolitan civic life reflected changes in power relations and social structures, such that the celebration of the feast changed over three distinct periods.

The first period of the popular feast lasted from Angevin rule in the thirteenth century to the 1570s. The Church of S. Giovanni a Mare, the real center of the saint's cult in the heart of the *popolo* quarter close to the old shoreline, had been founded early in the reign of the Angevin kings of Naples, who had special devotion to John the Baptist and had brought a vial of his blood to Naples in 1282–85.

In 1522 the *popolo*'s participation in city government was confirmed and linked to the celebration of St. John's Day. The first mention of the viceroy in procession through the streets of the merchant fair that I have found dates to a chronicle of 1543 when Pedro de Toledo, the long-reigning viceroy (1532–53), accompanied a visiting Tunisian king during the feast.[5] This procession was not in the first year of the viceroy's reign, nor does it follow the processional route later identified. It does visit most of the same places but in a loop beginning at the *seggio* of Porto to Piazza del Mercato and ending at the Molo Grande.

The appropriation by the Spanish viceroys from 1581 to the revolt of 1647 defined the second period. In 1576 after a long decline to near extinction, the confraternity of the Compagnia della disciplina di S. Giovan Battista, which dated from around 1440 at the beginning of the Aragonese period, was able to reform and reconstitute itself so that it began to expand its spiritual and corporal works of mercy beyond its past activities and to reestablish its former leadership during the feast and procession. The confraternity's revival coincided with the blood reliquary's translation to the Church of S. Maria Donnarómita in 1577. Immediately in 1577 and again in 1580 and 1581, S. Giovanni's blood liquefied when put in contact with the reliquary of the saint's rib. The Spanish viceroys in Naples quickly recognized the importance of the liquefaction miracle and tied their rule to the saint's feast. During the late sixteenth century, they came to jointly lead the procession on the saint's vigil in order to demonstrate their solidarity with the *popolo*, with the earliest evidence of the connection with S. Giovanni's Day in the first year of the rule of the viceroy Duke of Osuna (1582–86) in 1583.[6]

From two festival books in 1613 and 1614 during the viceroyalty of Pedro Fernández de Castro, Count of Lemos (1610–16), participation of the viceroy in the feast of San Giovanni appears to have become an annual affair.[7] Lemos's successor, the Duke of Osuna (1616–20), marched in the St. John festival parade every year of his four-year tenure; and, as part of the reconciliation of the political crisis after Osuna's failed conspiracy and recall, the new viceroy, Antonio Álvarez de Toledo, the Duke of Alba (1622–29), confirmed the normalcy of a decade earlier before Osuna by continuing this annual participation in the festival's procession from his first June in Naples in 1623 to his last in 1629. Eight printed festival books have been preserved describing the religio-civic feast of St. John the Baptist in the city of Naples from 1623 to 1631, and they provide an exceptional portrait of the ideology of the ruling elite and its public indoctrination on Spanish "good government."[8] Giulio Cesare Capaccio, secretary of the city of Naples, published five descriptions of the procession on St. John's vigil, one for each year from 1623 through 1627;[9] Giovanni Bernardino Giuliani, secretary of the Neapolitan *seggio del popolo*, published descriptions for 1628 and 1631;[10] and Francesco Orilia published a book for 1629, in which he describes the procession of the viceroy as the movement of the sun through the celestial signs of the zodiac and the embodiment of princely virtues. The festival reached its zenith in 1629, as the Duke of Alba took his final bow as viceroy, having restored the rapport between the civic components of Naples. In fact, the best description of this period can be found in the foot-long, Baroque title of Orilia's 501-page book: "The Zodiac, or, the idea of the perfection of princes; modeled from the heroic virtue of the most illustrious and most excellent Signor Don Antonio Álvarez di Toledo, duke of Alba, viceroy of Naples; represented as in a triumph by the most faithful Neapolitan *popolo*; through the labors of dottore Francesco Antonio Scacciavento its *eletto*; in the great pomp and circumstance feast of St. John the Baptist, celebrated on the 23rd of June 1629 in the seventh year of his governance; recorded by Francesco Orilia."[11]

The third period is marked by the reconfiguration and suppression of the feast from the revolt of 1647 until the ritual's disappearance by 1690. With the mounting problems of war and taxes during the mid-seventeenth century, public rituals became a flash point for the Spanish viceregal government. In 1647 the viceroy suspended the S. Giovanni feast for fear of a popular uprising, only to have the revolt break out two weeks later on the Sunday feast of S. Maria della Grazia on 7 July when the young boys' *compagnia degli Alarbi* ("Arabs") had their rehearsal for their annual mock-battle between "Christians" and "Moors" in Piazza del Mercato on the following Sunday feast of the Virgin of the Carmine conflate with a dispute in the piazza's market over the new fruit tax.[12] In the following year, although the nine-month revolt had been resolved in April, two and one-half months later in June 1648 the feast of S. Giovanni was again canceled because of continuing fears of unrest. The unpublished diary of Andrea Rubino, a priest in the Theatine milieu, recorded a detailed account of the St. John procession six times in the difficult twenty years following the 1647 revolt—in 1649, 1650, and 1654 before the plague of 1656, and in 1660, 1665, and 1668 after.[13] With the harsh repression after the revolt of 1647 and the devastating plague of 1656 that reduced population to perhaps as few as 150,000 inhabitants, the feast's suppression by the end of the seventeenth century fits a pattern of post-Tridentine clerical and state collaboration to control and discipline popular ritual practices.

The Cult of San Giovanni in Naples

In Naples, the cult of St. John had long and deep roots back to the earliest public foundations of Christianity in the Roman Empire. Constantine the Great was traditionally credited with constructing the Baptistery of S. Giovanni in Fonte, the oldest baptistery in Western Christendom.[14] It was part of the archbishop's cathedral, S. Restituta, which was later rebuilt and incorporated into the present duomo constructed by the Angevins in the thirteenth century. Adult catechumens knelt in a circular pool at the center of a square room with their heads above water looking at mosaics of gospel stories and martyrs offering their crowns of glory to God and the initiates. St. John the Baptist was venerated as the regenerative prophet of a new era, both a new solar and an agricultural year. His ceremonies of purification and passage carried the bivalent meaning of death as rebirth and of commencement as a time of ending and beginning.[15] The cult of S. Giovanni and public baptism for the rebirth of the Neapolitan people as Christians reinforced the importance of the bishop's church located at the city-center crossing of the cardo and decumanus.

Constantine was also credited with founding one of the four principal parishes in Naples, S. Giovanni Maggiore, located just above the *seggio del Porto*, in order to fulfill a vow made in the midst of a storm at sea. Having transferred his throne to Constantinople in 330, the apocryphal tradition has it that Constantine wished to return to Rome with his daughter Costanza to pay respects to Pope Sylvester's successor, Julius I (elected 6 February 337). Threatened by a storm rounding the cape of Trapani, he promised a church dedicated to John the Baptist; his daughter, one to S. Lucia. Arriving safely in Naples, they refurbished the ancient temple of Partenope and rededicated it to S. Giovanni, with chapels to him and S. Lucia. With the transformation of the cult site of the mythological ancient Greek foundation of Naples through the sanctification of the Siren Partenope's temple as an early parish church, the emperor Constantine reconnected late imperial Naples to his new Greek capital in the eastern empire.

The summer solstice birth of the precursor of Christ, John the Baptist, associated the birth of the New Testament and end of the Old Testament with pre-Christian festivals and the solar-agrarian year. Midnight was especially sacred for its divination rites with omens, signs, and prodigious prophecies. Small bonfires were lit in the fields to combat the night, and fire was as purifying as water in the mythology of the feast.[16] Such burning fires connected restorative pastoral-agrarian harvest rites ensuring fertility and fecundity to Christianity's baptismal rebirth. In the city, fireworks extended the practice of bonfire illumination. The feast of S. Giovanni came to play a central role in the ritual life of Naples because of the way the rising star of Spanish government during the inaugural year of a viceroy's rule was made to coincide with the saint's holiday on its appropriated agrarian and astrological summer solstice festival.

The center of the saint's cult in medieval and early modern Naples was neither the baptistery nor the parish; rather, it had migrated to the Church of S. Giovanni a Mare, just to the west outside Piazza del Mercato beyond the Arco dell'orologio. It is next to the Church of S. Eligio, the first great Gothic structure built in Naples, which was founded by the Angevins in 1270. S. Giovanni a Mare likewise had been founded under the Angevins and had a vial of the saint's blood brought to Naples in 1282–85. The Knights of St. John of Jerusalem became custodians of the church in 1386, with a hospice for pilgrims to the Holy Land. In the 1580s, the church had five chapels and provided dowries for a dozen poor young girls under lay confraternity patronage.[17] Among the many confraternities including the Gesù, S. Maria del bisogno, S. Maria dell'advocata, and S. Barbara delli Bombardieri, the oldest of these confraternities was the Compagnia della disciplina di S. Giovan Battista, founded about 1440. The St. John the Baptist Confraternity's traditional activities included praying in the church on feast days, marching in the vigil's procession, and providing aid to the poor (burying the dead, caring for the sick and needy, and providing dowries for poor young girls). When revived after 1576, it began to expand its activities in concordance with the revitalization of the celebration of the feast.

Many other Neapolitan churches owned relics of St. John the Baptist and had special devotion to him. Reliquaries of S. Giovanni's blood were kept at the monasteries of S. Giovanni a Carbonara, S. Ligorio (S. Gregorio Armeno), and S. Maria Donnarómita; a piece of the saint's face was in the duomo; and a rib also at S. Maria Donnarómita.[18] Early modern Naples venerated the blood not only of S. Gennaro but of numerous other blood relics. In his chronicle of 1552–96, the Jesuit Giovan Francesco Araldo lists the blood of eight saints in Naples (S. Gennaro, St. John the Baptist, St. Stephen, St. Bartholomew, St. Lawrence, St. Francis of Assisi, S. Nicola di Tolentino, and S. Patrizia).[19] In 1577, upon the blood reliquary's translation to Donnarómita, and again in 1580 and 1581, the blood of S. Giovanni had "prodigious liquefactions."[20] Capaccio reports that every time the vial with S. Giovanni's blood at Donnarómita came into contact with the reliquary of the saint's rib, the blood would liquefy.[21] The liquefaction of blood had special veneration in Naples, where the spontaneous changing from solid to liquid state or the "manna" or sweat that would appear on statues and relics were signs of the transference of "vital force," that is, *grazie* or favors.[22] Saints bodies in life and after death were considered to have efficacious healing powers, and their blood was believed to be able to transmit grace and virtue, a symbolism that connected aristocratic values and noble blood to the religious fervor of saintly virtue.[23]

Numerous other churches and chapels in Naples and its environs were dedicated to S. Giovanni, not surprising in a city that counted some 643 churches, chapels, monasteries, and oratories in the early seventeenth century.[24] In addition to S. Giovanni Maggiore in the *seggio* of Porto, each of the *seggi* had a church dedicated to S. Giovanni. S. Giovanni a Carbonara was a reformed Augustinian church and monastery that was especially patronized by the Caracciolo del Sole clan and the nobility of the *seggio* of Capuana. S. Giovanni a Porta inside the S. Gennaro Gate was one of the twenty-two ancient parishes of the city and was patronized by the Carmignana clan and the nobility of the *seggio* of Montagna. S. Giovanni di Chiaia was patronized by the Carafa clan of the *seggio* of Nido but was replaced by the Jesuit Church of S. Giuseppe after 1623. S. Giovanni Battista in via Portanova was a chapel of the noble family of the Mocci. S. Giovanni dei Fiorentini near S. Pietro Martire toward the Porta della marina del vino (Porta del Caputo) was originally the seat of the Florentine mercantile community in Naples, before the merchants transferred their church in 1557 and renamed the former S. Vincenzo near S. Maria Incoronata and S. Giorgio dei Genovesi in the heavily fortified Spanish center between S. Giacomo and the Castel Nuovo. Outside of the city, S. Giovanni (all'Arenaccia) or capo di Napoli was a chapel on the road called S. Genarello, which used to be the sight of a procession for good weather; and S. Giovanni a Teduccio, the suburb just to the east along the bay, had its own traditions of elaborate fireworks and a big horse race.[25]

The feast of St. John the Baptist in Naples was played out over a few days in four kinds of activities. First, on the morning of the 23 June vigil of the saint's day, a merchant fair was set up in the popular quarter of the city along about a one-kilometer parade route from the Castel Nuovo to S. Giovanni a Mare. The procession kicked off the annual celebration that extended through an eight-day octave by the end of the fifteenth century. The viceroy and the *eletto del popolo* led a procession that wove through the streets and squares near the bay as they received and recognized the captains of the *popolo*'s twenty-nine *ottine* and the consuls of the various mercantile and artisanal guilds at stops along the way. In the first mention of the viceroy in procession through a merchant fair in the streets of the popular quarter, Pedro de Toledo marched with a visiting Tunisian king during the feast of S. Giovanni in 1543.[26] The procession followed an elliptical route from the viceroy's palace past the *seggio di Porto, seggio di Portanova*, Piazza della Sellaria, Piazza del Mercato, Church of S. Giovanni a Mare, Loggia dei Genovesi, strada degli Orefici, Church of S. Pietro Martire, strada dei Lanzieri, Piazza dell' Olmo, the Molo Grande, and Rua Catalana to return to the viceroy's palace. The earliest evidence of.the connection with S. Giovanni's Day in the first year of a new viceroy dates from 1583 according to the nobleman Ferrante Carafa for the viceroy Duke of Osuna (1582–86).[27] The revival of the procession and its regularization related directly to the reconstitution of the confraternity at S. Giovanni a Mare in 1576, the translation of the saint's blood to Donnarómita a year later in 1577, and its liquefaction immediately thereafter and again in 1580 and 1581.

Second, three petitionary activities of contract, contrition, and courting related to the life-giving waters associated with the Baptist took place late into the evening on the vigil of St. John's Day. As to contracts, S. Giovanni was the patron of marital unions for their hoped-for fertility, and his feast continued the ancient Roman tradition of blessing the fecundity of June weddings. St. John the Baptist as a patron of fertility extended from the countryside to the city and from agricultural crops to human reproduction. St. John's Day on the summer solstice connected June weddings in unbroken tradition from antiquity to the present and made the feast a wedding anniversary for all married couples. An anecdote from the reign of the Aragonese conqueror Alfonso the Magnanimous in 1448 tells the story of the king's encounter with Lucrezia d'Alagno.[28] Only five years after Alfonso of Aragón had conquered the Kingdom of Naples, an audacious young girl begging an offering stopped the king's royal train in the city streets. Alfonso gave this girl a purse, but she took only a penny and returned the rest. She explained that it was the custom for young Neapolitan girls to stop passersby for small coins and to collect grains of wheat in small vases on the vigil of S. Giovanni in order to read their wedding-day fortunes. The eighteen-year-old girl in the story was Lucrezia d'Alagno, a young noblewoman of the *seggio* of Nido, to whom the king became enamored and eventually made his royal mistress, mother of his future successor in Naples, Ferrante. King Alfonso's offering to the young Lucrezia d'Alagno is credited with initiating the decoration of the statue of St. John the Baptist with gold, silver, and precious stones as it was carried in procession from the Church of S. Giovanni a Mare to the Rua Francesca.

Later in the evening of the 23rd, contrition became the dominant motive of supplicants. Fire and water marked the celebrations as bonfires and fireworks lit the sky and reflected off the bay in a purification ritual that included full immersion in the sea by naked male and female petitioners and penitents seeking cure for physical ailments and forgiveness of sins.[29] The earliest contemporary testimony by the poet Velardinello from the years around 1500, with his fond memories of the happy singing of naked female bathers, is reaffirmed in 1535 by Benedetto di Falco's description of the bathing near the Church of S. Giovanni a Mare.[30] Giovan Battista Del Tufo's poem *Il nuotare de la notte di San Giovanni* in 1588 and Tommaso Costo's *Il Fuggilozio* in 1600 confirm this practice, and as late as the 1650s a decree of the viceroy Count of Castrillo (1653–59) forbade bathing at night.[31]

As the night wore on, music and dancing, especially the lewd, naked *il ballo di S. Giovanni* (St. John's dance), evocative of Salome's performance for King Herod, along with excessive eating and drinking continued in the streets and linked the naked "rebaptism" to the local betrothal and courting customs. The courting ritual of the dance was clearly related to the wedding-day fertility customs of the summer solstice and the Baptist's efficacious waters, and it was slow to be suppressed in Naples, despite the ban against public dancing in the city streets by the Council of Trent in 1564. The singing and naked dancing continued through the night, as best described in 1632 by the French visitor to Naples, Jean-Jacques Bouchard.[32] Hoped-for marriage gave rise to a raft of popular superstitions, portents, and prognostications on fortune and fertility.[33] It was believed that a young maiden's grains of wheat would help her find her mate; that a great trail of fire shot across the night sky, dragging Salome and her cruel mother, Herodias, whom John the Baptist had rebuked for her adulterous and incestuous marriage to Herod; and that if one dropped a lead ball in boiling water, the resultant new shape could be used to foretell the future.

Third, on the day of the feast, 24 June, elections of the officers of the city's most important charitable body, the Santissma Annunziata, took place, as well as the investiture of the newly appointed *eletto del popolo*. Both of these political ceremonies dated to the early years of Spanish rule and can be found in the municipal statutes of 1522.[34]

In the fourth and final activity, on the day after the feast, the temporary statues were brought inside the saint's church for the coming year to continue and to ensure S. Giovanni's intercession.

St. John's Day and its associated beliefs were by no means limited to Naples. As the precursor of Christ, the only human being in addition to Mary the Mother of Jesus whose birthday rather than death day is celebrated in the church calendar, S. Giovanni was the object of widespread devotion at the time of the summer solstice in Italy and throughout Christendom. In medieval and Renaissance Florence, the city of S. Giovanni, Florentines held an elaborate and well-documented festival that has been skillfully interpreted by Richard Trexler as it was celebrated after 1343.[35] In Florence, Trexler explains how the festival of St. John's Day became a feast day of contract and sacrifice of the commune rather than voluntary small parties, of civic groups over feudal interests, and of the guildsmen as members of the military companies of their wards rather than as workers. Thus, as private celebrations became public festival, the communal power clique of the greater guilds brought both the old nobility and the artisanal laborers into civic celebration. Trexler emphasizes six aspects of the St. John's Festival in Florence: "a day of the merchant" with "wealth iconized as an altar" of praise, thanksgiving, and petition; the "procession of purification" for the city's clergy; "a day of the citizen-soldier" for all male citizens fifteen to sixty-five; "a day of moral laymen" for lay confraternities; "a day of the commune" when governmental subjugation and dominion over conquered peoples were flaunted; and the end of all the waiting and preparation with its culmination in the main horse race of the Florentine year. Thus, St. John's Day in republican Florence crystallized the world as one of contract in all human relations, of competition that tested society's limits and provided outlets to release pent up tensions, and of celebration that widened the world of work.[36]

In monarchical Naples, the same six themes can be identified, but customs differed. In Naples, contract and compact still dominated for private parties, merchants, artisans, guilds, and marriage partners, and between government and *popolo*, with the viceroy and the *eletto del popolo* playing significant roles in the merchant fair procession. The clergy, however, was notably absent (having made its annual profession of fealty earlier in the year on the Saturday before the first Sunday of May on the feast of the translation of S. Gennaro), and purification was instead sought individually by nude bathers in the bay. The captains of the *popolo*'s *ottine* met the viceroy, but the citizens did not march together in their neighborhood military units as in Florence. Local confraternities were active in the feast and procession. Under Spanish rule in sixteenth- and seventeenth-century Naples, royal and viceregal victories and exploits were commemorated, and provincial subjugation often portrayed; however, the city was not the center of imperium but only one jewel in the Spanish crown. Finally, the horse race was not as significant.

Amid all the erudite inventions and political posturing that attempted to manipulate and direct the feast's rituals in Naples, the popular superstitions on fortune and fertility that we have already seen—belief in the collection of grains of wheat, the fire ball of Salome and Herodias shooting across the sky, and lead balls in boiling water—continued to multiply. Above all, Naples and southern Italy held special devotion in the liquefaction of the blood of the saints. Just as S. Gennaro's liquefied blood on his feast days brought good fortune to Naples, so too S. Giovanni's liquefied blood and the myriad festivities practiced on his feast pointed to both an individual's and the city's *fortuna*. Fires and fireworks were ubiquitous, marriage engagements and amorous games were part of the order of the day and the disorder of the night in the "St. John's dance," the sea flanking the cult church provided easy access for purification through full immersion "rebaptism," and a mock battle between Saracens and *lazzari* (similar to the children's and court game "Li forasciute") took place in the Piazza del Mercato in front of S. Maria del Carmine whose bell tower spewed fireworks throughout the night. This ritual battle was the same one performed by the "Arabs" festive society on the feast of the Carmine.

Such public festivities could easily turn from celebration and ritual conflict to real violence, which was well known to the authorities who made preparations against violence around the time of the feast of S. Giovanni in 1647 before the revolt. When violence did erupt on 7 July, "Captain" Masaniello led his boy soldiers of the "Arabs " company armed with reeds into the fray with a battle cry extolling joyfulness and celebration for deliverance: "Allegrezza cari Compagni, e Fratelli. Rendete a Dio gratie. Et alla Gloriosa Vergine del Carmine della già venuta hora del vostra riscatto."[37] As this account by Liponari continues, "the coming of your ransom or redemption [*riscatto*] " refers specifically to "slavery " under Spanish rule. For Masaniello was the new Moses to lead the *popolo* from pharonic tyranny. He was another fisherman like Peter whose voice had freed Rome and the world from the slavery of Satan to the liberty of Christ. *Allegrezza!* Rejoice!

Another kind of political conflict played itself out on St. John's vigil in 1668. Despite the fact that an overflow crowd of more than five thousand people from the city and its environs packed the procession route so full that many visitors had to be satisfied seeing the *apparati* only the day before on 22 June or up to even the 25th, two days after the vigil's procession, many titled grandees and nobles boycotted the S. Giovanni procession in protest against the *eletto del popolo* Francesco Troise and the viceroy Pietro Antonio d'Aragona (1666–72), because of a dispute over meat provisioning in Naples that had split the town council and effectively blocked all its business from the previous month of May. During the procession itself, a large part of the cavalcade led by the viceroy's carriage, the royal trumpeters, and his German guards turned off the customary parade route near the beginning of the march at the strada dei Lanzieri to avoid the *popolo apparati* in the Loggia dei Genovesi and the Piazza della Sellaria. Instead, the rump procession marched directly to the end of the route at S. Giovanni a Mare, which the *popolo* interpreted, according to Fuidoro, as an act of disrespect for the *eletto* Troise.[38] Fuidoro never again records the procession, and the feast itself not again until 1671, when only the vigil's evening fireworks are noted without mentioning, as does an anonymous chronicler, that the celebration on the 24th took place in the safer confines of the Spanish-controlled city center at S. Giovanni dei Fioren-tini instead of S. Giovanni a Mare.[39]

Although the parish priest Carlo Celano's famous 1692 guidebook on Naples reports that the feast of S. Giovanni had become extinct some fifty years earlier because of its superstitious practices,[40] the real decline in the popular festival can be dated to the late 1660s. Fuidoro's description of the conflict in the city council over meat provisioning resulting in the division of the procession in 1668, and the feast's absence in his chronicle until the fireworks on the vigil three years later in 1671, albeit without De Blasé's reference of the change of venue to S. Giovanni dei Fiorentini, is clear evidence of how the feast was discon-nected from its local and unbridled Neapolitan *popolo* traditions. By redirecting the festival to a safer Florentine foreign merchants' holiday celebration in the heavily Spanish-garrisoned quarter near the Genoese national church S. Giorgio dei Genovesi, the feast of S. Giovanni became more controllable. Confuorto's chronicle confirms this change by continuing to indicate the election of the SS. Annunciata officers on 24 June through the 1680s and 1690s, but without men-tion of the procession and merchant fair on the 23rd.[41] When the movable feast of Corpus Christi interfered with St. John's Day—both feasts fell on the same day in 1666, and the octave of Corpus Christi fell on the 24 June feast day in 1661 and 1672—the calendar itself furthered the assimilation of the feast of S. Gio-vanni into the more acceptable Eucharistic holiday under clerical control.[42] Thus, formal patronage of the feast by the local clergy and the viceregal government eroded in the 1660s with the confluence of a number of festering causes: the con-tinued pressure from the post-Tridentine Church against the feast's oft criticized paganlike customs, the harsh repression of Spanish rule after the 1647 revolt of Naples that was ever wary of *popolo* power and crowds, the demographic decima-tion and sharp economic depression in the *popolo*'s mercantile and artisanal base after the 60 percent mortality of the 1656 plague, the gradual decline of Spanish fortunes after the 1659 Treaty of the Pyrenees, and the regency for the four-year old Charles II after the death of his father Philip IV in 1665. Finally, because the S. Giovanni vigil procession was so identified as the feast of the *eletto del popolo*'s accession, the immediate cause for its disappearance seems to have been the divi-sions and rivalries in city government that pitted the nobility against the viceroy, the old nobility of the three *seggi* of Capuana, Nido, and Montagna against the newer *seggi* of Porto and Portanova, and, above all, the nobility against the *eletto del popolo*, all of which came to a head in the vigil procession of 1668.

The Structure and Decorations of the Procession, 1623–1631

On the vigil of St. John's Day, some twenty identifiable city sites and their respective guild inhabitants marked the procession's itinerary through a mercantile bazaar of stalls and shops to the center of the saint's cult at S. Giovanni a Mare. As in most medieval and early modern cities, guildsmen and their trades along with foreign merchants were localized in specific geographic areas of the city and gave their names to particular squares and streets.[43] The number of guilds in working-class Naples was distributed as follows: Textiles and Clothing, 30 percent; Foodstuffs, 26 percent; Iron and Metal Workers, 20.4 percent; Liberal Arts, 14 percent; Carpenters, 3.6 percent; Housing and Construction, 3 percent; and others, 3 percent.[44] According to the 1606 census, the twelve *ottine* on the parade route numbered 64,567 *anime* (25 percent of the city population) from 10,030 *fuochi* (a density of 6.4 persons per hearth) and, together with the adjacent *ottina* of Mercato (which included the suburban *borgo* of S. Maria del Loreto), counted a total of 94,205 *anime* (36 percent of the city population) and 14,495 *fuochi* (a density of 6.5 persons per hearth).[45] In Naples, this *popolo* district occupied a low-lying area near the port and along the sea toward the southeast city walls, below the foundation of the ancient Greek town, which sloped up from the sea plain to higher ground. The parade on St. John's vigil joined the city's governing elite—the Spanish viceroy and the native Neapolitan nobility—in procession with the city council representative of the popular urban classes in procession through this densely populated working-class quarter between the old noble *seggi* and the shore.

By 1614 the viceroy and *eletto del popolo* led the procession every year, and its route through the *popolo* quarter had stabilized, with the only alteration in 1627 to accommodate the increasing need for space for the *apparati* of the wealthy silversmiths, goldsmiths, and jewelers (fig. 5.1). The viceroy, the vicereine in her carriage, and their cavalcade escort paraded out of the viceroy's palace on horseback and proceeded up the Via Toledo to Via S. Giacomo where they turned right along the notable monuments of the Spanish presence in the city, the jail of Santiago and the Church of S. Maria di Monserrato, to head down toward the Castel Nuovo. In the first of twenty stops, the *eletto del popolo* and his entourage met the viceroy and his party east of the Castel Nuovo at Guardiola, where the guard post of Spanish soldiers was maintained, in what is today Piazza del Municipio. In 1629 Orilia records that the *eletto* and captains of the *ottine* presented the viceroy with a floral bouquet, and "two consuls of the baker's guild walking beside his horse threw bread to the crowd with generous liberality from two large containers full of the whitest bread."[46] The procession moved through Piazza dell'Olmo into the heart of the city's dense *popolo* neighborhoods, where the *eletto* would stop to present each *ottina* captain to the viceroy. Capaccio's description of the 1626 procession gave the names of the *eletto del popolo* and ten *ottina* captains.[47]

The procession continued with stops at an additional eighteen stations to lay down a *popolo* itinerary that recognized the artisanal guilds in their workplace, before concluding at the twentieth. The full itinerary is as follows:

1. Guardiola, as noted above, east of Castel Nuovo
2. The corner of Rua Catalana, home of the hatters and shoemakers
3. The Dogana (or Customhouse), seat of the sword makers and cotton merchants
4. The fountain of Piazza di Porto, site of the button makers, those who turned animal guts into strings for musical instruments, and the fruit vendors
5. The Piazza di Maio, center of small-time vendors who serviced the nearby port
6. The street of the Lanzieri, center of rich wool and silk merchants whose brocades, gold-stitched silks, braids, and high-quality woolens were known on the international market
7. The Dominican Church of S. Pietro Martire, home to the wealthy silk merchants such as the silk stocking and fancy dress shirt manufacturers
8. Piazza Larga, the seat of the hatters
9. The street of the Orefici, the silversmiths, goldsmiths, and jewelers (whence, before 1627, the procession would proceed directly to the Spetiaria antica)
10. The wide Loggia dei Genovesi, site of a variety of activities from spice dealers, carpenters, cabinetmakers, woodworkers of all kinds, and food shops (where in 1627, because of the wealth of display of the Orefici, this wider and better venue for their valuable goods and elaborate statues was moved up in the order of the march from its previous position after the Armieri)
11. The fountain of the Pietra del Pesce, the city's wholesale fish market
12. The Spetiaria antica, center of the tailors, cloth merchants, spices, and drugs[48]
13. The street of the Gipponari, the tailors who made the *gipon* or waist vest
14. Next, a turn up into the Rua Francesca, the wool mattress merchants

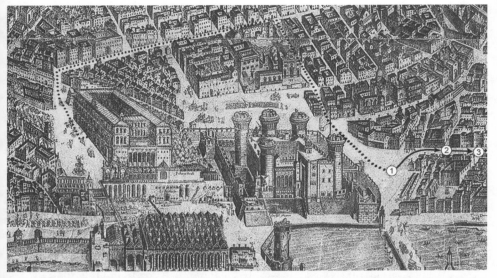

1 Piazza dell'Olmo	11 Fountain of the Pietra del Pesce
2 Rua Catalana	12 Spetiaria antica
3 Dogana	13 Street of the Gipponari
4 Fountain of Piazza di Porto	14 Rua Francesca
5 Piazza di Maio	15 Rua Campana
6 Street of the Lanzieri	16-17 Piazza della Sellaria
7 S. Pietro Martire	18 Street of the Armieri
8 Piazza Larga	19 Porta del Caputo
9 Orefici	20 Church of S. Giovanni a Mare
10 Loggia dei Genovesi	

Figure 5.1. Map of procession route for St. John the Baptist's Vigil on Baratta map.
© Archivio dell'Arte / Luciano Pedicini, Naples.

15. The Rua Campana, the copper, bronze, and other metal workers
16. A turn left into the Piazza della Sellaria, the wide and long political, institutional, and economic center of the *popolo* quarter
17. A departure from the Piazza della Sellaria
18. A turn left again that circles back along the street of the Armieri, where tailors were giving way to the silk drapers and where previously armorers had worked and given their name to the street in the Middle Ages (and where, before 1627, the Loggia dei Genovesi and the fountain of the Pietra del Pesce followed)
19. Arrival at the Porta del Caputo, the leatherworkers
20. Finally, a stop at the Church of S. Giovanni a Mare, before the procession returned, as it came, through the strada dei Lanzieri and Via dell'Olmo

The political trajectory for the feast of S. Giovanni grew out of proportion in the decade beginning with its celebration in the first year of the viceroyalty of the Duke of Alba in 1623 and culminating in the sumptuous ostentation of the 1629 procession and Orilia's commemoration of this farewell tribute to the departing viceroy, who had received news at the beginning of that year of his replacement viceroy. Orilia describes the 1629 festivities in twelve stages, with brief ceremonies of the gift giving of flowers, candies, and sweets at triumphal arches flanked by statues representing the virtues of good government and associated with one of the twelve signs of the zodiac at each of twelve stops along the way. Although the difficulties of Alba's successor, Fernando Afàn de Ribera, the Duke of Alcalá, which cut short his tenure to only two years (17 August 1629 to 9 May 1631), precluded a dedicatory book in 1630 for the lone St. John's Day of his viceroyalty,[49] the next viceroy, Manuel de Zuñiga y Fonseca, Count of Monterrey (1631–37), saw two books published for S. Giovanni during his first year in office in 1631.[50] The *popolo* secretary Giuliani again described the procession through the merchant fair, once again emphasizing abundance and plenty as well as Spanish good government and its virtues. The eight statues in the Sellaria proclaim the message in the personification of eight virtues—Religion, Justice, Providence, Magnanimity, Fortezza, Prudence, Magnificence, and Affability. And the representation of this last statue, Affability, with a lyre in her right arm and a cornucopia in her left, pulled together the two themes of joyful celebration and prosperity under Spanish rule as a consequence of the moral life of virtue. Pedro Martinez de Herrera, a Carmelite theologian, on the other hand, does not follow the vigil's procession; rather, its posted epigrams and mottoes provide the point of departure for a twenty-one-question Latin disquisition into the principles for princely rule.

The virtues—clemency, justice, wisdom, friendship, prudence, resolution, providence, liberality, modesty, nobility and integrity, honor and mercy—punctuate
this "mirror for princes" political treatise.

Unique in this extant literature is Orilia's treatise on "the idea of the perfection
of princes," not for its theme or descriptive content, but for its extensive engravings and its zodiacal organizing principle. Dozens of engravings fill Orilia's Baroque panoply of visual and verbal ephemeral decorations that include portraits
of twelve of the viceroy's distinguished ancestors in the Toledo clan, six judicial
figures from the Neapolitan courts, five offices in the Neapolitan bureaucracy,
ten offices in the viceroy's household, the seven high offices of the Kingdom
of Naples, six of Naples's patron saints including S. Gennaro and the five city
protectors newly elevated during Alba's viceroyalty,[51] allegorical figures of seven
Neapolitan island deities, the kingdom's twelve provinces, thirteen rivers, eight
sciences, and three statues of fame. A statue of Felicity at the sign of Cancer (the
sign of the zodiac governing the date of the saint's feast) overlooked the meeting
of the viceroy and *eletto del popolo* at the procession's first stop, Guardiola. Just as
the zodiac is a belt of stars within 9 degrees of the apparent path of the sun's orbit
above the earth, so too the processional route followed the zodiac's annual progression at each of its successive stops. The sun's guiding light shone the virtues
of "good government" upon the viceroy, who, in turn, bestowed them upon the
people. Thus, the thirty-six images of the twelve arches, twelve virtues, and twelve
portraits of the viceroy announce each of the twelve stops and signs of the zodiac
dividing the road of march. Orilia informs his readers that the association of the
twelve signs of the zodiac with "the twelve principal virtues," which "established
the idea of the feast and of the *apparati*," was derived from the *Civitate Cristi* by
Joannes Genesius Quaja of Parma (d. 1398) published in Reggio nell'Emilia in
1501.[52] Just as Quaja's book explicates Revelation 21 on the Heavenly City of the
New Jerusalem and specifies the names of its twelve gates and their twelve foundation stones, their associated twelve apostles, twelve directions, and twelve virtues,[53] so too in Orilia's zodiacal mirror for princes, the twelve astrological signs
are connected to the twelve virtues inscribed in the streets and piazza beginning
with the feast of St. John the Baptist and its summer sign of Cancer to specify
the requisite princely virtues of Felicity, Fortezza, Justice, Clemency, Prudence,
Wisdom, Pietas, Temperance, Concord and Zeal for Peace, Beneficence, Magnanimity, and Vigilance.

In the Duke of Alba's six previous years in office, in fact, six shorter books
published in Naples make it clear that the astral references that framed the 1629
festival were not unique. In the heart of the *popolo* district in the Piazza della

Sellaria near the seat of the *seggio del popolo* at the Church of S. Agostino, for example, a temporary stage in 1624 displayed eight statues in honor of the viceroy's ancestor, the 3rd Duke of Alba, Fernando Álvarez de Toledo (1507–82), whose renowned military exploits for Charles V and Philip II helped consolidate the Spanish Empire. Thus, statues of four of the provinces he commanded were linked with the four cardinal or moral virtues, with each standing under the influence of one of the planets—namely, Mercury reigned over Spain and Prudence, the Sun over Africa and Temperance, Mars over Germany and Fortitude, Venus over Italy and Justice.[54] And, of course, the Duke of Alba's name (a homonym for "dawn") is invoked in every one of the seven St. John the Baptist processions of his viceroyalty for having brought a new dawn to Spanish Naples with his arrival as viceroy on 24 December 1622.

What the audience of the 1623 to 1631 St. John's processions would have seen, according to the full iconographic descriptions provided by the city secretary Capaccio and the *popolo* secretary Giuliani, as well as by Orilia, differed each year (table 5.1). Nevertheless, some general composite profile can be created and the ephemeral *apparati* imagined from this ekphrasis and the engravings included in Orilia's tome.

First, triumphal arches, often *apparati* or machinery for fireworks, were ubiquitous. The arches were described according to the classical orders and the number of portals. Two arches were most important: the arch at the center of the *popolo* quarter in the Piazza della Sellaria, which was recycled from the feast of Corpus Christi and served as a fireworks *apparato*, and the comestible arch of ham, salami, and cheese at the end of the procession route at the Porta del Caputo. The arch of food and its adjacent fountain of wine were gifts to the *popolo* that made real all the propagandistic claims of *abbondanza*. Fireworks burst not only from the Sellaria arch of the Blessed Sacrament but also from mountains of plenty and pastoral landscapes, ships, dragons, and elm trees at the dogana, from pyramids, towers, and columns at the Piazza di Maio (both near the beginning of the procession), and from mechanical fish midway at the fish market Fontana della Pietra del Pesce.

Second, statues of the virtues—especially the four moral virtues of Justice, Temperance, Fortitude, and Prudence—connected abundance and good government through princely, viceregal virtue. Felicity, represented at the Guardiola starting point in 1623, 1624, and 1629, held in her arms the scepter of good government and a cornucopia of *abbondanza*, while her feet had stopped the wheel of Fortune, which had a stake through its hub.

Third, innumerable images of the viceroy Duke of Alba, his vicereine, the viceroy's ancestors and house of Toledo, their coat of arms, symbols of the sun or dawn, and the Spanish monarchs from Philip IV back to Charles V all emphasized the presence of the king in his absence. Through the surrogate vice-king, who was even presented in allegorical guise riding Pegasus above the Kingdom of Naples as one entered the Piazza della Sellaria in 1629, Neapolitan rulers would vanquish their enemies not unlike Bellerophon slayed the Chimera or perhaps even successfully guide the flying horse to the stars' end.[55]

Fourth, S. Giovanni is represented in painting, statuary, or even a *tableau vivant*.[56] An image of the Beheading of St. John the Baptist was displayed at the Fontana della Piazza di Porto, near the beginning of the parade route, in all five of Capaccio's books, 1623 to 1627. In Orilia's 1629 description, however, the decollation comes at the end of the march as the last image in the procession, where we see the fructifying blood of the saint spilled as salvific precursor and intercessor, whereas at the first stop of Guardiola is the birth of the Baptist. Capaccio's description of the 1626 procession reproduces an image of the birth of the Baptist in its preface, and his 1623 and 1624 books present a third image of St. John the Baptist in the desert as a frontispiece. Such images of S. Giovanni were common in Naples, with 148 paintings of ten different S. Giovanni scenes recorded in the death inventories of Neapolitan collectors from 1600 to 1780.[57]

Fifth, two of the competing guild displays were high points of every year's procession. In the first display, the jewelers, goldsmiths, and silversmiths at the Orefici stop expanded into the larger space of the Loggia dei Genovesi after 1627. In 1623 Capaccio described statues of Salus Publica (the goddess of Public Welfare), the viceroy, the three Graces, and Clemency; in 1624, fourteen statues including the two Muses Poinnia and Calliope, Fortuna, Partenope, Felicità, and Salute; and in 1626, Magnanimity, Partenope, and Prudence. In 1627 Capaccio praised the artists by name and claims that three statues of the Orefici exceeded one another in unbelievable values—a statue of the province of Navarre worth 600,000 to 700,000 ducats, a large globe worth 1 million ducats, and a statue of Hilarity (the richest of all) worth 1.5 million—when in 1626 total government income was 4.6 million ducats and the viceroy's annual stipend was 10,000 ducats.[58] In 1629 Orilia published engravings of the three gem-studded representations of Fame (Celebrity, Glory, and Eternity), and Orefici statues are constantly praised as outstripping the wealth and riches of Oriental India from Goa to Bengal. The second display, the real centerpiece of the parade route, however, came at the *seggio del popolo*'s political seat of the Piazza della Sellaria, where a stage set with eight statues would be constructed, resembling the statues of four provinces and four virtues already mentioned for 1624. In 1623 the eight statues represented

TABLE 5.1.
S. Giovanni *apparati*, 1623–1631

Procession Stops	Capaccio 1623	Capaccio 1624	Capaccio 1625	Capaccio 1626	Capaccio 1627	Giuliani 1628	Orilia 1629	Giuliani 1631
Guardiola	Aurora, Felicity	Felicity, Salute	Mars, Spain, Neptune	Immortality, Letitia	Viceroy, Sole, Pegasus	4 virtues, Ceres, Flora	St. John, Nativity, viceroy, Felicity, 12 Toledo clan ancestors	Mountain, Abundance
Rua Catalana	Justice	Neptune, Ceres, Partenope	Ship, elm tree	Viceroy, Hercules, Cerberus		Ship, elm tree		
Dogana	Ship			Ship, elm tree	Viceroy, arms			
Fontana di Porto	Mountain, Herodias	Nereid, St. John beheaded	St. John beheaded	St. John beheaded	St. John beheaded			St. John
Maio	Pyramid	Tower		Hydra, viceroy	Pyramid	Painting, fireworks		Viceroy, vicereine
Lanzieri	Sebeto, Siren, king & queen	Philip IV, eagle	Philip IV, queen, viceroy, 2 mountains	King & queen, arms of king, viceroy	Viceroy, vicereine	King & queen	Viceroy, Fortitude, 8 soldiers of different nationalities	*Apparati*, Sebeto, Partenope
San Pietro Martire	Partenope	Viceroy	Philip IV, queen	Pax, Abundance, Felicity, king & queen	Arch, Philip IV queen, viceroy	Justice, San Gennaro	Viceroy, Justice, 12 provinces of kingdom	Arch
Piazza Larga		Atlas	Viceroy	*Porta*, king & queen, viceroy; Peace	Philip IV, queen	Viceroy	Viceroy, Clemency, 6 judges	Viceroy, arms
Orefici	Salus Publica, viceroy, 3 graces, Clemency	2 Muses, 4 virtues, *apparati*			Philip IV, queen, St. John		Viceroy, Prudence, 5 magistrates	Arch, Ceres

Loggia dei Genovesi	To Armieri	After Fontana	After Fontana statues, imprese	Magnanimity, Partenope, Prudence	St. John, Navarra, Globe, Hilarity	Viceroy	Viceroy, Wisdom, 8 sciences, 3 statues of Fame	King, viceroy, vicereine, 2 mountains
Fontana della Pietra del Pesce	After Loggia	To Armieri, swordfish	To Armieri	After Armieri, fish	Justice	Shepherds, Eternity		
Spetiaria Antica	Philip IV	Philip III	Viceroy	King, viceroy	Rhetoric, King, viceroy	Mountain	Viceroy, Piety, 6 patron saints	
Gipponari	Siren, Spanish soldier	Arch, ship, Golden Fleece	*Imprese*	Silks, *imprese*	*Porta*, heaven		Viceroy, Temperance, 10 household offices	
Rua Francesca		Arch, altar	Fountain, Orpheus	*Porta*, viceroy	*Porta*, viceroy, pastoral		Viceroy, Concord, 7 places in Bay of Naples	Mountain
Rua Campana				Triton, 3 Sirens	Ceres		Partenope	
Pendino-Sellaria	8 Toledo members, Fame, Corpus Christi Arch, Siren, Felicity	Ibero Sebeto, 4 Spanish kingdoms, 4 virtues, Corpus Christi Arch, Partenope	3 Sirens, Faith, 4 Nymphs, 4 Neapolitan poets, Corpus Christi Arch, Argo	*Porta*, 6 gods, Zephyr, Corpus Christi Arch, 4 *apparati*	Neapolitan *popolo*, 8 Neapolitan provinces, *apparati*, Corpus Christi Arch, Partenope, Mercury	Viceroy, Bellerophon, 8 virtues, Corpus Christi Arch, Castle	Pegasus, St. John, viceroy, Beneficence, 13 rivers of kingdom	Glory, 8 virtues
Armieri	Barrel of sweets	city gate	Viceroy	Philip IV, 2 of viceroy	Viceroy, heaven		Viceroy, Magnanimity, 7 Great Offices	
Porta del Caputo	Food arch, wine font	Food	Food, wine font	*Apparati*, silks	Food	Food, wine	Viceroy, Vigilance, 6 seggi eletti	Food arch
S. Giovanni a Mare							St. John beheaded	Mountain, Charles V

Note: No festival was held in 1630.

members of viceroy Toledo's House; in 1625, four Neapolitan nymphs and four Neapolitan poets, as well as the three Sirens; in 1626, six maritime deities ex- ited the sea to praise the virtues; in 1627, the eight provinces of the Kingdom of Naples; and in 1628, the four moral virtues and four other virtues. In 1629 the number increased to thirteen statues of the principal rivers of the kingdom "in order to render sumptuous the triumph of Beneficence."[59] The river Sebeto, which runs underground through the city of Naples and is the origin or source of all earthly life as it feeds into Lake Avernus, the entrance to the underworld, is of special importance and appears almost every year. Similarly, Partenope, the founding Siren of Naples, might sound her string and sing her song "to invite the *popolo* to *allegrezza*," as Capaccio records for 1627.[60]

The Feast of St. John's Day after the Revolt of 1647

The three post-revolt and three post-plague St. John the Baptist processions re- corded by Rubino confirm that both the earlier themes of peace and prosperity and the same figures (religious, mythological, and political) continued to be cen- tral to the words and images of the merchant-fair decorations (table 5.2). Rubino, as in the 1620s books, emphasizes the precious cloths of silk, taffeta, and damask used for backdrops and canopies, which created an artificial sky over the streets and piazze. One new food item, macaroni, makes its way into the dreams of abundance, while in 1665 and 1668 the procession through the merchant fair began to make extended stops for plays or dramatic readings whose texts Ru- bino transcribes in great detail: five "Triumphs" in 1665 (for Neptune, Partenope, Ceres, Flora, and Pomona); and four plays in 1668 (*Gli Horti Esperidi*, *Il Monte Parnaso*, *The Triumph of Ceres*, and *Le Sireni baccanti*).[61] These are all plays prais- ing fertility and abundance, as nature's bounty reflects upon human creativity, beauty, and happiness in the paradisal garden of Naples. Portraits of the king and queen, viceroys and vicereines continued to preside over the invocation of S. Giovanni's blessing for the beginning of the year and for the favors of good harvest, good fortune, and godly virtue personified by the mythical Sirens and local Neapolitan deities.

Worth noting is the extraordinary list of ninety-six virtues identified as indi- vidual statues in the Largo del Castello staging-ground for the S. Giovanni pro- cession in 1668 (table 5.3). This extraordinary gallery of ninety-six statues would have been a dense forest of stone. One can imagine a formidable block of images if arranged eight by twelve. This concentration of virtues goes well beyond the usual incarnation of topoi, such as the theological virtues, the moral virtues, or even the thirty-five virtues on the frescoed ceiling in the refectory of S. Lorenzo Maggiore where the Neapolitan parliament used to meet. This virtuous contingent of ninety-six statues stood as a visual reminder of the spiritual goals of the S. Giovanni feast that had been pushed aside for its many other valences. But the statues' silent witnessing was a sign of the more aggressive plan of clerical control being launched to reform the excesses of the celebrations. More somber processions and more sober religiosity were becoming more diffused across early modern Catholicism in the seventeenth century. After the Council of Trent and its reaffirmation of the doctrine of the Eucharist, Corpus Christi took on added significance; and in late seventeenth-century Naples, after the movable feast of Corpus Christi fell on the same day as S. Giovanni in 1666, the clergy used the procession of Corpus Christi through the *popolo* quarter to assimilate the saint's feast and eliminate the vestigial pagan practices of S. Giovanni's Day.[62]

The feast of S. Giovanni in early modern Naples was enacted in a Baroque political lexicon of ephemeral structures, images, words, and music as an amalgam of religious and secular celebrations (the saint's protection, the merchant fair, and the procession), of pagan and superstitious practices (fireworks and bonfires, naked immersions in the sea, music and wild dancing), and of charitable and political office (election to the SS. Annunciata and *popolo* representative) that the Spanish viceroyalty appropriated as the paramount political ritual pledging felicity and fidelity between monarchy and *popolo*. The multiplicity of media in reinforcing registers created a harmony of these diverse interests but did not drown out their often discordant and conflicting agendas. The merchant fair, for example, was as much a display of thanks to St. John for his patronage in achieving success as it was a competition among the various guilds in their respective streets and piazze neighborhoods to impress the eyes and gain the ear of the viceroy over their rivals. Children, the most innocent of all, were manipulated as props to dress as angels or ancient gods and goddesses; to sing hymns and madrigals in praise of St. John, the Spanish monarchy, the viceroy, and *popolo* officials; and to hark their audience back to the mythical Greek founders of Neapolis (New City), who were lured there by the sirens' song even before the founding of Rome, and also forward to the messianic future promised by S. Giovanni in baptism. A beneficent and vigilant monarchy and its minister presided over the measured *allegria* of a golden age as it attempted to rewrite time and space from above—whether through the mythological lore of classical erudition, the obscure language of emblematic invention, the mannered poetry of *marinismo* conceits, and the conspicuous display of bourgeois pretension. The Baroque splendor of a feast like S. Giovanni in Naples, propped up and patronized as it was by its Span-

TABLE 5.2.
S. Giovanni *apparati*, after the revolt and the plague

Stops	1649	1650	1654	1660	1665	1668
Reggio Palazzo		Amore, Fideltà	*Porta*, drapery			
Strada Toledo	*Imprese*, viceroy, drapery	Drapery	Drapery		Arch, St. John, Music	
Trabaccari/Guardiola	Drapery, *imprese*	Drapery, *imprese*	Drapery	Arch, arms, Sebeto, Abundance		
Largo del Castello/ Olmo	Forest scene	Forest scene	Forest scene	King & queen, viceroy, *imprese*	Arms of king, viceroy, & Popolo, *imprese*	King, 96 statues of virtues
Strada di Porto	*Imprese*, fireworks	Drapery	Drapery, forest	Forest, *apparati*	Triumph of Neptune	*"Gli Horti Esperidi"*
Maio di Porto				Salami, cheese	Salami, cheese	Salami, cheese
Lanzieri	Fountain, arms of viceroy	Drapery, king & queen	Drapery	St. John, viceroy	Triumph of Partenope	Atlas & 4 parts of world
San Pietro Martire	Drapery	Drapery	Drapery	Drapery	Arms of king, Prince of Spain	King
Piazza Larga	Drapery	Drapery	Drapery	*Apparati*	Triumph of 3 Graces	Mount Parnassus
Orefice	3 statues in jewels	Cupid, Fame, Siren	Cupid, Fame, Siren	Fortuna, Peace	Minerva, Abundance, Prudence	6 statues

	Seafood to be sacked	Seafood to be sacked	Seafood to be sacked	Seafood to be sacked	Seafood to be sacked	Seafood to be sacked
Fontana della Pietra del Pesce	Seafood to be sacked	Seafood to be sacked	Seafood to be sacked	Seafood to be sacked	Seafood to be sacked	Seafood to be sacked
Armieri	Drapery	Drapery	Drapery	Arms	Arms	Arms
Spetiaria Antica	Drapery	Drapery		King, drapery	Drapery	Drapery
Gipponari	Drapery	Drapery	Drapery	Drapery	Drapery	Drapery
Rua Francesca	Macaroni	—	Nymphs, shepherds	Forest scene	Forest scene	Forest scene
Rua Campana				Macaroni	Macaroni	Macaroni
Pendino-Sellaria	Catafalque, *apparati*	Catafalque, *apparati*	Catafalque, *apparati*	Food, wine, Partenope, War/Peace	Food, wine, Triumph of Ceres	Luogo di Cuccagna, food, wine
Strada delli Scoppettieri	Forest scene	Forest scene	Forest scene	Forest scene	Forest scene	Forest scene
Porta del Caputo	Salami, cheese, *taralli*	Salami, cheese, *taralli*	Salami, cheese, *taralli*	Salami, cheese, *taralli*	Salami, cheese, *taralli*	Salami, cheese, *taralli*
Marina del Vino	Drapery, jewelry, food, viceroy symbols, forest scene	Amore, Fideltà	Zodiac, Seasons	Hill with Temple of Honor, 4 warriors dressed as 4 parts of world, Fame	Triumph of Flora	Triumph of Ceres
S. Giovanni a Mare				Peace over Tempest	Triumph of Pomona	Dance of satyrs and monkeys

TABLE 5.3.
The Ninety-six Virtues Represented in Statues at S. Giovanni's Feast in 1668

Curiosità	Fama chiara	Castore	Sincerità
Capriccio	Vigilanza	Abondanza	Augurio
Clio	Zelo	Concordia maritale	Speranza
Melpomene	Valore	Cerere	Concordia
Terpsicore	Fermezza	Amicitia	Nobiltà
Urania	Gloria	Chiarezza	Benignità
Euterpe	Istinto naturale	Eloquenza	Verità
Calliope	Liberalità	Inclinatione	Unione
Talia	Clemenza	Industria	Giove
Polinnia	Temperanza	Docilità	Zefiro
Erato	Inventione	Puntualità	Pace
Primavera	Attione virtuosa	Giuditia	Sicurezza
Estate	Remuneratione	Cortesia	Giustitia
Autunno	Senno	Esperienza	Perfettione
Fortezza	Splendor del nome	Gratitudine	Prudenza
Imitatione	Generosità	Esercitio	Ossequio
Costanza	Esculapio	Tempo	Confidenza
Buon essempio	Discretione	Umiltà	Temperanza
Decoro	Bontà	Compassione	Merito
Virtù	Sollecitudine	Lega	Stratagema militare
Ardire	Stabilità	Ragion di stato	Unione
Hospitalità	Nettuno	Vittoria	Eternità
Sapienza	Armonia	Dominio	Consiglio
Pietà	Lode	Diligenza	Fortuna

Source: Rubino, "Notitia," BSNSP, ms. XXIII.D.17, Festa di S. Giovanni Battista, 131–61. Note that Temperanza and Unione are listed twice.

ish lords, could not but ossify as such support wavered and such power waned with Spanish rule in defensive disarray and with a clerical offensive to regain control of excessive popular religiosity in full force in the last third of the seventeenth century confirmed by making S. Giovanni a city patron in 1695.

The Iconography of St. John's Day in Naples

To understand the iconography of St. John's Day in Naples, we should first remember that the art, literature, emblems, and ceremonies were intended for multiple audiences—both those present at the feast and those who could return to it in the words and images of printed books. The hierarchical patron-client networks began with the spiritual audience of the saint himself, who was praised, thanked, and petitioned. The political patrons invoked for the same purposes were the king together with his surrogate king, the viceroy, and their respective houses. Government officials in Naples were next in line as officers in the various councils or in the bureaucratic arms of the state machinery, as part of the viceroy's household, as judges and lawyers serving in the judicial system, and as members of the learned professions who might act as intermediaries between the people and the viceregal administration. *Popolo* officials, the *eletto*, the captains of the twenty-nine *ottine*, and the consuls of the numerous guilds would greet and make offerings to the viceroy for the artisan and merchant guildsmen and the people as a whole. Last and least were the lowly plebs, who were unincorporated and considered to be outside of the working-class members of urban society. For every group, the feast was above all a time of *allegrezza* or joyful celebration that reinforced their differentiation one from another and their articulation one with another.

Spiritual meanings grounded in biblical stories and their allegorical interpretation formed the bedrock upon which the feast was built. As the precursor of Christ, S. Giovanni prepared the way for the true Messiah just as the viceroy stood for the true king and the feast near the summer solstice pointed to the coming harvest. S. Giovanni's baptisms by water in the New Testament continued their purification power on his day in the Bay of Naples, and his prophecy of baptism by the Holy Spirit and fire was reenacted in countless St. John's fires and fireworks. St. John the Baptist's foretelling of Jesus as the Messiah extended to the prognostications of his feast day, his pronouncements against Herod and Herodias on the sanctity of marriage made him beloved of prospective brides, and his martyred blood fructified the barren earth just as his liquefied blood ensured the fruitfulness of Naples. Processions through the *popolo* quarter on Corpus Christi and St. John's vigil used the same triumphal arch in the Piazza della Sellaria. In 1629 a statue of S. Giovanni crowned this fireworks-machine arch borrowed from Corpus Domini, and it stood on a central pedestal above two friezes of Old Testament *figurae*—one of Moses delivering the Ten Commandments, the other of David singing and playing the harp before the Ark of the Covenant. The feast of S. Giovanni verified the fulfillment of the covenant between God and his Chosen People from Moses to David to John the Baptist to Christ, and it confirmed all new contracts with the same divine solemnity.

For the church and its ritual practices, the New Testament provided a direct link between John the Baptist and the celebration of the Eucharist. In the traditional Latin Mass of the Tridentine rite, after the Agnus Dei and the priest's communion, the priest turns toward the congregation with a ciborium of consecrated hosts in his hands; and, holding up one host in his consecrated fingers, he repeats three times, "Ecce Agnus Dei, ecce qui tollit peccata mundi."[63] These are the exact words of the Vulgate in John 1:29 when John the Baptist identified Jesus as "God's Chosen One" for whom he had borne witness and the reason why he had come, baptizing in water. In the mass, then, the congregation responds three times, "Domine, non sum dignus," and the priest distributes Holy Communion to the faithful. Every mass—defined by Trent as a sacrifice and sacrament—relied on the words of John the Baptist to acknowledge the miracle of the Incarnation, the central mystery of Christianity, that the Church affirmed not only happened once in historical time but was continually repeated at the consecration during every mass.

The biblical coming of the Messiah and the keeping of God's promise joined with the mythological founding of the city of Naples and its promised fertility. From the siren song of its founding goddess Partenope to the waters of its underground river of origin, the Sebeto, personifications of Naples's singing siren and sacred stream became commonplaces of the myth of Naples as the golden age.[64] Statues of Partenope and Sebeto in the strada dei Lanzieri in 1623 and 1631, or individually in every other year's displays in the 1620s, linked Naples to the goddesses of the golden age, Astrea and Virgo, to the winged-horse Pegasus and the discovery of the sweet inspirational spring of the Muses, and to Annona and Abbondanza, who, along with Ceres, brought the bounty of Naples. The myth engendered desire and nostalgia, for the Siren expressed the attraction that Naples holds over visitors who come near her shores and the longing that those far away feel pulling them back.

The mythology of the Sun and the Dawn with the golden age merged into the astrological underpinning of the reign of Philip IV, the "Planetary" King. Calderón de la Barca's *La Vida es sueño* of 1635 may be the most famous work that trumpeted the prophecies swirling around the king's birth in 1604.[65] The 1605 solar eclipse in Scorpio, the 1604 nova in the constellation of Ophiuchus, and the 1603 Jupiter-Saturn conjunction in Sagittarius presaged the heaven-sent ruler whose birth corresponded to the 33 C.E. death of Christ. Good rulership depended on such propitious horoscopes, and many ancient writers had connected the virtues with the signs of the zodiac such that Leo was identified with fortitude, Virgo with justice, and Sagittarius with wisdom. A dynasty's destiny was prophesized in the stars, and rulers vied for the best prognosticators.[66] Common folk, not only kings and courts, followed the stars, as a 1515 note by Gerard Listrius in Erasmus's *Praise of Folly* made clear that popular preachers might link the signs of the zodiac with the theory of bodily humors to explain why the Lenten fast began in Aries, the first sign of the zodiac.[67] Similarly, it would have been common knowledge that the sign of S. Giovanni's birth was Cancer, the Crab, a water sign, and also the "Gate of Men," that is, the gateway for the descent of souls from the heavens into human bodies and back again.

Birth and rebirth of the seasons with the fruits of abundance, as much as the birth and rebirth in baptismal waters and purification fires, connect John the Baptist with the promise of renewal and return of the heavens and the earth. The four elements reinforce a natural and a supernatural history whose promise is fulfilled with the coming feast. S. Giovanni's prophecy marks the end of the cycle of eternal return and announces the end of time itself.

The human body in both its spiritual attributes or virtues and its physical properties or senses is the steering metaphor throughout the S. Giovanni celebrations. In the displays of the merchant fair, the five senses are bombarded with the sights of art and architecture, the sounds of choirs and musicians, the smells of flowers and perfumes, the tastes of candies and sweets, and the touch of silks and satins, all of which are meant to lead to an experiential way of knowing the truths beyond the senses. The human body and the body politic speak the same language and share the same principles of good government through the moral and other virtues. Their goal, which is achieved in the enthusiasm of the festival, is the breaking of fortune's bonds, transcending the limits of the body in the earthly city, and literally making time stop. This fusing of time and space is achieved in the Heavenly City, and the golden age is inscribed in the streets, portrayed in the painting, sculptural, and architectural *apparati*, and flung to the sky in exploding bursts of light and color. Such *allegrezza* is the true happiness of paradise in the New Jerusalem found in Baroque Naples under Spanish rule.

Neapolitan Carnival and Forty Hours' Devotion

Laura Barletta, the leading expert on Neapolitan Carnival during the early modern period,[68] proposes the Italian South as a good model to explain the effect of modernization and secularization upon the daily sense of the sacred in a pluralistic society open to people and influences near and far. Her thesis emphasizes the unresolved tension between the attempted social control of popular practices and their unstoppable spontaneity, ambiguity, and creativity. In a nuanced, interdisciplinary approach, Barletta explores the boundaries between history, sociology, anthropology, and psychology to reveal the rich, often contradictory social and human realities in southern Italian formal and popular religion and culture. Barletta's polar opposition "between regulation and license" traces the complex, long-term decline of religious authority over the beliefs and practices of the common people and their growing alienation from the church after the Tridentine reform. For Barletta, the long-term trajectory of Carnival in Naples shows the co-option of popular celebration by elite civil and clerical powers in the early modern period and the eventual exhaustion of any authentic popular participation with the democratization of middle-class society after Italian Unification in the nineteenth century. From the city's central ceremonial place, the large open square in front of the royal palace (Largo di Palazzo) and the Via Toledo, the Neapolitan Carnival in the seventeenth and eighteenth centuries articulated a polyvalent communication system that crossed social barriers, rural/urban divisions, and native/foreigner distinctions. Neapolitan Carnival gave expression to societal sentiments, desires, and tendencies as it reasserted state power, promoted assent, allowed for dissent, and dissipated in the tension of contested power from the church, whose fragmented power-base was weakened by discordant and competing demands from the numerous churches, oratories, convents, hospitals, chapels, and religious houses in the old city.

Sixteenth-century records on Carnival are fragmentary and provide information only on noble participation and celebration. Seventeenth-century diaries and chronicles, on the other hand, provide a wealth of information on both noble and *popolo* Carnival practices. As in the 1620 celebration for Philip III's return to health, the birth of Philip IV's son Prospero in 1658, and the 1666 marriage of Emperor Leopold I to Margherita Maria Teresa, commemoration of royal life-cycle events could be co-joined to Carnival, as could, on the other hand, cancellation of Carnival festivities altogether in 1655 with the mourning of the death of Pope Innocent X and in 1666 on the death of Philip IV. Carnival celebrations were organized systematically with the *seggi* deputies in charge of the procession, masquerade, and games; the guilds each decorated a float of their own; and the *eletto del popolo* oversaw the free distribution of food.[69] "The frenzy of the plebs on the three last days of Carnival were full of excess in every city quarter such that they could not be controlled by the police," as in February 1675 when five or six homicides were reported.[70] Andrea Rubino's diary details Carnival celebrations for thirteen years between 1653 to 1669, with a typical entry from 2 February 1653 describing how "a band of a hundred masked revelers dressed as women, men, clowns, and demons with some dancing, some playing instruments, and others almost like bacchants raged about the city."[71] Fishermen, greengrocers, poultry sellers, tavern keepers (all the lower guilds) marched in cohorts, and Carnival maskers dressed and roamed the streets as witches, madmen, gypsies, lions, Sirens, rivers, Moors, black Ethiopians, old men and old women, the planets, gods and goddesses, gentlemen, and knights. Carriages and floats, riders on horse and men on foot pushed through the streets and crushed into the Fosse del grano, the Largo di Palazzo, the Via Toledo with typical Carnival license.

The civil and religious authorities attempted to counter the Carnival chaos and confusion with the establishment of the Forty Hours' Devotion (La Festa delle

Quarantore) in the sixteenth century. The practice of exposing the Blessed Sacrament for public view on a church altar seems to have been developed in Milan
and was fostered in Rome by Philip Neri and Ignatius Loyola by midcentury. The
earliest record of the Forty Hours' Devotion in the Kingdom of Naples dates from
1568 near Salerno at Cava dei Tirreni and followed soon afterward outside Naples
in 1569 at Nola, with the first explicit reference to it in Naples in 1588.[72] In 1592
Clement VIII issued the constitution *Graves et diuturnae*, which gave the devotion
its penitential focus and fixed its celebration on the last Sunday of Carnival; and
in 1623 Urban VIII issued the encyclical *Aeternus rerum*, which expanded its wor-
ship to the worldwide church. In addition to its role as an antidote to Carnival and
preparation for Lent, the devotion was also practiced in supplication and penance
at the time of war, economic crisis, the health of the king, plague, and natural
disasters such as floods, earthquakes, and eruptions of Vesuvius. The devotion's
central action consisted of a procession of the Blessed Sacrament to a church's
high altar for exposition, where it remained for forty hours before being returned
to its normal tabernacle with a closing ceremony and procession. The devotion
highlighted continuous prayer during its exposition and special indulgences for
those participating in the ceremonies. The devotion could be extended in circular fashion by rotating the sacramental exposition to one church after another
in succession. The Forty Hours' Devotion is closely related to the celebration of
Corpus Christi in which the viceroy always participated, and it reflects the heightened emphasis on Eucharistic devotion in response to the Protestant Reformation movements. Along with the usual sacred ornaments, music, cavalcades, and
fireworks, the devotion was accompanied by cannon salutes from Naples's three
castles and especially the display of innumerable lighted candles. The victory of
light over darkness symbolized the victory over sin with the perpetual exposition
of the Real Presence.

That visible exposition of the sacrament on the main altar inside churches
made its way into the streets during these regular processions but would also be
brought out precipitously into the streets in an attempt to quell rioting crowds
during the 1585 Starace riot and the early days of the revolt of 1647. The repetition of the Quarantore devotion as a regular response to Carnival and automatic
public spectacle at the time of crises routinized the presence of the Eucharist in
popular consciousness as a tool of supplication to God; but its ineffectiveness
as a form of pacification in 1585 and 1647 demonstrates that normal religious
devotion could not appease rioters in moments of extreme crowd anger and violence. The exposition of the Eucharist was a weapon of the weak in supplicating
God but could not be turned against the weak as a weapon of social control. The

language of the crowd makes it clear that its protest was not directed against God or the king; in both instances in 1585 and 1647, its complaint was against "bad government" and the king's ministers, with the common refrain "Viva il Re di Spagna e mora il mal governo."[73] Thus, for the *popolo*, God was on the people's side and the presence of the Eucharist in the streets was not a weapon to be used against them but a sign of God's standing with them against those who were exploiting them.

The Funeral of Masaniello

The spontaneity and creativity of popular devotion, which appropriated the form and content of religious and civic rituals, can best be seen in the unusual funeral afforded Masaniello after he was already dead, decapitated, and his head and body discarded and dispersed. The juxtaposition between Masaniello's madness, murder, and (what Musi coins) the "rites of degradation" on Tuesday 16 July 1647, the tenth day of the revolt, with the exhumation of Masaniello's body, the pomp and circumstance of the elaborate popular funeral cum state ritual, and the martyred hero's apotheosis on the very next day, Wednesday, 17 July, heightens the contrasts and contradictions between high and low culture in the mixed metaphors and blurred categories that make up "the history, myth, legend, divine authority, and earthly authority" invoked in the telling of the ten-day story of Masaniello.[74] The movement of the story of Masaniello from hero to villain and martyr to saint is plotted as a drama in its retelling. The narrative traces his rise from fishmonger to military commander and his fall from the insanity of power and responsibility to assassination, from the relief of the people over deliverance from a madman decapitated and dishonored to the rehabilitated holy body of a martyr, saint, and prophet in a triumphant apotheosis. Fuidoro's single sentence summarizing Masaniello's funeral cortege—"The funeral was conducted as if it were to honor the corpse of the killed first dictator Julius Caesar"—captures the ambiguity and ambivalence of the obsequies in a metaphor reincarnating great Caesar's ghost and the long-standing debate over his identity as patriot or traitor, republican or dictator, martyred savior or justly executed tyrant.[75]

Donzelli gives the fullest account of the spontaneous funeral ceremonies for Masaniello with the narrative structure and emotive tone of a formal civic obsequy.[76] After the body was recovered and washed "diligently" in the Sebeto, the bier was filled with many candles and carried afterward, "accompanied by a great quantity of the *popolo* armed, who impetuously went to the Fosse del grano," where his head had been displayed on a stake. Sewing the head back on the body, they returned to the Church of the Carmine "as in procession . . . impassioned with a sadness mixed with anger" and bystanders along the way were already calling for prayers to "beato Masaniello."

The cardinal-archbishop, who had earlier licensed the exhumation, "ordered upon the insistence of the *popolo* that all the salaried priests subject to his jurisdiction, under penalty of six *scudi*, were to go two hours before sunset with wax candles to assist at the obsequies." Some four hundred priests arrived at the Church of the Carmine, and they were joined by one hundred orphan boys from the Conservatory of Santa Maria di Loreto. Masaniello's body was covered with a white silk sheet so that his head could be seen; his right hand held a sword, and his left hand held the staff of the Captain General del Popolo.

The funeral procession left the Carmine for the street of the Lavinaio and the Piazza della Sellaria to the sound of muffled martial drums, "conforming to the custom in funeral rites for a Captain General" with the priests, orphan boys, many companies of soldiers of the *popolo*, swelled by the squads of armed soldiers posted in each piazza as they passed—to some forty thousand—and followed by four thousand women carrying candles, sobbing, and chanting the rosary for the deceased. The funeral ceremonies took the traditional triumphal route with the cortege marching in front of the Vicaria, *seggio di Capuana*, the Duomo, S. Lorenzo, the *seggio* di Montagna, S. Domenico, the *seggio* di Nido, along the decumanus inferior to the Via Toledo, Largo del Castello, the *seggio* di Porto, the *seggio* di Portanova, and the Sellaria, before returning to S. Maria del Carmine. The cortege then proceeded slowly to the Royal Palace, with mourners singing the litany of the saints and church bells pealing as the cortege passed along the way. At the Royal Palace, ringed with lit torches, the viceroy was filled with disdain but simulated his grief for the crowd in viewing the body. He ordered eight pages to carry the bier and the Spanish soldiers to lower their banners and arms before the coffin in performance of all ceremonies customary for an honored war hero. The funeral procession went on to the Castel Nuovo, past the palace of the Corriere Maggiore, Piazza dell'Olmo, Piazza del Porto, strada dei Lanzieri, *seggio* di Porto, *seggio* di Portanova, the Selleria and Pendino, strada della Campana, Rua Francesca, la Conciaria, and Piazza del Mercato, where they arrived about three hours after sunset to return the body to the Church of the Carmine for solemn burial.

The most significant detail of the obsequies was the fact that the corpse held sword and staff in hand in the rites afforded to Masaniello as the Captain General of the *popolo* militia. Shouts went out from the crowds, "Sancte Mas'anelle, Ora pro nobis"[77] and "Viva Masaniello."[78] Masaniello was addressed in death as both saint and king. Fuidoro makes it clear that "this triumph showed the *popolo* that it was not very far from [fulfilling] the vendetta against the nobles, by the sign that they had found a Saint in the form of Cavaliers,"[79] because both the cardinal-archbishop and the viceroy had now conceded to all their demands as a result of the overwhelming response of the people. This point is underlined by Villari in his emphasis on the complicity of the clergy and cardinal for the "large and elaborate funeral" in response to wide popular support as "the moment, then, that the gravity of the crisis began to be understood." For "tumult and emotive reaction" had given way to "disciplined organization and a united political purpose."[80] The revolutionary zeal of the early days of the revolt had now crossed over with a renewed level of popular support after the murder of Masaniello. It was a unified support, however, that was not to last in the divisions and disagreements to follow. The galvanizing moment of Masaniello's funeral turned out in the long run to be as ephemeral as the usual ritual floats and fireworks, with only the formal appearance of similarity to royal obsequies. Its memory lived on, but its effects were soon quashed. The future of the *popolo* did not lead to inclusion but rather alienation, as the crowd remained outside looking in upon the restored viceroy, the occupying Spanish troops, and the complicit Neapolitan nobility.

Popolo Participation: From *Allegrezza* to Alienation

In the face-to-face culture of early modern European towns, citizens of the "ceremonial city" constantly paraded through the streets in recurrent performances of religious processions, devotional rites, civic festivals, and popular demonstrations.[81] Cavalcades of horse-backed ranks of nobility, city aldermen, and government officers celebrated royal entries and commemorated military victories, while somber funeral marches bore the dead to burial and expiatory processions accompanied prisoners to execution. Monuments, images, writings, and emblems of religious, mythological, astrological, and political allegories conveyed polyvalent messages to the urban polity's audience of diverse caste, class, age, and gender; and such visual and verbal ephemera formed part of the ritual process that created and reinforced group identity, hierarchical structures, and urban solidarity, as well as fanning and fomenting rivalries, competition, and contestation among families, friends, and neighbors.[82] The visible manifestations of stage-set backdrops transformed the mundane places of streets, squares, and buildings into theaters, just as the act of marching itself on feast days turned participants costumed in their finery into dramatic actors and ecstatic dancers prancing on horseback or preening in scripted formation, all playing their part in a larger-than-life story to outdo one another. Equally significant, if not more so, were the preparations for and anticipation of the festival day that stretched out over time and changed daily routines into a reaffirmation of the order of the world and one's place in it.[83] The whole world—the suspension of time and space, the linkage of all time and space into a single moment and place, fervor and excitement, engagement and comunitas (to use Victor Turner's word for the heightened consciousness of group behavior), the definition of who one is and one's place in the highly formal, ordered society of rank, occupation, and neighborhood—passed before one's eyes in parade along the road of march and was crystallized in the blinking-of-an-eye horse race in the city's central square or along its main street to structure every other day for the remainder of the year and the rest of one's life.[84]

In early modern Europe, marching through the streets was not only common but always political and a form of propaganda, as was the printing of festival books commemorating the ritual practices, because other forms of mass-media communication were obviously still far in the future.[85] Most difficult of all is to penetrate inside the feast's finery and frenzy to the common people themselves. What did they see and what did they do in city ceremonies? How did popular participation change over time? Whereas the game-playing ethic of the nobility at court led to detachment and disengagement from ritual, as sincerity gave way to dissimulation, the appropriation of ritual by church and state from above estranged commoners' spontaneity and enthusiasm, as social control eroded any authentic attachment to the festivities by those below. In the flickering light of ephemeral urban decoration, we can see that the iconic content and popolo reception of the Neapolitan festivals' art and architecture, poems and epigrams, or spirited songs and sonorous music were like the faint echoes of the cannon salutes and the fireworks bombardments blown out to sea by the wind, so that by the end of the Spanish viceroyalty in Naples, such festive propaganda had become no more than shopworn stage props discarded at the end of the play; and Spanish rule itself had become a disapproved memory whose lightning flashes had dissipated into the dark night.[86]

The Spectacle and the Citizen

Early modern Neapolitan rituals provide a lens to view how the city represented itself. Constructing its self-image from its ancient founding myths of the alluring Siren Partenope's song, the Cumaen connection from the Campi Flegrei to the west, the waters of the river Sebeto flowing through the city to the entrance of the underworld at Lake Avernus, ever-present Vesuvius's brooding majesty and mystery hovering a stone's throw away to the east, and the beauties and bounties of the bay's blue waters bathing its shore, Naples fashioned itself as the Heavenly City of the New Jerusalem, intermediary between heaven and hell. On earth, Naples and its *Campania felice* garden of the Mediterranean grounded itself in the traditions of its natural landscape—"the fecundity of its land, the amenity of its site, the salubrity of its air, and the temperateness of its climate."[1] A terrestrial paradise of plenty, which boasted a ruling class that claimed ancient republican rights and promised fidelity in return, had also become the urban refuge for countless rural commoners from Calabria, Puglia, the Abruzzi, and the Amalfi Peninsula fleeing feudal dues and taxes.[2] Three of the city's eleven foreign "national" churches, in fact, were built and governed by provincials from the three Amalfi Peninsula towns of Agérola, Cetara, and Massa Lubrense.[3] The amalgam of traditions between high and low was matched by an infusion of imported rites and customs from foreign communities of Jews (since expelled), Catalans, French, English, Ragusans, Florentines, Venetians, Lombards, Germans, Greeks, and Genoese as enumerated in Capaccio's chapter "On the Inhabitants of Various Nations in the City of Naples," to which Parrino added Romans, Dutch, and Flemings; and from foreign rulers, who patronized men and ideas they brought from Normandy, Germany, Anjou, Aragón, Burgundy, and Castile.[4] All were leavened in the warm embrace of a church, whose competing religious orders and saint cults made Naples a hothouse combining and recombining popular beliefs and practices with ancient, rural, and foreign traditions. The first church dedicated to San Giovanni replaced the temple of Partenope according to legend at the time of Constantine, while the new Theatine Church of San Paolo Maggiore built between 1583 and 1603 was constructed from the spolia of the ancient Roman temple of the Dioscuri. On the ground, the monarchical state and religious hierarchy ruled over citizens (both nobles and commoners) imbued with a sense of their ancient rights and privileges.

The distinctive feature defining citizenship was place—whether one was in or of the city versus those who were not. Neapolitan citizens were created de jure; they became Neapolitans de facto, through public ritual. The city walls and gates, thus, marked not only a physical but also a legal and symbolic boundary.[5] The *possesso* of the king in absentia and of his viceroys upon their taking office required their oath to abide by the city's privileges and prerogatives. Entries of distinguished visitors became matters of state, out of both the honor a host bestows upon a guest and the show of power and authority of rulers over a place and its people. The ceremonies developed to cross this threshold and to present such guests keys of the city gates allowed them to pass through the liminal spaces outside the gates and be welcomed with special status as honored guests rather than simply as resident foreigners. Such entrances and liminal crossings were ritually negotiated. In the same way, marching through the streets in processions and cavalcades inscribed a ritual geography into the city's physical fabric. The routes became sacred ways, blessed and honored through repetition; and the stops along the way—the noble and *popolo seggi*, the cathedral, churches, royal palace, and city's piazze—all assumed a monumental character. While the ephemeral draperies and decorations, trumpets and drums provided passing sights and sounds, they altered the perception and meaning of the city and its parts. As city space was reordered, so too city time stopped. The social divisions in the city merged at the same time that the social hierarchy was reinforced. The spectacle of such ceremonies fostered the making of a public, citizen culture.

The spectacle turned myth into ritual as it made visible and concrete the various stories that Neapolitans told about their collective identities.[6] The spectacle borrows from the central mystery and everyday miracle of Christianity in the mass, that is, "the Word made Flesh." This embodiment of language goes beyond mere visualization, because the spectacle transforms representation into lived experience. Its theatrical illusions seduce observers to become active participants because of the spectacle's immediacy, transparency, and accessibility. The normal boundaries of time, space, and reality collapse in the spectacle, as it authorizes a new and often false consciousness in the fashioning of new identities. The spectacle absorbs and resolves contestations of power by reorganizing divisions and fissures into new structures of power and resistance that give new meaning to the relationship of past, present, and future. In the end, as observers become actors, they engage in a reciprocal exchange in the creation of citizen identity.

The stereotypical Neapolitan persona of bravura, cleverness, and insouciance could be equally assigned to nobleman or *lazzaro*, a self against society whose mask of independence belied the absence of social bonds. In reality, nothing could be farther from the truth of the local political organization of *seggi* or *ottine*, or the concerted religious revival fostered by the amalgamation of church and Spanish rule from the mid-sixteenth century. That anti-stereotype, the persona of the good citizen, was not only represented in action during the recurrent cycle of rituals but visualized in stone funerary monuments throughout the city's churches and in the numerous paintings circulating in private noble households. What did the self-representation of the Neapolitan citizen look like? What kind of civic culture engaged him and what kind of urban identity did he assume in early modern Naples? The persona represented by Neapolitan artists allows us to see how Neapolitans conceived of themselves across their three primary social divisions of nobility, *popolo*, and plebs.

The similarity between old and new nobility in religious adherence to the post-Tridentine program of the Counter-Reformation is striking in its conformity without any difference across caste or class, before or after the 1647 revolt, before or after the 1656 plague.[7] The ideal secular persona of the old nobility as represented in the Firrao Chapel in S. Paolo Maggiore between the 1630s and the 1640s contrasts sharply, however, with the aspirations of the "new men" of the professional classes as represented in the Cacace Chapel constructed between the 1640s and the 1650s across the street at S. Lorenzo Maggiore.[8] What differs between the old nobility in its emphasis on traditional military virtues, birth, and blood and the "new men" of office, worth, intelligence, and learning is visible in their respective iconographic attributes of sword, helmet, and armor against toga and book. The old nobility was born to rule, whereas the new nobility was self-made.

We can see the much greater divergence in the Neapolitan social fabric in Gargiulo's stereotypical depiction of the relationship between elites and the *popolo* in the *Eruption of Vesuvius in 1631*.[9] Long misinterpreted as part of a series of paintings with Gargiulo's *Piazza del Mercato during the Revolt of Masaniello* and *Piazza Mercatello during the Plague of 1656* that were supposedly anti-Spanish and "informal, journalistic notations of contemporary events," Christopher Marshall has shown that these paintings were not associated in the seventeenth century, that they were painted as artful syntheses of historical narratives, and that their noble patrons' political sympathies were clearly pro-Spanish. The mistaken interpretation of these paintings, based upon Bernardo de Dominici's 1742–43 *Vite de' pittori, scultori ed architetti napoletani* description of the collection of Gargiulo's paintings owned by Don Antonio Piscicelli, has given way to new evidence from *The Getty Provenance Index*. A 1690 death inventory list of paintings owned by Giovanni Battista Capece Piscicelli, nobleman of the *seggio* of Capuana and resident in a palazzo behind the monastery of SS. Apotoli, proves that this forerunner of the later mid-eighteenth-century collection described by Dominici did not include either of Gargiulo's paintings on the 1631 Vesuvius eruption or on the plague of 1656, and thus both were later additions not related to the revolt.[10]

Marshall argues that Gargiulo's *Eruption of Vesuvius* and the *Plague of 1656* both share an interpretive key for the deliverance from natural disasters through the intercession of supernatural forces. S. Gennaro miraculously stops the lava flow and rain of rocks from Vesuvius to save the city, while the Virgin's prayer during the plague moves Christ to stay the sword of the angel of death over the Largo Mercatello. In the *Eruption of Vesuvius*, Gargiulo portrays the response to the panic and terror of the eruption and earthquake that convulsed Naples in the night of 15–16 December 1631. The orderly procession of clerics and noblemen together with Cardinal Boncompagni and the newly arrived viceroy Count of Monterrey circles in a piazza outside the Porta Capuana. Marching in rows of threes and fours, they carry a monstrance with the Eucharist and the reliquary of S. Gennaro under a baldachin, and reliquaries of the eleven other city patrons officially recognized at that time were distributed among their respective followers in parade. The calm confidence of the processing elites is juxtaposed against the agitation and anxiety of the crowds of commoners gesticulating and pointing, begging and beseeching both inside and outside or on balconies and rooftops around the tight circle of the procession (fig. C.1). Penitential practices read from left to right in the foreground—two worried women with babes in arms in animated conversation, two bare-footed supplicants with outstretched arms approaching the procession who cause the marchers to turn their heads, a dog barking at a self-abasing petitioner licking the ground, two hooded flagellants kneeling before the passing Eucharist and relics, a hooded penitent carrying a cross behind the procession, and another being absolved in confession from a mendicant friar—structure the swirling throng in a chaotic, yet submissive stereotype of the plebs in confusion and disarray. Understood in Marshall's reading of "the rituals of unity and decorum" presented in the painting, the *popolo* remains "latently violent and unstable," but here "the people humbly defer to their superiors and to the socially controlling power of religion ... positively channeled into acts of penitence and devotion."[11]

Such inclusive pacification and co-option characterized prerevolt rituals and festivals. Whether in doleful penitence or joyful celebration, religious devotion undergirded citizen culture. The most visible expression of the kind of public display aimed at placating the *popolo* can be seen in the comestible arches and wine fountains that had become part of the procession on the vigil of S. Giovanni. Orilia's engravings of the 1629 procession include two ephemeral constructions that signaled the end of the march at the Porta del Caputo: an arch of food with round wheels of cheese forming pillars with stuffed pigs on their pediments and cured hams and salamis hanging to form the arch, and a fountain of wine with the coat of arms of the viceroy Duke of Alba that was modeled on a fountain he built near the royal palace.[12] The earliest reference to such largesse in the distribution of free food is found in Capaccio's description of the 1614 S. Giovanni procession, where "cheeses of every kind and so abundant, with a great number of various salamis" were seen at the end of the route as signs "of the providence of the good Prince, who at all times and with so much solicitude supplies the provisioning of the Citizens."[13] Similarly, the ritual pillage of the gangway when royals and viceroys arrived by boat at the port had the utilitarian purpose of distributing free cloth to the *popolo* and, as was seen when not made available for sacking in the arrival of the princess Maria d'Austria in 1630, could create a stir. In prerevolt Naples, such magnanimous generosity of the prince as enacted by his viceroy was a mechanism to maintain the image and power of good government through royal virtue.

In post-revolt, post-plague Naples, as wealth and power were consolidated in fewer hands, the church and state exerted greater control over public celebrations and rituals, the old nobility became more subordinate, and the *popolo*'s resistance was broken. In the slow recovery that began between 1660 and 1680, the "new men," upwardly mobile members of the state bureaucracy, emerged as the clear winners. Their self-representation is best portrayed by Michele Regolia in his painting of the antechamber of a Neapolitan nobleman's palace circa 1670 (fig. C.2). Regolia allows us to see the kinds of public rooms that numerous Neapolitan inventories record.[14] Three sight lines or strata define the room: a high border of trompe l'oeil busts and niches at the base of a feigned lacunar soffit; a middle register of six clearly identifiable religious paintings dominating the whole scene; and a lower level of miscellaneous paintings of battle scenes, landscapes, and portraits as well as two finely made monetiere and four waiting-room chairs on

Figure C.1. Detail from Domenico Gargiulo, *Eruption of Vesuvius in 1631*. Soprintendenza per i Beni Architettonici e Paesaggistici e per il Patrimonio Storici, Artistici ed Etnoantropologici per Napoli e Provincia, Naples.

a majolica pavement, which fill in the remaining viewing surfaces. On the literal level, as a reflection of taste and status, Regolia's nobleman's room portrays the ordered arrangement of art objects that fit into specified spaces.[15] Gérard Labrot's study of Neapolitan art inventories reveals a passion for symmetry in such reception rooms, often a binary organization of design and a pairing of like objects, themes, or artists, and the determinative role of the size of the painting in its placement—with greater size a reflection of a family's grandeur.[16] Inventories also reveal that art objects were exhibited in private palaces with the public in mind. Smaller, mediocre works, often by anonymous artists and on pietistic themes, were kept in family rooms away from public viewing, whereas one's best paintings were proudly displayed in public rooms as status symbols.[17]

The Regolia room displays the same decorative organizational principles and

Figure C.2. Michele Regolia, *Antechamber of a Nobleman's Room.* © Archivio dell'Arte /
Luciano Pedicini, Naples.

the same kinds of themes recorded in the Neapolitan inventories, an integration of religious paintings, landscapes, and still lifes. The origin of this kind of
interior palace decoration in Naples dates back to an émigré Antwerp merchant-
financier Gaspar Roomer, who had already settled in his grand palace (Monteoliveto) where he established a *Kunstkamer* by 1630 when Capaccio described this
great art patron's paintings.[18] Deep connections between Flanders and Naples
have been seen with Spanish Netherlander artists at work on the intarsia panels
in the Certosa di S. Martino in the 1590s and through a long history of exchange
between Burgundy and Naples from the time of Charles V, with Charles Leclerc,
president of the Chamber of Accounts in Lille, appointed commissioner general
for Naples in 1517; Philibert de Châlons, Prince of Orange, viceroy, 1528–30; and
Antoine Perrenot, Cardinal Granvelle, viceroy, 1571–75. Throughout Roomer's
career in Naples, he commissioned, imported, exported, exhibited, and collected
art works, especially of the Flemish and Neapolitan schools, with Rubens's *Feast
of Herod*, depicting at its focal point Salome presenting St. John the Baptist's
head on a platter to Herod, perhaps the best example of the Spanish Netherlands'
influence on Spanish Naples.[19] This Rubens painting arrived in Naples around

1640; and, with its resonance in the Neapolitan devotion to S. Giovanni, it had a singular importance for the development of the later Neapolitan Baroque style as seen in the Mattia Preti painting of the same theme dated 1657–58. By Roomer's death in 1674, he had collected some fifteen hundred paintings, with seventy of them passing to his son-in-law, Ferdinand Vandeneinden, whose father had been Roomer's business partner and whose 1688 inventory included both the Rubens and Preti *Feast of Herod*.

The visual core of the Regolia painting, the center row of six religious works that most attracts the viewer's attention, should help us decipher the painting's overall intent.[20] From left to right, we see a *Denial of Peter* and *Judith and the Maidservant with the Head of Holofernes*, both showing the strong influence of Caravaggio's chiaroscuro technique, with candles in the hands of the servants. The *Denial of Peter* is based on a Guercino that was then in Naples and here is reproduced in a reversed copy probably made from an engraving. The *Judith* is a French or Roman Caravaggesque type. A *Supper at Emmaus*, the lone painting to be definitively identified, is a copy of an early Stanzione painting, also in a Cara-vaggesque mode.[21] It is paired with the fourth painting, a *Christ and the Woman of Samaria at the Well*, which was one of the subjects commissioned for a side altar at the Monte della Misericordia.[22] An *Immaculate Conception* in the style of Murillo and *St. Anthony of Padua with the Christ Child* possibly by Ribera or An-drea Vaccaro complete this dominant motif line. All six paintings appear to be in the Neapolitan-Spanish Baroque style contemporary with the mid-seventeenth-century date of Regolia's painting, and Neapolitan artists such as Stanzione and Cavallino painted all six themes often.[23]

Among the eighty-three Neapolitan inventories from 1600 to 1780 cataloged in the Getty *Documents for the History of Collecting*, these six themes are all repre-sented:[24]

— Immaculate Conception, 76 times
— St. Anthony of Padua, 31 times[25]
— Judith with Holofernes' head and the sword, 38 times
— Jesus and the Samaritan woman, 23 times
— Supper at Emmaus: blessing or breaking bread, 9 times[26]
— Peter denies Christ with a girl servant and soldiers, 6 times

Paintings of all six themes are found in only one of the eighty-three inventoried collections, while two inventories include five of the six themes and four other inventories include four. Antonio Lauro (1713), a lawyer or magistrate who seems to have lived as a rentier, for example, left a 220-item inventory arranged by the twelve rooms in his apartment.[27] Although the six themes were not displayed in the same room, three of them, however—a Judith (item 203), one of four paintings on this theme that he owned; *Jesus and the Samaritan Woman* (item 200), identified as the work of Francisco Antonio Altobello; and an Immaculate Conception (item 199), one of five owned by Lauro—are in close proximity, albeit in one upstairs private room. The rare theme of the Denial of Peter, identified as the work of Domenico Viola in the Lauro collection, is the lone theme missing in the inventories of Santo Maria Cella, Duke of Frisa (1680), and Giovanna Battista d'Aragon Pignatelli, Duchess of Terranova e Monteleone (1723).[28] The inventories listing four of the paintings are also equally divided between old aristocrats and bourgeoisie: Ottavio Orsini, Prince of Frasso (1704), owned neither a *Judith* nor a *Samaritan Woman*; Carlo de Cardenas, Count of Acerra, Marquis of Laino (1699), owned no *Denial of Peter* and no *Supper at Emmaus*, the two rarest of the six themes; Francisco Cavallino (1677) owned no *Judith* and curiously no *Immaculate Conception*; and Ignazio Provenzale, Duke of Collecorvino (1693), owned no *Peter* and no *Samaritan Woman*.[29] Obviously, none of these seven collections was the actual model for the Regolia *Kunstkamer*. Nevertheless, there should be no doubt that one like them could have been.

From the painting itself we may infer that Regolia's nobleman collector was a member of the nouveau riche, office-holding class of lawyers and orators, Naples's *togati*. The line of sight defined by the trompe l'oeil sculptures should caution us from assigning this room to the old nobility. While there are a few soldiers with batons represented, the majority of busts are of togated philosophers or orators holding rolled papyrus scrolls indicative of a long line of lawyers and magistrates watching over this room's affairs.

The moral message defining the public persona put forward by the iconographic content of Regolia's subjects, however, is unmistakable. The paired themes present the viewer with a schema of knowledge and a model for practice: virtue (both religious and civic) comes from faith and works. Just as the portrait of an individual should reveal the soul of the inner man, this portrait of a noble's room defines who he is—a nobleman of religious virtue, a virtuous nobleman defined by deeds, not blood, who displays his personal spiritual journey. The *Denial of Peter* in his failure of faith during the Passion narrative (Mark 14:61–72) is an example of man's sinful nature, despite being forewarned, and also of the power of penance. *Judith and the Maidservant with the Head of Holofernes*, celebrating her decapitation of the Assyrian tyrant in defense of her people's long hoped-for liberation (an allegory of Christ and the church with the moral trope of victory over sin), likewise emphasizes the importance of faith and forgiveness. The third painting, the *Supper at Emmaus*, when the risen Christ revealed himself by breaking bread with some disheartened disciples departed from Jerusalem after the Crucifixion (Luke 24:28–32), and the fourth scene, *Christ and the Woman of Samaria at the Well*, as the Lord discusses the fallen, foreign woman's past life and makes His call to faith (John 4:1–30), both follow the theme of the previous two paintings dedicated to faith by representing good works. The *Supper at Emmaus* is often explicated as an example of feeding the hungry, with the added sacramental reference to the Eucharist. *The Samaritan Woman*, similarly, involves charity to a stranger by giving drink to the thirsty and also the sacrament of Baptism, since Christ tells the fallen woman that his water will never again make her thirsty. Two devotional paintings more appropriate for a private room than a public gallery, an *Immaculate Conception*[30] and *St. Anthony of Padua with the Christ Child*,[31] with their invocation of charity complete this paired theme on the redemptive cycle, faith and good works. As the antithesis of sin, Mary of the Immaculate Conception is a special patron of redemption and a sign of the Apocalyptic Woman's coming to announce the end of the world (Revelation 12:1–2). St. Anthony of Padua, the Apostle of Charity popular especially for giving alms to the poor, is shown in ecstasy before the Christ Child in a conventional pose to stimulate prayer and private devotion. Taken together with the *virtù* of the sage philosophers and orators portrayed by the classical busts in the cornice niches above, the invocation of faith, hope, and charity, good works, and prayer proclaims the dedication of a household of a devout lawyer or magistrate to Counter-Reformation ideals.

In seventeenth-century Naples, faith is to good works what noble birth is to virtuous deeds: both define the context and the content of the pictorial narrative portrayed by Regolia in his *Inside a Nobleman's House*. Similarly, the visual, musical, and literary arts performed and displayed during religious and civil rituals set a model to live lives fulfilling the theme of nobility in the same terms as the religious ideals of Counter-Reformation spirituality. In the city and the kingdom, then, the Neapolitan noble citizen (both sword and robed nobleman) presented himself born to rule—from antiquity and past service in battle or from professional training and present service in the state bureaucracy, from religious fidelity, and from moral rectitude. The citizen frame made virtue its goal, which in Regolia's eye became the formal, moral facade between the ordered life inside and the uncertain chaos outside.

The overall message of Neapolitan rituals emphasized the virtues in all their manifestations and attributes. The public and private, religious and civic festivals all highlighted virtue as the goal of the individual and the binding ties of society at large. Rituals were idealized exchanges and communications that were meant to refresh and reunite participants to an ancient tradition around the commonalities of the myth of Naples and the allure of the Siren's song. It was a trickle-down theory of virtue and citizenship disseminated from above by church and state for the elites, both nobles and the upwardly aspiring members of the higher *popolo*, to the exclusion of the people at large. Especially after the revolt and plague, the mass of the *popolo* and plebs became more and more marginalized and alienated. No celebration demonstrates the bifurcation of rituals into two-track festivals better than the Neapolitan festivities for the birth of Philip IV's son Prospero in 1658. The imagery of the four continents in the festival's great floats flouted the Spanish imperial ideology at a time when its territories were slipping away. The spectacle lacked the spontaneity and resonance of earlier days and had become more of a time for insider, elite play than citizen solidarity. The more the state tried to push its agenda from above, the less it reached the people below. Ritual time no longer reinforced the structure of things but rather revealed the separateness of things. Ritual from above without faith from below went through the motions without any of the meaning that gave action its purpose. Form without matter mattered little at all as Spanish Naples became Spanish no more.

TABLE A.I.
Two Rural Neapolitan Ritual Calendars

	Amalfi (1594)[a]	Conza (1597)[b]
	IMMOVABLE FEASTS	
January		
1	Circumcision	Circumcision
6	Epiphany	Epiphany
17	St. Anthony Abbot	
20	St. Fabian	
24	St. Macarius	
February		
2	Purification	Purification
24	St. Matthias	St. Matthias
March		
7	St. Thomas Aquinas	St. Thomas Aquinas
12	St. Gregory	
25	Annunciation	Annunciation
April		
2	S. Francisco di Paola	
25	St. Mark	St. Mark
May		
1	Sts. Philip & James	Sts. Philip & James
3	Invention of the Holy Cross	Invention of the Holy Cross
8	Translation of St. Andrew	
26	Translation of St. Macarius	
June		
11	St. Barnabas	
13	St. Anthony of Padua	
15	Sts. Vito & Modesto	
24	St. John the Baptist	St. John the Baptist
27	Miracle of St. Andrew[3]	
29	Sts. Peter & Paul	

TABLE A.I.   *(cont'd.)*

	Amalfi (1594)[a]	Conza (1597)[b]
July		
2	Visitation	Visitation
22	St. Mary Magdalene	
25	St. James	St. James
August		
5	St. Mary of the Snows	
6	Transfiguration	
10	St. Lawrence	St. Lawrence
15	Assumption	Assumption
20		St. Erbert[d]
25	St. Bartholomew	St. Bartholomew
28		St. Augustine
September		
8	Nativity of the Blessed Virgin	Nativity of the Blessed Virgin
19	S. Gennaro & Companions	S. Gennaro & Companions
21	St. Matthew	St. Matthew
29	St. Michael Arch.	St. Michael Arch.
30	St. Jerome	
October		
18	St. Luke	
28	Sts. Simon & Jude	Sts. Simon & Jude
November		
1	All Saints	All Saints
11	St. Martin	St. Martin
25	St. Catherine	St. Catherine
30	St. Andrew	St. Andrew
December		
7	St. Ambrose	
8	Immaculate Conception	Immaculate Conception
13	St. Lucy	St. Lucy
21	St. Thomas	St. Thomas
25	Nativity of Lord	Nativity of Lord
26	St. Stephen	St. Stephen
27	St. John the Evangelist	St. John the Evangelist
28	Holy Innocents	
30		St. Sylvester

MOVABLE FEASTS

All Sundays	All Sundays
Holy Thursday	Holy Thursday
Easter + 2 days following	Easter + 2 days following
Ascension Thursday	Ascension Thursday
Pentecost + 2 days following	Pentecost + 2 days following
Corpus Christi	Corpus Christi

[a] Rossini, *Constitutioni et decreti*, provides the calendar from the diocesan synod of Amalfi, January 1594. The metropolitan seat of Amalfi consisted of the dioceses of Lettere, Capri, Minori, and Scala-Ravello.

[b] Gesualdo, *Constitutiones et decreta dioecesanae synodi*, provides the calendar from the diocesan synod of Conza, 19 October 1597. The metropolitan seat of Conza consisted of the dioceses of Muro, Cangiano, Monteverde, Cedonia, and S. Angelo dei Lombardi-Bisaccia.

[c] St. Andrew is the patron of Amalfi and its cathedral. The miracle is the passing of the armada of Barbarossa.

[d] S. Erberto (St. Herbert Hoscam) was archbishop of Conza, 1169–81.

The Neapolitan Ritual Calendar: Fall–Winter and Spring–Summer

	De Feriis (1555–56)[a] Legal Holidays	De Feriis (added)[b] Legal Holidays	De Feriis (1656)[c] Legal Holidays	Raneo (1634)[d] Viceroy's Holidays
FALL–WINTER				
Autumnal equinox				
September				
8	Nativity of Blessed Virgin Mary (Piedigrotta)			Nativity of Blessed Virgin Mary (Piedigrotta)
10		S. Nicola da Tolentino	S. Nicola da Tolentino	
14	Triumph of the Holy Cross		Triumph of the Holy Cross	Triumph of the Holy Cross
15		Image of St. Dominic of Sora		
17		Holy Name of Mary		
19	S. Gennaro*			S. Gennaro*
21	St. Matthew			
23		S. Sossio	S. Sossio	
27		Sts. Cosmas & Damian	Sts. Cosmas & Damian	
29	St. Michael Archangel**			
30	St. Jerome		St. Jerome	
October				
2		Guardian Angel	Guardian Angel	
4	St. Francis of Assisi**		St. Francis of Assisi**	St. Francis of Assisi**
5		Francis Borgia**		Blessed Borja**
7		S. Maria della Vittoria	S. Maria della Vittoria	S. Maria della Vittoria
15		St. Teresa**	St. Teresa**	St. Teresa**
18	St. Luke		St. Luke	
19				St. Ursula
20		St. Peter of Alcantara		
21				St. Ursula & the 11,000 Virgins
28	Sts. Simon & Jude			

TABLE A.2. *(cont'd.)*

	De Feriis (1555–56)[a] Legal Holidays	De Feriis (added)[b] Legal Holidays	De Feriis (1656)[c] Legal Holidays	Raneo (1634)[d] Viceroy's Holidays
November				
1	All Saints Day			All Saints Day
2	All Souls Day		All Souls Day	
4		St. Charles Borromeo	St. Charles Borromeo	
6	S. Leonardo		S. Leonardo	S. Leonardo
9	S. Agrippino*		S. Agrippino*	
10		B. Andrea di Avellino**	B. Andrea di Avellino**	B. Andrea di Avellino**
11	St. Martin		St. Martin	St. Martin
12		S. Diego di Alcalá	S. Diego di Alcalá	S. Diego di Alcalá
21	Presentation of Blessed Virgin Mary		Presentation of Blessed Virgin Mary	
25	St. Catherine		St. Catherine	St. Catherine
28		B. Giacomo della Marca**	B. Giacomo della Marca**	S. Giacomo della Marca**
30	St. Andrew			
December				
3		S. Francis Xavier**	S. Francis Xavier**	
4		St. Barbara	St. Barbara	
6	St. Nicholas**		St. Nicholas**	
7	St. Ambrose		St. Ambrose	
8	Immaculate Conception		Immaculate Conception	Immaculate Conception
13	St. Lucy		St. Lucy	St. Lucy
14	S. Agnello*		S. Agnello*	S. Agnello*
16		Patrocinio of S. Gennaro	Patrocinio of S. Gennaro	Patrocinio of S. Gennaro
20			St. Francis Xavier	St. Francis Xavier
Winter solstice				
December (End of month)				Novena to Our Lady of the Angels

248

Date				
24	St. Thomas Apostle			
25	Nativity of the Lord			
26		St. Stephen	St. Stephen	St. Stephen
27		St. John the Evangelist	St. John the Evangelist	
28		Holy Innocents		
31		St. Sylvester		
January				
1	Circumcision			Circumcision
2		Epiphany		
3		Epiphany		
4		Epiphany		
5		Epiphany		
6	Epiphany			
7		S. Maria del Principio	St. Raymond	
8		Translation of Thomas Aquinas	S. Maria del Principio	
17	St. Anthony Abbot**		St. Anthony Abbot**	St. Anthony Abbot**
19			Translation of Thomas Aquinas	
20	Sts. Fabian & Sebastian		Sts. Fabian & Sebastian	
23		St. Raymond of Peñafort		
25	Conversion St. Paul		Conversion St. Paul	
31		St. Peter Nolasco		
February				
2	Purification/Presentation			Purification/Presentation
3	St. Blaise		St. Blaise	
5	St. Agatha		St. Agatha	[Suor Orsola Benincasa]
25	St. Matthias			
March				
7	St. Thomas Aquinas**		St. Thomas Aquinas**	St.Thomas Aquinas**
9		St. Frances of Rome	St. Frances of Rome	St. Frances of Rome
12	St. Gregory of Armenia**		St. Gregory of Armenia**	
19	St. Joseph			

TABLE A.2. (cont'd.)

	De Feriis (1555–56)[a] Legal Holidays	De Feriis (added)[b] Legal Holidays	De Feriis (1656)[c] Legal Holidays	Raneo (1634)[d] Viceroy's Holidays
March				
20		St. Joachim	St. Joachim	
21	St. Benedict		St. Benedict	St. Benedict
Movable feasts		Ash Wednesday + 6 days before (6 days not feasts, but law-courts closed)	Septuagesima Sexagesima Quinquagesima Five Sundays of Lent: Quaresima	Septuagesima Sexagesima Quinquagesima
SPRING–SUMMER				
Vernal equinox				
March				
25	Annunciation			Annunciation
April				
2		S. Francisco di Paola**	S. Francesco di Paola**	S. Francesco di Paola**
23	St. George		St. George	
25	St. Mark		St. Mark	
29	St. Peter Martyr**		St. Peter Martyr**	St. Peter Martyr**
30	S. Severo*		S. Severo*	
May				
1	Sts. Philip & James			Sts. Philip & James
3	Invention of the Holy Cross			Invention of the Holy Cross
8	Apparition of St. Michael		Apparition of St. Michael	
15		St. Isidore		
17	S. Restituta		S. Restituta	

19		S. Ivo of Helory		S. Ivo of Helory
23	S. Eufebio*		S. Eufebio*	
26		St. Philip Neri**	St. Philip Neri**	
30		St. Ferdinand III of Castile		
June				
11	St. Barnabas		St. Barnabas	
13	St. Anthony of Padua		St. Anthony of Padua Our Lady of the Afflicted	St. Anthony of Padua
Summer solstice				
June				
23				Eve of St. John the Baptist
24	St. John the Baptist**			
29	Sts. Peter & Paul			
July				
2	Visitation		Visitation	Visitation
14 July–4 Oct		Harvest & vindemia		
15	S. Atanasio*		S. Atanasio*	
16	S. Maria del Carmine		S. Maria del Carmine	S. Maria del Carmine
22		St. Mary Magdalene**	St. Mary Magdalene**	St. Mary Magdalene**
25	St. James			S. James
26	St. Anne			
27	S. Martha			
29		St. Martha	St. Martha	
31		St. Ignatius	St. Ignatius Loyola	St. Ignatius
August				
1	St. Peter in Chains		St. Peter in Chains	
2		Portiuncula (S. Francis of Assisi Chapel)	Portiuncula (S. Francis of Assisi Chapel)	
3	S. Aspreno*		S. Aspreno*	Invention of the relics of S. Stephen
4	St. Dominic**			St. Dominic**
5	S. Maria delle Neve		S. Maria delle Neve	
6	Transfiguration		Transfiguration	
7		Blessed Gaetano**	Blessed Gaetano**	Blessed Gaetano**

TABLE A.2. (cont'd.)

	De Feriis (1555–56)[a] Legal Holidays	De Feriis (added)[b] Legal Holidays	De Feriis (1656)[c] Legal Holidays	Raneo (1634)[d] Viceroy's Holidays
August				
10	St. Lawrence			St. Lawrence
15	Assumption + 2 days following			Assumption
16		S. Rocco	S. Rocco	
17		Octave of S. Lawrence	Octave of S. Lawrence	
20	St. Bernard		St. Bernard	
25	St. Bartholomew			St. Bartholomew
26		S. Patrizia**	S. Patrizia**	
28	St. Augustine**		S. Augustine**	St. Augustine**
29	Beheading of St. John the Baptist		Beheading of St. John the Baptist	Beheading of St. John the Baptist
September				
4		S. Rosalia		
7		Victory Cardinal Infante at Battle of Nördlingen, 1634	Victory Cardinal Infante at Battle of Nördlingen, 1634	Victory Cardinal Infante at Battle of Nördlingen, 1634
Movable feasts	Easter + 2 days following Ascension	Easter + 7 days before & after	Easter	Easter
	Pentecost + 2 days following Corpus Christi	Pentecost + 2 days following	Corpus Christi	
		Octave of Corpus Christi (not feast, but lawcourts closed)		
		1st Saturday of May, translation of S. Gennaro	1st Saturday of May	1st Saturday of May
			1st Sunday of July	1st Sunday of July

* Sallmann, *Naples et ses saints*, 85–86, n. 2. Naples had seven original patron saints.

** Ibid. There were twenty-eight newly elected patron saints of Naples, 1605–1731. The following five saints had been elected patrons by the 1634 and 1656 calendars: 1605: Thomas Aquinas; 1625: Andrea Avellino and Patrizia; 1626: Giacomo della Marca and Franceso di Paola; the sixth by the 1656 calendar, 1640: Dominic. The remaining twenty-two were not yet patrons in the 1634 and 1656 calendars: 1657: Francis Xavier; 1664: Teresa of Avila; 1667: Philip Neri; 1671: Gaetano da Thiene; 1675: Gregory of Armenia and Nicholas of Bari; 1688: Michael the Archangel; 1689: Clare of Assisi; 1690: Peter Martyr, Maria Maddalena de' Pazzi, and Blaise; 1691: Francis of Assisi and Cecilia; 1695: Francis Borgia and John the Baptist; 1697: Candida; 1698: John of Capistrano and Anthony Abbot; 1699: Mary of Egypt; 1705: Mary Magdalene; 1711: Augustine; and 1731: Irene of Thessalonica.

a Vario, *Pragmaticae edicta, decreta*, 2: 8–10, "De Ferriis," Titulus LXXVIII, Prammatica II (15 April 1556), 8–10.
b Ibid.
c Rubino, "Notitia," BSNSP, XXIII.D.14 (25 April 1656), Prammatica XXIV, "De Ferriis," 214–17.
d Raneo, *Etiquetas de la corte*, 69–73.

TABLE A.3.
Games Listed in Basile's *Pentamerone*

Accosta palla (Get near the ball): Day 4 introduction: "A primitive form of bocce." Canepa, 295. "One throws a first ball, and the players throw the others in turn, trying to make them go as near as possible to the first." Penzer, 2:1.

Anca Nicola: Day 2 introduction: "One boy bending over and putting his head in the lap of another, who then with his hands hides the eyes of the first. A third boy then jumps astride on his back and sings: 'Anca Nicola, si' bella e si' bona, E si' maretata: Quanta corna tiene ncapa?' (Anca Nicola, you're beautiful and you're good, And you're married: How many horns do you have on your head?) putting a hand on his head and raising as many fingers as he wishes," with first boy guessing the number of fingers. Penzer, 1:132; Canepa, 143 .

Anola tranola, pizza fontanola: Day 2 introduction: Words are used as a magic spell in tale 5.3.

Aprite le porte a povero farcone (Open the door to the poor falcon): Tale 1.10; day 2 introduction: "A game in which all hold hands and go round in a circle, leaving one in the middle [the falcon] who has to try to escape by passing under the arms of one of the couples." Penzer, 1:134.

Auciello auciello maneca de fierro (Bird, bird, iron handle): Day 2 introduction; tale 2.7: "Bears some relation to the *covalera* game." Penzer, 1:134.

Banco fallito (Bankrupt): Tale 1.2; day 5 introduction: A card game in the game of games.

Banno e commannamiento (Edict and proclamation): Day 2 introduction: "A game in which the catchwords are taken from the formula of court proclamations, which began 'Edict and commandment on the part of the Grand Court of the Vicaria, by which it is notified.'" Penzer, 1:132.

Beneficiata (Beneficiary): Tale 2.7: Take one's turn.

Ben venga lo mastro (Welcome the master): Day 2 introduction; tale 4.8: also a dance. Canepa, 144.

Binte fegure (Twenty lords): Day 5 introduction: A card game in the game of games.

Capo o croce (Heads or tails): Day 4 introduction.

Carrettuso (Carrettuso): Day 5 introduction: A card game in the game of games.

Che tiene 'n mano, l'aco e lo filo (What's in your hand? Needle and thread): Day 2 introduction: Possibly a variant of Stone in your lap. Canepa, 145.

Chiammare (Calling): Day 5 introduction: A card game in the game of games.

Chioppa o separa (Pairs or singles): Day 4 introduction: Variety of odds and evens. Penzer, 2:1.

Compagno mio, feruto so' (My friend, I'm wounded): Day 2 introduction; tale 3.3: Two children lie face-down head to head and completely covered. Other players stand and hit, one at a time. The child who is hit tries to guess who hit him, and if correct, changes places with the hitter.

Covalera (The brooding hen): Day 2 introduction; a game of hide-and-seek with the "brooding hen" the seeker, Penzer, 1:132.

Cucco o viento (Egg or wind, or Something or nothing): Day 4 introduction: "One holds out a closed hand telling one's opponent to guess." Penzer, 2:1.

Gatta cecata (Blind puss): Day 2 introduction: Variation of blindman's bluff. Canepa, 145.

Grieco o acito (Greco wine or vinegar): Day 2 introduction.

Guarda mogliere (Guard your wife): Day 2 introduction: One person (the wife) kneels as the "mother" and other players walk around her. The mother defends the wife's head from their blows; and if she touches one of the hitters, that person is it and becomes the wife with the previous wife becoming the mother.

Iste e veniste e lo luoco te perdiste (You came and you went, and your spot is spent.): Tale 1.3: "A rhyme used by children in a game, usually when one takes the place left vacant by another, and the other on returning finds it occupied." Penzer, 1:39–40.

TABLE A.3. *(cont'd.)*

La campana (Bell) Day 4 introduction: Hop-scotch game with eight compartments in the shape of a bell; the goal is to throw an object such as a key or disc into the sections and then hop on one foot to kick it out without it or one's foot touching the line. Penzer, 2:1.

La gabella (The tax game) Day 5 introduction: A card game in the game of games.

La lampa a la lampa (To the lamp, to the lamp) Day 2 introduction: "The usual beginning to a game. One places the index finger in the palm of another child, while singing. . . . If the latter suddenly closes his hand and holds the finger, the former 'goes under.'" Penzer, 1:133.

La morra: Day 4 introduction: A game to see whose turn it is to do something. Played with two people to predict the number of fingers the other player will hold up. Penzer, 2:1; Canepa, 295.

La palla: ball; Day 4 introduction.

La passara muta (Mute sparrow): Tale 1.2.

La penetenza (Penalty) Day 5 introduction: A game of games in which speaker "suggests some kind of game to each lady in turn, and she, without stopping to think, must say that it does not please her and give the reason why."

Le castellucce (Little castles) Day 4 introduction: Piles of nuts, chestnuts, etc., which one must try to hit and knock down with another nut or chestnut. Penzer, 2:1.

Le gallinelle (The little hens): Day 2 introduction.

Le norchie: a card game: Day 4 introduction.

Li forasciute (The outlaws) Day 2 introduction:; "A game similar to that of the 'Turks and Christians' . . . or rather similar to 'soldiers and brigands,'" thus, similar to "Cops and robbers" or "Cowboys and Indians." Penzer, 1:133.

Li sbriglie: skittles; Day 4 introduction.

Lo malecontento (Discontented): Day 5 introduction: A card game in the game of games.

Lo tuocco (Touching): Day 4 introduction: "A variety of the 'morra' game that is played to see whose turn it is to do something (particularly paying for wine that is in front of one, played by those drinking at bars)." Penzer, 2:1.

Lo viecchio no è venuto (The old man has not come): Day 2 introduction.

Mammara e nocella (Mammara and hazel nuts): Day 2 introduction: "Two hold hands and stretch out their arms, forming a hollow like a chair, clasping their hands as if pledging their faith; then one sits, and they carry him (or her) dangling through the house, and sing." Penzer, 1: 133.

Mazz'e piuzo (Staff and stick): Day 4 introduction: "making the *piuzo*, a wooden cylinder with pointed ends, jump in the air, hitting it and keeping it up with a bat." Canepa, 295.

Paro o sparo (Odds or evens): Tale 1.10; day 4 introduction.

Pesce marino 'ncagnalo (At him, sea fish): Day 2 introduction.

Picchetto (Piquet): Day 5 introduction: A card game in the game of games.

Preta 'nsino (Stone in the apron, or Stone in your lap): Tale 1.2; day 2 introduction: "Somewhat similar to the so-called game of the ring. One person, with some object (a small stone, ring, etc.) hidden between his hands, goes round and pretends to let it drop into the hands or on to the lap of each: then he asks one of them to whom he really gave it." Penzer, 1:133.

Quattro mentune (Four rams): Day 5 introduction: A card game in the game of games.

Re mazziero (King mace-bearer): Day 2 introduction: The mace-bearer led processions with a long club; also a card dealer. Canepa, 145.

Rentinola, mia rentinola (Swallow, my swallow): Day 2 introduction: "One girl kneels while others place their hands on her head and one other goes around singing." The song is an invitation to dance as a prelude to marriage. "When the song is ended, one girl is taken aside and the song recommences, until they are all taken except the girl who is kneeling." Penzer, 1:132; Canepa, 144.

Rota de li cauce (Circle of heels, or Wheel of kicks): Frame tale. Day 2 introduction; "A game played by children joining hands to form a circle. They kick away one of the players who tries to get inside, and he who lets him in has then to go outside the circle." Penzer, 1:3.

Sagliepengola (Seesaw): Day 2 introduction.

Sauta parmo (Jump a palm's length): Day 2 introduction.

Sbaraglino: backgammon. Tale 4.5.

Sbracare (Stripping): Day 5 introduction: A card game in the game of games.

Scarreca l'aseno (Unload the ass): Tale 4.5: A dice game.

Scarreca la votta (Unload the cask): Day 2 introduction; tale 3.3: "It is played by placing the child astride the knees and tossing it in imitation of a horse's trot. . . . When repeating the last verse, one separates the knees so that the child falls between." Penzer, 1:132.

Scarreca varrile (Unload the barrel): Day 2 introduction: "Two children stand back to back, lock arms, and then take turns lifting each other off the ground." Canepa, 145.

Scarriglia Mastrodatto (Argue the case, court clerk): Day 2 introduction: A game imitating court proceedings. Canepa, 145.

Seca mautone (Saw the brick): Day 4 introduction.

Stienne mia cortina (Stretch my curtain): Day 2 introduction; tale 2.3: Similar to "London Bridges."

Tafaro e tamburro (Butt and drum): Day 2 introduction: Magic words in tale 5.3. Variation on blindman's bluff, with children touching and pinching the one in the middle who has to guess the last one to touch him. Canepa, 145.

Travo luongo (Long beam): Day 2 introduction: Version of leapfrog.

Trinfiello (Triumph): Tale 1.2; tale 1.10; day 5 introduction: A card game in the game of games.

Viata te co la catena (Lucky you with the chain): Tale 1.10.

Vienela vienela (Come, oh come): Tale 1.10; day 2 introduction: "variation of the *covalera* game," Penzer, 1:134.

Source: Basile, *Lo Cunto de li cunti*, ed. Rak; Basile, *Giambattista Basile's* The Tale of Tales, trans. Canepa; and Basile, *The Pentamerone of Giambattista Basile*, ed. Penzer.

Abbreviations

ACDF	Archivio per la Congregazione della dottrina della fede
AGS	Archivo General, Simancas
ASMN	Archivio Storico del Muncipio di Napoli
ASN	Archivio di Stato, Napoli
ASV	Archivio Segreto Vaticano
BAV	Biblioteca Apostolica Vaticana
BNF	Bibliothèque nationale de France, Paris
BNM	Biblioteca Nacional Madrid
BNN	Biblioteca Nazionale di Napoli
BSNSP	Biblioteca di Società Napoletana di Storia Patria
DBI	*Dizionario biografico degli italiani.* Rome: Istituto della Enciclopedia italiana, 1960–.

Introduction. Urbs et Orbis

1. Notar Giacomo, *Cronica di Napoli*, 190–91: "li dicesse che haueano apontato con la Christianissima Maesta deli capitoli et ordinacioni delacita: dove li fo resposto dicendole che voleua sapere dequesto che hauite ad fare vuy dequesta terra nui simo ientilomini et citidini de napoli et vuy non vence hauite ad impazare in alcuna cosa. vermi decani fetenti." English translation follows von Reumont, *The Carafas of Maddaloni*, 58–59.

2. Weissman, "Reconstructing Renaissance Sociology," 39–46, and "The Importance of Being Ambiguous," 269–80.

3. Ventura, "Le ambiguità di un privilegio," 385–416; "Governo urbano e privilegio di cittadinanza," 95–110; "Mercato delle risorse e identità urbana," 268–304; and "Il Linguaggio della cittadinanza," 347–75.

4. Ventura, "Il Linguaggio della cittadinanza," 348–49, cites the Muscettola manuscript (AGS, *Estado, Nápoles*, leg. 1050, f. 23), which names these four types of Neapolitan citizens: "Napoletani proprii e nativi," the "Oriundi Napolitani," gli "Alletti," and the "Napoletani in virtù della Regia Pragmatica."

5. For rights and duties of Neapolitans, ibid., 347–60; Parrino, *Teatro eroico*, 1:32.

6. *Machiavelli's* The Prince. *A Bilingual Edition*, 8–27.

7. Tutini, *Dei origine e fundatione de' seggi*, 2 and 35.

8. Muir and Weissman, "Social and Symbolic," 81–103, on "social geography, particularly networks of space-based sociability, and symbolic geography, the use of place to delineate, comment on, and transform the social order of the Renaissance Italian city."

9. Martines, *Violence in Italian Cities*.

10. Albéri, *Relazioni degli ambasciatori veneti*, ser. 1, 3:333–78, partially translated in J. Davis, *Pursuit of Power*, 35–69, esp. 46–47.

11. Porzio, "Relazione del Regno," Pontieri's commentary and the document, CXXXV–CXL, 309–40. See also Calabria, 9–11, for a similar anonymous 1570s "Delectable and Useful Discourse of the Things that are in the Kingdom of Naples," and p. 9, n. 3, for its resonance in the 1575 report to the Venetian senate by their ambassador Girolamo Lippomano.

12. Porzio, "Relazione del Regno," 339. See Galasso, "Lo stereotipo del napoletano e le sue variazioni regionali," in *L'altra Europa*, 171–225.

13. Strazzullo, *Edilizia e urbanistica a Napoli*, 115–17, and De Seta, *Storia della cittá di Napoli*, 235–41, explain that decrees beginning in the 1560s aimed to control and ban new construction around the city walls to dampen population growth from immigration.

14. Botero, *Relationi universali,* was first published in two books in 1591, and later expanded to three and four books. The English translation, Botero, *Relations of the most Famous Kingdomes and Common-wealths*, 330; see Gioda, *La vita e le opere di Giovanni Botero*.

15. Parrino, *Teatro eroico*, 1:32–34, describes city privileges, especially the exemption from paying the hearth tax (*fiscali*) assessed on subjects in the kingdom at large.

16. Botero, *Relations of the most Famous Kingdomes and Common-wealths*, 334–35.

17. Liponari, *Relatione delle rivolutioni popolari*, 14–15: "poiche qual maggior contaggio per una città trovarsi può, che la disunione tra cittadini? . . . In somma quello, che è la cõtinua febbre ad un corpo è la disunione degli animi nelle città, e ne' Regni. La città è una Nave, e la disunioni l'aperture, e li buchi, per li quali, mentre quelli, che sono dentro, combattono con disparità de voleri, entra l'acqua dell'aperta guerra in tal' abbundanza, che sommerge la Nave con tutte quante le merci."

18. On the metaphor of contagion and fever, see D'Alessio, *Contagi*; on the metaphor of the ship of state, see Niccoli, "Images of Society," 111–13.

19. Liponari, *Relatione delle rivolutioni popolari*, 10, "E che? Siamo noi meno di Palermo? Non è forse il nostro Popolo più formidabile, e bellicoso? Non habbian forse piu ragione noi altri, come piu aggravti, e oppresi? Sù sù all'armi, resolutione ci vuole, il tempo è pretioso, non è bene differir l'impresa, chi doverebbe sollevarci, odo le nostre querele, e le trascura, quel hà promesso, e non ci attende la parola. Queste e simili doglianze fatte in diverse coventicoli erano hor mai publiche."

20. Beloch, *Bevölkerungsgeschichte Italiens*, 1:172; and Petraccone, *Napoli del Cinquecento all'Ottocento*. Kingdom population is estimated from hearth counts of towns in its twelve provinces in 1505, 1563, 1595, and 1669 by multiplying index numbers of 4.5 to 5.5.

21. Vittorio Conti, *Le leggi di una rivoluzione*, XXXIV–LXII. Musi, *La rivolta*, 236–38, rejects Conti's suggestive hypothesis that the revolt of 1647 had four phases reflecting four republican models, because it "presupposes an organic political development and the

correspondence between governmental form and content"; but Musi does not deny the presence of the four republican models. On the 1647 revolt, see Villari, *The Revolt of Naples*; on political models, see Fasano Guarini, "La crisi del modello repubblicano," 553–84.

22. Giambattista Marino, *Lettere*, 553–57, with English translation from Braudel, *Out of Italy*, 163–66.

23. Beloch, *Bevölkerungsgeschichte Italiens*, 1:172, adds uncounted population in the bread census (religious communities, guests of monasteries and hospices, nobles and their servants, and children under three years of age) to estimate 240,000 inhabitants.

24. Petraccone, *Napoli del Cinquecento all'Ottocento*, for a review of Neapolitan demography.

25. AGS, *Estado, Nápoles*, leg. 1038, f. 139, "Bando de la Vicaria contro los vagabundos de la ciudad de Napoles" (29 April 1550); Villari, *The Revolt of Naples*, 214, nn. 20–21, on immigration from the countryside and "vagrants"; Muto, "The Form and Content of Poor Relief," 213–14.

26. Strazzullo, *Edilizia e urbanistica a Napoli*, 71–73, 235.

27. Parrino, *Teatro eroico*, 1:13, "La prospettiva di essa sembra un' artificioso Teatro, poiche cominciando dal piano, si va insensibilmente innalzando sù le colline, che le servono graziosamente d'appogio."

28. De Cavi, "'Senza causa, et fuor di tempo,'"187–208.

29. Valerio, *Piante e vedute di Napoli dal 1486 al 1599*, 35–38, map 8, "Quale e di quanta Importanza è Bellezza sia la nobile Cita di Napole in Italia."

30. Galasso, "Da 'Napoli gentile' a 'Napoli fedelissima,'" 61–110.

31. Muto, "Gestione politica e controllo sociale," 90–91. The seven *borghi* were Santa Maria di Loreto, San Antonio di Vienna, Santa Maria delle Vergini, Santa Maria della Stella, Gesù Maria, Santa Maria del Monte, and Chiaia.

32. Ibid., 91–93. See also De Seta, *I Casali di Napoli*.

33. De Seta, *Napoli*, 107–21.

34. Caroline Bruzelius, introduction to Bacco, *Naples: An Early Guide*, lxv–lxxix.

35. Divenuto, *Napoli sacra del XVI secolo*, 91–92.

36. Strazzullo, *Edilizia e urbanistica a Napoli*, 157–71.

37. Muto, "The Form and Content of Poor Relief," 229, gives 71 monasteries and 29 convents with 3,050 monks and 1,972 nuns in 1606; 95 monasteries and 29 convents with 5,030 monks and 2,725 nuns in 1629; and 103 monasteries and 32 convents with 5,367 monks and 2,845 nuns in 1671.

38. Rosa, "L'onda che ritorna," 398. Rosa provides a detailed geography of ecclesiastical and sacred space inside and outside the walls of Counter-Reformation Naples. On the religious culture of street corner society, see Muir, "The Virgin on the Street Corner," 25–40.

39. Lutio di Castiglione, *I Sedili di Napoli*, 149–52, gives the five confraternities and their founding dates, with the Holy Cross the earliest founded in 1367.

40. Tutini, *Dei origine e fundatione de' seggi*, 171.

41. Borrelli, "Concetto di popolo," 377–95, and this whole special issue, "Essere popolo. Prerogative e rituali d'appartenenza nelle città italiane d'antico regime," *Ricerche Storiche* 32:2–3, especially articles by Giorgio Chittolini, Mario Ascheri, Claudio Donati, and Gérard Delille.

42. Comparato, "Toward the Revolt," in Calabria and Marino, *Good Government in Spanish Naples*, 296–300.

43. Capaccio, *Il Principe*, "Ottimo Cittadino," Avvertimento 128, p. 269: "Ottimo cittadino è colui, che vuole il giusto per convenienza; & aborrisce il contrario senza scandalo. Euripide fà tre qualità di cittadini, la prima de i ricchi, ma inutili. La seconda di poveri invidiosi a i ricchi. L'altra di quei, che sono in mezzo, che conserva quella disciplina, che constituisce la città."

44. Capaccio, *Il Forastiero*, 692: "Tutti questi distinguo in nobili, popolati, e plebei. I primi, di Piazza, e fuor di Piazza. I secondi, in megliori, e di mezzana conditione. I terzi in gente bassa."

45. Ibid., 777–85. On the *popolo*, 783: "Napoli hà un Popolo di nome ma più di effetto. Per che un popolo è di Gentil'homini che per antichità, per ricchezze, per possessione di feudi, per stile nobile di vivere, han fatto acquisto di nome, e popolo primario. . . . Hà poi un'altro popolo di persone stimate di Tribunali, e si vede che i Dottori ascendono gradi di Magistrati supremi, che ponno comandare, alla nobiltà, e tanto più sarebbero grandi, quando fussero fatti Baroni. Et ultimamente un popolo, che nelle mercature e ne i commerci esercitandosi, ritiene un grado venerabile trà citadini, e massime quando giunti alla possessione de gli haveri, si fanno spettabili, e magnifici nel cumolo di dinari, di fabrica, di splendori nell'Economia, dilungandosi dalla bassezza, sempre si vanno avantaggiando ad un viver civile, e generoso."

46. Ibid., 785: "E così formar anco tre gradi di plebe ove alcuni con lor arti vivono più civilmente, alcuni van declinando assai dalla civiltà, & alcuni con gli infimi esercitii si riducono a tanta bassezza che non ponno ergersi a nessuna maniera di vero stato popolare."

47. Ibid., 539: "Questa mal nata plebe ad ogni modo non può oscurar la fama di così inclita città . . . Ma come dico, la vil plebe seditiosa, e sopra tutto ignorante, è bastevole di dar qualche macchia la qual però lavano a lungo andare col sangue loro stesso." On competing theories of republican citizenship circulating in Naples, see Comparato, "Toward the Revolt," in Calabria and Marino, 290–96.

48. Rykwert, *The Idea of a Town*.

49. Tutini, *Dei origine e fundatione de' seggi*, 40–45, provides the coats of arms of all *seggi*, active and defunct. The coats of arms of the major *seggi* can still be seen on the bell tower of S. Lorenzo, where the city council met. Lutio di Castiglione, *Sedili di Napoli*, p. 74, n. 4, explains that Capuana's horse became bridled in 1250 when the Hohenstaufen king Conrad, upon his entrance into Naples, imposed it on the *seggio* for its opposition to his conquest.

50. Faraglia, "Le ottine ed il reggimento popolare in Napoli," 1–31.

51. Bacco, *Naples: An Early Guide*, 48, notes that S. Agostino enjoyed special patronage from its closest noble district, the *seggio* of Capuana.

52. Muto, "Il regno di Napoli sotto la dominazione spagnola," 233–47. See also, Muto, "Noble Presence and Stratification in the Territories of Spanish Italy," 274–85.

53. Musi, *La rivolta*, 169, reports that during the later months of the 1647 revolt of Naples, the nobles outside the *seggi* sent a proposal to the *popolo* suggesting suppression of the three smaller *seggi* and their reincorporation with these nobles *fuori piazza* into a new *seggio*. This new noble *seggio*, more favorable to the *popolo*, would have shared city rule with

Capuana and Nido. If the two older *seggi* were unwilling to share governance in this way, as this proposal continued, the new *seggio* would rule with the *popolo* alone.

54. The starting point for such studies in Naples is Mancini, *Feste ed Apparati civili e religiosi*. See also Galasso, "La festa," in *L'altra Europa*, 121–42; Rak, "A dismisura d'uomo," 259–312, and "Il sistema delle feste nella Napoli barocca," 2:301–27; Fabris, "Musical Festivals at a Capital without a Court, 270–86, and *Music in Seventeenth-Century Naples*, chap. 1, "La città della festa," 1–49.

55. Guarino, "The Politics of Appearances," now *Representing the King's Splendour*, and his summary article, "Spanish Celebrations in Seventeenth-Century Naples," 25–41.

56. Cocco, "Vesuvius and Naples: Nature and the City."

57. De Cavi, "Spain in Naples: Building, Sculpture, and Painting under the Viceroys (1585—1621)" (Ph.D. dissertation, Columbia University, 2007), now published as *Architecture and Royal Presence*.

58. Dauverd, "Mediterranean Symbiotic Empire."

59. Trexler, *Public Life in Renaissance Florence*; Muir, *Civic Ritual in Renaissance Venice*; and Visceglia, *La città rituale: Roma e le sue cerimonie in età moderna*. Two early works that set the terms of inquiry into ritual are Jacquot, *Le fêtes de la Renaissance*; and Strong, *Art and Power: Renaissance Festivals (1450–1650)*. See also Schneider, *The Ceremonial City: Toulouse Observed, 1738–1780*; Muir, *Ritual in Early Modern Europe*; and Fenlon, *The Ceremonial City: History, Memory and Myth in Renaissance Venice*.

60. De Cavi, *Architecture and Royal Presence*, 85–132. On the artistic preservation and restoration of the Aragonese sarcophagi in the sacristy of S. Domenico, see *Le Arche dei Re Aragonesi*.

61. Fabris, "Musical Festivals at a Capital without a Court."

62. Burke, "The Virgin of the Carmine and the Revolt of Masaniello," 3–21; and the expanded rejoinder, Villari, *The Revolt of Naples*, afterword one, "Masaniello, Contemporary and Recent Interpretations," 153–70.

63. Vario, *Pragmaticae*, 2:8–10, *De Ferriis*, Titulus LXXVIII, Prammatica II (13 November 1555).

64. Galasso, "Da 'Napoli gentile' a 'Napoli fedelissima,'" 61–110.

65. Calaresu, "Images of Ancient Rome," 641–61.

66. J. Marino, "Economic Idylls and Pastoral Realities," 215–16, quotes the Venetian ambassador to Naples, Alvise Lando, in 1580.

67. Ibid., 216–19; Hernando Sánchez, "Naturaleza y mito," 66–73; and Calabria, *The Cost of Empire*.

68. On Neapolitan guidebooks, see Amirante, *Libri per vedere*; for saint cults and saint lives, see Sallmann, *Naples et ses saints*.

69. Bacco, *Naples: An Early Guide*, 45–49.

70. Toschi and Penna, *Le Tavolette votive*, "Le Origini del culto alla Madonna dell'Arco," 39–54; and Rak, "Lo squardo devoto," 31–59, lists a sixth category of ex-votos as unspecified or unidentified petitions.

71. Villari, *The Revolt of Naples*, 42–46.

72. Strazzullo, *Edilizia e urbanistica a Napoli*, 187–98, provides a chronological catalog of churches and religious institutions built in Naples in the seventeenth century.

73. Caputi, *La Pompa funerale . . . Filippo II.*

74. J. Marino, "Celebrating a Royal Birth," 53–67, and, "The Zodiac in the Streets," 203–29; and on Carnival, Barletta, *Fra regola e licenza.*

75. Orilia, *Lo Zodiaco.*

76. Garnica, "The Ceremonial of the Neapolitan Court," 9–60, is partially transcribed in Cherchi, "Juan de Garnica," 213–24. On Diéz de Aux, see De Cavi, *Architecture and Royal Presence,* 217–21 and 223–24. Raneo, *Etiquetas de la corte.*

77. Bouchard, *Voyage dans le Royaume de Naples,* 2:159–475.

78. Montemayor, *Diurnali di Scipione Guerra;* Rubino, "Notitia," BSNSP, ms. XXIII.D.14–17; Fuidoro, *Giornali di Napoli;* Confuorto, *Giornali di Napoli.*

79. Campanella, *La Monarchia di Spagna: Prima stesura giovanile,* 25: "Dico dunque che il fine delle monarchie é già venuto, ed ogni cosa ha da resolversi nell'imperio felicissimo de Santi e della Chiesa, il che sarà finite le Quattro monarchie e morto l'Antecristo, secondo Lattanzio, santo Ireneo, Tertulliano, Origene, Vittorino, santo Bernardino, l'abbate Gioachino e infiniti altri teologi, filosofi e poeti, come altrove dichiarai." Ernst dates this early draft between the conversion of Henry IV (June 1593) and his benediction by Clement VIII (September 1595).

80. Telesio had published the first two books of his *De natura juxta propria principia* in 1565, with the complete edition of the *Rerum natura* in 1586. Della Porta first published *Magiae naturalis* in four books in 1558 and a revised, second Neapolitan edition in twenty books in 1589. Tasso traveled between courts in Ferrara, Mantua, Rome, and Naples. His pastoral drama *L'Aminta* was first performed in 1573 in Ferrara, where he completed the *Gerusalemme liberata* in 1575 and later published it in 1581. He published his *Discorsi del poema eroico* in Naples in 1594.

Chapter 1. Myth and History: From Italy to Naples

1. Machiavelli, *Il principe e Discorsi,* ed. Bertelli, 125–26: "Coloro che leggeranno quale principio fusse quello della città di Roma, e da quali latori di leggi e come ordinato, non si maraviglieranno che tanta virtù si sia per più secoli mantenuta in quella città." English translations Machiavelli, *Discourses on Livy,* trans. Mansfield and Tarcov, 7–10. See Mansfield, *Machiavelli's New Modes and Orders,* 28–32.

2. Baldassarri and Saiber, *Images of Quattrocento Florence,* xix–xxii, 3–36.

3. On humanist thought on the origins of cities, see Jacks, *The Antiquarian and the Myth of Antiquity,* esp. chap. 2, " *Urbs* or *Civitas*: The Humanists' Debate," 74–124.

4. Veyne, *Did the Greeks Believe in Their Myths?,* emphasizes that, for the ancients, "historical truth was tradition and vulgate." On Livy and Dionysius of Halicarnassus, for example, "the materials of a tradition are not the tradition itself, which always emerges as a text, a tale carrying authority. History is born as tradition, not built up from source materials" (7).

5. Weber, *The City,* 97–98.

6. Botero, *The Greatness of Cities,* bk. I.2, p. 228. See Guazzo, *La civil conversazione;* and for its context, see Miller, "Friendship and Conversation in Seventeenth-Century Venice," 1–31.

7. Botero, *The Greatness of Cities*, bk. I.i, p. 227.

8. Ibid., bk. I, 227–43.

9. Schumpeter, *History of Economic Analysis*, 254–55.

10. Weber, *The City*, 71.

11. Vernant, *Myth and Thought among the Greeks*, 256.

12. Vernant and Vidal-Naquet, *Myth and Tragedy in Ancient Greece*, 260.

13. Vernant, *Myth and Society in Ancient Greece*, 235–40.

14. Biondo, *Roma Ristaurata et Italia Illustrata*, 64–241. See Cochrane, *Historians and Historiography*, 34–40.

15. Hyde, "Medieval Descriptions of Cities," 4–5; also see 28–30, "List of Medieval Descriptions of Cities, c. 738–1340" for thirteen cities.

16. I have consulted the first edition of Alberti, *Descrittione di tutta Italia* (1550), and the modern edition, Petrella, *L'officina del geografo*, but I have used extensively a later Venetian edition (1596). After the first edition, eight editions followed in the next twenty-five years; two Latin editions were published in Cologne in 1566 and 1567; and in the 1561 edition, Alberti added a description of the Italian islands. See Cochrane, *Historians and Historiography*, 305–8; and Redigonda, "Alberti, Leandro," *DBI* 1: 699–702.

17. Alberti, *Descrittione di tutta Italia* (1596), 179v: "Una delle Sirene quivi sepolta, la quale (come narrano le favole) quindi si gettò nel mare per il gran cordoglio c'hebbe, non havendo potuto ingannare con le sue lusinghe Ulisse, & compagni, & poi fu sepolta in questo luogo qual fu poi fabricato da i Cumani, & dal nome di questa vergine, anzi meretrici (come dicono alcuni) talmente Partenope nominate." This part of the Siren's story gave rise to beliefs and practices that include the Sirens in funerary rituals, with a role in mourning the dead and helping to fulfill the promise of life after death.

18. Ibid., 364v–365r: "Da chi la fosse fabricata in piu modi si narra, de i quali alcuni ne rammentarò, lasciando però dar sentenza al giudicioso lettore, di quel che li parerà piu verisimile. Io durò qui una parola. Nella narratione del principio delle città, e de i luoghi, sovente io descrivo alcune cose, che paiono a me non solamente favole, anzi bugie, et ciò faccio per dimostrace haverle vedute, acciò che non sia ripreso ò d'ignoranza, o di negligenza, o di malignità."

19. Ibid., 365r: "Altri altrimenti scrivono circa la edificatione di essa, e perche à me paiono di poco momento, e da far ridere i Lettori tal narrationi, per non esser tedioso a quelli, le lascierò ad altri scrivere. Quanto alle openioni descritte, par a me, che siano alcune di quelle, che habbino poco colore di verità."

20. McNeill, *Mythistory*, "Mythistory, or Truth, Myth, History, and Historians," 3–22.

21. Alberti, *Descrittione di tutta Italia* (1596), 365r: "Perche spese volte, tanta è la cupidità de'mortali di voler'esser istimati, et esser divenuti d'antichi, e nobili avoli, credendo alcuni alle narrationi delle favole, che tassano gli scrittori, che non fanno memoria di essi, si come ignoranti, o invidiosi, o negligenti. Et per tanto gli spirti gentili, et giudiciosi non mi noteranno in questo, se ben io descrivo tali favole, benche possono avvertire s'io li presto fede, o nò, quando dico, ch'io le lascio nel giudicio del prudente lettore."

22. Ibid., 397v: "Non ritrovo cosa certa del principio di essa città. Ben'è vero, che ho letto una cronica molto antica, qual dice, che fu fatta da Ercole compagno di Giasone, nominandola Troia, il qual passando per Italia con molti compagni Greci per andare in Ispagna,

e dimostrando maravigliose opere di sua fortezza (et massimamente in questi luoghi) superò un forte, e terribile Gigante presso al Pò, che portava seco una palla di metallo, di peso di 300 libre, la qual talmente maneggiara, che leggermente la gettava ovunque li piaceva. Havendo adunque Ercole superato costui, volle che si edificassi quivi una città in memoria di tanta vittoria nominandola Climena dal nome della madre (la qual città fu poi detta Cremona.) Poscia (edificata essa città) vi condusse in quella ad habitare alquanti de i vicini populi, che habitavano in quà, et in là fra il Po, & Adda fiumi. Et per questa cagione a perpetua memoria, fu fatta una statua, che rappresenta il Gigante con la palla in mano, la quale ogni anno è vestita da i Cremonesi."

23. Nora, "Between Memory and History," 7–25. See Nora, *Realms of Memory*.

24. Gatti Perer, *"La dimora di Dio con gli uomini" (Ap 21,3)*.

25. Bairoch, *The Population of European Cities from 800 to 1850*.

26. J. Marino, "Administrative Mapping," 5–25, emphasizes the expansion of the market for printed maps after the 1560s in Venice, Florence, Rome, and Naples. For a contrary view on an earlier map market already present in turn-of-the-century Florence, see Woodward, *Maps as Prints*, 76 and 119, nn. 6 and 101. For maps of Naples in sixteenth-century city-map collections, see Valerio, *Piante e vedute di Napoli dal 1486 al 1599*: map 9, Paolo Forlani, *Il primo libro delle cittá, et fortezze principali del mondo* (Venice, 1567); map 15, Georg Braun and Frans Hogenberg, *Civitates Orbis Terrarum*, vol. 1 of 6 (Cologne, 1572–1617); map 16, François de Belleforest, *La Cosographie Universelle* (Paris, 1575); map 17, Gerard de Jode, *Speculum Orbis Terrarum* (Antwerp, 1578); map 25, Francesco Valegio, *Raccolta di le piu illustri et famose citta di tutto il mondo* (Venice, ca. 1590); and map 26, Pietro Bertelli, *Theatrum Urbium Italicarum* (Venice, 1599).

27. Braun and Hogenberg, *Beschreibung und Contrafactur*, map insert between 48 and 49.

28. Nuti, "I 'teatri' di città," 105–23.

29. Bellucci and Valerio, *Piante e vedute di Napoli dal 1600 al 1699*, map 9. See Benevolo, *La città italiana nel Rinascimento*, frontispiece and introduction, "I motivi delle trasformazioni cittadine nel Rinascimento italiano," 11–40.

30. Nuti, "I 'teatri' di città."

31. Discussion of the twin sons of Remus can be found in the many treatments of Lorenzetti's fresco of *Good and Bad Government* in Siena's Palazzo Publico. See Bowsky, *A Medieval Italian Commune*, 287–89; Greenstein, "The Vision of Peace," 492–510; and Starn and Partridge, *Arts of Power*, 10–80.

32. Baldassarri and Saiber, *Images of Quattrocento Florence*, 12–17, translates the preface and introduction to book 1 of Bruni, *Historiarum Florentini populi*. See Brown, "The Language of Empire," 32–47.

33. See the classic argument on "civic humanism" in Baron, *The Crisis of the Early Italian Renaissance*, chap. 3, "A New View of Roman History and of the Florentine Past," 47–78, which examines Bruni's *Dialogi* and *Laudatio Florentinae Urbis* as "the birth of a new civic sentiment and a new attitude toward the past" in a comparison of "republicanism versus Dante's glorification of Caesar" (48).

34. Lanzoni, *Genesi svolgimento e tramonto*, 36.

35. Natale Conti, *Natale Conti's* Mythologiae, "Introduction," 1:xxv. Conti's *Mythologiae*

saw at least twenty-five Latin editions and six French translations published in numerous international locations in Italy, Germany, France, and Switzerland.

36. Ibid., 1:3.

37. Lanzoni, *Genesi svolgimento e tramonto*, 36.

38. Muir, *Civic Ritual in Renaissance Venice*, 68, on the Attila foundation myth for Venice.

39. Bizzocchi, *Genealogie incredibili*.

40. M. Tanner, *The Last Descendant of Aeneas*, 17–19.

41. Ibid., 67–69.

42. Capaccio, "Napoli descritta ne' principii del secolo XVII," 73. Often attributed to Giulio Cesare Capaccio, Quondam, *La parola nel labirinto*, 224, n. 54, dismisses the attribution as erroneous or at least uncertain on the basis of a disparity between its statistics and those in *Il Forastiero*, day 9 and its divergence from the method of organization found in Capaccio's historical works.

43. Muir, *Ritual in Early Modern Europe*, 232–39.

44. Rykwert, *The Idea of a Town*, 199–200 and 231, n. 35a; also note the Filarete description of the astrological conditions necessary and foundation ceremonies invented for the founding of the ideal town Sforzinda (*Filarete's* Treatise on Architecture, 22 and 43–44). See Rubinstein, "Vasari's Painting on the Foundation of Florence," 64–73.

45. Muir, *Civic Ritual in Renaissance Venice*, 71 for 25 March; Filarete, *Filarete's* Treatise on Architecture. See Quinlan-McGrath, "The Italian City as a Living Entity."

46. Alberti, *Descrittione di tutta Italia* (1596), Brescia, 391r–v; (1550), frontispiece. In the 1596 edition, the frontispiece has David slaying Goliath.

47. Collenuccio, *Compendio de le istorie del Regno di Napoli*; and the study of Masi, *Dal Collenuccio a Tommaso Costo*.

48. See Samantha Kelly's forthcoming translation of the fourteenth-century vernacular history of Naples known as the "Cronaca di Partenope"; and Altamura, *Cronaca di Partenope*.

49. Collenuccio, *Compendio de le istorie del Regno di Napoli*, 12.

50. Pontano, *Historia della guerra di Napoli*. On Pontano's historiographical heirs in Naples, see Cochrane, *Historians and Historiography*, 270–72; on Camillo Porzio (c. 1527–80), *La congiura dei Baroni*, and his unpublished work.

51. Guicciardini, *The History of Italy*, 3.

52. Bentley, *Politics and Culture in Renaissance Naples*; and Santoro, "Humanism in Naples," 1:296–331.

53. Costo, *Addizioni e note*; Masi, *Dal Collenuccio a Tommaso Costo*, appendix I.

54. Costo, *Giunta di tre Libri*, 135r–43v. The quotation is from Villari, *The Revolt of Naples*, 218, n. 37.

55. Costo, *Il Fuggilozio*. For biographical details, xxxvi–xlv; and Lettere, "Costo, Tommaso," *DBI* 30:411–15.

56. On Tasso in Naples, see Quondam, *La parola nel labirinto*, 25–61.

57. Costo and Benvenga, *Il Segretario di lettere*, originally published in Costo's *Lettere*.

58. Costo, *La apologia istorica*, 4: "Torno dunque a dire che la città di Napoli, per non essersi curata di havere scritta proprio delle sue cose, è in corsa nella calumnie de gli

stranieri, i quail e male informati, e poco amorevoli di lei ne hanno parlato non conforme al vero, ma secondo le loro varie passioni."

59. Cochrane, *Historians and Historiography*, 275, summarizes the general thrust of publications in both content and format. Bacco, *Effigie di tutti i Re*, and the numerous editions of his later popular guidebooks are a good example. Cochrane is mistaken, however, about the purpose of these late sixteenth-century books, because newly appointed Spanish viceroys prepared themselves with Spanish-language *avvertimenti*. See Rivero Rodríguez, "Doctrina y práctica política en la monarquía hispana," 197–213, with examples of the genre transcribed in Coniglio, *Declino del viceregno*, "Istruzioni di Filippo III al vicerè conte di Lemos" (20 April 1599), 71–143, and "Istruzioni di Filippo III al vicerè di Napoli conte di Benavente" (17 September 1602), 174–241.

60. Mazzella, *Descrittione del Regno* and *Le vite dei re*. For the *Descrittione*, I have used the 1601 reprint edition (1981).

61. Mazzella, *Sito et antichità della città di Pozzuolo*.

62. Mazzella, *Descrittione del Regno*, 15–16: "Finalmente si previene alla bella, e Real città di Napoli detta prima dal nome della Sirena, che v'arrivò portata dall'onde, Partenope; la quale cambiatosi il nome per esser stata rihabitata, secondo l'oracolo da i Cumani, che l'haveano avanti distrutta."

63. Costo, *Ragionamenti*, esp. 1–5.

64. Zappullo, *Sommario Istorico . . . di tre gran Città, cioè Gerusalem, di Roma, e di Napoli*. In the second and subsequent editions (1602; 1603; 1609), Zappullo adds Venice because of its long history of liberty not subject to its enemies and the Indies as the hope and fulfillment of the spread of God's word to all mankind. I have used the 1609 edition, ix–x and 253–330.

65. Summonte, *Dell' Historia della Città e Regno di Napoli*, 1:27, "un'altro marmo con l'iscrittione che nel suo luogo si ponerà, à noi dato dal Signor Scipion Mazzella diligentissimo perscrutatore dell'antichità di questa Città: & amator di virtù."

66. Ibid., vol. 3 (1640) and vol. 4 (1643), 446–79, on the "acerbic and cruel death of Gio. Vincenzo Starace."

67. Ibid., 1:3: "Vorrei in questa mia Historia circa l'origine della edificatione di si nobil Città, parlarne breve, e risoluto: ma per la diversità dell'openioni degli antichi scrittori, è necessario per maggior chiarezza, ch'io qui le narri, acciò ciascuno possa ben'intenderla, & tener poi quello che più gli aggrada"; and 1: 5–6, "Dico dunque che la fondatrice della Città nostra fù Partenope non la favolosa Sirena, ó meretrice come alcuni han figurato (perche l'allegoria, e verità, che sotto questa figura stà nascosta diremo appresso). Ma fu veramente donna, e Signora pudicissima, seguita da molta gente, che con lei vennero da Calcide dell'isola d'Euboa, hor detta Negroponte."

68. Ibid., 1:3: "Seguito da molti: quali dicono che la Città di Napoli fù edificata da Cumani venuti dall'Isola d'Euboa, hor detta Negroponte; imperoche 170 anni doppo la roina di Troia, e 260 prima che Roma edificata fusse, e del mondo 4213 seguendo questa opinione. E secondo un altra correndo gli anni del mondo 4036. E prima del nascimento di N.S. Giesu Christo 1168."

69. Nigro, "Capaccio, Giulio Cesare," 18:374–80; and Quondam, "Dal mannerismo al barocco," 5:368–72 and 503–33.

70. Capaccio, *Il Secretario*. See Nigro, "The Secretary," 82–99.

71. Wilcox, *The Development of Florentine Humanist Historiography*.

72. Capaccio, *Napolitanae Historiae*.

73. Ibid., unnum. iii–iv. See Novellino, "Le filigrane culturali della 'fedeltà,' " 7–10. Note that in Capaccio the attributes of Naples are assigned to nature and fortune, as opposed to Pontano's figuration art and nature a century earlier.

74. Capaccio, *Il Forastiero*, author's preface "To the Curious Reader," unnumbered vii: "mi si offerì una sì gran vastità di novi pensieri, e furono tante le cose che giudicai degne di tenersene conto da gli omini curiosi in questa occasione, che mi ritrovai immerso dentro il pelago d'una Enciclopedia che nell'universal varietà di descrittioni, relationi, accidenti Regali, governi, guerre, memorie di cose antiche, successi di Stato, encomij di famiglie, e di persone degne di onore, e mille altre cose simili che trattengono nella lettione i belli ingegni, e che sono utili alla varietà del sapere, mi ferono dubitare se dovessi formarne istoria, o pure con altro genere di dire spiegare i concetti miei." For an explication of this passage as a reflection of the concept "patria," see Novellino, "Le filigrane culturali della 'fedeltà,' " 5–6.

75. Snyder, *Writing the Scene of Speaking*, 185–97. Manso's treatise on dialogue appears as an appendix in *Erocallia*, 1033–64. For Tasso on dialogue, see Snyder, *Writing the Scene of Speaking*, 146–80; for the Italian text of Tasso's *Discorso dell'arte del dialogo* with facing English translation, Tasso, *Tasso's Dialogues*, 15–41. For Manso in Capaccio, *Il Forastiero*, 8–9, 750–51; for Tasso in Capaccio, *Il Forastiero*, 3–4, where he is equated with Homer, Virgil, and Ariosto.

76. Capaccio, *Il Forastiero*, 1–2: "Forastiero: poi c'havend'io questo capriccio di andar atorno per il mondo per curiosità di saper molte cose di che non tutti han gusto, come sono origine, e belezze di città, costumi di popoli, usanze di genti, movimenti di guerra, varietà di dominij, maneggi di governi, provedimenti di leggi, esercitij di Cavalieri, andamenti di cittadini, fabriche, pitture, statue, politia di habitanti, & ogni altra simil cosa che ad inclita città convenga, e particolarmente à Napoli città famosa che fa invidia à tutte l'altre famosissime di Europa. . . . Conosco molto bene che siete deli'humor mio; e che siete sicuro che se un virtuoso da tutte le discipline può salire ad alcun grado di gloria . . . Cittadino: Molto bene. E chi non può saper quest'universale, attenda almeno ad esser benissimo informato della sua patria; che tal'hor sapendo esser buon relatore dell'origine, riti, costumi, antichità, nobiltà, vaghezze, commode, e che so io?"

77. Tasso, *Tasso's Dialogues*, 151–91, provides the Italian text and facing English translation.

78. Colapietra, "La storiografia napoletana," 16 (1960): 415–36 and 17 (1961): 416–31; and Cochrane, *Historians and Historiography*, 155–59, 270–75.

79. Capaccio, *Il Forastiero*, 64. On the cult of the ancient god Hebone, associated with the sun, see Novellino, "Il culto di Hebone," 106–36.

80. Capaccio, *Il Forastiero*, 14.

81. Ibid, 56–58: "E vero che i curiosi van considerando per cosa di maraviglia che Napoli città qual dopo il Romano Imperio mai non potè esser vinta col ferro, fusse finalmente soggiogata con una sola parola."

82. For Capaccio's understanding of *favola*, see *Gli Apologi*, 1602, "Ai lettori," unnum.

4v–10v: "la Favola mescolarsi con una certa narratione ritrovata per diletto, ma che fusse però ella di cose ne vere, ne verisimili; come ne vero fù . . . E pure sotto quei veli mistica-mente alle volte i gravi significati di varie cose andavano comprendo que'curiosi Antichi, che non potendo penetrar quegli occlti Simboli della Teologia, ne i sentieri de i quali ciecamente eglino andavan caminando senza lume di Fede, la quale à quelle maniere as-cose andò porgendo poi nuova apparenza; andavano quasi imitatori adombrando le varie fantasie, e i varii capricci che non veleano che al volgo ignorante così chiari apparissero" (5r).

83. Capaccio, *Il Forastiero*, 64–65: "La Lira fù chiaro simbolo della consonanza di tutte le cose che si fussero potuto imaginare in questa Città così del governo che dovea con tanto ordine di varij dominij, acquistar la sua perfettione, in che si ritrova in questi tempi, sotto la perfettissima armonia del Regno di Spagna; come della volontà de i vassalli, con-cordemente uniti à servire in qualisvoglia modo il padrone, che se bene e plebe, e popolo, e nobiltà differiscono in stato, come differenti sono le corde della Lira, tutta volta come l'istesse accordandosi in diversità, fanno perfettissima unione di fede." The tripartite divi-sion of Neapolitan society has been represented differently by various observers. Porzio's "Relazione del Regno di Napoli al Marchese di Mondesciar," 239–340, explicates his three "sorti di uomini" as plebs, nobles, and barons. See Muto, "Il regno di Napoli sotto la domi-nazione spagnola," 228–33.

84. Capaccio, *Delle Imprese*, 1:23, "La Lira, significò la Concordia, che per quell celeste simolacro se la dipingono propria i Napolitani in braccio d'una Sirena, e di sei corde, per l'unione di cinque piazze di Nobili, & una Popolare."

85. Alciati, *Emblemata cum commentariis*, 60–65, and *Emblematum liber*; Capaccio, *Il Principe*, 15–17.

86. Alciato, *Emblemata cum commentariis*, 64b, "Discant praeterea hinc Principes, qua ratione amore potius & benevolentia subditos gubernare, quā vi & armis debeant; siq-uidem constans pax, indubitata fides, prompta obedientia, non alia clavi melius ad harmo-niam tenditur, quam amore."

87. Capaccio, *Il Principe*, 17: "Adimandato Agesilao, per qual cagione non cingea Sparta di mura? Rispose, che i Cittadini concordemente uniti erano ottimo presidio a difender la Città. Et Agasicle a colui, che gli disse, come senza satelliti può star sicuro il Principe? Rispose; s'egli comandarà come il padre a i figli."

88. Ibid. Capaccio translates Alciato's Latin, *Emblemata cum commentariis*, 65a: "Vetam ac stabilem civium benevolentiam, optimam esse Principis, custodiam."

89. Capaccio, *Il Forastiero*, 65: "L'esser partecipe poi della natura di uccello, altro non significò che la felicità de i loro ingegni Napolitani, veloci a spargere in servigio de i loro Re, velocissimi all'acquisto di tutte le grandezze; & al volare con la contemplatione al cielo, ov'era per fonder la nova Religione Cristiana per farsene superiori a qualsivoglia natione."

90. Capaccio, *Delle Imprese*, 1:23–24: "Ma non parve a me buona mai l'Impresa di Si-rena, mai di cosa buona significatrice, sempre fraudolenta, e che inganna; e direi che più tosto è Impresa per significar le delitie, e i gusti della Città, alludendo alla dolce, e delitiosa Partenope. Cõ tutto ciò, nel tempo de'suoi Rumori, dòpò l'essersi ridotta a stato di quiete fù fatta questa, d'una Sirena che in mezzo a Vesevo acceso fà stillar latte dalle mamme, col

motto, DUM VESUVII SIREN INCENDIA MULCET." For images of Partenope, see Fabris, "La città della Sirena," 2:473–501, figs. 1–7.

91. Corsi, "Musica reale e immaginaria nelle feste," 24–27.

92. Celano, *Notize del bello dell'antico*, 4:125–26. For a detail of the street, see De Seta, *Storia della città di Napoli*, 283, tav. 67, marked on the map at 201, which is taken from the Baratta map of 1670, but is clearly identified on the earlier Baratta map of 1629 in Baratta, *Fidelissimae urbis Neapolitanae*, schema, 26–27 at 149 and 150.

93. Corsi, "Musica reale e immaginaria nelle feste," 7–9, esp. n. 6, which quotes a description of the *apparati* in the Sellaria by Giovanni Domenico De Lega.

94. Divenuto, *Napoli L'Europa*, 117r–v.

95. Capaccio, *Il Forastiero*, 65: "Questa Dea [Partenope] adunque fù ne i primi honori tra Napolitani."

96. Ibid., "E con questi vi dirò gli altri geroglifici co i quali Napoli adorò il Sole, e prima, il chiamarono Hebone."

97. Novellino, "Il culto di Hebone," 111, n. 10.

98. Ibid., 132, n. 42.

99. Capaccio, *Il Forastiero*, 65–79.

100. Ibid., 70, "In alcune si vede dipinta una Cetera, che risguarda la proprietà de i giri celesti, ch' è l'armonia; e di tutti i giri è Principe, e moderatore il Sole." Cf. Capaccio, *Delle Imprese*, 1:54v, "Così per significar il Principe, havremo il Sole, per l'operatione del continuo moto."

101. Capaccio, *Il Principe*, Avvertimento CXXXIX, "Maestri di Principi. Chirone," 293: "E fiera, mentre danni / Reca ai compagni, e dà scompiglio a l'hoste, / E huomo poi, mentre lontano da Dio, / Finge esser huomo pio."

102. Ingman, "Machiavelli and the Interpretation of the Chiron Myth," 217–25.

103. Capaccio, *Il Principe*, Avvertimento CXXXVIII, "Consiglieri del buon Principe. Senato," 290–91: "Sedenti elle si veggon; che conviene / Che i Giudici sian gravi, e di quieta / Mente; e che no sian di animi leggieri. / E non han mani, che non piglia doni. / E se il primo di lor è cieco, sappi, / Che'l Principe è costui, che senza affetto / Ascolti solo, e faccia / Quel, che'l Senato con le leggi abbraccia."

104. Ibid., 194–95.

105. Capaccio, *Incendio di Vesuvio*, 2nd num., 1: "Quando li mesi à dietro successe l'horribilissimo accidente dell'incendio di Vesuvio, venni subbito à ritrovarvi così sbigottito, & attimorato che non seppi anco ritrovar principio di ragionarvi, ch'in vero novità cosi maravigliosa haveria stordite le menti de i più coragiosi homini del mondo, mi ridussero à credere che all'hora fusse venuto il fine di quello"; and 85–86: "Et in tanto arda Vesuvio, per far perpetua luminaria alla grandezza della Chiesa; che durarà insino alla consumatione del secolo eternamente, alla Maestà di casa d'Austria che per infiniti secoli farà padrona; alla Maestà dell'Imperio coronata da quelle due eccelse Corone; & alla fidelissima Città di Napoli, la qual sempre erutta fiàme di carità, di amore, e di divotione, e queste sono la vera rivolutione di pianeti."

106. Baker, "Inventing the French Revolution," 203–7, explains that before the eighteenth century, "revolution" and more frequently "revolutions" meant literally "a cycle in human affairs that brings things back to their point of departure (in an analogy with the

astronomical meaning of the term)," and thus, figuratively, "changes in fortune, accidental mutations in human affairs, innovations and disorders erupting within the flow of human time"; but not yet "a radical break with the past achieved by the conscious will of human actors, an inaugural moment for a drama of change and transformation projected indefinitely into the future."

107. Capaccio, *Il Forastiero*, 770–87, esp. 742 and 783–84.

108. Ibid., 484–89. See Corona, "La morte di Giovan Vincenzo Starace." Two detailed descriptions of the incident drawn from wider sources are available in English: Villari, *The Revolt of Naples*, 19–29; and Muir, "The Cannibals of Renaissance Italy," 5–14.

109. Capaccio, *Il Forastiero*, 487: "All'hora come cani arrabbiati, e come fiere indomite . . . e strascinandolo usciti da S. Agostino, se'l porarono per tutta la cità, aspergendo ogni loco del suo sangue . . . Passò oltre quella mal nal nata gente, e ridussero il cadavero a tal termine, che non trovandosi, ne carne, ne pelle, ne ossa, ne se gli potè dar sepoltura, se non vogliamo dire che gli fù sepolcro tutta la cità di Napoli"; and 488: "Tremo in sentir queste parole piene di giusta vendetta, e così proprie, e significanti."

110. Ibid., 561 at the beginning of the excursus 561–73: "ma ce n'andiamo superficialmente per narrationi delle cose occorse in varij tempi; si potrebbe dire che si accosta assai alla natura di Ragion di Stato, per che si sono proposti modi fantastichi di governi esercitati non secondo la Ragione, ma secondo la volontà de i padroni de gli Stati. E per questo dal ragionar che faremo hoggi scopriremo i due veri modi di governo che stabiliscono la grandezza del Re, & il bisogno di vassalli in una città qual'è Napoli." Cf. on Capaccio's digression, Comparato, *Uffici e società*, 406–8.

111. Capaccio, *Il Forastiero*, 561: "l'uno consiste nel vero e ragionevole governare fondato senza soffisticherie, nelle Leggi Imperiali che comandano il dovere; l'altro nella prattica civile compresa ne gli statuti, e regole ordinate sotto l'istesse leggi per non deviare, ma che mantenghi la citadinanza cō quell che le viene permesso dal padrone. Quello si esercita ne i tribunali del Re; e questo nella raunanza del publica."

112. Ibid., 563: "uno impuro Machiavelli, e suoi seguaci, peste del mondo, fabrica sopra l'instabilità dell'Heresia, essendo tutto ciò che si ratta intorno a questa materia." On *ragion di stato*, cf. Borrelli, "Ragion di Stato. L'arte italiana della prudenza politica."

113. Capaccio, *Il Principe*, 9–11: "La congregatione de gli huomini reprobi, che meretrice con proprio nome chiamar si può, siede sopra una impura, e formidabil bestia, quando con illecito culto in tanti inimici della Christiana religione, o favella, o scrive, o pur opera cose illecite, enormi falsità, e cō una tazza di finta sapienza, sotto pretesto di vera pieta inebria, & uccide. . . . Procurano in questa maniera gli impuri Macchiavelli d'ingannare con dolci apparenze i Signori del Mondo."

114. Capaccio, *Il Forastiero*, 563: "Chiesa è vera ragion di Stato. Ragion di Stato, vuol dire cosa ragionevole, e che sta ferma, e non crolla, e non sdrucciola come gli stati secolari, che star fermi non ponno."

115. Capaccio, *Il Principe*, 11: "è pure un notabilissimo precetto quello di Aristotele nella Politica, che quei, che governano, se attenderano alla Religione, perche manco temeranno i popoli, che non si faccia alcuna cosa contra la Giustitia, vedendo che'l padrone teme Dio; e contra un c'haverà Dio favorevole, no havranno ardire d'insorgere temerariamente." Costo, *La apologia*, 5–6, had expressed similar opinions: "secondo Aristotile, è quel, che

vien creato da un numero d'homini buoni e Giusti, un di loro cioè per bontà, ò per virtù eroiche proprie, e de' suoi maggiori sopravanzi tutti gli altri . . . l'honesto Tiranno per dovere, appara grande amator della religiones, timoroso di Dio, di honestissimi costumi e virtuose e che sopr'a tutto si guardi da offender altrui nell'honore."

116. Capaccio, *Il Forastiero*, 566: "Questa è la Ragion di Stato, fratel mio, obedire alla Chiesa Cattolica, e sottoporre il capo a i piedi di Sommi Pontefici, i quali havendo due spade, così riserbano la loro nel rigor dell'Ecclesiastica disciplina, che porgono l'altra a i Re . . ."

117. Novellino, "Il culto di Hebone," 110, n. 8, on Capaccio's exile.

118. Capaccio, *Il Forastiero*, 568–69: "l'una fù, un nido dell'Alcione sopra uno scoglio in mare, l'altro un Cimiero dentro il quale faceano il mele l'Api, . . ."

119. Alciato, *Emblemata cum commentariis*, 737–47.

120. Capaccio, *Il Principe*, Avvertimenti CLXIX and CLXX, "Dalla Guerra la pace" and "Dalla pace l'abondanza," 370–75: "Pace sempre deve esser desiderata, e procurata . . . Il vero stabilimento di pace co i popoli è la provisione dell'annona, che ad ogni modo stà a carico del Principe . . .che niente differisce il buon Principe dal buon padre."

121. Alciato, *Emblemata cum commentariis*, 734–37; and Capaccio, *Il Principe*, Avvertimento CLVIII, "La Pace," 367–69.

122. Alciato, *Emblemata cum commentariis*, 718–34; and Capaccio, *Il Principe*, Avvertimenti CLXIII–CLXVII, "Giusta vendetta: Polifemo," "Giusta vendetta: Corvo e Scorpione," "Equal pena hà'l delinquente, e'l persuasore: Trombettiero," "Altri pecca, & altri è castigate: Cane," "Spada di pazzo: Aiace," 355–66.

123. Capaccio, *Il Principe*, 375: "Et in fine è verissimo quel, che scrive Dione Crisostomo, che se nella nave tutti i passaggieri dormono, giocano, mangiano, & al nochiero è necessario osservar tempeste future, venti, che spirano, scolgi ove non urti." Niccoli, "Images of Society," 101–22, examines "metaphor as political creation language" with reference to the image of the ship of state, 111–13.

124. Capaccio, *Il Principe*, 375: "il popolo nella Republica vive spensierato, ma tocca al Principe il governare, e'l provedere ad ogni futuro male, e di lui solo è il travaglio, e pure la plebe un giorno volse lapidare Antonino Pio, perche mancò il vitto."

125. Capaccio, *Il Forastiero*, 484–89. Cf. Villari, *The Revolt of Naples*, 25–27 and esp. 217–19, nn. 34–43 with n. 37 explaining how Costo had modified his views on the culpability of the plebs.

126. Capaccio, *Il Forastiero*, 780–81: "con grave danno di così inclita città, è rimasto questo disordine di disparità . . . dalla disparità nasce quella discordia civile che consiste in varij pareti, per che ne i negotij che si trattano ogniuno affetta superiorità onde la Lira comincia a far dissonanza."

127. Capaccio, *Il Principe*, Avvertimento XLV, 85: "E caminando lo Stato Aristocratico in Italia, quanto ha sempre caminato di bene in meglio nel governo della Republica Veneta, mentre con tanta sua gloria si vede per lo spacio di tanti anni star in piedi, trà impetuose onde di travagli, e trà flutti di mille persecutioni? Tutto perche camina innanzi, senza volgersi in dietro al pertubato, e confuso governo di Odocratia, facendo poco conto della bassa plebe." Cf. Rovito, *Il Viceregno Spagnolo di Napoli*, 25, n. 56.

128. Capaccio, *Il Forastiero*, 569: "nell'historie i disordini che questa Ragione hà cagionato infin dall'anno '400."

129. Ibid., 570–71.

130. Ibid., 571–72: "di esser tiranno con gli homini, e con Dio."

131. Alciato, *Emblemata cum commentariis*, 65, "Stultitiae est index linguaque voxque suae."

132. Capaccio, *Il Principe*, 18–19; and Alciato, *Emblemata cum commentariis*, 69b–70a. See Snyder, *Dissimulation and the Culture of Secrecy*, "Harpocrates' Finger," 10–16.

133. Petrarca, "La festa di San Giovanni Battista a Napoli," 16, cites Capaccio's books in 1613, 1614, 1623, 1624, 1625, 1626, 1627.

134. Capaccio, *Il Forastiero*, 660–62.

135. D'Agostino, *Parlamento e società*.

136. Celano, *Notize del bello*, 3:1, 201–3. See also Hernando Sánchez, "El Parlamento del Reino de Napoles," 333.

137. On the Neapolitan historians, see Colapietra, "La storiografia napoletana." See Cochrane, *Historians and Historiography*, 155–59, 190–97, 270–75, 285–92. For a similar interest in the late Neapolitan Enlightenment, see Calaresu, "Images of Ancient Rome," 641–61.

138. Comparato, *Uffici e società a Napoli*, 355–86; and Galasso, "Una ipotesi di 'blocco storico' oligarchico-borghese," 507–29.

Chapter 2. Ritual Time and Ritual Space

1. Capaccio, *Il Forastiero*, 690: "Hora aggiungete mò tanti altri habitatori, del Regno istesso Calabresi, Pugliesi, Apruzzesi, e più vicini Costaioli, Cavaioli, c'hanno ripiena tutta la cità con tanta frequenza che quasi fanno il terzo di quella, e mi direte quell che poco fà udiste, che gli habitatori fa equentando, & ingrandendo le cità le nobilitano. Ma non lasciarei di dire che la cità di Napoli nobilita anco tutti quelli che vengono ad habitarla. Per che parlando di questi del Regno, quando alcuni sono quà, par che rinascono, e mutano costumi, e quella rozzezza del paese diventa civiltà; & una libertà propria di Napoli, si fan sentire, e'l pane vogliono a più bon mercato, e più bianco, e più grosso, ne si ricordano del pan d'orgio, o di miglio che mangiavano prima. Queste sono le proprie grandezze, e gli allettamenti di questa Sirena."

2. Bouchard, *Voyage dans le Royaume de Naples*, 2:437. See also Marchiex, *Un Parisien à Rome et à Naples*.

3. Burke, *Popular Culture in Early Modern Europe*, 178–204.

4. Bouchard, *Voyage dans le Royaume de Naples*, 2:438–39.

5. Turner, *The Ritual Process*.

6. Bouchard, *Voyage dans le Royaume de Naples*, 2:446.

7. Vario, *Pragmaticae*, 2: 8–10, "De Ferriis."

8. Braudel, *The Mediterranean*, pt. 1, "The Role of the Environment," 1:23–354.

9. Galasso, "La festa," in *L'altra Europa*, 124–25.

10. Rappaport, *Ritual and Religion*, 184–86, summarizes the debate between E. E. Evans-Pritchard and Edmund Leach over the meaning of repetition through the metaphors of cyclicity or alternation. For an anthropological study of 1990–91 fieldwork in a mountain village in Basilicata, see Tak, *South Italian Festivals*, 97–101.

11. Mancini, *Feste ed apparati*, 12, cites Celano, *Notizie del bello*, 1: 277–85.

12. Lanternari, "Cristianesimo e religioni etniche," 329–60, and *La Grande festa*; Galasso, "La festa," in *L'altra Europa*.

13. Tak, *South Italian Festivals*, 99.

14. Bouchard, *Voyage dans le Royaume de Naples*, 2:182ff.

15. Ibid., 2:282.

16. Zappullo, *Sommario Istorico*, 330: "Laonde quanto il Regno di Napoli è il più dovitioso d'ogni altra parte d'Italia, tanto meno diventa misero, et infelices, et in esso si verifica quel, che dice il Savio nell' Ecclesiaste al cap. 3: 'Vidi afflictionem, quam dedit Deus filiis hominum, ut distendantur in ea. Cuncta fecit bona in tempore suo, et mundum tradidit disputationi eorum, ut non inveniat homo opus, quod operatus est Deus ab initio usque ad finem.'" The citation is Ecclesiastes 3:10–11 with the Vulgate in Zappullo and the King James Version in translation. The whole biblical passage is relevant, and its knowledge is assumed by Zappullo.

Ecclesiastes 3:1–15

For everything there is a season, and a time for every matter under heaven:
a time to be born, and a time to die;
a time to plant, and a time to pluck up what is planted;
a time to kill, and a time to heal;
a time to break down, and a time to build up;
a time to weep, and a time to laugh;
a time to mourn, and a time to dance;
a time to throw away stones, and a time to gather stones together;
a time to embrace, and a time to refrain from embracing;
a time to seek, and a time to lose;
a time to keep, and a time to throw away;
a time to tear, and a time to sew;
a time to keep silence, and a time to speak;
a time to love, and a time to hate;
a time for war, and a time for peace.

What gain have the workers from their toil? I have seen the business that God has given to everyone to be busy with. He has made everything suitable for its time; moreover, he has put a sense of past and future into their minds, yet they cannot find out what God has done from the beginning to the end. I know that there is nothing better for them than to be happy and enjoy themselves as long as they live; moreover, it is God's gift that all should eat and drink and take pleasure in all their toil. I know that whatever God does endures for ever; nothing can be added to it, nor anything taken from it; God has done this, so that all should stand in awe before him. That which is, already has been; that which is to be, already is; and God seeks out what has gone by. (New Revised Standard Version)

17. De Blassis, "De precedentia nobelium sedilium," 543–77, summarizes the no-longer-extant first volume of the *Praecedentiarum*. Note that at least three occasions are

missing between 12 December 1508 and 24 October 1509, and on eleven occasions two entries for general parliaments' convocation and commencement employed the same *sindaco*.

18. By way of comparison with Rome, Fagiolo dell'Arco, *Bibliografia*, divides festival books from 1585 to 1721 into eight categories: papal elections, sacred festivals at court, entrances or visits to Rome, Forty Hours' Devotion, secular festivals, funerals, Jubilees, and papal funerals.

19. ASMN, Parlamenti Generali, *Praecedentiarum*, vols. 1–10 (1488–1556), have been badly damaged. Volumes 1 (earlier transcribed by De Blassis, "De precedentia nobelium sedilium") and 9 are missing; volumes 5, 6, and 10 are badly burned and illegible. BNN, Branc. V.B.4–9, "Parlamenti e Gratie della Città di Napoli," are copies of the seven volumes 2–8 of the *Praecedentiarum* in 6 volumes for the eighty-nine years, 1554–1642.

20. Such frequency can be corroborated in other sources. Zazzera, "Narrazioni . . . duca d"Ossuna," 473–617, diary of the four-year tenure of the viceroy Duke of Osuna (1616–20) records four such occasions with noble cavalcades 1.2 times over the forty months: 23 August 1616; 8 November 1616; 13 March 1617; and 1 January 1620.

21. BNN, Branc. V.B.4, "Parlamenti e Gratie della Città di Napoli," 7r–v (31 October 1554) records the entrance of the Marchese di Pescara into Naples; Branc. V.B.9, 45r–68r (14 September 1642) for the parliamentary *gratie.*

22. Muto, "Apparati e cerimoniali di corte," 113–49.

23. Mancini, *Feste ed apparati*, 11–21; Boccadamo, "Il linguaggio dei rituali religiosi," 151–66.

24. *Donativi* were parliamentary aides, that is, a tax "given freely" by the city and kingdom to the king along with parliamentary requests (*grazie*) for special favors or rights.

25. BNN, Branc. V.B.6, "Parlamenti e Gratie della Città di Napoli," 2nd num., vol. 4, 120v–121r (4 July 1614) on the visit of Don Emanuel Filiberto, son of the Duke of Savoy.

26. BNN, Branc. V.B.4, "Parlamenti e Gratie della Città di Napoli," 124v (11 June 1562) on the recovery of Philip II's son Don Carlos and Branc. V.B.7, 117r–119v (18 January 1620) on the recovery of Philip III.

27. BNN, Branc. V.B.4, "Parlamenti e Gratie della Città di Napoli," 96r (25 November 1560) on the obsequies for the French king Henry II and 181v (28 November 1564) for the Habsburg Holy Roman Emperor Ferdinand of Austria; Branc. V.B.4, 10v (26 May 1555) on Paul IV's election and Branc. V.B.5, 36v (23 May 1572) on Gregory XIII's election.

28. BNN, Branc. V.B.4, "Parlamenti e Gratie della Città di Napoli," 10v (3 May 1555) on the surrender of Siena, Branc. V.B.5, 35r–v (25 October 1571) on the victory of the Holy League at Lepanto under Don Juan of Austria. Branc. V.B.5, 84v (2 May 1574) and 250r (29 July 1579) on numerous victories in Flanders. Branc. V.B.5, 284v (25 September 1582) and 312r (25 September 1583) on the naval victory in the Azores securing the accession of Portugal with the Battle of Terceira in the Azores.

29. BNN, Branc. V.B.6, "Parlamenti e Gratie della Città di Napoli," 2nd num., vol. 4, 34r (September 1605) for rain.

30. De Cavi, *Architecture and Royal Presence*, 217–24.

31. Ibid., document 82, 436–41. My thanks to Sabina de Cavi for personal communication describing Diéz de Aux's manuscript.

32. Raneo, *Etiquetas de la corte de Nápoles 1634.*

33. Visceglia, "Nobiltà, città, rituali religiosi," 204–5.

34. Raneo, *Etiquetas de la corte de Nápoles 1634*, 74–79.

35. Hernando Sánchez, "El parlamento del Reino de Napoles," 329–87.

36. De Cavi, "El Possesso de los virreyes españoles en Nápoles." My thanks to Sabina de Cavi for sharing this paper.

37. Britonio, *Ordene et recollettione de la festa*, and partially transcribed by Megale, "'Sic per te superis gens inimica ruat,'" 587–91. See also Hernando Sánchez, *El reino de Nápoles*, 254–56, for further descriptions from the humanists Pietro Gravina's and Marin Sanudo's diaries.

38. Hernando Sánchez, *El reino de Nápoles en el Imperio de Carlos V*, 256; and Toscano, "Carlo V nella letteratura e nella publicistica napoletane," 5:265–82.

39. Montemayor, *Diurnali di Scipione Guerra*, 45.

40. BNN, Branc. V.B.5, "Parlamenti e Gratie della Città di Napoli," 33v (Granvelle), 286r–v (Osuna); Montemayor, *Diurnali di Scipione Guerra*, 45 (Miranda), 46 (Olivares), 74 (Lemos). Scipione Guerra also mentions the *ponte*, but not its sack for the entry of Cardinal Zapata in 1620. Bulifon, *Giornali di Napoli*, 44 and 51, also mentions the *ponte*, but not its sack for the entries of Cardinal Granvelle in 1571 and the Duke of Osuna in 1582.

41. Vitale, *Ritualità monarchica*, 66–74 and 126–27.

42. BNN, Branc. V.B.5, "Parlamenti e Gratie della Città di Napoli," 33v. For analysis of the gangway's symbolic meaning as a "bridge" or passage and its sack in ritual pillages, Guarino, "The Politics of Appearances," 49–52, argues that "ritual pillages, also known as *allegrezze*, were a common feature of Italian princely courts during intervals of power" and that these sacks during the interregnum transition ceremony can be interpreted either as signs of devotion to possess the spiritual power of the viceroy's royal presence or as warning to the new viceroy in keeping with assault on the ruler's property after a period of "bad government." See Ginzburg, "Ritual Pillages," 20–41.

43. Parker, *Philip II*, 196.

44. Ibid., 20–22, 39; and Kamen, *Philip of Spain*, 35–49, 56–78.

45. Kamen, *Philip of Spain*, 57, n. 30, cites the letter of Juan de Figueroa to Charles V: Winchester, 26 July 1554, in *Collección de Documentos Inéditos para la Historia de España*, 3:519. Figueroa was a regent of the Kingdom of Naples and personal ambassador between Charles and his son Philip.

46. BNN, Ms. XIV.C.21, cc. 108r–v.

47. *Aviso de la sollennità e festa.*

48. Lega, *Il glorioso triomfo*, which is transcribed in Toscano, "Le Muse e i Colossi," 377–410.

49. Toscano, "Le Muse e i Colossi," 382–83.

50. De Cavi, "El Possesso de los virreyes españoles en Nápoles," includes a transcription from the Archivio Storicio Diocesano di Napoli, *Diari dei Cerimonieri* in the appendix.

51. Coniglio, *I Vicerè*, 226–31, and Guarini, "The Politics of Appearances," 88–92, provide short summaries of the visit. For the original sources, see Raneo, *Etiquetas de la corte de Nápoles 1634*, 196–200; Bucca, "Aggionta alli diurnali di Scipione Guerra"; Fellecchia, *Viaggio della maestá*; Capaccio, *Il Forastiero*, 952–62; and Parrino, *Teatro eroico*, 1:201–9.

52. Capaccio, *Il Forastiero*, 959: "E credo che dovesse mirabilmente esser sodisfatta in quella Maschera che di volontà ferono tanti segnalati Cavalieri, e d'inventione del Cavalier Gio. Battista Basile, dove non sò qual maggior cosa potesse comparire per vaghezza, per splendore, per diletto, per varietà di ciò che si ritrova nel tesoro della poesia." See also, Fellecchia, *Viaggio della maestá*, 54–56, "una maschera all'usanza Unghera, la più vaga, & numerosa di quante se ne potessero mai vedere, il cui numero fino al giorno di hoggi, non fù mai ne equalato, ne superato:; Bucca, "Aggionta alli diurnali di Scipione Guerra," 365–68; and Parrino, *Teatro eroico*, 2:241ff. See Basile, *Monte Parnaso*.

53. Fellecchia, *Viaggio della maestá*, 54: "Stando S. M. nella famosa Città di Napoli, ch'è la più antica, & nobil Madre d'Heroi, Arsenale dell'armi, & steccato di Marte, quella Napoli, che ne i suoi ordini rassembra un bellissimo Cielo, il cui primo mobile è la nobiltà, il cui Polo Artico è la scienza, il cui Antartico è la magnanimità, la cui base è la fede, le cui Zone sono i sensi, i cui circoli sono le potenze, i cui moti sono i pensieri, le cui stelle sono le virtù, i cui segni sono i meriti, fatta albergo de sì alta Regina."

54. *Argomento della festa*; *Relatione delle sontuose feste.*

55. Galasso, *Napoli Spagnola dopo Masaniello*, 1:22–23, with the quotation cited from Parrino, *Teatro eroico*.

56. Raneo, *Etiquetas de la corte de Nápoles 1634*, 263–76, on the obsequies for Philip II; 255–63, for the Count of Lemos; 277–84, for Margherita d'Austria; 276, for Don Carlos; and 105–7, on royal births.

57. Costo, *Della rotta di Lepanto*, was republished "amplified and improved" as *La Vittoria della Lega*. See Capuozzo, "Tomaso Costo e la battaglia di Lepanto."

58. Cocco, "Vesuvius and Naples," 273–82, cites twenty-four books published in 1631–32 in his bibliography; and the BNN has three bound books (Sez. Nap. XXIX*A.90; Sez. Nap. XXIX*D.129(4; and 136.F.32), which contain twenty-six additional books concerning the 1631 eruption. See also Riccio, "Nuovi documenti sull'incendio Vesuviano." Forni reprint edition binds two of the contemporary books together, Braccini, *Dell'incendio*; Giuliani, *Trattato del Monte Vesuvio*.

59. *Micco Spadaro*, 126–27 and 184–85.

60. Clifton, "Mattia Preti's Madonna of Constantinople," 336–64. See also Clifton, "Images of the Plague."

61. Clifton, "Mattia Preti's Madonna of Constantinople," 341–42 and 361, figs. 9–10, explains how the spelling and orthography on this print have been changed from "La Madonna de Costantinopli" to "LA MADONNA DE COSTANTINapoli" in order to attach "this particular manifestation of the Madonna securely to the city of Naples."

62. Bellucci and Valerio, *Piante e vedute di Napoli*, map 11 (1611), map 31 (1626), and map 52 (1648).

63. *Micco Spadaro*, 150–51 and 152–53. See also Marshall, "'Causa di Stravaganze,'" 482 and 484.

64. Parrino, *Teatro eroico*, 3:31–32: "sopra tutto pel numero troppo grande de' giorni feriali, erano divenuti poco meno ch'eterni."

65. Galasso, *Napoli Spagnola dopo Masaniello*, 1:41–50, chap. 4, "La peste."

66. Raneo, *Etiquetas de la corte de Nápoles 1634*, 47–48.

67. Ibid., 46; and Vario, *Pragmaticae edicta, decreta*, 2:10, 14 July "Incipiunt feriae messium, & vindemiarum, & durant usque ad diem 4. mensis Octob."

68. Bouchard, *Voyage dans le Royaume de Naples*, 2:419, with the summer months of July and August described, 402–26.

69. Costo, *Nomi delle prouincie*, 36–37.

70. Giustiniani, *Dizionario geografico-ragionato*, 4:122, gives only seventy-four hearths for Conza in 1595; instead, I have used the hearth figures in Mazzella, *Descrittione del Regno di Napoli*, 110. Hearth counts for the diocesan seats are given by Giustiniani (Mazzella in parenthesis): Muro, 486 (722); Cangiano not listed; Monteverde, 185 (191); Cedonia, 327 (299); Sant'Angelo de' Lombardi, 346 (281); and Bisaccia, 593 (409).

71. Gesualdo, *Constitutiones et decreta*.

72. Rossini, *Constitutioni et decreti*.

73. Costo, *Nomi delle prouincie*, 36. Giustiniani, *Dizionario geografico-ragionato*, 1:167, and Mazzella, *Descrittione del Regno di Napoli*, 84, for hearth counts in Amalfi. Giustiniani (Mazzella in parenthesis) give hearth counts for the diocesan seats as follows: Lettere, 313 (179); Capri, 349 in 1561 (349); Minori, 128 (126); and Scala, 272 (227).

74. Delille, "Agricultural Systems and Demographic Structures," 79–126.

75. Vario, *Pragmaticae edicta, decreta*, 2:8–10, "De Feriis," Titulus LXXVIII, Prammatica II (15 April 1556).

76. Ibid., 2:8, "De Feriis," Titulus LXXVIII, Prammatica I (20 June 1534): "con pleggeria di soddisfare, o ritornare nelle carceri in certo termine."

77. Ibid., 2:10, "De Feriis," Titulus LXXVIII, Prammatica III (14 May 1587): "conseguire I loro crediti; e seguendo l'abilitazione durante le ferie."

78. Ibid., 2:10, "De Feriis," Titulus LXXVIII, Addenda to Prammatica II (15 April 1556).

79. Ibid., 2:10–11, "De Feriis," Titulus LXXVIII, Prammatica IV establishes the feast of S. Diego on 12 November 1590.

80. Rubino, "Notitia," BSNSP, XXIII.D.14 (25 April 1656), Prammatica XXIV "de Feriis," 214–17.

81. Raneo, *Etiquetas de la corte de Nápoles 1634*, 69–73.

82. "Notizie. Delle cose principali," 797: "Le Feste principali e vistose in ogni anno."

83. Bouchard, *Voyage dans le Royaume de Naples*, 2:266.

84. Celano, *Notize del bello*, 1:345–49.

85. Two seventeenth-century devotional books provide an introduction to the Christological, Marian, and saints' cults in Naples. See Giovan Battista Caracciolo, *Nelle feste del Signore e della Madonna*, and *Nelle feste de Santi Apostoli*.

86. "Notizie. Delle cose principali," 797: "Le Feste principali e vistose in ogni anno."

87. Faraglia, "Le ottine," 17–20.

88. Visceglia, "Nobiltà, città, rituali religiosi," 173–205.

89. Ibid., 177–79.

90. Hernando Sánchez, *El reino de Nápoles en el Imperio de Carlos V.*

91. Imperato, *Privilegi, capituli, e gratie*, 56–57, cap. 29; Tutini, *Del Origine e fundatione de' seggi*, gives the "Gratie concesse dal Rè Cattolico alla Piazza del Popolo nel 1507" (291–

96), and the "Capituli per lo regimento della Piazza del Popolo fatti nel 1522" (297–301), with cap. 18 at 299. See Vitale, "La nobiltà di seggio," 1–19, for information on reforms in the internal organization of the *seggi*.

92. Dauverd, "Mediterranean Symbiotic Empire," chap. 7, "The Eye of the Storm: The Genoese Church."

93. Divenuto, *Napoli L'Europa*, 266–67, gives Araldo's *Chronicle* entry.

94. For a similar phenomenon in rural France, see Hoffman, *Church and Community*, 108–14, where "the new devotional brotherhoods [like that of the Blessed Sacrament] were considered a potent weapon in the Tridentine Church's struggle against the village festivals, banquets, and excessive boisterous *royaumes*, for in the countryside the somber processions these confraternities held and their sober exercises of piety were designed to supplant the old communal celebrations, which the church viewed as sources of scandal and debauchery." In his survey of 108 northeastern parishes reporting devotional confraternities during pastoral visits, Hoffman finds that the Blessed Sacrament confraternity grew from one in 1613–14 and nine in 1654–62, to forty-two in 1700–1719.

95. Vitale, *Ritualità monarchica*, 186–97.

96. On the Starace episode, see Villari, *The Revolt of Naples*, 19–33; here p. 27, n. 42, quotes an anonymous account, Faraglia, "Il tumulto napoletano": "O populo storduto, hai incominciato et non hai fenuto, al dì dello Corpo de Christo ogne homo stia listo, al dì de Santo Joanne ogni homo lassa le panelle et piglia l'arme."

97. Montemayor, *Diurnali di Scipione Guerra*, 41.

98. Ibid., 77–78.

99. Giraffi, *Ragguaglio del tumulto*, 8–9, is partially translated as "The Neapolitan Revolution" in Dooley, *Italy in the Baroque*, 241; and Rubino, BSNSP, XXIII.D.14, 24–26. For a classic study of the relationship between ritual and revolt in Naples, see Burke, "The Virgin of the Carmine," 3–21; and Villari's rejoinder in its expanded version, "Masaniello, Contemporary and Recent Interpretations," in *The Revolt of Naples*, 153–70.

100. Rubino, "Notizie," BSNSP, XXIII.D.14, 24–26.

101. Garnica, "Un memoriale sul cerimoniale," partially transcribed in Cherchi, "Juan de Garnica." On Garnica and his manuscript, see J. Marino, "An Anti-Campanellan Vision," 367–93.

102. Garnica in Cherchi, "Juan de Garnica," 222–24. My thanks to Anna Varela Lago for her translation. Such chaos continued to plague festivals. Almost a century later a 1685 pragmatic ordered that the processional streets used for Corpus Christi through its octave be closed to carriages, wagons, and all vehicles because of "the irreverence and scandal they caused." *Nuovo collezione delle Prammatiche*, 3:294–95, "De Cultis Sacramento, Tit. LIX, Prammatica II (15 June 1685).

103. Villari, *The Revolt of Naples*, 22–29. Burke, "Southern Italy in the 1590s," 177–90. For an examination of the "Adviertimentos" outlining the continuing problems confronting Spanish rule in the city and kingdom of Naples prepared by the departing viceroy Juan de Zuñiga, Count of Miranda (1586–95), for his successor viceroy in 1595, see J. Marino, "The Rural World in Italy," 405–29.

104. Garnica in Cherchi, "Juan de Garnica," 222–24.

105. Garnica, "The Ceremonial of the Neapolitan Court," concluding section (47r–60v)

is not transcribed by Cherchi, 49r: "Demanera que la procession sobredicha no es de tanta importancia, comparada con to que se aventura haziendola."

106. Parrino, *Teatro eroico*, 1:201: "il desiderio del Duca d'Alba di ritornare in Napoli, per oscurare con la sua presenza l'autorità del vicerè, à lui poco amorevole."

107. Talucci, *Il passaggio di D. Maria d'Austria*.

108. Capaccio, *Panegirico*, dedication by Andrea di Gennaro, 4: "questa fedelissima Città per la venuta di S. Maestà in Napoli havendo veduto una del sangue de i Serenissimi nostri Padroni, e Regina di tanta grandezza, che di lei pur gran tempo no s'è vista cosa maggiore." Capaccio's fictional Citizen expounds upon these words in *Il Forastiero*, 955, "lascio le continue, & allegrissime visite de tanti Signori titolati, e'l concorso di notte, e di giorno di tutto il popolo Napolitano bramoso di vedere sì gran Regina, della quale non vidde il nostro cielo la maggiore per molti anni, che non può narrarsi con quanto numero comparvero in quel mare, che non mare, ma un bosco si rapresentava a gli occhi di tutti con tanti legni."

109. Capaccio, *Panegirico*, 14.

110. Fellecchia, *Viaggio della maestá*, 40; Raneo, *Etiquetas de la corte de Nápoles 1634*, 196–97; Capaccio, *Il Forastiero*, 956. The *seggi*'s petition is preserved, BNN, MS. XIX.C.21, cc. 277r–285v, undated, "Memoriale della fidelissima Città di Napoli."

111. Capaccio, *Il Forastiero*, 954: "da i quali [il Ponte] fù conchiuso che per eceder di magnificenza gli altri ponti fatti a persone Regali, e particolarmente quello che fù fatto a Filiberto Principe de Savoia, che fù lungo 250 palmi, e largo 24 questo della Regina fusse lungo 50 passi, e fusse coverto di lama d'argento di color bianco, e rancino come veramente fù, e poi donato da detta Signora al monistero di S. Maria de Costantinopoli." The elaborate *ponte* can be seen in Domenico Gargiulo's painting, *Desembarco de Maria de Austria en Napoles* (Madrid, Banco Hispano Americano), reproduced in Moli Frigola, "El ingreso de la future esposa," 361, fig. 21.

112. Fellecchia, *Viaggio della maestá*, 20–31, for the catalog of "le Dame più belle," and 31–37, for the five songs of greeting and amorous battle in the "battaglia amorosa"; and Bucca, "Aggionta alli diurnali di Scipione Guerra," 343, for the "pochissima cortesia" shown to the grandes dames of Naples, with only Anna Carafa, Princess of Stigliano; Isabella Gonzaga, Duchess of Sabbioneta; Elena Aldobrandini, Duchess of Mondragone; Giovanna Branciforte, Princess of Butera; and Margherita d'Aragona, Princess of Bisignano deigned to receive full acknowledgment upon their visit inside the palace.

113. Bucca, "Aggionta alli diurnali di Scipione Guerra," 344, describes the popular acclamation for Alba.

114. Bacco, *Naples: An Early Guide*, 110–21.

115. Mitchell, *Italian Civic Pageantry*, 99–100. Notar Giacomo, *Cronica di Napoli*, 290–93.

116. Lega, *Il glorioso triomfo* in Toscano, "Le Muse e i Colossi," 388–410; Sala, *La triomphale entrata di Carlo V*; Castaldo, *Dell'historia*, 49–55; Summonte, *Dell' Historia*, 4:91–123; De' Dominici, *Vite de' pittori*, 2:12–20; Mitchell, *Italian Civic Pageantry*, 101–4. See also Hernando Sánchez, "El Virrey Pedro de Toledo," 9–15, *Castilla y Nápoles*, 283–297, and "El *Glorioso Triumfo* de Carlos V," 447–521; Visceglia, "Il viaggio cerimoniale di Carlo V dopo Tunisi," 2:172–33; Megale, "'Sic per te superis gens inima ruat,'" 587–610; and Corsi, "Musica reale," 5–27.

117. Lega, *Il glorioso triomfo*, in Toscano, "Le Muse e i Colossi," 398, gives Philip and Ferdinand, instead of Philip; Sala, *La triomphale entrata di Carlo V*, c. 21r, and Castaldo, *Dell'historia*, 52, give Sigismund, and Summonte, *Dell' Historia*, 4:104, Rudolph, instead of Ferdinand; Sala, *La triomphale entrata di Carlo V*, c. 21, Castaldo, *Dell'historia*, 52, and Summonte, *Dell' Historia*, 4:104, give Albert.

118. For an image of the Palazzo Te ceiling and the context of the emperor's image, Burke, "Presenting and Re-presenting Charles V," 431.

119. Croce, "I seggi di Napoli," 17. See also, Sigismondo, *Descrizione della città*, 2:47.

120. On the *Regia Razza*, see Mantelli, *Burocrazia e finanze pubbliche*, 239–40. On the *chinea* procession under Philip II, see Dandelet, *Spanish Rome*, 55–57, 78.

121. Valerio, *Piante e vedute di Napoli*, map 22 (1578–85 ca.), 69–70, "Neapolitanus," is an engraving of a bridled horse rampant above the city and bay.

122. Cortese, *Feudi e feudatari*, transcribes AGS, *Visitas d'Italia, Nápoles*, lib. 58. See Hernando Sánchez, *El reino de Nápoles en el Imperio de Carlos V*, 383–84.

123. Coniglio, *Il regno di Napoli*, 25–26.

124. De Seta, *Storia della città di Napoli*, 245–47, tav. 56–57: Alessandro Baratta, "Fidelissimae urbis neapolitanae cum omnibus viis accurate et nova delineatio aedita in lucem ab Alexandro Baratta, 1629." See also Baratta, *Fidelissimae urbis Neapolitanae*; and Bellucci and Valerio, *Piante e vedute*, map 33 (1627), 66–70; map 36 (1629), 73; map 76 (1670), 128; and map 83 (1679), 136–37. The 1629 map is in Italian rather than Spanish and substitutes the Virgin and Child in the upper-right corner for an original political-military dedication to the viceroy Duke of Alba. For an analysis of the political intent of the Baratta map, see Naddeo, "Topographies of Difference," 23–47.

125. De Seta, *Storia della città di Napoli*, tav. 56–57: "Vero disegno della nobilissma cavalcata che si suol fate in questa fidelissima città di Napoli cose nell'ingresso di ciascheduno vicerè come in ogn'altra occasioni di donativi alla cattolica real maestà d'altri allegrezze e particolari accidenti ne quail si dimostra la fedeltà e magnificenza di tuti il Regno."

126. Ibid., 298–304; and Bellucci and Valerio, *Piante e vedute*, map 40 (1632), 80–81; and map 84 (1680), 138–39: Alessandro Baratta in 1630, "La fedelissima città di Napoli con la nobilissima cavalcata che si fece il 19 dicembre del 1630 della Serenissima Infante D. Maria d'Austria Regina di Ungheria cui entro 8 d'Agosto del 1630"; Baratta in 1680, "Cavalcata che si fà in questa Fid^{ma} Città di Napoli nelle Nozze Reali delle Cattoliche Maestà di Carlo Secondo Re delle Spagne e della Regina Maria Luisa Borbone."

127. Parrino, *L'ossequio tributario . . . Carlo Secondo*, 32–33, prints the foldout map.

128. Archivio di Stato di Venezia, *Senato Dispacci, Roma*, filza 218, design. 1: Paolo Petrini, "Ordine della Cavalcata fatta per l'entrata del Re Filippo V nella città di Napoli il di vinti Magio l'anno, 1702."

129. Capasso, *Catalogo ragionato*, 2:337–38, gives d'Anna's dates in office. He was *eletto* twice, from 20 November 1687 to 18 August 1689 and again from 5 July 1702 to 20 November 1703. This newly appointed *eletto* claimed extraordinarily high titles, and in fact the *eletto* of the people had ceased to be a bourgeois office after the sixteenth century.

130. Parrino, *Teatro eroico*, 1:56–57.

131. Kantorowicz, *The King's Two Bodies*; Muir, *Ritual in Early Modern Europe*, "Regal

Ceremonies," 271–87; and on Spanish royal funerary rites, Eire, *From Madrid to Purgatory*, 265, 287–99; Varela, *La muerte del rey*; and Orso, *Art and Death*.

132. Summonte, *Dell'historia*, 4:308: "le cui esequie furono di grandissimo stupore, giamai ad altro Principe le simili celebrate."

133. Evidence is from a late source, a biography of the emperor by the Milanese historian Gregorio Leti in Protestant exile in Amsterdam in 1700, cited in Anderson, "'Le roi ne meurt jamais,'" 5:379, 385, cites Leti, *Vita dell'invittissimo Imperadore Carlo V*, 4:411. Summonte, *Dell'historia*, 4:308: "Tutte le Città all'Imperio soggette con ogni possibil sollennità l'esequie di un tanto Imperadore celebrarono."

134. Strong, *Art and Power*, 95–96.

135. Eire, *From Madrid to Purgatory*, 288–91, esp. 288 n. 14.

136. For the elaboration of the royal funeral catafalque (*Castrum doloris*) in the seventeenth century, see Tozzi, *Incisioni barocche di feste*, 70–93.

137. *Descrittione della pompa funerale*, 8–9, 12; *La magnifica, e suntuosa pompa funerale*, pl. 5.

138. Rosenthal, "*Plus Ultra, Non Plus Ultra*," 204–28.

139. Summonte, *Dell'historia*, 4:308–30.

140. Panico, *Il carnefice e la piazza*, 21–36.

141. Ibid., 119–37.

142. Ibid., 120–21.

143. De Simone et al., *Masaniello nella drammaturgia Europea*, 37–43.

144. Panico, *Il carnefice e la piazza*, 125–27.

145. Rak, "Lo squardo devoto," 34–35, cites Arcangelo Domenici, "Compendio dell'Historia, Miracoli, et Gratie della Madonna SS. Dell'Arco," ms. Biblioteca del Santuario della Madonna dell'Arco, pp. 14–15: "grande fu il concorso del populo da Santo Anastasio, Somma et suoi casali, da Resina, Portici et la Barra da una parte, da Ottaiano, Marano, Marigliano, la Fraola la Cerra et Ponticello et altre terre e casali senza conto dell'altra. Ma molto piú fu la moltitudine delle persone nobili et plebe che venivano a far reverenza a questa Regina grande da tutte le città circumvicine, come da Nola, Sarno, Santo Severino, Nocera, Castell'a Mare et Capri et dall'altra banda faceva a gara Caserta, Capua, Aversa, Pozzuolo. Ma che diremo della nobilissima e divotissima città di Napoli? . . . fu tanta la moltitudine della nobiltà et del populo, di carrozze, cocchi et cavalli ch'uscì da Napoli che per molti et molti giorni dalla porta del Carmine fin'alla Madonna Santissima dell'Arco che sono quattro miglia et più era difficile poter passare et caminare avanti et indietro. Dalla taverna della Cerqua poi fin alla Madonna Santissima, che son due miglie bone, et molto più intorno a quella casa santa, era necessario appasso appasso vi stessero labardieri et huomini armati per trattenere la calca, soffocandosi l'un l'altro, anzi era tale il rumore della multitudine che parea un mare grande, sta in fortuna et finalmente nissuno si ricorda né di aver visto né letto concorso tale come questo et ha sequitato et sequita, per gratia del Signore, se non in tanta grandissima copia in gran parte et il nome di questa Madre Santissima . . . non solo è sparso in questo regno e in tutta l'Italia ma in Spagnia, in Francia, in Polonia, in Ungaria et fin in Costantinopoli."

146. Toschi and Penna, *Le Tavolette votive*, 39–40; but Rak, "Lo squardo devoto," 33, gives variant dates for the first miracle as 1450, 1590, or 1500.

147. Giannone, *Plaza Mayor in Castelnuovo*.

148. Machiavelli, *The Discourses*, I:55, argues that symmetrical social relationships produced republics; asymmetrical social relationships, monarchies. On "good arms," see Machiavelli, *The Prince*, chap. 12.

149. Braudel, *The Mediterranean*, 1:345–46.

150. Muto, "The Form and Content of Poor Relief," 214. For a list of guilds in Naples, see Muto, "Il regno," 254.

151. Orilia, *Lo Zodiaco*, references Tutini on the *seggi*, a clear indication that his work was already circulating (perhaps in manuscript) almost fifteen years earlier by 1630.

152. Musi, *La rivolta di Masaniello*, 119.

153. Bacco, *Naples: An Early Guide*, 39–45.

154. For Florence, see Trexler, "Le célibat à la fin du Moyen Age," 1337, 1346–47.

155. For Venice, see Rapp, *Industry and Economic Decline*, 24, 103.

156. Mols, "Population in Europe," 43–44, discusses population density, with a density of 300 to 500 inhabitants per hectare typical of working-class districts in major towns.

157. Bentley, *Politics and Culture*, 3–6. For the text, De Rosa, "Lodi di Napoli," 183–94.

158. See J. Marino, *Pastoral Economics*, 191–92; Petraccone, "Manifattura e artigianato tessile," 101–57; Muto, "The Form and Content of Poor Relief," 232–33.

159. Galasso, "Da 'Napoli gentile,'" 61–110.

Chapter 3. Patronage: The Church and the Heavenly City

1. Musi, "Le rivolte italiane," 209–20. See also Musi, *Italia dei Viceré*; and Kettering, *Patrons, Brokers, and Clients*.

2. F. W. Kent with Simons, "Renaissance Patronage," 2–21; and Weissman, "Taking Patronage Seriously," 25–45. See also D. Kent, *Cosimo de' Medici*, 8 and 392.

3. Regio, *Vita dei sette santi protettori*, 28.

4. Regio, *Dell'Opere spirituali*, 2:577–609.

5. Toschi and Penna, *Le Tavolette votive*, 39, 42–43, with a photo of the relic. See Freedberg, *The Power of Images*, 105–7.

6. Regio, *Dell'Opere spirituali*, title page, subtitle.

7. Sallmann, *Naples et ses saints*.

8. Quondam, *La parola nel labirinto*, 107–11.

9. Regio, *Dell'Opere spirituali*, biographical information gleaned from the author's introduction.

10. Manzi, *La tipografia napoletana*.

11. Olgier, "Paolo Regio," appendix, 279–84.

12. Toppi, *Biblioteca Napoletana*, 347.

13. Regio, *Dialoghi intorno*, 1r–23r.

14. Ibid., 18r.

15. Ibid., 23v–66v.

16. Ibid., 24v.

17. Ibid., 32v–33r; see de Cavi, *Architecture and Royal Presence*, 117–23.

18. Regio, *Dialoghi intorno*, 24v, lists in addition: Giovanni Albino, Michael Reccio,

Bartolomeo Fatio, Giovanni Tarcagnotta, Giovanni Battista Carafa, Agnoli di Costenzo, Antonio Terminio, Camillo Porzio, Tristano Caracciolo.

19. Ibid., 42v.

20. Ibid., 48v.

21. Ibid., 52v.

22. Ibid., 92v.

23. O'Malley, *Trent and All That*.

24. Regio, *Delle osservanze Catholica; Della felicità e della miseria; Della consolatione e del consiglio.*

25. Toppi, *Biblioteca Napoletana*, 238.

26. Quattromani, *La philosophia di Berardino Telesio*; Troilo, *La philosophia di Berardino Telesio.*

27. Sirri, *Bernardino Telesio.*

28. Regio, *Delle osservanze Catholica*, 133ff.

29. Ibid., 136.

30. See Villari, *The Revolt of Naples*, 42–46.

31. See McGinness, *Right Thinking and Sacred Oratory.*

32. Sallmann, *Naples et ses saints*, 15.

33. Gigli, *Diario Romano*, 32–33.

34. Costo, *Memoriale delle cose più notabili*, 88–91 (23 August 1614) and (9 August 1615).

35. Montemayor, *Diurnali di Scipione Guerra*, 90–91.

36. Fiorella, *Una santa della città*; and Seidel Menchi, "Benincasa, Orsola," *DBI*, 8: 527–30.

37. Coniglio, *I Vicerè*, 185.

38. Fiorelli, *Una santa della città*, 29–32; Novi Chavarria, "Un'eretica alla corte del conte di Lemos," 79.

39. Schutte, *Aspiring Saints*, 65.

40. Sallman, *Naples et ses saints*, 202–10; and Amabile, *Il Santo Officio della Inquisizione in Napoli*, 2:23–34.

41. Novi Chavarria, "Un'eretica alla corte del conte di Lemos," 77, and BNN, MS XIV.E.58, lists Neapolitan spiritualist-heretics from Juan de Valdez, Peter Martyr Vermigli, Bernardino Occhino, Marco Antonio Flaminio against the Theatine hero-saints Gaetano Thiene, Marinorio Veneziano, and Gian Pietro Carafa.

42. Sallmann, "Di Marco, Giulia," *DBI*, 40:78–81; Amabile, *Il Santo Officio della Inquisizione in Napoli*, 2:23–34; and BNN, MS XIV.E.58.

43. Novi Chavarria, "Un'eretica alla corte del conte di Lemos," cites new documentation in BNN, MS XV.G.26, "Parte seconda che contiene l'eresie di Suor Giulia de Marchis," 271–73; BAV, Vat. Lat. 12731; and ACDF, MS. I.4.b, inc. 21.

44. An itinerary for the Kingdom of Naples according to travel days between towns is provided in BNM, MS 2857, "Itinerario del Reyno de Napoles." Cerreto Sannita is 73 km northeast of Naples.

45. Sallmann, "Di Marco, Giulia " *DBI*, 40:78–81.

46. Novi Chavarria, "Un'eretica alla corte del conte di Lemos," 82–83.

47. Ibid., 79 and 83.

48. Bell, *How to Do It.* 57–63.

49. Novi Chavarria, "Un'eretica alla corte del conte di Lemos," 89–93.

50. Ibid., 85. Camillo de Lellis (1550–1614) founded the order, which received papal approval in 1591 and had some three hundred members in Italy at the time of his death.

51. Ibid.

52. Ibid., 90.

53. For Neapolitan convents and membership, I have used the anonymous 1607–8 city description attributed to Capaccio, "Napoli: Descritta ne' principii," 89–93. See also the 1595–96 history of the Jesuits in late sixteenth-century Naples by Giovan Francesco Araldo transcribed in Divenuto, *Napoli Sacra,* 92–93; and Bacco's *Nuova descrittione,* 72–75, in the revised 1629 edition, but originally published in 1609. Araldo gives 27 female convents with more than 3,000 nuns; the anonymous description, 29 convents with 1,972 nuns; and Bacco, 31 convents with 2,725 nuns.

54. The list of followers is in Novi Chavarria, "Un'eretica alla corte del conte de Lemos," appendice, 109–18, and transcribed from ACDF, MS. I.4.b, inc. 21.

55. Novi Chavarria, "Un'eretica alla corte del conte di Lemos," 97.

56. Ibid., appendice, 109–18.

57. Ibid., 83. On the Lemos reform policy in Naples, see Galasso, "Le riforme del conte di Lemos," 199–229; and on the Lerma patronage network, Benigno, *L'ombra del Re.*

58. Novi Chavarria, "Un'eretica alla corte del conte di Lemos," 99.

59. Ibid., 78–79.

60. Antonio Astrain, "Congregatio de Auxiliis," in *The Catholic Encyclopedia;* and Von Pastor, *The History of the Popes,* 24:281–366 and 25:230–52.

61. Galasso, "Ideologia e sociologia," 213–49.

62. Stoll, "Napoli-Tarragona andanta e ritorno," 1:297–336, p. 300, notes that the play had "precocious public success, [where] it probably already had been performed in 1623 in remote Lima and in 1625 in Madrid, Seville, and Naples."

63. For the text, Molina, *El burlador de Sevilla y convidado de piedra.*

64. Cervantes, *Don Quixote,* pt. I, bk. 51: "las mas rica y mas viciosa ciudad que habia en todo el universo." See Elias de Tejada, *Napoles Hispanicos,* 4:46–48.

65. Coniglio, *I Vicerè,* 176; Alonso-Muñumer, "La corte y el virreinato," 467–84.

66. Novi Chavarria, "Un'eretica alla corte del conte di Lemos," cites BNN MS. S. Martino 62.

67. Galasso, *Napoli spagnola dopo Masaniello,* 1:49–50, identifies the competition in Naples between the thaumaturgic saints St. Francis Xavier for the Jesuits and S. Gaetano for the Theatines.

68. ASV, Segretario di Stato Napoli, 20 D (1615–1616), cc. 60–62, letter of Deodato Gentile, Bishop of Caserta (20 February 1615), 60r: "E quanto al primo delli quadri che si espongono in chiesi di Religiosi, di Padri semplici fra il numero di Beati i questo per quanto ho potuto raccogliere, e vedere da molti anni che sono in questa città, non succede ad altri, che alli Padre Gesuiti, li quali ordinnamente nelle sue sollennità adornano quasi tutta la chiesa di diversi quadri di suor religiosi. Che essi à li secolari, che frequentano le chiese loro li chiamano per Beati, e le maggior parte, e forsi tutti con l'insigne di Beatitu-

dine, e Santità come sono diademe, reggi, insegne di martiri, rapresentationi di rapimenti, e miracoli, e cose simili, pero questo e costume antico di sudetti Padri, il quale ogni anno va crescendo con la moltitudine di quadri, e mi ricordo, che se ne comincio a fare costi romore, sin sotto la b[eata] m[emoria] di Clemente Ottavo, usando essi Padri quasi altre tanto in Roma, quanto qui pero ne alli hora si pascò più oltre nella prohibitione, ne io ho creduto essere caso di doverne dare costo contostante la notorietà del fatto, non potendo però negare, che non lo stimi anco io per grande, e pericoloso abuso. è da poter un giorno partorire qualche inconveniente."

69. Sallmann, *Naples et ses saints*, 85–86.

70. Hills, *Invisible City*, 128–32; and expanded in her "Enamelled with the Blood of a Noble Lineage," 1–40.

71. Hills, *Invisible City*, 129.

72. Strazzullo, *Edilizia e urbanistica*, 97–102.

73. Del Pesco, "Alla ricerca di Giovanni Antonio Dosio," 15–66.

74. On the Carthusians' "sense that the monastic life is to be seen as the threshold of paradise," Mursell, *The Theology of the Carthusian Life*, 159–65. On the Renaissance ideal city, Garin, "La città ideale," 57, and Firpo, *Lo stato ideale della Controriforma*. On Carthusian architecture, Leoncini, "Il monastero certosino" 1:47–58 De Cunzo, "La Certosa di San Martino," 1:139–46; and Porter, "The 'Prophetic' Dozen," 249–311. On religious architecture and religious orders in Naples, see Hills, *Invisible City*.

75. For a description and bibliography on the sacristy, Galante, *Guida sacra*, 273, 286–87. On S. Martino in general, with special focus on the decoration of the church interior with polychrome revetment as part of an effort to make the church into the embodiment of the Heavenly Jerusalem, see Napoli, "From Social Virtue to Revetted Interior," 523–46. My thanks to Nick Napoli for sharing this article, as well as his conversation and communication on the Certosa.

76. D'Addosio, "Documenti inediti di artisti napoletani," 165–66, 178–79.

77. Peters, *German Masters*, 106–276. Stimmer (Schaffhausen, 1539–Strasbourg, 1584) worked in Zurich until 1570, when he transferred to Strasbourg, where he prepared his 170 illustrations of the Old and New Testament "for the pious pleasure of the devòut." See also P. Tanner, "Neue Künstliche," 185–200, and Bucher, *Weltliche Genüsse*.

78. Mielke, "Hans Vredeman de Vries," 18–20, 125–33. Born of a German mother in Leeuwarden in 1527, Vredeman de Vries designed engravings of perspectival constructions, classical building style, and architectural views, which established his reputation at Antwerp, where he came to the attention of William of Orange and eventually worked for Prince Maurice of Nassau in Amsterdam and The Hague, before his death in Hamburg in 1606.

79. Knipping, *Iconography*. See Strumwasser, "Heroes, Heroines, and Heroic Tales."

80. Porter, "The 'Prophetic' Dozen," 259–60, fig. 6–48.

81. Forcellino, *Il Cavaliere d'Arpino*.

82. Klein, "Introduction," 196–99.

83. Stratton, *The Immaculate Conception*, 35–66; Willette and Conelli, "The Tribune Vault of the Gesù Nuovo," 169–213.

84. Schütze, "The Politics of Counter-Reformation Iconography," 555–68; Pacheco, "The Iconography of the Virgin of the Immaculate Conception," 165–72.

85. Klein, "Introduction," 163–64.

86. I have consulted two editions in the Getty Library and the Bibliothèque national de France, Paris, both dated 1560, each with twenty illustrations. In each, fifteen of the twenty illustrations, for a total of eighteen of the twenty-six S. Martino intarsia, are exact or similar copies.

87. A Vredeman de Vries effigy of Cardinal Granvelle is included in Vredeman de Vries, *Pictores, Statuarii, Architecti*, 18r. On Granvelle's library, see Piquard, "Le livres du Cardinal de Granvelle," 301–23.

88. Amabile, *Fra Tommaso Campanella*.

89. Deleón-Jones, *Giordano Bruno*, 72. Bruno's Heavenly Jerusalem is a symbol of "the order and vision brought about by Wisdom for those who seek out the Truth through the path of the chosen. . . . The symbol of Jerusalem associated with the ass is the entry of Christ into the Holy City, which represents the triumphant entry of the humble to the final vision of the divine. Entrance into Jerusalem is part of the prophecies surrounding the coming of the Messiah." The image derives from two evangelical sources: Christ's entry into Jerusalem, now to be the Second Coming; and the idea that God dwells within us.

90. Campanella, *La Città del Sole/The City of the Sun*, 116–19.

91. Badaloni, "I fratelli Della Porta"; and Villari, *The Revolt of Naples*.

92. Clubb, *Giambattista Della Porta*, 311; and Della Porta, *Gli duoi fratelli rivali/The Two Rival Brothers*, 90–91.

93. Zotta, "Agricultural Crisis," 127–203.

94. Hamilton, "The Apocalypse Within," 269–83.

95. Chastel, "Marqueterie et perspective," 141–54; and Krautheimer, "The Panels in Urbino, Baltimore and Berlin Revisted," 232–57.

96. Causa, "Giovan Francesco d'Arezzo," 123–34.

97. Krautheimer, "The Panels in Urbino, Baltimore and Berlin Revisted," with the original article, "The Tragic and Comic Scene of the Renaissance."

98. Garin, "La città ideale," 52–54.

99. Rossi and Rovetta, "Indagini sullo spazio," 104–13.

100. Rabil, *Humanism in Italy*, 1:141–331.

101. Puppi, "Venezia tra Quattrocento e Cinquecento," 55–66.

102. Hersey, *The Aragonese Arch at Naples*.

103. De Seta, "The Urban Structure of Naples," 348–71; and Hersey, *Alfonso II*.

104. De Seta, *Napoli fra Rinascimento e Illuminismo*, 36, 37, 164.

105. Zappullo, *Sommario Istorico*.

106. Ibid. (1598), 318, describes how lightning ignited the munitions stored in the Castel S. Elmo, and verified in the Jesuit visitation text, Divenuto, *Napoli Sacra*, 185; and Costo, *Memoriale delle cose più notabili* (1618), 66.

107. Caputi, *La Pompa funerale . . . Filippo II*.

108. Zappullo, *Sommario Istorico* (1598), 317.

109. Braudel, *The Mediterranean*, 1:355–71, on news and distance, with news of Lepanto on 7 October 1571 reaching Naples seventeen days later on 24 October. Despite the short-

term displacement of information caused by the time it took for the news to travel the far-off distance, the local experience of grief was not diminished.

110. Anelli, *Oratione*.

111. Imbriani, *In Philippi II*.

112. Caputi, *La Pompa funerale . . . Filippo II*. The dedication is dated 26 February 1599, with an apology for the lack of polish in the text because of the shortness of time for publication.

113. Davila, *Oratio*.

114. Capaccio, *Oratio*; and Lotterio, *In funere Augustissimi*.

115. Decio Caracciolo, *Oratione*; and Turamini, *Orazione*.

116. Filante, *Oracion*.

117. Gemma, *In Serenissimi*.

118. McManamon, *Funeral Oratory*.

119. Ippolití, "Domenico Fontana," *DBI*, 48:640.

120. Caputi, *Relatione della pompa funerale . . . Margherita d'Austria*.

121. Davila also delivered the funeral oration on the death of the Neapolitan viceroy, Ferdinand Ruiz di Castro, Count of Lemos, in 1601. Davila, *Attione funerale*.

122. Caputi, *La Pompa funerale . . . Filippo II*, 4.

123. Ginzburg, *Occhiacci di legno*. See Giesey, *The Royal Funeral Ceremony*.

124. Caldwell, *The Sixteenth-Century Italian Impresa*, 18; Rosenthal, "Plus Ultra, Non Plus Ultra," 204–28.

125. Caputi, *La Pompa funerale . . . Filippo II*, 12–24.

126. Strong, *Art and Power*, fig. 63, shows Philip II's entry into Antwerp in 1549 with Charles V and the still Prince Philip bearing up the world.

127. This *impresa* had been published in all four editions of Ruscelli, *Le imprese illustri*.

128. Cicero's oration *Post reditum in senatu* (57 BCE), 7,9: "quos neque terror nec vis, nec spes nec metus, nec promissa nec minae, nec tela nec faces a vestra auctoritate, a populi Romani dignitate, a mea salute depellerent ("che né il terrore né la violenza, né la speranza né la paura, né le promesse né le minacce, né le armi né le fiaccole fecero allontanare dalla vostra autorità, dalla dignità del popolo romano e dalla mia salvezza."

129. Parker, *The World Is Not Enough*, 10–11.

130. Caputi, *La Pompa funerale . . . Filippo II*, 25.

131. Ibid., 28–30.

132. Hardie, "Aeneas," 145–50. The Latin text is:

Aspice bis senos laetantis agmine cycnos,
aetheria quos lapsa plaga Iovis ales aperto
turbabat caelo; nunc terras ordine longo
aut capere, aut captas iam despectare videntur:
ut reduces illi ludunt stridentibus alis,
et coetu cinxere polum, cantusque dedere,
haud aliter puppesque tuae pubesque tuorum
aut portum tenet aut pleno subit ostia velo.
(*Aeneid* 1.393–400)

133. Caputi, *La Pompa funerale . . . Filippo II*, 116–27.

134. Ibid., 34–71.

135. Villari, *The Revolt of Naples*, 19–33.

136. Kamen, *Philip of Spain*, 91–92.

137. Turamini, *Orazione*, 10.

138. Chartier, "Text and Images," 32–70.

139. Decio Caracciolo, *Oratione*.

140. Strong, *Art and Power*, 95–96, cites *Les Obsèques . . . de l'Empereur Charles* (Paris, 1559).

141. Vitignano, *Vera genealogia*.

142. Ibid., introduction dated 1 January 1599, cites the letter of praise from Philip II dated 29 October 1597, in ASN, *Partium 46*, fol. 206, and the Philip III letter dated 29 November 1598, in *Partium 1*, fol. 18.

143. De Cavi, *Architecture and Royal Presence*, 101–5, shows that Vitignano was the first Neapolitan chronicle to use genealogical trees rather than a portrait series in his chronicle of Neapolitan kings, which traces Spanish Habsburg ancestry back to the ancient Roman family of the Giulii. See M. Tanner, *The Last Descendant of Aeneas*.

144. *The Jesuit Ratio Studiorum of 1599*, 77, 78, and 47.

145. Dimler, *The Jesuit Emblem*, 701–71.

146. Capaccio, *Delle imprese*, 21. See Caldwell, *The Sixteenth-Century Italian Impresa*, 178–79.

147. Manning, Introduction, xv.

148. Ibid., xvii–xviii.

149. Caputi, *Relatione della pompa funerale . . . Margherita d'Austria*, 23–24. See Mauro, "'Sontuoso benchè funesto,'" 113–30.

Chapter 4. The Rule of the Games: Playing Court

1. Certeau, *Culture in the Plural*, viii. See also, Certeau's *The Practice of Everyday Life*, for further thoughts on the individual's creative and inventive making and remaking of culture.

2. Pietro Carrera, *Il gioco degli scacchi* (Trento: Militello, 1617), as reported in Parlett, *The Oxford History of Board Games*, 95–98.

3. Lucas, *The French Revolution Research Collection and Videodisk*, pt. 2: *Themes in Culture and Art*. The anonymous watercolor print is in BNP, collection of the Belgian diplomat Baron de Vinck de Deux-Orp #2735.

4. Macry, *Giocare la vita*.

5. See Asor-Rosa, "Basile," Nigro, "Capaccio," and Lettere, "Costo," in *DBI*, 7:76–80, 18:374–80, 30:411–15.

6. See for orientation, Jannini, *La "Bibliotheque Bleue" nel Seicento*, esp. Peter Burke, "The 'Bibliotèque bleue' in Comparative Perspective," 59–66.

7. Rak, *Napoli gentile*, 293–330. See also, Canepa, "'Quanto 'nc'è da ccà a lo luoco dove aggio a ire?'" 37–80, and *From Court to Forest*. For the text, Basile, *Lo Cunto de li cunti*, ed. Rak, provides a bilingual Neapolitan-Italian edition; the important English edition and

notes, with a review of Basile's writings, *The Pentamerone of Giambattista Basile*, ed. Penzer, appendix 5, 2: 259–64; and the recent English translation, *Giambattista Basile's The Tale of Tales; or, Entertainment for Little Ones*, trans. Canepa.

8. N. Z. Davis, "Women on Top," 131. The public sphere also provided the arena for the transmutation of cultural forms such as court cases and polemical scandals into a form of popular literature, the cause célèbre, with the result of eroding faith and undermining trust in the traditional authority of the Old Regime. See Maza, *Private Lives and Public Affairs*.

9. Basile, *Lo Cunto de li cunti*, ed. Rak, Nota bibliografica, 1042–47, traces later editions, expansion of the audience, and transformations of the tales inside and outside of Italy.

10. Rak, *Napoli gentile*, 293–330.

11. On court studies, Filippi, "Corti Europee e civiltà moderna," 258–63.

12. Castiglione, *The Book of the Courtier*, 18.

13. For critical interpretation, Rebhorn, *Courtly Performances*; for reception, Burke, *The Fortunes of the Courtier*.

14. Basile, *Lo Cunto de li cunti*, ed. Rak, 198–221, nn. 4, 9, 25, 32, 37.

15. Ibid., 216: "Si pazzo tu che non canusce la fortun toia . . . si na cosa me resce 'm paro."

16. Basile, *The Pentamerone of Giambattista Basile*, ed. Penzer, 2:105; Basile, *Lo Cunto de li cunti*, ed. Rak, 888: "ma, con tutta sta negra vita, non era possibele che la palla de la necessità, truccando chella de lo 'nore, la mannasse fora."

17. Basile, *The Pentamerone of Giambattista Basile*, ed. Penzer, 1:26, and *Lo Cunto de li cunti*, ed. Rak, 56.

18. Rabelais, *Oeuvres complètes*, 1:83–87, "sessé, passé et beluté temps."

19. Snow, *Inside Bruegel*, 6, 14, 165–66.

20. Ibid., 141–60, for Snow's thesis of assurances and ambiguities. See Turner, *The Ritual Process*.

21. Basile, *Lo Cunto de li cunti*, ed. Rak, 1100–1101, outlines the structure of each tale in relation to proverbs: summary of the tale, ideological opening with proverbial frame of tale's moral, the tale, and ideological close in a proverb.

22. See Propp, "Ritual Laughter in Folklore."

23. On the popular "Italian Style" in late sixteenth- and early seventeenth-century dance, see Sparti, "Breaking Down Barriers," 255–76.

24. Basile, *Lo Cunto de li cunti*, ed. Rak, 878: "Fu sempre 'nsipeto, signure mieie, chillo gusto che no ha quarche rammo de iovamiento. Però non foro trovate li trattenemiente e le veglie pe no piacere dessuetele, ma pe no guadagno gostuso perzì, pocca non sulo se vene a passare lo tiempo co sta menera de iuoche, ma se scetano e fanno prunte li 'nciegne a saperse resorvere e a responnere a chello che se demanna."

25. Guazzo, *La civil conversatione*, bk. 4 1.21, 269, 258v–259v: "daremo forma al giuoco della solitudine, col fare elezzione ciascuno di noi d'un luogo convenevole alla vita solitaria, assegnando la cagione ch ci avrà mossi a ridurci in solitudine e confermandola con qualche proverbio o altra sentenza."

26. Basile, *Lo Cunto de li cunti*, ed. Rak, 886, n. 1, argues that the game of games is "a species of game of truth called *spropositi* (cf. Lippi, *Il Manmantile racquistato*, II, 47) char-

acterized by the same structure as the *gioco di solitudine* in Guazzo. Canepa, *From Court to Forest*, 91–95, also examines the game of games in its relationship to truth telling.

27. On the role of gender in court play, see McClure, "Women and the Politics," 750–91. He examines the condescension of false courtesy, with Tasso's arguments emphasizing that women at court challenged "male tyranny" and wanted to win "true victory" in games and beyond.

28. Basile, *Lo Cunto de li cunti*, ed. Rak, 536–55. For an English translation, see Basile, *The Pentamerone of Giambattista Basile*, ed. Penzer, 1:257–64. Translations in the text are my own. Canepa, *From Court to Forest*, 193–97, has an interpretation of the tale similar to my own.

29. The Vomero is the hill above Naples, which was at the time of our story rich farmland already covered with country homes and villas, and which, by means of nineteenth-century funicular technology, would later join the old city as a newly urbanized quarter west from the Certosa of S. Martino.

30. J. Marino, "L'agricoltura pratica," 235–48.

31. Legman, *Rationale of the Dirty Joke*, 811–12: "Scatological jokes and tales are among the most primitive and direct, requiring nothing more than the mere mention of the taboo object or action to achieve the effect of anger, terror, shock, offense, or laughter—that is to say, *humor*—upon persons controlled by the taboo and thus responsive to its verbal flouting"; and 891: "Scatology is the weapon of choice or court-of-last-appeal, when a crushing insult is wanted, and this not only in our culture but in almost all. . . . The deepest level, insofar as jokes and insults are concerned, is that of the inevitable and hostile infantile anality of almost all humor."

32. Petrarch, *Petrarch's Lyric Poems*, 330, Sonnet 185: "d'amor trasse inde un liquido sottile."

33. Ibid., 514, Sonnet 327: "l'aura, l'odore, il refrigerio e l'ombra."

34. Dundes, *Life Is Like a Chicken Coop Ladder*.

35. Bettelheim, *The Uses of Enchantment*, 37, with objections in Darnton, "Peasants Tell Tales," 12–13, 266. For Bettelheim, fairy tales speak in the language of symbols that represent conscious and unconscious content, appealing to all three of its aspects—id, ego, and superego—and to the need for ego ideals as well. Freudians have concerned themselves with showing what kind of repressed or otherwise unconscious material underlies such tales, whereas Jungians have stressed in addition the archetypical psychological phenomena necessary for gaining a higher state of selfhood.

36. Elias, *The Civilizing Process*; Castiglione, *The Courtier*, 40–44.

37. Basile, *The Pentamerone of Giambattista Basile*, ed. Penzer, 1:261, n. 1.

38. Parrino, *Teatro eroico*, 1:54, describes the viceroy's guard: one company of 100 lancers, two companies of 50 cavalry, one company of 70 Germans, one company of Spanish infantry. Orilia, *Lo Zodiaco*, 88, includes an engraving of a German soldier among a group of eight engravings of soldiers of different nationalities.

39. Douglas, "Pollution," 12:336–41, and *Purity and Danger*.

40. Basile, *The Pentamerone of Giambattista Basile*, trans. Penzer, notes, 1:264. See also, Thompson, *Motif-Index*, "B312: Friendly animals, Helpful animals obtained by exchange"; and Darnton, "Peasants Tell Tales," 9–72.

41. Leach, "Anthropological Aspects of Language."

42. See Gundersheimer, "Trickery, Gender, and Power," 121–41, for an examination of the suppressed game of a practical joke at the Este court of Ferrara in 1584, which emphasizes the tension between valor and intellect in the court's gender-charged relationships.

43. Caillois, *Man, Play, and Games.*

44. Ibid., 55.

45. Tasso, "Il Gonzaga secondo overo del giuoco," 217–56; Garzoni, "De' Giocatori in universale et in particolare," disc. lxix. On ancient games, Beca de Fouquières, *Les jeux des Anciens.*

46. Greene, "Ceremonial Play and Parody in the Renaissance," 281–93, follows an itinerary that includes the *Decameron*, Erasmus's *Praise of Folly*, John Skelton's "Phillip Sparrow," Rabelais's *Third Book*, Cervantes's *Don Quixote*, Shakespeare's *Richard II*, Dryden's "MacFlecknoe," Pope's *Dunciad*, and Spencer's *Faerie Queene.*

47. Della Porta, *Della fisonomia dell'uomo.*

48. Aldorisio, *La Gelotoscopia*, 42–53. See also, Courtine and Vigarello, "La physionomie de l'homme impudique," 85–86.

49. *Breve racconto della festa a ballo.* I have viewed a microfilm copy of the Bibliothèque nationale de France, Paris original, 3–13. A transcription of the libretto in bilingual translation and the musical score are in *A Neapolitan festa a ballo*; and a nearly complete transcription in a bilingual edition is included in *The Sylvan and Oceanic Delights of Posilipo*. My thanks to Margaret Murata for introducing me to this work. MusicSources of Berkeley, California, in collaboration with the University of California, Santa Cruz Theater Arts Department staged performances on 4 and 26 May 2007.

50. *A Neapolitan festa a ballo*, vii.

51. Ibid., xiii; and *The Sylvan and Oceanic Delights of Posilipo*, 23.

52. *A Neapolitan festa a ballo*, xiv; and *The Sylvan and Oceanic Delights of Posilipo*, 23.

53. *A Neapolitan festa a ballo*, xiv.

54. Ibid., xiv–xv.

55. Costo, *Il Fuggilozio*, 6; and Sarnelli, *Posilecheata*, 209–14. See also Ianella, *Posilecheata di Pompeo Sarnelli*, "Il cratere della Sirena," 233.

56. Costo, *Il Fuggilozio*, 16–17, "Questo è quel tanto celebrato Posilipo, questo è quello che ne' caldi della state fa dimenticare a Napoli tutte l'altre sue delizie; qui, poiché la sua distanzia non è di piú che due miglia, le bellissime Gentildonne e i nobilissimi Cavalieri vengono a far di loro pomposa vista; qui e paesani, e forestieri a sollazzarsi concorrono; e qui tutte le passate noie di dolce oblio si cuoprono."

57. Sarnelli, *Posilecheata*, 210–13.

58. Antonio Bulifon, "Teatro que el excellentissimo senor marques del Carpio mi senor hizo para celebrar el nombre dela reyna madre nuestra senora el dia de santa Ana . . . En Napoles a 26 de julio 1685," in Bellucci and Valerio, *Piante e vedute*, map 87, 142–43.

59. Bulifon, *Giornali di Napoli*, 1:139. See also Coniglio, *I Vicerè*, 222–23.

60. Croce, *I teatri di Napoli*, 103–4.

61. Bulifon, *Giornali di Napoli*, 1:173–74. The Orsini di Gravina Palace is the lone example of a great Tuscan Renaissance palace in Naples, built a hundred years earlier (1513–49)

across the street from Piazza Monteoliveto; it is the present seat of the Facoltà di Architettura.

62. Intorcia, *Magistrature*, 253, 79, 134.

63. *Relatione delle feste* (1639). See J. Marino, "Celebrating a Royal Birth," 233–47; and Chaves, "El duque de Medina de las Torres y el teatro," 37–68.

64. *The Commedia dell'Arte*, transcribes 176 dramatic plots in the Neapolitan stage tradition around 1659–1700 from a manuscript in the BNN.

65. *Relatione delle feste* (1639), 10. On the *burla* in its literary context, see Close, *Cervantes*.

66. Pitt-Rivers, *The Fate of Shechem*, 92–96, "Don Juan, the destroyer of reputations—this is the basic sense of his title *burlador*—whose aspirations to self-aggrandizement were founded upon the notion that the honor you strip from others becomes yours. In an agonistic society such as this, not only marriage but all romantic relations between the sexes have implications in the political realm even though they are seldom recognized. Thus the tenderest sentiments come together in the complex of honor with considerations of ethics, religion, prestige, economics and social pre-eminence to form a system of behavior that determines the distribution and redistribution of respect among the families of which the community is composed."

67. *Feste celebrate* (1658).

68. Ibid., 43: "Erano piene le strade, e dale fenestre pendendo drappi ricchissimi, con la pompa delle Dame, e Cavalieri, che per tutto amiravano, e con l'infinto numero de' popoli, pareva trionfasse ad onte della Peste, e della Morte, la Città del Sole." The population of Naples, estimated between 400,000 and 450,000 inhabitants before the plague of 1656, was reduced by one-half to two-thirds, to around 150,000 to 200,000 people, in that year. See Petraccone, *Napoli del Cinquecento all'Ottocento*; and Galasso, *Napoli Spagnola dopo Masaniello*, 1:41–50.

69. Rak, "A dismisura d'uomo," 277–301.

70. Ibid., 278, reproduces the frontispiece with female personifications of the four continents seated around the globe and coats of arms of the king and the viceroy, as well as the *carri* of the continents (300–301) and the *teatro* with the allegorical *carri* of the continents (p. 298). See Mancini, *Feste ed Apparati*, 26–27, for much clearer reproductions of the four *carri*, and tav. A between pp. 38 and 39 for a sense of the very large engraving 128 by 59 centimeters inserted at the end of the festival book.

71. *Feste celebrate* (1658), 16.

72. *Relatione delle feste* (1639), 2: "che augurandosi l'accrescimento delle sue grandezze nella moltiplicatione de'suoi Signori, stimò doverle spendere prodigamente per tributo di gratitudine, e di vassallaggio."

73. *The Commedia dell'Arte*, 1:13.

74. Accetto, *Della dissimulazione onesta*; Snyder, *Dissimulation and the Culture of Secrecy*.

75. Sarnelli, *Posilecheata*, 175–76. Celano, *Notize del bello*, 4:232, describes the colossal head; and 1: 14 gives the inscription, "Parthenopes Eumeli Phalerae Thessaliae Regis filiae, Pharetis Creteique regum neptis proneptis quae Eubaea colonia deducta civitati prima

fundamenta iecit et dominate est Ordo et Populus Neapolitanus memoriam ab orco vindicavit. MDLXXXXIIII."

76. Tasso, "Il Gonzaga secondo overo del giuoco," 222.

77. Ibid., 235–36: "Annibale Pocaterra: Io non so qual possa esser questa commune cagione, se forse non è il diletto per lo quale furono tutti i giuochi, se non m'inganno, ritrovati: percioché la severità de la vita attiva e de la contemplative eziandio aveva bisogno d'alcun temperamento che la rendesse piacevole, e le fatiche de l'una e de l'altra con alcun piacere doveva esser mescolato: e questo non si poteva da alcuna cosa più convenevolmente prendersi che da' giuochi, i quail, comeché possano esser faticosi a chi gli fa, alcuni d'essi particolarmente, sono sempre nondimeno alleggiamento de le fatiche di chi gli riguarda. . . . Trattenimento dico io il diletto de l'animo, del quale i giuocatori, e talora i riguardanti, ingannati, non s'accorgono del fuggir de l'ore: e trattenimento si dice perch'egli ci trattiene da l'operazioni, e fra lor si frapone acciochè più volentieri ad esse, che faticose ci paiono, ritorniamo."

78. *Passare il tempo.*

79. Sutton-Smith, *The Ambiguity of Play*, 9–12, outlines the seven rhetorics explicated in his study—the rhetoric of play as progress, fate, power, identity, the imaginary, the self, and frivolous—which are developed from William Epson's classic *Seven Types of Ambiguity* (New York: Meridian Books, 1955).

80. Cashman, "Performance Anxiety," 333–52, in its theoretical frame employs anthropological "practice theory" in order "to suggest that rank and culture constrained a ritual participant's ability to act creatively while jockeying for position at court, and diminished the possibility of attaining social and material satisfaction."

Chapter 5. Allegrezza: *The City Rules*

1. Orilia, *Lo Zodiaco*, 338, 340, 342, 344; and Petrarca, "La festa," 50–52, 54. My thanks to Dinko Fabris for identifying the instruments and pointing out that the unusual seven-string lute illustrates the metaphor of harmony among Naples's seven city council representatives (two from Montagna, and one each from the other *seggi*).

2. Capaccio, "Napoli descritta," 797; and Celano, *Notize del bello.*

3. Four important studies are the starting points for an understanding of the Feast of St. John the Baptist in Naples: Petrarca, "La festa"; Iannella, "Les fêtes," 131–85; Megale, "Gli apparati napoletani," 191–213; and Muto, "Spazio urbano e identità sociale," 305–25.

4. Rubino, "Notitia," BSNSP, ms. XXIII.D.14–17.

5. Capaccio, "Napoli descritta," 520–21.

6. Megale, "Gli apparati napoletani," 192, n. 4; and Torraca, "Sacre rappresentazioni," 159.

7. Petrarca, "La festa," 16, references the two Capaccio festival book manuscripts of 1613 and 1614 in BSNSP as destroyed during World War II. A 1614 manuscript copy is extant: Capaccio, "Relatione dell' apparato," BNN, MS. XIX.97.

8. Petrarca, *La festa*; Iannella, "Les fêtes"; Megale, "Gli apparati napoletani"; and Muto, "Spazio urbano e identità sociale."

9. Capaccio, *Apparato della festività del glorioso S. Giovan Battista* (1623, 1624, 1626, [1626], 1627). Capaccio also has an unpublished *relatione* on the feast for 1614.

10. Giuliani, *Descrittione dell'apparato di San Giovanni* (1628 and 1631).

11. Orilia, *Lo Zodiaco*.

12. D'Alessio, Masaniello, 44–53; and Burke, "The Virgin of the Carmine," 10–11.

13. Rubino, "Notitia," BSNSP, MS. XXIII.D.14–17.

14. Divenuto, *Napoli l'Europa*, 301–6, attributes eleven church foundations to the emperor Constantine after 325. In reality, the baptistery was probably founded by Bishop Severo in the late fourth century but still at least a generation before that of S. Giovanni in Laterano.

15. Lupieri, *Giovanni e Gesù*, explains the rivalry between the cults of Jesus and John the Baptist.

16. See Tak, *South Italian Festivals*, 85–104, for an analysis of 1990–91 fieldwork in the mountain town of Calvello in Basilicata, where broom fires made from collected broom branches marked local feasts: "The first summer festival was for San Giovanni Battista on 24 June, when the sun reaches its highest course. Around 1748 the holiday of San Giovanni Battista was a real festival. There were fireworks and a procession with the saint's image through town. During the eighteenth and nineteenth centuries this procession was still held only to disappear around 1900. . . . Broom fires were lit too on the eve of 24 June and disappeared along with the procession. . . . Many magical powers were attributed to the night of his holiday, especially to water and morning dew" (90).

17. Divenuto, *Napoli l'Europa*, 165–66.

18. Divenuto, *Napoli sacra*, 89, 97; Capaccio, "Napoli descritta ne' principii del secolo," 89; and Bacco, *Nuova descrittione*, 85–86.

19. Divenuto *Napoli sacra*, 97; Capaccio, "Napoli descritta ne' principii del secolo," 89, lists six (not St. Bartholomew, St. Lawrence, or St. Francis, but includes S. Pantaleone); Bacco, *Nuova descrittione*, 86, lists seven (not St. Francis); and the translation of Bacco's 1671 edition, *Naples: An Early Guide*, 49, adds an eighth (Blessed Andrea Avellino).

20. Sodano, " 'Sangue vivo,' " 309, n. 66.

21. Capacco, *Il Forastiero*, 990, "ogni volta che'l sangue di quell santo s'incontra con la Costa dell'istessa Reliquia che in detto loco si conserva, fa l'istesso effetto che fa il sangue del glorioso S. Gennaro."

22. On the idea of "vital force," see Binde, *Bodies of Vital Matter*, 49–54.

23. Sodano, " 'Sangue vivo,' " 293–310, describes the peculiar Neapolitan miracle of blood liquefaction in four canonization processes of Andrea Avellino in 1608, Giovanni Leonardo de Fusco in 1620, Geremia da Valacchia in 1625, and Francesco De Geronimo in 1718.

24. Muto, "Sacred Places," 103, cites the anonymous seventeenth-century list in D'Aloe, "Catalogo." The various churches of S. Giovanni are described in D'Aloe and Divenuto, *Napoli Sacra*.

25. Galasso, "La festa," 121.

26. Capasso, "Breve Cronica," 520–21: "Die xxiii junii 1543 Neapoli. La sera de San Joan il Re de Tunse cavalcò insieme colo Vecerrè per la cità, et lo Vecerrè lo andò ad incontrare fi al palazzo dove stava il Re et se salutaro, cavalcandono per segio de porto, per segio de

portanova, per la sellaria, per lo mercato, per San Joan ad mare, per la logia, per li orifici, per san Petro martiro, per li lanzeri, piazza delulmo, per lo molo grande, vedendo tutte gioize et rechize et alter gentilize per la cità; de po voltando per la roa (*rua*) catalana sende è andato al palazzo suo insieme co lo Vecerrè."

27. Megale, "Gli apparati napoletani," 192, nn. 3–4 cite Ferrante Carafa's description in BNN, MS.X.A.16, 66r. See Torraca, "Sacre rappresentazioni del napoletano," 157.

28. Capaccio, *Illustrium Mulierum*, 225–27.

29. Binde, *Bodies of Vital Matter*, 52–53, describes the ethnography concerning the beneficial properties of baths and dew on Ascension and S. Giovanni. Two effects were pronounced: purification came from water that cleaned the skin and cured skin disease, rheumatism, headaches, and bad humors; fertilization and vitalization came from water as necessary for organic life and affected the fertility of women and hair growth, filled the udders of female animals with milk, and was good for general health by providing renewed strength and vigor.

30. Iannella, "Les fêtes," 174–75. Velardinello's verses are part of a longer poem:

Le femmene, la sera de San Gianne
Levano tutt'n chietta a la marina
Allere se ne jeano senza panne,
Cantanno sempe maie la romanzina.

Falco, *Descrittione de i luoghi*, 32–33: "In una parte populosa della Città, giace la Chiesa consecrata à San Gio: Battista Gierosolimitano, chiamato San Giovanni à Mare. Era un'antica usanza, hoggi non al tutto lasciata, che la Vigilia di S. Giovanni verso la sera, e lo scuro del dì, tutti huomini, e donne andare al mare, e nudi lavarsi, persuasi purgarsi de' loro peccati alla foggia de gli antichi, che peccando andavano al Tevere à lavarsi, e come S. Gio: Battista per la lavatione del Battesimo ne ammaestra."

31. Del Tufo, *Il nuotare de la notte di San Giovanni* in Volpicella, *Giovan Battista Del Tufo. Illustratore*, 107–9; and Costo, *Il Fuggilozio*, day 7. See Iannella, "Les fêtes," 175.

32. Bouchard, *Voyage dans le Royaume de Naples*, 2:419: "Presque toutes les veilles de feste les enfants allument à une heure de nuit de grands feux le long de l'eau par resjouissance et dancent nuds tout autour. A quoy l'on peut aussi adjouter une autre particularité fort extravagante: à une heure de nuit toutes les femmes sortent de leurs maisons et vont en trouppes à la marine vider les cantari."

33. Celano, *Notizie del bello*, 4:234.

34. Imperato, *Privilegi, capituli, e gratie*, 56–57, cap. 29; Tutini, *Del origine*, 291–296, gives the "Gratie concesse dal Rè Cattolico alla Piazza del Popolo nel 1507," and 297–301 the "Capituli per lo regimento della Piazza del Popolo fatti nel 1522" with cap. 18 at p. 299.

35. Trexler, *Public Life in Renaissance Florence*, 216–78, esp. 240–78. Trexler's analysis of St. John's Day enriches Gregorio Dati's early fifteenth-century diary description of the feast as the merchant city's ideology of "communality over familial individually, and sacrifice over conflict" by showing "that public feast was quintessentially private, that private festivities were very political."

36. Mackenney, *Tradesmen and Traders*, 141–49, documents "the economies of display"

to show how important medieval and early modern festivals were in stimulating economic activity.

37. Liponari, *Relatione delle rivolutioni popolari*, 25.

38. Fuidoro, *Giornali di Napoli*, 2:81–83 (23 June 1668), "Quando la cavalcata fu alli Lanzieri, buona parte di essa, con la prima carrozza di Sua Eccellenza, trombette regie e parte della guardia de' tedeschi, pigliorno la strada delli Scoppettieri e per la Marina del vino, ma, avvisato l'eletto del Popolo e l'usciero di Sua Eccellenza, proseguirono per la strada di San Pietro martire, com'era il solito; e cosi, benchè fusse poco numerosa di titolati e nobili, nondimeno diede questo disordine impressione nel popolo che fusse procurato da essi nobili, per dispetto di esso eletto per le cause accennate di sopra. Concorsero dalle città e luoghi convecini dentro Napoli più di cinquemila persone, e cominciorno a godere l'apparato sin dal giorno avanti, ancorchè non fusse complito, e quasi non si poteva caminare per le strade nel giorno preciso, e seguitò sino alla domenica e lunedi seguente." The cause of the dispute over the sale of meat is described in ibid, 2:78 (May 1668), and the whole episode is examined in context in Galasso, *Napoli Spagnola dopo Masaniello*, 2:143–54.

39. Fuidoro, *Giornali di Napoli*, 2:211 (23 June 1671). De Blasé, "Frammento d'un diario," *ASPN* 14 (1889), 51 (24 June 1671), "Mercordi 24 detto festa di s. giov. battista l'eccllenze del Viceré et Vicereine si trasferirno a pigliar l'indulgenze nella chiesa di s. giov. de Fiorentini, dove si celebrò la festività con gran sollennità, et concorso di popolo."

40. Celano, *Notizie del bello*, 4:233, and repeated in Galante, *Guida sacra*, 300.

41. Confuorto, *Giornali di Napoli*, lists the feast of S. Giovanni each 24 June but only notes the election of the SS. Annunziata governor and *eletto del popolo*.

42. For 1672, neither Fuidoro nor De Blasé mentions the feast of S. Giovanni, which is erased in favor of the octave of Corpus Christi. Fuidoro, *Giornali di Napoli*, 3:43–44 (23 June 1672), and De Blasé, "Frammento d'un diario," 311 (23 June 1672): "Essendosi fatte per tutta l'ottava del Santissimo Corpus Domini le solite processioni dale consuete Chiese parrochiali, venne chiusa tal solennità dalla processione, che si fece Giovedì 23 doppo pranzo dalla chiesa di s. giacomo dei Spagnoli, dove intervene il Viceré con tutti I regij ministry, et si goderno Quattro bellissimi et pomposi altari ricchi d'argento e tapezzaria."

43. Filarete, *Filerete's Treatise on Architecture*, 292–93, follows this model even in the ideal city.

44. Scognamiglio Cestaro, *Le istitutzioni della moda*, 41.

45. Capaccio, "Napoli descritta ne' principii del secolo XVII," 86–87. For a description of the *ottine*, see D'Agostino, "Il governo spagnolo," 5:182–88.

46. Orilia, *Lo Zodiaco*, 16.

47. Capaccio, *Apparato della festività del glorioso S. Giovan Battista* ([1626]).

48. The Spetiaria antica connects to the Via Scalesia, and before the 1627 change of route, the procession continued from the Spetiaria antica into Via degli Armieri. These two streets (Scalesia with twenty-nine shops and seventy-three workers, and Armieri with twenty-eight and fifty-eight workers) had the largest concentration of tailors in the city, 4.7 percent of the city's shops. See Scognamiglio Cestaro, *Le istitutzioni della moda*, 394–98.

49. Coniglio, *I Viceré*, 219–32, describes Alcalá's numerous problems and conflicts.

50. Giuliani, *Descrittione dell'apparato* (1631); and Herrera, *Principe advertido*.

51. Orilia, *Lo Zodiaco*, 267–77, includes illustrations of S. Gennaro (the first among the

seven original patrons of Naples), Blessed Andrea Avellino (the ninth, confirmed in 1625), Blessed Giacomo Marchigiano (the tenth, 1625), S. Francesco di Paola (the eleventh, 1626), S. Patrizia (the twelfth, 1526), and S. Antonio di Padua (the thirteenth, 1629).

52. Ibid., unnumbered 4v.

53. Quaja, *Liber de civitate Christi*, lists the twelve signs of the zodiac in traditional annual order from Aries (21March–19 April) associated as the first attribute with each of the twelve gates of the New Jerusalem, which are named Virginalis et Pudicitiae, Pastoralis et eminentiae, Doctoralis et sapientiae, Sacerdotalis et clericalis et diligentiae, Regularis et obedientiae, Legistalis et eloquentiae, Imperialis et praesidentie, Militaris et resistentie, Coniugalis et amicitiae, Salutaris et convalescentiae, Manualis et Mercimonialis, Seculariis et penitentialis.

54. Capaccio, *Apparato della festività del glorioso S. Giovan Battista* (1624), 71–78. Fernando Álvarez, 3rd Duke of Alba, (1507–82), had first come to prominence fighting the French at Fuenterabía in 1524 and was appointed its military governor, led a part of Charles V's army in the conquest of Tunis in 1535, commanded the imperial armies against the German princes of the Schmalkaldic League at Mühlberg in 1547, and was commander in chief of imperial forces in Italy in 1552 and viceroy of Naples (1556–59). Alba was most famous, however, for his harsh policies and as head of Spanish forces in the Low Countries (1567–73) during the Dutch Revolt. In 1580 Alba led his final campaign in the conquest of Portugal.

55. Pegasus also appears in the Guardiola first stop in 1627, and the winged horse is an apt mythological figure connected with St. John the Baptist because of their shared association with water. The name Pegasus came from his appearance near the source of Oceanus, he was captured by Bellerophon while drinking at the fountain of Pirene, and his hoof marked the spot of the Muses' fountain of inspiration. In Orilia, *Lo Zodiaco*, 358, Pegasus, with Alba astride is tapping for the source of water (the Muses' spring) from the rocks.

56. Capaccio, *Apparato della festività del glorioso S. Giovan Battista* (1626), 13, says the decollation at the Fontana di Porta, "rapprentava al vivo."

57. Labrot, *Collections of Paintings in Naples*, 624–25 (John, 34 items), 625–26 (John the Baptist, 44 items), 626 (John the Baptist Sleeping, 1 item), 759 (John the Baptist identifies Christ as the Lamb of God, 1 item), 759 (Baptism of Christ in the river Jordan: John the Baptist pouring water on Christ's head; the Holy Ghost descends, 21 items), 759 (John the Baptist reproaches Herod and Herodias, 1 item), 759–60 (Beheading of John the Baptist, 24 items), 760 (Salome with the head of John the Baptist on a dish, 19 items), 760 (Salome gives the head to her mother, 1 item), 760 (the head of John the Baptist on a platter, 1 item).

58. Calabria, *The Cost of Empire*, 62 and 86, gives total government income and expenditure for the kingdom in 1626 as 4,584,444 and 4,720,845 ducats respectively. The viceroy was the highest paid officer in Spanish Naples, AGS, *Secretarías provinciales*, Libro 44 (22 March 1594), 1r.

59. Capaccio, *Apparato della festività del glorioso S. Giovan Battista* (1623), 40–48, Signori of the Casa del Toledo include D. Pietro, D. Luigi, D. Fernando, D. Federico, D. Garsia, D. Pietro Juniore,. D. Antonio, and Donna Leonora; Capaccio, *Apparato* (1626), 60ff., the Sirens (Partenope, Lecuosia, Ligia), a Simulacro della Fede, the nymphs (Mergel-

lina, Egla, Leucopetra, Antiniana), and the poets (Sannazaro, Pontano, Bernardino Rota, and Epicuro); Capaccio, *Apparato* [1626], 44–46, the maritime deities (Galatea, Glauco, Teti, Nettuno, Dori, Proteo); Capaccio, *Apparato* (1627), 43ff., the eight provinces (counting the double provinces of the Abruzzi, Principato, and Calabria as one each, and not including Capitanata); Giuliani, *Descrittione dell'apparato* (1628), 60ff., moral virtues (Fortitude, Prudence, Justice, Temperance) and four other virtues (Modesty, Magnanimity, Counsel, and Equity); and Orilia, *Lo Zodiaco* (1629), 375–404, the rivers, of which thirteen are named (Volturno, Silare, Ofanto, Crate, Galeso, Satito, Sebeto, Fiterno, Sarno, Sibari, Aterno, Truentum, Garigliano) and 372 (for the quotation).

60. Capaccio, *Apparato della festività del glorioso S. Giovan Battista* (1627), 55.

61. Rubino, "Notitia," BSNSP, MS. XXIII.D.16, 321–41, and MS. XXIII.D.17, 131–61.

62. For a similar phenomenon in rural France, see Hoffman, *Church and Community*, 108–14, where "the new devotional brotherhoods [like that of the Blessed Sacrament] were considered a potent weapon in the Tridentine Church's struggle against the village festivals, banquets, and excessive boisterous *royaumes*, for in the countryside the somber processions these confraternities held and their sober exercises of piety were designed to supplant the old communal celebrations, which the Church viewed as sources of scandal and debauchery." In his survey of 108 northeastern parishes reporting devotional confraternities during pastoral visits, Hoffman finds that the Blessed Sacrament confraternity grew from one in 1613–14 and nine in 1654–62, to forty-two in 1700–1719.

63. Priest: "Behold the Lamb of God, behold Him who takes away the sins of the world." All: "Domine, non sum dignus et intres sub tectum meum; sed tantum dic verbo, et anabitur anima mea" (Lord, I am not worthy that You should come under my roof. But say the word and my soul will be healed). The Latin Mass of the Tridentine rite is available on line as part of the Internet Medieval Sourcebook located at the Fordham University Center for Medieval Studies Web site (www.fordham.edu/halsall/basis/latinmass2.html).

64. Rak, "*Napoli no plus*," 2:267–95; and Fabris, "La città della Sirena," 2:473–93.

65. De Armas, "Segismundo/Philip IV," 83–100.

66. Cox-Rearick, *Dynasty and Destiny*.

67. Erasmus, *The Praise of Folly*, 102, n. 8, on the rhetorician's use of the exordium.

68. Barletta, *Il Carnevale del 1764*, and *Fra regola e licenza*.

69. Barletta, *Fra regola e licenza*, 218–19.

70. Ibid., 288 cites Fuidoro, *Giornali di Napoli*, 3:228: "Le pazzie della plebe in questi tre ultimi giorni del carnevale sono date in eccesso in ogni quartiero, né sono state sufficienti le guardie di reprimerle."

71. Rubino, "Notitia," BSNSP, MS. XXIII.D.14, 82–94, describes the first masquerade to go out into the street of S. Giovanni a Carbonara on 2 Februrary, "una schiera di cento mascheri, vestiti chi da donne, chi da homini, chi da varie sorte de zanni, e chi da demoni, quail parte ne danzavano, parte andavan percontendo sonori istrumenti, et parte tanti baccanti furiavano per la città."

72. Ussia, "La festa delle Quarantore," 253–65.

73. Fuidoro, *Successi historici*, 77.

74. D'Alessio, *Masaniello*, 179–91, weaves together numerous accounts, especially privileging previously unused manuscript sources from the BAV. Musi, *La rivolta di*

Masaniello, 145–54, calls the events of 16–17 July "the sacred drama" told as a "stereotypical construction" and analyzed as "a psychological history" with a clinical vocabulary such as schizophrenia and sublimation. He follows the important pro-Spanish text of Tommaso De Santis. I have followed Giuseppe Donzelli's anti-Spanish account with reference and confirmation in nine other of the some twenty contemporary sources (De Santis, Fuidoro, Giraffi, Liponari, Nicolai, Rosso, Sauli, Tontoli, and Tutini-Verde): De Santis, *Historia del tumulto*, 151; Donzelli, *Partenope Liberata*, 104–06; Fuidoro, *Successi historici*, 72–73; Giraffi, *La rivolutioni di Napoli*; Liponari, *Relatione delle rivolutioni*, 275–79; Nicolai, *Historia*, 91–97; Capograssi, "La Rivoluzione di Masaniello," 184–86; "Copia di lettera . . . Ottaviano Sauli," 380; Tontoli, *Il Mas'Aniello*, 142; Tutini and Verde, *Racconto della sollevatione*, 82–83.

75. Fuidoro, *Successi historici*, 72: "Posero in ordine li funerali come si dovesse honorar il cadavere dell'occiso Giulio Cesare primo dittatore."

76. Donzelli, *Partenope Liberata*, 104–6.

77. "Copia di lettera . . . Ottaviano Sauli," 380.

78. Capograssi, "La Rivoluzione . . . [Andrea Rosso]," 185.

79. Fuidoro, *Successi historici*, 73: "In questo trionfo che mostrava il Popolo non era ancor lontano dalla vendetta contro nobili, a segno che se havesse trovato un Santo in forma di Cavalieri."

80. Villari, *The Revolt of Naples*, afterword one, 156.

81. Schneider, *The Ceremonial City*.

82. San Juan, *Rome: A City Out of Print*, examines the role of printed ephemera in constructing Baroque Rome, ca. 1580–1660.

83. Gregorio Dati's diary from late fourteenth-century Florence describes the anticipation for St. John's Day; see "An Occasion of Solidarity," in Brucker, *The Society of Renaissance Florence*, 75–78. In their book *La Terra in Piazza*, the folklorist Alan Dundes and anthropologist Alessandro Falassi have captured this enthusiasm in their evocation and analysis of the *palio* in Siena.

84. Turner, *The Ritual Process*. For Renaissance and early modern Italy, see Trexler, *Public Life in Renaissance Florence*; Muir, *Ritual in Early Modern Europe*; and Visceglia, *La città rituale*.

85. Darnton, "A Bourgeois Puts His World in Order," 107–43. For early U.S. parades, see Ryan, "The American Parade"; and S. Davis, *Parades and Power*. Architectural historians often draw links between Baroque display and fascist art and architecture as propaganda.

86. Celano, *Notizie del bello*, 4:233; and Galante, *Guida sacra*, 300.

Conclusion. The Spectacle and the Citizen

1. Parrino, *Teatro Eroico*, 1:13.

2. Capaccio, *Il Forastiero*, 690.

3. Divenuto, *Napoli sacra del XVI secolo*, 92.

4. Capaccio, *Il Forastiero*, 671–90; and Parrino, *Teatro eroico*, 1:33.

5. Jackson and Nevola, introduction to *Beyond the Palio*, 1–10.

6. Barzman, "Early Modern Spectacle," 282–302; and Debord, *The Society of the Spectacle*.

7. Pacelli, "L'Ideologia del potere nella ritrattistica napoletana," 225.

8. Ibid., 218–41.

9. Marshall, " 'Causa di Stravaganze,' " 478–97.

10. Ibid., 480–84, esp. 494, n. 12, on the paintings' provenance and a transcription of the 1690 inventory from *The Getty Provenance Index on CD-ROM* (Malibu: The J. Paul Getty Trust, 1996), Inv. I–245. De' Dominici, *Vite de' pittori*, 3:196–97 describes the *Eruption of Vesuvius*, as does a near-contemporary manuscript of Giannone, *Giunte sulle vite de' pittori napoletani*, 139–40.

11. Marshall, " 'Causa di Stravaganze,' " 492.

12. Orilia, *Lo Zodiaco*, 456, 491; reproduced in Petrarca, "La festa di San Giovanni Battista," 48, 49.

13. Capaccio, "Relatione dell'apparato . . . nell'anno 1614," BNN MS. XIX.97, 19r.

14. Labrot, *Collections of paintings in Naples*, 1–42.

15. Labrot, "Des saints à la nature," 267–342.

16. Ibid., 281.

17. Ibid., 281, 302.

18. Haskell, *Patrons and Painting*, 205–8. Capaccio, *Il Forastiero*, day IX, 863–64; and De' Dominici, *Vite de' pittori*, 3:35, cites Roomer's role in spreading the knowledge of contemporary Netherlandish painting in Naples.

19. Whitfield and Martineau, *Painting in Naples, 1606–1705*, 215–16, 239–40. Labrot, *Collections of Paintings in Naples*, 28–29, concludes that seventeenth- and eighteenth-century inventories of Neapolitan painting collections include three main groups of northern artists' works: the northern followers of Caravaggio—Louis Finson, Honthorst, Stomer, and van Somer; works by Rubens (Giuseppe Maria della Leonessa, Principe di Supino [1772], alone owned twenty-one works by Rubens!), Van Dyck, and their followers, in originals, copies, and workshop paintings; and still lifes and landscapes of northern paintings— Brueghel, Poelenburgh, and van Bloemen among the better-known names. The Spanish Netherlands–Spanish Naples art network, in fact, had been in existence from at least the late fifteenth century, with evidence from the late sixteenth century that some northern artists were actively working in Naples itself and carrying their experience and Neapolitan works back north. This late sixteenth-century circulation of art commodities coincides with the circulation of news and ideas on the Revolt of the Netherlands in Spanish Naples and thus provides further evidence of the vitality of the public sphere in linking material life to politics and ideas.

20. My thanks to Tom Willette for sharing his detailed analysis of the Regolia painting, and to Renato Ruotolo for arranging access to view the painting, which is held in a private collection.

21. Schütze and Willette, *Massimo Stanzione*, 191, scheda A7; 273, fig. 102, identifies this *Supper at Emmaus* as an original, a version, or a copy in the Vatican collection. It owes much of its inspiration to Caravaggio's version in the Brera in Milan. A smaller format version of this painting (sheda A7.a) was also in the Pio Monte della Misericordia.

22. Tuck-Scala, "Caravaggio's 'Roman Charity,' " 130, identifies the Monte della Misericordia painting as the work of Fabrizio Santafede.

23. The theme of St. Peter appears in a work by Cavallino (cat. 9); Judith in works by

Stanzione (cat. A45, A67) and Cavallino (cat. 45, 46, 82); Emmaus in a work by Stanzione (cat. A7); Samaritan Woman by neither artist; the Immaculate Conception in works by Stanzione (cat. A99) and Cavallino (cat. 26, 51); and St. Anthony in works by Cavallino (cat. 56–57). For Stanzione, autographed works are listed in Schütze and Willette, *Massimo Stanzione*; for Cavallino, Lurie, and Percy, *Bernardo Cavallino*.

24. Labrot, *Collections of Paintings in Naples*, 764, 746, 773, 761–62, 590–92, and 609–10. See also Pigler, *Barockthemen*, who lists a huge number, 158 Italian paintings, of the Immaculate Conception ("Die Unbefleckete Empfängnis," 2:497–505); gives no listing for St. Anthony of Padua with the Christ Child; identifies 59 Italian paintings of Judith ("Judith und Holofernes, 1:191–96); gives no listing for the Samaritan Woman; lists 109 Italian paintings of the Supper at Emmaus ("Christus in Emmaus," 1:346–54); and gives 36 Italian out of 90 total paintings for Peter Denies Christ ("Die Verleugnung Petri," 1:333–36).

25. Because the Getty inventory lists thirty-nine unspecified St. Anthony paintings, they may have been by either St. Anthony of Padua or St. Anthony Abbot. The local Neapolitan favorite St. Anthony Abbot, whose feast day marked the beginning of Carnival, had his shrine outside the Capuana Gate. His cult may have inspired an almost equally large veneration, with twenty-eight inventory paintings of his own.

26. None of the inventoried items is identified as a Stanzione.

27. Labrot, *Collections of Paintings in Naples*, 254–63. Lauro must have been older at the time of death in 1713, since the 1687 inventory of his brother-in-law, the obscure artist Lorenzo Ruggi (1687), lists Lauro as the guardian to his sister Camilla's seven children (164–67). If we subtract a conservative ten years for the birth of the seven children and assume that to be named ward Lauro himself had reached legal adulthood, we would be back before the 1670s, the approximate date of the Regola *Kunstkamer*.

28. Ibid., 144–49 and 309–28. Cella, a Florentine merchant who arrived in Naples before 1656, was the Grand Duke of Tuscany's agent in Naples and married into the high Neapolitan aristocracy—Maria des Cespedes, Duchessa di Frisa, the sister of the *cappellano maggiore* of the kingdom. His enormous fortune was the result of a wide range of economic activity: silk exporting, money changing, and investing capital for aristocrats and other wealthy bourgeoisie like himself. Giovanna Battista Pignatelli, on the other hand, was the daughter and wife of Spanish grandees, the last of the Duchi di Bellosguardo branch of the d'Aragona Cortes family and wife of Niccolò Pignatelli di Monteleone (1648–1725), who was *cavallerizzo maggiore* to the Queen of Spain in 1699, viceroy of Sicily and later of Sardinia.

29. Ibid., 224–31, 202–13, 135–38, and 176–81. Ottavio Orsini, among the highest Neapolitan nobility, distinguished himself in the active life as one of the city's foremost lawyers in the second half of the seventeenth century. Carlo de Cardenas, from an old fifteenth-century Aragonese family in Naples, maintained a number of fiefs in Terra di Lavoro, the province around Naples, and patronized literary-scientific matters according to the Jesuit Nicola Partenio Giannatasio's dedication in *Halieutica*, a ten-canto treatise on fish breeding. Francisco Cavallino, described as *magnifico* in the notarial document, is rather obscure, perhaps the son of the painter Bernardo Cavallino. Ignazio Provenzale, a member of the robed nobility who purchased an Abruzzi fief, was a lawyer-magistrate who held a number of bureaucratic offices—in 1678 *avvocato fiscale* of the Sommaria (the

kingdom's chief economic council), one of its ten presidents in 1683, and governor of the Abruzzi.

30. Stratton, *The Immaculate Conception in Spanish Art.*

31. The Paduan Franciscan was among the most popular of Italian saints. Sallmann, "Il santo patrono cittadino," 195 and 209, finds that St. Anthony of Padua was named a city's patron thirty-five times between 1630 and 1699, more than twice as much as any other saint.

Archival and Manuscript Sources

Archivio di Stato, Napoli

Archivio di Stato, Venezia

Senato Dispacci, Roma, filza 218, design. 1: Paolo Petrini, "Ordine della Cavalcata fattta per l'entrata del Re Filippo V nella città di Napoli il di vinti Magio l'anno, 1702."

Archivio per la Congregazione della dottrina della fede

MS I.4.b, inc. 21

Archivio Segreto Vaticano

Segretario di Stato Napoli 20 D (1615–1616)

Archivio Storico del Muncipio di Napoli

Parlamenti Generali, *Praecedentiarum,* vols. 1–10 (1488–1556)

Archivo General, Simancas

Estado, Nápoles, leg. 1038, f. 139, "Bando de la Vicaria contro los vagabundos de la ciudad de Napoles" (29 April 1550)

Secretarías provinciales

Biblioteca Apostolica Vaticana

Vat. Lat. 12731

Biblioteca di Società Napoletana di Storia Patria

Rubino, Andrea. MS. XXIII.D.14–17. "Notitia di quanto è occorso in Napoli dall'anno 1648 per tutto l'anno 1669"

Biblioteca Nacional Madrid

MS 2857, "Itinerario del Reyno de Napoles di tutto lo circuito del Regno cominciando dalla prima terra di marina, et circuendo tano il mare come la terra fatto l'anno 1559"

Biblioteca Nazionale di Napli

MS. XIV.C.21, cc. 108r–v

MS XIV.E.58

MS XV.G.26, "Parte seconda che contiene l'eresie di Suor Giulia de Marchis," 271–73

MS. XIX.C.21, cc. 277r–285v, undated. "Memoriale della fidelissima Città di Napoli al Re di Spagna dove s'espone la precedenza dell' Sindico di essa Città"

Branc. V.B.4–9, "Parlamenti e Gratie della Città di Napoli"

University of Chicago Library, Special Collections

Garnica, Juan de. MS. 1120, 2nd num. "The Ceremonial of the Neapolitan Court," recto only 9–60. Rome, 1595. "Para las cosas tocantes al officio de Virrey de Napoles." Partially transcribed in Paolo Cherchi, "Juan de Garnica: un memoriale sul cerimoniale della corte napoletana." *Archivio storico per le province napoletane*, 3rd ser., 13:92 (1975): 213–24.

Published Primary Sources

Accetto, Torquatto. *Della dissimulazione onesta.* Naples: Egidio Longo, 1641. Ed. Salvatore S. Nigro. Genoa: Costa & Nolan, 1983.

Albéri, Eugenio, ed. *Relazioni degli ambasciatori veneti al Senato.* 1st ser., vol. 3. Florence: Società editrice fiorentina, 1839–63.

Alberti, Leandro. *Descrittione di tutta Italia.* Bologna: Anselmo Giaccarelli, 1550. *Descrittione di tutta l'Italia, et isole pertinenti ad essa.* Venice: Paulo Ugolino, 1596. Giancarlo Petrella, ed., *L'officina del geografo: la "Descrittione di tutta Italia" di Leandro Alberti e gli studi geografico-antiquari tra Quattro e Cinquecento; con un saggio di edizione (Lombardia-Toscana).* Milan: V & P università, 2004.

Alciati, Andrea. *Emblemata cum commentariis.* Padua: Petro Paulo Tozzio, 1621. Reprint, New York: Garland Publishing, 1976.

———. *Emblematum liber.* 1621 ed. www.mun.ca/alciato/index.html, accessed 26 December 2009.

Aldorisio, Prospero. *La Gelotoscopia.* Naples: Tarquinio Longo, 1611.

Anelli, Francesco. *Oratione . . . nell'esequie dell'invittiss. e gloriossis. Filippo II Re di Spagna.* Naples: Stigliola, 1599.

Argomento della festa fatta nel Real Palazzo di Napoli da i gentilhomini della Corte dell'Eccellentissimo Signor Conte di Ognatte Viceré per il felice arrivo in Milano della Real Sposa del Cattolico, e Gran Rè Filippo Quarto Nostro Signore. Naples: Egidio Longo, n.d.

Aviso de la sollennità e festa fatta in la città di Napoli in lo giuramento et homaggio dato al serenissimo Filippo de Austria re d'Inghilterra e di Napoli. Naples, 1554.

Bacco, Enrico. *Effigie di tutti i Re, che han dominato il Reame di Napoli da Ruggiero I Normano in sino ad oggi.* Naples: Carlino, 1602.

———. *Naples: An Early Guide.* Trans. E. Gardner. Introd. Caroline Bruzelius. New York: Italica, 1991.

———. *Nuova descrittione del Regno di Napoli diviso in dodici Province.* Naples: Secondino Roncaglio, et ristampato per Ottavio Beltrano, 1629. Reprint, Bologna: Arnaldo Forni Editore, 1997.

Baratta, Alessandro. *Fidelissimae urbis Neapolitanae cum omnibus viis accurata et nova delineatio.* Ed. Cesare De Seta. Facsimile, Naples: Electa, 1986.

Basile, Giambattista. *Lo Cunto de li cunti.* 1634–36. Ed. Michele Rak. 3rd ed. Milan: Garzanti, 1989. Eng. Trans.: *The Pentamerone of Giambattista Basile.* Ed. N. M. Penzer.

Vol. 2. London: John Lane the Bodley Head Ltd, 1932. *Giambattista Basile's The Tale of Tales; or, Entertainment for Little Ones.* Trans. Nancy L. Canepa. Detroit: Wayne State University Press, 2007.

———. *Monte Parnaso. Mascarata da Cavalieri Napoletani.* Naples: n.p., 1630.

Biondo, Flavio. *Roma Ristaurata et Italia Illustrata.* Trans. Lucio Fauno. Venice: Domenico Giglio, 1558.

Botero, Giovanni. *Della ragion di stato. Libri dieci con tre libri delle cause della grandezza, e magnificenza delle città.* Venice: Gioliti, 1589. Translated by P. J. Waley and D. P. Waley as *The Reason of State.* London: Routledge & Kegan Paul, 1995.

———. *The Greatness of Cities.* 1588. Trans. Robert Peterson. London: Routledge & Kegan Paul, 1955.

———. *Relationi universali.* 1591. Translated as *Relations of the most Famous Kingdomes and Common-wealths thorowout the World.* London: John Haviland, 1630.

Bouchard, Jean-Jacques. *Voyage dans le Royaume de Naples.* In *Journal,* 2:159–475. Turin: G. Giappichelli editore, 1976–77.

Braccini, Giulio Cesare. *Dell'incendio fattosi nel Vesuvio e delle sue cause ed effetti.* Naples, 1632. Reprint, Bologna: Arnaldo Forni Editore, 2006.

Braun, Georg, and Franz Hogenberg. *Beschreibung und Contrafactur der vornembster Stät der Welt.* Preface and commentary, Max Schefold. 6 vols. Facsimile, Plochingen: Müller und Schindler, 1965–70.

Breve racconto della festa a ballo. Naples: Costantino Vitale, 1620. Bilinugal eds.: *A Neapolitan festa a ballo and Selected instrumental ensemble pieces.* Ed. Roland Jackson. Madison: A-R Editions, 1978; and *The Sylvan and Oceanic Delights of Posilipo.* New London Consort directed by Philip Pickett. CD-ROM. L'oiseau-Lyre 425-610-2, 1990.

Britonio, Girolomo. *Ordene et recollettione de la festa fatta in Napoli per la nova havuta de lo Imperadore Carlo de Austria.* [Naples, 1519].

Bruni, Leonardo. *Historiarum Florentini populi libri XII.* Translated in Baldassarri and Saiber, *Images of Quattrocento Florence.*

Bucca, Ferrante. "Aggionta alli diurnali di Scipione Guerra." *Archivio storico per le province napoletane* 36:2 (1911): 336–82 and 36:3 (1911): 507–14.

Bulifon, Antonio. *Giornali di Napoli del MDXLVII al MDCCVI.* Ed. Nino Cortese. Naples: Società napoletana di storia patria, 1932.

Campanella, Tommaso. *La Città del Sole/The City of the Sun.* Trans. Daniel J. Donno. Berkeley and Los Angeles: University of California Press, 1981.

———. *La Monarchia di Spagna: Prima stesura giovanile.* Ed. Germana Ernst. Naples: Istituto Italiano per gli Studi Filosofici, 1989.

———. *Ordinis praedicatorum philosophia.* Naples: Salviani, 1591.

Capaccio, Giulio Cesare. *Apparato della festività del glorioso S. Giovan Battista.* Naples, 1623.

———. *Apparato della festività del glorioso S. Giovan Battista . . . à 23 di Giugno 1624.* Naples, 1624.

———. *Apparato della festività del glorioso S. Giovan Battista . . . à XXIII di Giugno MDCXXV.* Naples, 1626.

———. *Apparato della festività del glorioso S. Giovan Battista . . . à XXIII di Giugno MDCXXVI.* Naples, [1626].

———. *Apparato della festività del glorioso S. Giovan Battista . . . à XXIII di Giugno MDCXX-VII.* Naples, 1627.

———. *Delle Imprese.* Naples: Gio. Giacomo Carlino and Antonio Pace, 1592.

———. *Il Forastiero.* Naples: Gio. Domenico Roncagliolo, 1634.

———. *Gli Apologi.* Naples: Gio. Giacomo Carlino, 1602; Naples: Gio. Giacomo Carlino and Costantino Vitale, 1607; Venice: Barezzo Barezzi, 1619.

———. *Illuustrium Mulierum et illustrium Litteris virorum elogia.* Naples: Gio. Giacomo Carlino, 1608; 1609.

———. *Incendio di Vesuvio.* In *Il Forastiero.* 2nd num.

———. (Attrib.) "Napoli descritta ne' principii del secolo XVII." Ed. Bartolommeo Capasso. *Archivo storico per le province napoletane* 7 (1882): 68–103, 531–54, 776–97.

———. *Napolitanae Historiae.* 2 vols. Naples: Jacobo Carlino, 1607.

———. *Oratio in Obitu Philippi II Hispaniarum Regis Catholici.* Naples: Carlino and Pace, 1599.

———. *Panegirico in lode della serenissima D. Maria D'Austria Regina di Boemia e di Ongheria.* Napoli: Gio. Domenico Roncagliolo, 1630.

———. *Il Principe . . . tratto da gli emblemi dell'Alciato, con ducento, e più avvertimenti politici e morali utilissimi à qualunque Signore per l'ottima eruditione di Costumi, Economia, e Governo di Stati.* Venice: Barezzo Barezzi, 1620.

———. "Relatione dell' apparato fatto dal popolo Nap.no nella festività del Glorioso S. Gio. Battista all'Ecc.ze di Don Pietro di Castro, e D. Caterina Sandoval nell'anno 1614." Biblioteca Nazionale di Napli, MS. XIX.97.

———. *Il Secretario.* Rome, 1589; Venice, 1591, 1594, 1597, and 1607.

Capasso, Bartolomeo. "Breve Cronica dai 2 giugno 1543 a 25 maggio 1547 di Geronimo de Spenis da Frattamaggiore." *Archivio storico per le province napoletane* 2 (1877): 511–31.

Capograssi, A. "La Rivoluzione di Masaniello vista dal residente Veneto a Napoli [Andrea Rosso]." *Archivio storico per le province napoletane,* n.s., 33 (1952): 167–235.

Caputi, Ottavio. *La Pompa funerale fatta in Napoli nell'essequie del Catholico Re Filippo II di Austria.* Naples: Stigliola, 1599.

———. *Relatione della pompa funerale che si celebrò in Napoli, nella morte della Serenissima Reina Margherita d'Austria.* Naples: Tarquinio Longo, 1612.

Caracciolo, Decio. *Oratione ne' funerali di Filippo Secondo Re Cattolico.* Naples: Carlino and Pace, 1599.

Caracciolo, Giovan Battista. *Nelle feste de Santi Apostoli e di vari altri santi. Ragionamenti spirituali, encomiastici.* Naples: Camillo Cavallo, 1650.

———. *Nelle feste del Signore e della Madonna. Ragionamenti spirituali, encomiastici.* Naples: Camillo Cavallo, 1649.

Castiglione, Baldasare. *The Book of the Courtier.* Trans. Charles S. Singleton. New York: Anchor Books, 1959.

Castaldo, Antonio. *Dell'historia in Raccolta da tutti i più rinomati scrittori dell'historia generale del regno di Napoli.* Naples: Gravier, 1769.

Celano, Carlo. *Notize del bello dell'antico e del curioso della città di Napoli.* Ed. Giovanni Battista Charini. 5 vols. 1692. Reprint, Naples: Edizioni dell'Anticaglia, 2000.

Cervantes, Miguel de. *Don Quixote*. Trans. John Rutherford. New York: Penguin Books, 2001.

Collenuccio, Pandolfo. *Compendio de le istorie del Regno di Napoli*. Ed. Alfredo Saviotti. 1539; Bari: Laterza, 1929.

The Commedia dell'Arte in Naples: A Bilingual Edition of the 176 Casamarciano Scenarios. La Commedia dell'Arte a Napoli: Edizione Bilingue dei 176 Scenari Casamarciano. Ed. and trans. F. Cotticelli, A. Goodrich Heck, and T. F. Heck. 2 vols. Lanham, Md.: Scarecrow Press, 2001.

Confuorto, Domenico. *Giornali di Napoli dal MDCLXXIX al MDCIC*. Ed. Nicola Nicolini. 2 vols. Naples: Società Napolitana di Storia Patria presso Luigi Lubrano, 1930.

Conti, Natale. *Natale Conti's Mythologiae*. Trans. and annotated John Mulryan and Steven Brown. 2 vols. 1567; 1581 Frankfurt ed. Medieval and Renaissance Texts and Studies, vol. 316. Tempe: Arizona Center for Medieval and Renaissance Studies, 2006.

"Copia di lettera del Maestro di Campo Ottaviano Sauli all'Eccmo signor Marchese Spinola." *Archivio storico per le province napoletane* 15:1 (1890): 355–87.

Corona, Silvio, and Ascanio Corona. "La morte di Giovan Vincenzo Starace." Biblioteca Nazionale di Napoli, MS. XV.F.47, 100–115. Transcribed in *Archivio storico per le province napoletane* 1 (1876): 131–38.

Cortese, Nino. *Feudi e feudatari Napoletani della prima metà del Cinquecento*. Naples: Società Napoletana di Storia Patria, 1931. Transcribes Archivo General, Simancas, *Visitas d'Italia, Nápoles*, lib. 58.

Costo, Tommaso. *Addizioni e note al Compendio dell'istoria del Regno di Napoli*, scritto da P. Collenuccio, M. Roseo e C. Pacca. Naples, 1583; Naples, 1588; Venice, 1613.

———. *La apologia istorica del Regno di Napoli contra la falsa opinione di coloro che biasimarono i Regnicoli di inconstanza e d'infedeltà*. Naples: Gio. Domenico Roncaglio, 1613.

———. *Della rotta di Lepanto*. Naples: Giovanni Battista Cappelli, 1573. Revised as *La Vittoria della Lega*. Naples: Giovanni Battista Cappelli, 1582.

———. *Il Fuggilozio*. Ed. Corrado Calenda. Naples: Carlino and Pace, 1596. Mod. ed., Rome: Salerno editrice, 1989.

———. *Giunta di tre Libri . . . al Compendio dell'historia del Regno di Napoli*. Venice: Cappelli and Peluso, 1613.

———. *Memoriale delle cose più notabili accadute nel Regno di Napoli dell'incarnazione di Cristo per tutto l'anno MDLXXVI*. Naples: Salviani, 1592; 1594; 1618.

———. *Nomi delle provincie, citta, terre, e castella: E de' Vescovadi, & Arcivescovadi del Regno di Napoli. De i Re, che vi regnarono, con le lor discendenze figurate in alberi; De'Vicerè stativi da Bellisarlio in quà. e de'Sette offici di esso. Con un'Indice de'Signori titolati, che vi sono, e delle Famiglie de' Seggi di Napoli. E nel fine un Memoriale di tutti i successi piu notabili d'esso Regno dalla natività di Cristo in quà, non più dato in luce*. Naples: Per Gio. Iacomo Carlino & Antonio Pace, 1593.

———. *Ragionamenti intorna alla descrizzione del Regno di Napoli et all'antichità di Pozzuolo di Scipione Mazzella*. Naples: Stigliola à Porta Regale, 1595.

Costo, Tommaso, and Michele Benvenga. *Il Segretario di lettere*. Ed. Salvatore S. Nigro. Palermo: Sellerio editore, 1991. Originally published in Tommaso Costo, *Lettere*. Venice, 1602; Naples, 1604.

Cronaca di Partenope. Ed. Antonio Altamura. Naples: Società editrice napoletana, 1974.

The "Cronaca di Partenope": A Critical Edition of the First Vernacular History of Naples (c. 1350). Ed. Samantha Kelly. Leiden: Brill, Forthcoming.

D'Addosio, G. B. "Documenti inediti di artisti napoletani dei secoli xvi e xvii dalle polizze dei banchi." *Archivio storico per le province napoletane* 45 (1920): 165–66, 178–79.

Davila, Ferdinando. *Attione funerale fatta l'ultimo d'ottobre MDCI . . . nelle essequie dell'illust. et eccellent. Sig. D. Ferdinando Ruiz di Castro, Conte di Lemos*. Naples: Gio. Iacomo Carlino, 1601.

———. *Oratio in Funere Philippi II Austriaci Potentissimi, Hispaniarum Indiarum ac Utriusque Siciliae Regis Catholici*. Naples: Carlini and Pace, 1599.

Davis, James C., ed. *Pursuit of Power. Venetian Ambassadors' Reports on Turkey, France, and Spain in the Age of Philip II, 1560–1600*. New York: Harper Torchbooks, 1970.

De Blasé, G. "Frammento d'un diario inedito napoletano." *Archivio storico per le province napoletane* 13 (1888): 788–820 and 14 (1889) 34–68, 265–352.

De Blassis, Giuseppe. "De precedentia nobelium sedilium in onoribus et dignitatibus occurrentibus Universitati Neapolis." *Archivio storico per le province napoletane* 2 (1877): 543–77.

De' Dominici, Bernardo. *Vite de' pittori, scultori ed architetti napoletani*. 4 vols. Naples: Stamperia del Ricciardi, 1742–43. Reprint, Bologna: Arnaldo Forni Editore, 1971.

De Rosa, Loise. "Lodi di Napoli." In *Napoli Aragonese nei ricordi di Loise de Rosa*, ed. Antonio Altamura. Naples: Libreria Scientifica Editrice, 1971.

De Santis, Tommaso. *Historia del tumulto di Napoli*. Leyden: Stamperia d'Elsevir, 1652.

Della Porta, Giambattista. *Della fisonomia dell'uomo*. Ed. Mario Cicognani. Parma: Ugo Guanda, 1988.

———. *Gli duoi fratelli rivali/The Two Rival Brothers*. Ed. and trans. Louise George Clubb. Berkeley and Los Angeles: University of California Press, 1980.

Descrittione della pompa funerale fatta in Brussele alli xxix. di Decembre M.D.LVIII. per la felice, & immortal memoria di Carlo V. Imperatore, con una naue delle vittorie di sua Cesarea Maesta. Milan: Francesco Moschenio, 1559.

Divenuto, Francesco, ed. *Napoli L'Europa e la Compagnia di Gesù nella "Cronica" di Giovanni Francesco Araldo*. Naples: Edizioni Scientifiche italiane, 1998.

———. *Napoli sacra del XVI secolo: Repertorio delle fabriche religiose napoletane nella cronic del Gesuita Giovan Francesco Araldo*. Naples: Edisioni Scientifiche Italiane, 1990.

Donzelli, Giuseppe. *Partenope Liberata*. Ed. Antonio Altamura. Naples: Fausto Fiorentino, 1970.

Dooley, Brendan, ed. and trans. *Italy in the Baroque*. New York: Garland Publishing, 1995.

Erasmus, Desiderius. *The Praise of Folly*. Trans. Clarence H. Miller. New Haven: Yale University Press, 1979.

Falco, Benedetto di. *Descrittione de i luoghi antique di Napoli, e del suo amenissimo distretto*. Naples: Giovvani Battista Cappelli, 1589. Ed. Tobia R. Toscano. Rome: CIEN, 1992.

Fellecchia, Alessandro. *Viaggio della maestá della regina di Bohemia, e d'Ungheria da Madrid sino a Napoli con descrittione di Pausilipo, e di molte Dame Napoletane*. Naples: Secondino Roncagliolo, 1630.

Ferraro, Pirro Antonio. *Cavallo Frenato*. Naples: Antonio Pace, 1602.

Feste celebrate in Napoli per la nasita del Serenissimo Prencipe di Spagna Nostro Signore. Naples: Faggioli, 1658.

Filante, Filippo. *Oracion . . . Hecha en la muerte del Alto Rey de las Españas Don Phelipe d'este nombre segundo.* Naples: Stigliola, 1599.

Filarete, Antonio Averlino. *Filarete's* Treatise on Architecture. Trans. John R. Spencer. New Haven: Yale University Press, 1965.

Fuidoro, Innocenzo. *Giornali di Napoli dal MDCLX al MDCLXXX.* Ed. Franco Schlitzer et al. 4 vols. Naples: Società Napolitana di Storia Patria, 1934–43.

———. *Successi historici raccolti dalla sollevatione di Napoli dell'anno 1647.* Ed. Anna Maria Giraldi and Marina Raffaeli. Milan: FrancoAngeli, 1994.

Garzoni, Tomaso. "De' Giocatori in universale et in particolare." In *La Piazza universale di tutte le professioni del mondo.* Venice, 1585. 2 vols., ed. Giovanni Battista Bronzini. Florence: Olschki, 1996.

Gemma, Francesco. *In Serenissimi atque Catholici semperq. Invictissimi regis nostri Philippi II. Obitum.* Naples: Carlino and Pace, 1599.

Gesualdo, Scipione. *Constitutiones et decreta dioecesanae synodi in Metropolitana Ecclesia Conzana celebrata del xix Octobris MDXCVII.* Naples: Carlino, 1600.

Giannone, Onofrio. *Giunte sulle vite de' pittori napoletani.* Ed. Ottavio Morisani. Naples: R. Deputazione di Storia Patria, 1941.

Gigli, Giacinto. *Diario Romano (1608–1670).* Ed. Giuseppe Ricciotti. Rome: Tumminelli editore, 1958.

Giraffi, Alessandro. *La rivolutioni di Napoli.* Venice: per il Baba, 1647.

———. *Ragguaglio del tumulto di Napoli.* Venice: Baba, 1647.

Giuliani, Giovanni Bernardino. *Descrittione dell'apparato di San Giovanni . . . L'anno M.D.XXVIII.* Naples, 1628.

———. *Descrittione dell'apparato fatto nella festa di San Giovanni . . . L'anno M.D.XXXI.* Naples, 1631.

———. *Trattato del Monte Vesuvio.* Naples, 1632. Reprint, Bologna: Arnaldo Forni Editore, 2006.

Grisone, Federico. *Ordini di cavalcare, et modi di conscere le nature de' cavalli, emendar I vitti loro, et ammaestrargli per l'uso della guerra & commodita de gli huomini.* Venice: Vincenzo Valgrisi, 1551.

Giustiniani, Lorenzo. *Dizionario geografico-ragionato del Regno di Napoli.* Vol. 12. Naples, 1797–1805. Reprint, Bologna: Forni editore, 1970.

Guazzo, Stefano. *La civil conversazione.* Ed. Amedeo Quondam. 2 vols. 1574; Modena: Pannini, 1993.

Guicciardini, Francesco. *The History of Italy.* Ed. and trans. Sidney Alexander. New York: Collier Books, 1969.

Herrera, Pedro Martinez de. *Principe advertido y declaracion de las Epigramas de Napoles la Vispera de S. Iuan.* Naples: por Lazaro Scorriggio, 1631.

Imbriani, Julii Caesari. *In Philippi II Hispaniarum Regis Catholici Obitu. ad Fidellissimum Campanorum Senatum Oratio.* Naples: Carlino and Pace, 1599.

Imperato, Francesco. *Privilegi, capituli, e gratie, concesse al fedelissimo populo Napolitano, & alla sus piazza.* Naples: Gio. Domenico Roncagliolo, 1624.

The Jesuit Ratio Studiorum of 1599. Trans. Allan P. Farrell. 1970. www.bc.edu/bc_org/avp/ ulib/digi/ratio/ratio_web.html, accessed 17 February 2008.

Lega, Giovan Domenico. *Il glorioso triomfo et bellísimo aparato ne la felicísima entrata di la maestà cesarea in la nobilísima città di Partenope fatto con lo particolare ingresso di essa Maestà ordinatissimamente descritto*. Naples: Giovanni Sultzbach, 1535; Naples: Mattia Cancer, 1535.

Leti, Gregorio. *Vita dell'invittissimo Imperadore Carlo V*. Vol. 4. Amsterdam, 1700.

Liponari, Nescopio. *Relatione delle rivolutioni popolari successe nel distretto e regno di Napoli: nel presente anno 1647 alli 7 Luglio*. Padua: per il Sarti, 1648.

Lippi, Lorenzo. *Il Manmantile racquistato*. 1670; Venice: Stefano Orlandini, 1748.

Lotterio, Gabriele. *In funere Augustissimi Catholici Regii nostri Philippi II Austriae*. Naples Carlino and Pace, 1599.

Lucas, Colin, ed. *The French Revolution Research Collection and Videodisk*. Pt. 2: *Themes in Culture and Art*. Paris and London: Bibliothèque Nationale and Pergamon Press, 1989.

Machiavelli, Niccolò. *Il principe e Discorsi sopra la prima deca di Tito Livio*. Ed. Sergio Bertelli. 5th ed. Milan: Feltrinelli, 1977. *Machiavelli's* The Prince. *A Bilingual Edition*. Trans. and ed. Mark Musa. New York: St. Martin's Press, 1964. *Discourses on Livy*. Trans. Harvey C. Mansfield and Nathan Tarcov. Chicago: University of Chicago Press, 1996.

La magnifica, e suntuosa pompa funerale, fatta in Burselle il di xxix. di Decembre, l'anno M.D.LVIII. nell' essequie dello 'nuittissimo Carlo Quinto, Imperadore Massimo. Antwerp: Cristophoro Plantino, 1559.

Manso, Giambattista. *Erocallia, ovvero dell'amore e della bellezza*. Venice, 1628.

Marino, Giambattista. *Lettere*. Ed. Marziano Guglielminetti. Turin: Einaudi, 1966.

Mazzella, Scipione. *Descrittione del Regno di Napoli*. Naples, 1586; 1597; 1601. Reprint of 1601 edition, Bologna: Arnaldo Forni Editore, 1981.

———. *Sito et antichità della città di Pozzuolo e del suo amenissimo distretto*. Naples: Salviani, 1591; Naples: Stigliola à Porta Regale, 1595.

———. *Le vite dei re di Napoli con le loro effigie naturale*. Naples: Giuseppe Bonfadino, 1594.

Molina. Tirso de. *El burlador de Sevilla y convidado de piedra*. Ed. James A. Parr. Binghamton: Medieval and Renaissance Texts and Studies, 1994.

Montemayor, Giuseppe de, ed. *Diurnali di Scipione Guerra*. Naples: Società Napolitana di Storia Patria, 1891.

Nicolai, Agostino. *Historia, overo narrazione giornale dell'ultime rivoluzioni della citta e regno di Napoli*. Amsterdam: Jodoco Pluymer, 1660.

Notar Giacomo. *Cronica di Napoli*. Ed. Paolo Garzilli. Naples: Dalla Stamperia Reale, 1845. Reprint, Bologna: A. Forni, 1980.

"Notizie. Delle cose principali della città di Napoli circa il 1600." *Archivio storico per le province napoletane* 7 (1882): 797: "Le Feste principali e vistose in ogni anno."

Nuovo collezione delle Prammatiche del Regno di Napoli. Naples: Nella Stamperia Simoniana, 1803.

Orilia, Francesco. *Lo Zodiaco, over, idea di perfettione di prencipi: formata dall'heroiche virtù dell'illustriss. Et eccellentiss. Signore D. Antonio Alvarez di Toledo, duca d'Alba vicerè di Na-*

poli: rapresentata come in un trionfo dal fidelissimo popolo napoletano: per opera del dottore Francesco Antonio Scacciavento suo eletto: nella pomposissima festa di San Gio. Battista, celebrata à 23 di giugno 1629 per il settimo anno del suo governo raccolta per Francesco Orilia. Naples: Ottavio Beltrano, 1630.

Pacheco, Francisco. "The Iconography of the Virgin of the Immaculate Conception" (1628). In *Italian and Spanish Art, 1600–1750: Sources and Documents*, ed. Robert Enggass and Jonathan Brown, pp. 165–72. Evanston: Northwestern University Press, 1992.

Parrino, Domenico Antonio. *L'ossequio tributario della fedelissima Città di Napoli per le dimostranze giulive nei Regii Sponsali del Cattolico ed Invittissimo Monarca Carlo Secondo colla Serenissima Principessa Maria Anna di Neoburgo Palatina del Reno sotto i felicissimi auspicii dell'Eccellentissimo Signore D. Francesco di Benavides Conte di S. Stefano Vicerè, e Capitan Generale nel Regno di Napoli. Ragguaglio historico.* Naples: nella nuova stamp di Dom. Ant. Parrino e Michele Luigi Mutii, 1690.

———. *Teatro eroico e politico de' governi de' vicere de Regno di Napoli dal tempo del Re Ferdinando Il Cattolico fino al presente.* 3 vols. Naples: Parrino and Mutii, 1692–94. 2 vols. Naples: Gravier, 1770.

Petrarca, Francesco. *Petrarch's Lyric Poems: The* Rime sparse *and Other Lyrics.* Trans. and ed. Robert M. Durling. Cambridge, Mass.: Harvard University Press, 1976.

Pontano, Giovanni Gioviano. *Historia della guerra di Napoli.* Naples: Giuseppe Cacchi, 1590.

Porzio, Camillo. *La congiura dei Baroni.* Rome: Paolo Manuzio, 1565. Reprint, Venosa (PZ): Edizioni Osanna Venosa, 1989.

———. "Relazione del Regno di Napoli al Marchese di Mondesciar viceré di Napoli tra il 1577 e il 1579." In *La congiura de' Baroni del Regno di Napoli contra il Re Ferdinando primo e gli altri scritt*, ed. Ernesto Pontieri. Naples: E.S.I., 1964.

Quaja, Joannes Genesius. *Liber de civitate Christi.* Reggio nell'Emilia: per Ugone[m] de Rugeriis, 1501.

Quattromani, Sertorio. *La philosophia di Berardo Telesio ristretta in brevitia.* Naples: G. Cacchi, 1589.

Rabelais, François. *Oeuvres complètes.* Ed. P. Jourda. 2 vols. Paris: Garnier Frères, 1962.

Raneo, José. *Etiquetas de la corte de Nápoles 1634.* Ed. A. Paz y Mélia. Abstract from *Revue Hispanique* 27. New York and Paris, 1912.

Regio, Paolo. *Della consolatione e del consiglio. Dialoghi sette. Terza parte degli Opuscoli Morali.* Naples: Carlino and Pace, 1598.

———. *Della felicità e della miseria. Dialoghi sette. Seconda parte degli Opusculi Morali.* Naples: Carlino and Pace, 1597.

———. *Delle osservanze Catholica. Dialoghi sette. Prima parte degli Opusculi Morali.* Naples: Carlino and Pace, 1597.

———. *Dell'Opere spirituali.* 2 vols. Naples: Giuseppe Cacchii, 1592–93.

———. *Dialoghi intorno la felicità, et la miseria, et la fragilità della vita humana.* Naples: Cacchii, 1591.

———. *Discorsi del Regio intorno le virtu morali.* Naples: Salviani, 1576.

———. *Sermoni intorno le tre virtù teologiche.* Naples: Stigliola, 1595.

———. *Siracusa: Pescatoria.* Naples: Giovanni de Boy, 1569.

————. *La Sirenide. Poema Spirituali*. Naples: Pace, 1603.

————. *Vita dei sette santi protettori di Napoli*. Naples: Giuseppe Cacchii, 1573; 1579.

Relatione delle feste fatte in Napoli dall'eccellen.mo signor duca di Medina de las Torres, viceré del regno, per la nascita della serenissima infanta di Spagna. Naples: Egidio Longo, 1639.

Relatione delle sontuose feste con che celebrò le nove del felice Desposorio del Rè Nostro Signore D. Filippo IV et il compimento d'anni 14 della Regina Nostra Signora. Naples: Francesco Antonio Orlando, 1649.

Rossini, Carlo. *Constitutioni et decreti fatti e pubblicati da Giulio Rossini arcivescovo d'Amalfi nella diocesana sinodo fatta nella metropolitana chiesa d'Amalfi, sotto il di 12 et seguenti del mese di Gennaro 1594*. Naples: Aulisio, 1594.

Ruscelli, Girolamo. *Le imprese illustri con espositioni, et discorsi*. Venice, 1566, 1572, 1580, 1584.

Sala, Andrea. *La triomphale entrata di Carlo V Imperadore augusto en la inclita città di Napoli et di Missina*. Naples, 1535.

Sarnelli, Pompeo. *Posilecheata*. Ed. Enrico Matao. Naples: Edizioni di Gabriela e Maria Teresa Benincasa, 1986.

Sigismondo, Giuseppe. *Descrizione della città di Napoli e suoi borghi*. 1788. Reprint, Bologna: Arnaldo Forni editore, 1989.

Stimmer, Tobias. *Nueu künstliche Figuren Biblischer Historien*. Basel: T. Gwarin, 1576.

Summonte, Giovan Antonio. *Dell' Historia della Città e Regno di Napoli*. Vols. 1–2. Naples: Carlino, 1601–2. Vol. 3. Naples: Francesco Savio, 1640. Vol. 4. Naples: Giacomo Gaffaro, 1643.

Talucci, Celio. *Il passaggio di D. Maria d'Austria Regina di Ungheria per lo stato ecclesiastico. L'anno 1631*. [Rome, 1631].

Tasso, Torquato. "Il Gonzaga secondo overo del giuoco." In *Prose*, ed. Ettore Mazzali. 1582; Milan: Ricardo Ricciardi editore, 1959.

————. *Tasso's Dialogues. A Selection, with the Discourse on the Art of the Dialogue*. Trans. Carnes Lord and Dain A. Trafton. Berkeley and Los Angeles: University of California Press, 1982.

Tontoli, Gabriele. *Il Mas'Aniello, overo discorsi narrativi la Sollevatione di Napoli*. Naples: Per Roberto Mollo, 1648.

Troilo, Erminio, ed. *La philosophia di Berardino Telesio restretta in brevita et scritta in lingua Toscana del Montano Academico cosentino all eccellenza del Sig. Duca di Nocera*. Naples: Cacchi, 1589. Mod. ed., Bari: Società Tipografica Editrice Barese, 1914.

Turamini, Alessandro. *Orazione in morte dell'invitt.mo e gloriosiss.mo Don Filippo d'Austria II Re di Spagna*. Naples: Stigliola, 1599.

Tutini, Camillo. *Dei origine e fundatione de' seggi di Napoli*. Naples: Appresso il Beltrano, 1644. Reprint, Paolo Piccolo, *Dell'origine e fondazione de Sedili di Napoli*. Naples: Luciano Editore, 2005.

Tutini, Camillo, and Marino Verde. *Racconto della sollevatione di Napoli accaduta nell'anno MDCXLVII*, ed. Pietro Messina. Rome: Istituto Storico Italiano per l'età moderna e contemporanea, 1997.

Vario, Domenico Alfeno, et al. *Pragmaticae edicta, decreta, interdicta, regiaeque sanctiones regni neapolitani*. 4 vols. Naples: Sumptibus Antonii Cervonii, 1772.

Vitignano, Cornelio. *Vera genealogia descendenza della serenissima et invittissima prosapia d'Austria.* Naples: Carlino and Pace, 1599.

Volpicella, Scipione. *Giovan Battista Del Tufo, Illustratore di Napoli del secolo XVI.* Naples: Stamperia della Regia Università, 1880.

Vredeman de Vries, Jan. *Pictores, Statuarii, Architecti.* [1560s].

———. *Scenographiae sive perspectivae.* Antwerp: En la maison de Hieronymus Cock, 1560.

Zappullo, Michele. *Sommario Istorico . . . di tre gran Città, cioè Gerusalem, di Roma, e di Napoli.* Naples: Carlino and Pace, 1598; Naples, 1602; Vicenza: Giorgio Greco, 1603; Naples: Carlino and Vitale, 1609.

Zazzera, Francesco. "Narrazioni tratte dai Giornali del Governo di Don Pietro Girone duca d'Ossuna, vicerè di Napoli." Ed. Francesco Palermo. *Archivio Storico Italiano* 9 (1844): 473–617.

Secondary Sources

Alonso-Muñumer, Isabel Enciso. "La corte y el virreinato: El Mecenazgo de Don Pedro Fernández de Castro, VII Conde de Lemos, y su Política cultural en Nápoles a comienzos del XVII." In *El Área del Mediterráneo.* Ed. Rosario González Martínez. Vol. 3 of *Congreso Internacional Las Sociedades Ibéricas y el Mar a Finales del Siglo XVI.* 6 vols. Madrid: Los Centenarios de Felipe II y Carlos V; Lisbon: Pabellón de España, Expo '98, 1998.

Amabile, Luigi. *Fra Tommaso Campanella.* Vol. 3. Naples: Antonio Morano, 1882.

———. *Il Santo Officio della Inquisizione in Napoli.* 2 vols. Città di Castello: S. Lapi, 1892.

Amirante, Francesca, et al., eds. *Libri per vedere. Le guide storico-artistiche della città di Napoli: fonti testimonianze del gusto immagini di una città.* Naples: Edizioni Scientifiche Italiane, 1995.

Anderson, Jaynie. "'Le roi ne meurt jamais': Charles V's Obsequies in Italy." In *El Cardenal Albornoz y el Colegio de España,* ed. Evelio Verdera y Tuells. Vol. 5. Bologna: Publicaciones del Real Colegio de España, 1979.

Le Arche dei Re Aragonesi. Naples: Elio de Rosa editore, 1991.

Asor-Rosa, A. "Basile, Giambattista." *Dizionario biografico degli Italiani,* 7:76–80. Rome: Istituto della Enciclopedia italiana, 1960–.

Badaloni, N. "I fratelli Della Porta e la cultura magica e astrologica a Napoli nel '500." *Studi storici* 1:4 (1959–60): 677–715.

Bairoch, Paul, et. al. *The Population of European Cities from 800 to 1850. Data Bank and Short Summary of Results.* Geneva: Librairie Droz, 1988.

Baker, Keith Michael. "Inventing the French Revolution." In *Inventing the French Revolution: Essays on French Political Culture in the Eighteenth Century.* Cambridge: Cambridge University Press, 1990.

Baldassarri, Stefano Ugo, and Arielle Saiber, eds. *Images of Quattrocento Florence: Selected Writings in Literature, History, and Art.* New Haven: Yale University Press, 2001.

Barletta, Laura. *Il Carnevale del 1764 a Napoli. Protesta e integrazione in uno spazio urbano.* Naples: Società Editrice Napoletana, 1981.

———. *Fra regola e licenza: chiesa e vita religiosa, feste e beneficenza a Napoli e in Campania (secoli XVIII–XX).* Naples: Edizioni Scientifiche Italiane, 2003.

Baron, Hans. *The Crisis of the Early Italian Renaissance: Civic Humanism and Republican Liberty in an Age of Classicism and Tyranny*. Rev. ed. Princeton: Princeton University Press, 1966.

Barzman, Karen-edis. "Early Modern Spectacle and the Performance of Images." In *Perspectives on Early Modern and Modern Intellectual History: Essays in Honor of Nancy S. Struever*, ed. Joseph Marino and Melinda W. Schlitt. Rochester: University of Rochester Press, 2001.

Beca de Fouquières, L. *Les jeux des Anciens. Leur description, leur origine, leur rapports avec la religion, l'histoire, les arts et les moeurs*. Paris: C. Reinwald, 1869.

Beloch, Karl J. *Bevölkerungsgeschichte Italiens*. 3 vols. Berlin: De Gruyter, 1947–61.

Bell, Rudolph M. *How to Do It: Guides to Good Living for Renaissance Italians*. Chicago: University of Chicago Press, 1999.

Bellucci, Ermanno, and Vladimiro Valerio. *Piante e vedute di Napoli dal 1600 al 1699: la città teatro*. Naples: Electa Napoli, 2007.

Benevolo, Leonardo. *La città italiana nel Rinascimento*. Milan: Edizioni Il Polifilo, 1969.

Benigno, Francesco. *L'ombra del Re. Ministri e lotta politica nella Spagna del Seicento*. Venice: Marsilio, 1992.

Bentley, Jerry H. *Politics and Culture in Renaissance Naples*. Princeton: Princeton University Press, 1987.

Bettelheim, Bruno. *The Uses of Enchantment: The Meaning and Importance of Fairy Tales*. New York: Alfred A. Knopf, 1976.

Binde, Per. *Bodies of Vital Matter. Notions of Life Force and Transcendence in Traditional Southern Italy*. Gothenburg Studies in Social Anthropology 14. Göteborg: Acta Universitatis Gothoburgensis, 1999.

Bizzocchi, Roberto. *Genealogie incredibili. Scritti di storia nell'Europa moderna*. Bologna: il Mulino, 1995.

Boccadamo, Giuliana. "Il linguaggio dei rituali religiosi napoletani (secoli XVI–XVII)." In *I linguaggi del potere nell'età barocca. 1. Politica e religione*. Ed. Francesca Cantù. Rome: Viella, 2009.

Borrelli, Gianfranco. "Concetto di popolo e rappresentazioni dei soggetti nelle scritture politiche italiane del Seicento." *Ricerche Storiche* 32:2–3 (May–December 2002): 377–96.

———. "Ragion di Stato. L'arte italiana della prudenza politica." www.filosofia.unina.it/ragiondistato/intro-i.html, accessed 1 August 2008.

Bowsky, William M. *A Medieval Italian Commune: Siena under the Nine, 1287–1355*. Berkeley: University of California Press, 1981.

Braudel, Fernand. *La Méditerranée et le monde méditerranéen á l'époque de Philippe II*. Paris: Librarie Armand Colin, 1949; 2nd ed., 2 vols., Paris: Librarie Armand Colin, 1966. Translated by Siân Reynolds as *The Mediterranean and the Mediterranean World in the Age of Philip II*. 2 vols. New York: Harper & Row, 1972–73.

———. *Out of Italy, 1450–1650*. Trans. Siân Reynolds. Paris: Flammarion, 1991.

Brown, Alison. "The Language of Empire." In *Florentine Tuscany: Structures and Practices of Power*, ed. William J. Connell and Andrea Zorzi. Cambridge: Cambridge University Press, 2000.

Brucker, Gene, ed. *The Society of Renaissance Florence. A Documentary Study*. New York: Harper Torchbooks, 1971.

Bucher, Gisela. *Weltliche Genüsse: Ikonologische Studien zu Tobias Stimmer (1539–1584)*. Bern: Peter Lang, 1992.

Burke, Peter. *The Fortunes of the Courtier*. University Park: Pennsylvania State University Press, 1995.

———. *Popular Culture in Early Modern Europe*. New York: Harper & Row, 1978.

———. "Presenting and Re-presenting Charles V." In *Charles V, 1500–1558, and His Time*, ed. Hugo Soly. Antwerp: Mercatorfonds, 1999.

———. "Southern Italy in the 1590s: Hard Times or Crisis?" In *The European Crisis of the 1590s: Essays in Comparative History*, ed. Peter Clark. London: Allen and Unwin, 1985.

———. "The Virgin of the Carmine and the Revolt of Masaniello." *Past and Present* 99 (1983): 3–21.

Caillois, Roger. *Man, Play, and Games*. Trans. Meyer Barash. New York: Free Press of Glencoe, 1961.

Calabria, Antonio. *The Cost of Empire: The Finances of the Kingdom of Naples in the Time of Spanish Rule*. Cambridge: Cambridge University Press, 1991.

Calabria, Antonio, and John A. Marino, eds. and trans. *Good Government in Spanish Naples*. New York: Peter Lang, 1990.

Calaresu, Melissa. "Images of Ancient Rome in Late Eighteenth-Century Neapolitan Historiography." *Journal of the History of Ideas* 58:4 (1997): 641–61.

Caldwell, Dorigen. *The Sixteenth-Century Italian Impresa in Theory and Practice*. Brooklyn: AMS Press, 2004.

Canepa, Nancy L. *From Court to Forest: Giambattista Basile's* Lo cunto de li cunti *and the Birth of the Literary Fairy Tale*. Detroit: Wayne State University Press, 1999.

———. " 'Quanto 'nc'è da ccà a lo luoco dove aggio da ire?': Giambattista Basile's Quest for the Literary Fairy Tale." In *Out of the Woods: The Origins of the Literary Fairy Tale in Italy and France*, ed. Nancy L. Canepa. Detroit: Wayne State University Press, 1997.

Capasso, Bartolommeo. *Catalogo ragionato . . . dell'archivio municipale di Napoli (1387–1806)*. 3 vols. Naples: Stabilmento tipografico del Cav. Francesco Giannini, 1876–1916.

Capuozzo, Stefania. "Tomaso Costo e la battaglia di Lepanto. Edizione e studio de *La vittoria della Lega*." Dottorato di ricerca in Filologia moderna Ciclo XIX (2004–7). Dipartimento di Filologia moderna, Università degli Studi di Napoli Federico II, 2007. www .fedoa.unina.it/2720/01/Capuozzo_Filologia_Moderna.pdf, accessed 22 August 2008.

Cashman, Anthony B., III. "Performance Anxiety: Federico Gonzaga at the Court of Francis I and the Uncertainty of Ritual Action." *Sixteenth Century Journal* 33:2 (1001).

The Catholic Encyclopedia. New York: Robert Appleton Company, 1908. www.newadvent .org/cathen/index.html.

Causa, Raffaello. "Giovan Francesco d'Arezzo e prospero maestri di commesso e prospettiva. Le tarsie del Coro dei Conversi nella Certosa di S. Matino." *Napoli Nobilissima*, ser. 3, 1 (1961–62): 123–34.

Certeau, Michel de. *Culture in the Plural*. Ed. Luce Giard and trans. Tom Conley. Minneapolis: University of Minnesota Press, 1997.

————. *The Practice of Everyday Life*. Trans. Steven Rendall. Berkeley: University of California Press, 1984.

Chartier, Roger. "Text and Images. The Arts of Dying, 1450–1600." In *The Cultural Uses of Print in Early Modern France*, trans. Lydia G. Cochrane. Princeton: Princeton University Press, 1987.

Chastel, André. "Marqueterie et perspective au XVe siècle." *La Revue des Arts* 3:3 (1953): 141–54.

Chaves, Teresa. "El duque de Medina de las Torres y el teatro. Las fiestas de 1639 en Nápoles." In *Percorsi del teatro spagnolo in Italia e Francia*, ed. Fausta Antonucci. Florence: Alinea editrice, 2007.

Clifton, James. "Images of the Plague and Other Contemporary Events in Seventeenth-Century Naples." Ph.D. dissertation, Princeton University, 1987.

————. "Mattia Preti's Madonna of Constantinople and a Marian Cult in Seventeenth-Century Naples." In *Parthenope's Splendor: Art of the Golden Age in Naples*, ed. Jeanne Chenault Porter and Susan Scott Munshower. Papers in Art History, vol. 7. University Park: Pennsylvania State University, 1993.

Close, A. *Cervantes and the Comic Mind of His Age*. Oxford: Oxford University Press, 2000.

Clubb, Louise George. *Giambattista Della Porta Dramatist*. Princeton: Princeton University Press, 1965.

Cocco, Sean Fidalgo. "Vesuvius and Naples: Nature and the City, 1500–1700." Ph.D. dissertation, University of Washington, 2004.

Cochrane, Eric. *Historians and Historiography in the Italian Renaissance*. Chicago: University of Chicago Press, 1981.

Colapietra, Raffaele. "La storiografia napoletana del secondo '500." *Belfagor* 15 (1960): 415–36 and 16 (1961): 416–31.

Comparato, Vittor Ivo. *Uffici e società a Napoli (1600–1647). Aspetti dell'ideologica del magistrato nell'età moderna*. Florence: Leo S. Olschki, 1974. The last chapter is translated as, "Toward the Revolt of 1647," in *Good Government in Spanish Naples*, ed. and trans. Antonio Calabria and John A. Marino. New York: Peter Lang, 1990.

Coniglio, Giuseppe. *Declino del viceregno di Napoli (1599–1689)*. Naples: Giannini, 1990.

————. *Il Regno di Napoli al tempo di Carlo V: amministrazione e vita economic-sociale*. Naples: Edizioni Scientifiche Italiane, 1951.

————. *I Vicerè Spagnoli di Napoli*. Naples: Fausto Fiorentino, 1967.

Conti, Vittorio. *Le leggi di una rivoluzione. I bandi della Repubblica Napolitana dall'ottobre 1647 all'aprile 1648*. Naples: Jovene, 1983.

Corsi, Cesare. "Musica reale e immaginaria nelle feste per la visita a Napoli di Carlo V." In *Napoli musicalissima. Studi in onore del 70° compleanno di Renato Di Benedetto*, ed. Enrico Careri and Pier Paolo De Martino. Lucca: Libreria Musicale Italiana, 2005.

Courtine, J.-J., and G. Vigarello. "La physionomie de l'homme impudique." *Communications* 46 (1987): 85–86.

Cox-Rearick, Janet. *Dynasty and Destiny in Medici Art: Pontormo, Leo X, and the two Cosimos*. Princeton: Princeton University Press, 1984.

Croce, Benedetto. "I seggi di Napoli." *Napoli Nobilissimi*, n.s., 1:2 (1920): 17–19.

————. *I teatri di Napoli secolo XV–XVIII*. Naples: Luigi Pierro, 1891.

D'Agostino, Guido. "Il governo spagnolo nell'Italia meridionale (Napoli dal 1503 al 1580)." In *Storia di Napoli*, 5:1–278. Naples: Società editrice Storia di Napoli, 1967–78.

———. *Parlamento e società nel regno di Napoli. Secoli XV–XVII.* Naples: Guida editori, 1979.

D'Alessio, Silvana. *Contagi. La rivolta napoletana del 1647-'48: linguaggio e potere politico.* Florence: Centro Editoriale Toscano, 2003.

———. *Masaniello.* Rome: Salerno editrice, 2007.

D'Aloe, S. "Catalogo di tutti gli edifici sacri della città di Napoli e suoi sobborghi." *Archivio storico per le province napoletane* 8 (1883): 111–52, 287–315, 499–546, 670–737.

Dandelet, Thomas James. *Spanish Rome, 1500–1700.* New Haven: Yale University Press, 2001.

Darnton, Robert. "A Bourgeois Puts His World in Order: The City as a Text." In *The Great Cat Massacre and Other Episodes in French Cultural History.* New York: Vintage Books, 1984.

———. "Peasants Tell Tales: The Meaning of Mother Goose." In *The Great Cat Massacre and other Episodes in French Cultural History.* New York: Vintage Books, 1985.

Dauverd, Céline. "Mediterranean Symbiotic Empire: The Genoese Trade Diaspora in the Spanish Kingdom of Naples, 1460–1640." Ph.D. dissertation, University of California, Los Angeles, 2007.

Davis, Natalie Zemon. "Women on Top." In *Society and Culture in Early Modern France.* Stanford: Stanford University Press, 1975.

Davis, Susan. *Parades and Power: Street Theatre in Nineteenth-Century Philadelphia.* Philadelphia: Temple University Press, 1986.

De Armas, Frederick A. "Segismundo/Philip IV: The Politics of Astrology in *La Vida es sueño.*" *Bulletin of the Comediantes* 53:1 (2001): 83–100.

De Cavi, Sabina. *Architecture and Royal Presence: Domenico and Giulio Cesare Fontana in Habsburg Naples (1592–1627).* Newcastle upon Tyne: Cambridge Scholars Publishing, 2009.

———. "El Possesso de los virreyes españoles en Nápoles." In *El legado de Borgoña: Fiesta y ceremonia cortesana en la Europa de los Austrias,* ed. Bernardo García García and Krista De Jonge. Conference papers, Madrid, 2007. In press.

———. " 'Senza causa, et fuor di tempo': Domenico Fontana e il Palazzo Vicereale Vecchio di Napoli." *Napoli Nobilissima,* ser. 5, 4:5–6 (2003): 187–208.

De Cunzo, Mario A. "La Certosa di San Martino." In *Certose e Certosini in Europa. Atti del Convegno alla Certosa di San Lorenzo Padula 22, 23, 24 settembre 1988.* 2 vols. Naples: Sergio Civita Editore, 1990.

De Seta, Cesare. *I Casali di Napoli.* Bari: Laterza, 1984.

———. *Napoli.* Naples: Editori Laterza, 1981.

———. *Napoli fra Rinascimento e Illuminismo.* Naples: Electa, 1991.

———. *Storia della cittá di Napoli dalle origini al Settecento.* Rome: Laterza, 1973.

———. "The Urban Structure of Naples: Utopia and Reality." In *Renaissance from Brunelleschi to Michelangelo: The Representation of Architecture,* ed. Henry Millon. New York: Rizzoli, 1994.

De Simone, Roberto, et al., eds. *Masaniello nella drammaturgia Europea e nella iconografia del suo secolo.* Naples: Gaetano Macchiaroli editore, 1998.

De Vries, Jan. *European Urbanization, 1500–1800.* Cambridge, Mass.: Harvard University Press, 1984.

Del Pesco, Daniela. "Alla ricerca di Giovanni Antonio Dosio: gli anni Napoletani (1590–1610)." *Bollettino d'Arte* 27, ser. 6 (January–February 1992): 15–66.

Debord, Guy. *The Society of the Spectacle.* Trans. Donald Nicholson-Smith. 1967; New York: Zone Books, 1995.

Deleón-Jones, Karen Silvia. *Giordano Bruno and the Kabbalah: Prophets, Magicians and Rabbis,* New Haven: Yale University Press, 1997.

Delille, Gérard. *Agricoltura e democrafia nel Regno di Napoli nei secoli XVIII e XIX.* Naples: Guida, 1977. The last chapter is translated as, "Agricultural Systems and Demographic Structures in the Kingdom of Naples," in *Good Government in Spanish Naples,* ed. and trans. Antonio Calabria and John A. Marino. New York: Peter Lang, 1990.

Dimler, G. Richard. *The Jesuit Emblem: Bibliography of Secondary Literature with Select Commentary and Descriptions.* Brooklyn: AMS Press, 2005.

Douglas, Mary. "Pollution." *International Encyclopedia of the Social Sciences,* ed. David L. Sills, 12:336–41. New York: Macmillan Free Press, 1968.

———. *Purity and Danger.* New York: Praeger, 1969.

Dundes, Alan. *Life Is Like a Chicken Coop Ladder: A Portrait of German Culture through Folklore.* New York: Columbia University Press, 1984.

Dundes, Alan, and Alessandro Falassi. *La Terra in Piazza: An Interpretation of the Palio of Siena.* Berkeley and Los Angeles: University of California Press, 1975.

Eire, Carlo M. N. *From Madrid to Purgatory: The Art and Craft of Dying in Sixteenth-Century Spain.* Cambridge: Cambridge University, 1995.

Elias, Norbert. *The Civilizing Process.* Trans. Edmund Jephcott. 1939; Oxford: Blackwell, 1994.

Elías de Tejada, Francisco. *Napoles Hispanicos.* 5 vols. Madrid. Montejurra, 1958–64.

Fabris, Dinko. "La città della Sirena. Le origini del mito musicale di Napoli nell'età Spagnola." In *Napoli Viceregno Spagnolo: Una capitale della cultura alle origini dell'Europa moderna (sec. XVI–XVII),* ed. Monika Bosse and André Stoll. 2 vols. Naples: Vivarium, Istituto Italiano per gli Studi Filosofici, 2001.

———. *Music in Seventeenth-Century Naples: Francesco Provenzale (1624–1704).* Aldershot: Ashgate, 2007.

———. "Musical Festivals at a Capital without a Court: Spanish Naples from Charles V (1535) to Philip V (1702)." In *Court Festivals of the European Renaissance: Art, Politics and Performance,* ed. J. R. Mulryne and Elizabeth Goldring. Aldershot: Ashgate, 2002.

Fagiolo dell'Arco, Maurizio. *Bibliografia della festa barocca a Roma.* Rome: Antonio Pettini, 1994.

Faraglia, N. F. "Le ottine ed il reggimento popolare in Napoli." *Atti del Accademia Pontaniana* 28:21 (1898): 1–31.

———, ed. "Il tumulto napoletano dell'anno 1585." *Archivio storico per le province napoletane* 11 (1886): 433–41.

Fasano Guarini, Elena. "La crisi del modello repubblicano: patriziati e oligarchie." In *La Storia. I grandi problemi dal medioevo all'età contemporanea,* ed. Nicola Tranfaglia and Massimo Firpo. Vol. 5: *L'Età moderna.* 1. *I quadri generali.* Turin: UTET, 1987.

Fenlon, Iain. *The Ceremonial City: History, Memory and Myth in Renaissance Venice*. New Haven: Yale University Press, 2007.

Filippi, Bruna. "Corti Europee e civiltà moderna. Un bilancio storicografico (9–10 maggio 1997)." *Quaderni Storici*, n.s., 97 (April 1998).

Fiorella, Vittoria. *Una santa della città: Suor Orsola Benincasa e la devozione napoletana tra Cinquecento e Seicento*. Naples: Editoriale Scientifica, 2001.

Firpo, Luigi. *Lo stato ideale della Controriforma*. Bari: Laterza, 1957.

Forcellino, Maria. *Il Cavaliere d'Arpino. Napoli 1589–1597*. Milan: Angelo Guerini e Associati, 1991.

Freedberg, David. *The Power of Images: Studies in the History and Theory of Response*. Chicago: University of Chicago Press, 1989.

Galante, Gennaro Aspreno. *Guida sacra della città di Napoli*. Naples: Stamperia del Filreno, 1872. Reprint, Naples: Società Editrice Napoletana, 1985.

Galasso, Giueseppe. *L'altra Europa: per un antropologia storica del Mezzogiorno d'Italia*. Milan: Mondadori, 1982.

———. "Da 'Napoli gentile' a 'Napoli fedelissima.'" In *Napoli capitale: identità politica e identità citadina. Studi e ricerche 1266–1860*. Naples: Electa Napoli, 1998.

———. "Ideologia e sociologia del patronato di San Tommaso d'Aquino su Napoli (1605)." In *Per la storia sociale e religiosa del Mezzogiorno d'Italia*, ed. Giuseppe Galasso and Carla Russo. Vol. 2. Naples: Guida, 1982.

———. *Napoli Spagnola dopo Masaniello*. Vol. 2. Florence: Sansoni Editore, 1982.

———. "Le riforme del conte di Lemos e le finanze napoletane nella prima metà del Seicento." In *Mezzogiorno medievale e moderno*. Turin: Giulio Einaudi editore, 1965.

———. "Una ipotesi di 'blocco storico' oligarchico-borghese nella Napoli del Seicento: i 'Seggi' di Camillo Tutini fra politica e storiografia." *Rivista Storica Italiana* 90 (1978): 507–29.

Garin, Eugenio. "La città ideale." In *Scienza e vita civile nel Rinascimento italiano*. 3rd ed. Rome: Laterza, 1975.

Gatti Perer, M. L., ed. *"La dimora di Dio con gli uomini" (Ap 21,3). Immagini della Gerusalemme celeste dal III al XIV secolo*. Milan: Vita e pensiero; pubblicazioni della Università Cattolica, 1983.

The Getty Provenance Index on CD-ROM. Malibu: The J. Paul Getty Trust, 1996.

Giannone, Enrico. *Plaza Mayor in Castelnuovo. Ovvero I giuochi dei tori nella Napoli del Seicento*. Naples: Comune di Napoli, 2005.

Giannone, Onofrio. *Giunte sulle vite de' pittori napoletani*. Ed. Ottavio Morisani. Naples: R. Deputazione di Storia Patria, 1941.

Giesey, Ralph. *The Royal Funeral Ceremony in Renaissance France*. Geneva: E. Droz, 1960.

Ginzburg, Carlo. *Occhiacci di legno*. Milan: Feltrinelli, 1998.

———. "Ritual Pillages: A Preface to Research in Progress." In *Microhistory and the Lost Peoples of Europe*, ed. Edward Muir and Guido Ruggiero. Baltimore: Johns Hopkins University Press, 1991.

Gioda, Carlo. *La vita e le opere di Giovanni Botero: con la quinta parte delle Relazioni universali e altri documenti inediti*. Milan: U. Hoepli, 1894–95.

Greene, Thomas M. "Ceremonial Play and Parody in the Renaissance." In *Urban Life in the*

Renaissance, ed. Susan Zimmerman and Ronald F. E. Weissman. Newark: University of Delaware Press, 1989.

Greenstein, Jack. "The Vision of Peace: Meaning and Representation in Ambrogio Lorenzetti's *Sala della pace* Cityscapes." *Art History* 11:4 (1988): 492–510.

Guarino, Gabriel. "The Politics of Appearances: State Representations and Images of Power in Spanish Naples during the Seventeenth Century." Ph.D. dissertation, Churchill College, Cambridge University, 2004.

———. *Representing the King's Splendour: Communication and Reception of Symbolic Forms of Power in Viceregal Naples.* Manchester: Manchester University Press, 2010.

———. "Spanish Celebrations in Seventeenth-Century Naples." *Sixteenth Century Journal* 37:1 (2006): 25–41.

Gundersheimer, Werner L. "Trickery, Gender, and Power: The *Discorsi* of Annibale Romeik." In *Urban Life in the Renaissance*, ed. Susan Zimmerman and Ronald F. E. Weissman. Newark: University of Delaware Press, 1989.

Hamilton, Alastair. "The Apocalypse Within: Some Inward Interpretations of the Book of Revelation from the Sixteenth to the Eighteenth Century." In *Tradition and Re-Interpretation in Jewish and Early Christian Literature: Essays in Honour of Jurgen C. H. Lebram*, ed. J. W. Van Henten et al. Studia Post-Biblica, no. 36. Leiden: E. J. Brill, 1986.

Hardie, P. R. "Aeneas and the Omen of the Swans (Verg. *Aen.* 1. 393–400)." *Classical Philology* 82:2 (April 1987): 145–50.

Haskell, Francis. *Patrons and Painting: Art and Society in Baroque Italy.* Rev. and enlg. ed. New Haven: Yale University Press, 1980.

Hernando Sánchez, Carlos José. *Castilla y Nápoles en el siglo XVI. El Virrey Pedro de Toledo.* Salamanca: Junta de Castilla y León, Consejería de Cultura y Turismo, 1994.

———. "El *Glorioso Triumfo* de Carlos V en Napoles y el humanismo de corte entre Italia y España." In *Carlo V, Napoli e il Mediterraneo*, ed. Giuseppe Galasso and Aurelio Musi. *Archivio storico per le province napoletane 119* (2001): 447–521.

———. "Naturaleza y mito en el Napoles espanol del Renacimiento: El Virrey Pedro de Toledo." *Album Letras Artes* 31 (1991): 66–73.

———. "El Parlamento del Reino de Napoles bajo Carlos V: Formas de representacion, faciones aristocraticas y poder virreinal." In *Rappresentanze e territori. Parlamento friulano e istituzioni rappresentative territoriali nell'Europa moderna*, ed. Laura Casella. Udine: Forum, 2003.

———. *El reino de Nápoles en el Imperio de Carlos V. La consolidación de la conquista.* Madrid: Sociedad Estatal para la Conmemoración de los Centenarios de Felipe II y Carlos V, 2001.

———. "El Virrey Pedro de Toledo y la entrada de Carlos V en Nápoles." *Investigaciones históricas* 7 (1988): 9–15.

Hersey, George L. *Alfonso II and the Artistic Renewal of Naples, 1485–1495.* New Haven: Yale University Press, 1969.

———. *The Aragonese Arch at Naples, 1443–1475.* New Haven: Yale University Press, 1973.

Hills, Helen. "Enamelled with the Blood of a Noble Lineage: Tracing Noble Blood and Female Holiness in Early Modern Neapolitan Convents and Their Architecture." *Church History: Studies in Christianity and Culture* 73:1 (2004): 1–40.

———. *Invisible City: The Architecture of Devotion in Seventeenth Century Neapolitan Convents.* Oxford: Oxford University Press, 2004.

Hoffman, Philip T. *Church and Community in the Diocese of Lyon, 1500–1789.* New Haven: Yale University Press, 1984.

Hyde, J. K. "Medieval Descriptions of Cities." In *Literacy and Its Uses: Studies on Late Medieval Italy,* ed. Daniel Waley. 1966; Manchester: Manchester University Press, 1993.

Iannella, Gina. "Les fêtes de la Saint-Jean à Naples (1581–1632)." In *Les fêtes urbaines en Italie a l'époque de la renaissance: Vérone, Florence, Sienne, Naples,* ed. Françoise Decroisette and Michel Plaisance. Paris: Klincksieck, 1993.

———, ed. *Posilecheata di Pompeo Sarnelli M.DC.LXXXIV.* Naples: Domenico Morano librajo-editore, 1885.

Imbriani, Vittorio. "Della *Siracusa* di Paolo Regio. Contributo alla storia della novellistica nel secolo XVI." Presentato alla Real Accademia di Scienzi Morali e Politiche. Naples: Tip. degli Regia Università, 1885.

Ingman, Heather. "Machiavelli and the Interpretation of the Chiron Myth in France." *Journal of the Warburg and Courtauld Institutes* 45 (1982): 217–25.

Intorcia, G. *Magistrature del Regno di Napoli. Analisi prosopografica secoli xvi–xvii.* Naples: Jovene, 1987.

Ippolití, A. "Fontana, Domenico." *Dizionario biografico degli Italiani,* 48:638–43. Rome: Istituto della Enciclopedia italiana, 1960–.

Jacks, Philip. *The Antiquarian and the Myth of Antiquity: The Origins of Rome in Renaissance Thought.* Cambridge: Cambridge University Press, 1993.

Jackson, Philippa, and Fabrizio Nevola, eds. *Beyond the Palio: Urbanism and Ritual in Renaissance Siena.* Malden, Mass.: Society for Renaissance Studies and Blackwell Publishing, 2006.

Jacquot, Jean. *Le fêtes de la Renaissance.* 3 vols. Paris: CNRS, 1956–75.

Jannini, P. A., et al., eds. *La "Bibliotheque Bleue" nel Seicento o della Letteratura per il Popolo.* Vol. 4 of *Quaderni del Seicento Francese.* 1981.

Kamen, Henry. *Philip of Spain.* New Haven: Yale University Press, 1997.

Kantorowicz, Ernst. *The King's Two Bodies.* Princeton: Princeton University, 1975.

Kent, Dale. *Cosimo de' Medici and the Florentine Renaissance.* New Haven: Yale University Press, 2000.

Kent, F. W., with Patricia Simons. "Renaissance Patronage: An Introductory Essay." In *Patronage, Art, and Society in Renaissance Italy,* ed. F. W. Kent and Patricia Simons. Oxford: Clarendon Press, 1987.

Kettering, Sharon. *Patrons, Brokers, and Clients in Seventeenth-Century France.* New York: Oxford University Press, 1986.

Klein, Peter K. "Introduction: The Apocalypse in Medieval Art." In *The Apocalypse in the Middle Ages,* ed. Richard K. Emmerson and Bernard McGinn. Ithaca: Cornell University Press, 1992.

Knipping, John B. *Iconography of the Counter Reformation in the Netherlands: Heaven on Earth.* 2 vols. Nieuwkoop: B. de Fraaf, 1974.

Krautheimer, Richard. "The Panels in Urbino, Baltimore and Berlin Revisited." In *Renaissance from Brunelleschi to Michelangelo: The Representation of Architecture,* ed. Henry Millon. New York: Rizzoli, 1994.

———. "The Tragic and Comic Scene of the Renaissance: The Baltimore and Urbino Panels." *Gazette des Beaux-Arts* 33 (1948): 327–46.

Labrot, Gérard. *Collections of Paintings in Naples, 1600–1780*. The Provenance Index of the Getty Art History Information Program. Munich: K. G. Sauer, 1992.

———. "Des saints à la nature: structure et évolution des collections napolitaines." In *Études Napolitaines. Villages, palais, collections XVIe–XVIIIe siècles*. Seyssel: Champ Vallon, 1993.

Lanternari, Vittorio. "Cristianesimo e religioni etniche in Occidente. Un caso concreto d'incontro: la festa di San Giovanni." In *Occidente e Terzo Mundo*. Bari: Dedalo libri, 1972.

———. *La Grande festa. Vita rituale e sistemi di produzione nelle società tradizionali*. 2nd ed. Bari: Edizioni Dedalo, 1983.

Lanzoni, Francesco. *Genesi svolgimento e tramonto delle leggende storiche*. Rome: Tipografia Poliglotta Vaticana, 1925.

Leach, Edmund R. "Anthropological Aspects of Language: Animal Categories and Verbal Abuse." In *New Directions in the Study of Language*, ed. E. H. Lenneberg. Cambridge, Mass.: MIT Press, 1964.

Legman, G. *Rationale of the Dirty Joke: An Analysis of Sexual Humor*. New York: Bell Publishing, 1975.

Leoncini, Giovanni. "Il monastero certosino: attuazione di un ideale." In *Certose e Certosini in Europa. Atti del Convegno alla Certosa di San Lorenzo Padula 22, 23, 24 settembre 1988*. 2 vols. Naples: Sergio Civita Editore, 1990.

Lettere, S. "Costo, Tommaso." *Dizionario biografico degli Italiani*, 30: 411–15. Rome: Istituto della Enciclopedia italiana, 1960–.

Lupieri, Edmondo. *Giovanni e Gesù: storia di un antagonismo*. Milan: A. Mondadori, 1991.

Lurie Anne T., and Ann Percy. *Bernardo Cavallino of Naples, 1616–1656*. Bloomington: Cleveland Museum of Art and Kimbell Art Museum, 1984.

Lutio di Castiglione, L. *I Sedili di Napoli*. S. Giorgio a Cremano: Morano, 1973.

Mackenney, Richard. *Tradesmen and Traders: The World of the Guilds in Venice and Europe, c. 1250–c. 1650*. London: Croom Helm, 1987.

Macry, Paolo. *Giocare la vita. Storia del lotto a Napoli tra Sette e Ottocento*. Rome: Donzelli editore, 1997.

Mancini, Franco. *Feste ed apparati civili e religiosi in Napoli dal viceregno alla capitale*. Naples: Edizioni Scientifiche Italiane, 1968.

Manning, John. Introduction to *Aspects of Renaissance and Baroque Symbol Theory 1500–1700*, ed. Peter M. Daly and John Manning. New York: AMS Press, 1999.

Mansfield, Harvey C. *Machiavelli's New Modes and Orders: A Study of the Discourses on Livy*. Chicago: University of Chicago Press, 2001.

Mantelli, Roberto. *Burocrazia e finanze pubbliche nel Regno di Napoli*. Naples: Lucio Pironti Editore, 1981.

Manzi, P. *La tipografia napoletana nel '500*. 8 vols. Florence: Olschki, 1968–75.

Marchiex, Lucien. *Un Parisien à Rome et à Naples en 1632. D'après un manuscrit inédit de J.-J. Bouchard*. Paris: Ernest Leroux, 1897.

Marino, John A. "Administrative Mapping in the Italian States." In *Monarchs, Ministers, and Maps: The Emergence of Cartography as a Tool of Government in Early Modern Europe*, ed. David Buisseret. Chicago: University of Chicago Press, 1992.

———. "L'agricoltura pratica italiana nell'età moderna: 'dai loro frutti li conoscerete.'" In *Nel sistema imperiale: l'Italia spagnola*, ed. Aurelio Musi. Naples: Edizioni Scientifiche Italiane, 1994.

———. "An Anti-Campanellan Vision on the Spanish Monarchy and the Crisis of 1595." In *A Renaissance of Conflicts: Visions and Revisions of Law and Society in Italy and Spain*, ed. John A. Marino and Thomas Kuehn. Toronto: University of Toronto Centre for Reformation and Renaissance Studies, 2004.

———. "Celebrating a Royal Birth in 1639: The Rape of Europa in the Neapolitan Viceroy's Court." *Rinascimento* 44 (2004): 233–47.

———. "Economic Idylls and Pastoral Realities: The 'Trickster Economy' in the Kingdom of Naples." *Comparative Studies in Society and History* 24:2 (1982): 211–34.

———. *Pastoral Economics in the Kingdom of Naples*. Baltimore: Johns Hopkins University Press, 1988.

———. "The Rural World in Italy under Spanish Rule." In *Spain in Italy: Politics, Society, and Religion, 1500–1700*, ed. Thomas James Dandelet and John A. Marino. Leiden: Brill, 2007.

———. "The Zodiac in the Streets: Inscribing 'Buon Governo' in Baroque Naples." In *Embodiments of Power: Building Baroque Cities in Austria and Europe*, ed. Gary B. Cohen and Franz A. J. Szabo. Oxford: Berghahn Books, 2007.

Marshall, Christopher R. "'Causa di Stravaganze': Order and Anarchy in Domenico Gargiulo's *Revolt of Masaniello*." *Art Bulletin* 80:3 (September 1998): 478–97.

Martines, Lauro, ed. *Violence in Italian Cities, 1200–1500*. UCLA Center for Medieval and Renaissance Studies, no. 5. Berkeley and Los Angeles: University of California Press, 1972.

Masi, Giorgio. *Dal Collenuccio a Tommaso Costo: vicende della storiografia napoletana fra Cinque e Seicento*. Naples: Editoriale Scientifica, 1999.

Mauriello, Adriana. "Metamorfosi di temi e statuti narrativi nella *Siracusa* di Paolo Regio." In *Rinascimento meridionale e altri studi in onore di Mario Santoro*, ed. Maria Cristina Cafisse et al. Naples: Società Editrice Napoletana, 1987.

Mauro, Ida. "'Sontuoso benchè funesto.' Gil apparati per le esequie di Filippo IV a Napoli (1665–1666)." *Napoli Nobilissima*, ser. 5, 9:3–4 (July 2008): 113–30.

Maza, Sarah. *Private Lives and Public Affairs: The Causes Célèbres of Prerevolutionary France*. Berkeley and Los Angeles: University of California Press, 1993.

McClure, George W. "Women and the Politics of Play in Sixteenth-Century Italy: Torquato Tasso's Theory of Games." *Renaissance Quarterly* 61 (2008): 750–91.

McGinness, Frederick. *Right Thinking and Sacred Oratory in Counter-Reformation Rome*. Princeton: Princeton University Press, 1995.

McManamon, John M. *Funeral Oratory and the Cultural Ideals of Italian Humanism*. Chapel Hill: University of North Carolina Press, 1989.

McNeill, William H. *Mythistory and Other Essays*. Chicago: University of Chicago Press, 1986.

Megale, Teresa. "Gli apparati napoletani per la festa di San Giovanni Battista tra cinque e seicento." *Comunicazioni sociali* 1–2 (1994): 191–213.

———. "'Sic per te superis gens inimica ruat.' L'ingresso trionfale di Carlo V a Napoli (1535)." In *Carlo V, Napoli e il Mediterraneo*, ed. Giuseppe Galasso and Aurelio Musi. *Archivio storico per le province napoletane* 119 (2001): 587–610.

Micco Spadaro. *Napoli ai tempi di Masaniello*. Naples: Electa Napoli, Ministero per i Beni e le Attività Culturali, Soprintendenza per il Polo Museale di Napoli, 2002.

Mielke, Hans. "Hans Vredeman de Vries. Verzeichnis der Stichwerke und Beschreibung seines stils sowie Beiträge zum Werk Gerard Groennings." Ph.D. dissertation, Freien Univeristät, Berlin, 1967.

Miller, Peter N. "Friendship and Conversation in Seventeenth-Century Venice." *Journal of Modern History* 73 (March 2001): 1–31.

Mitchell, Bonner. *Italian Civic Pageantry in the High Renaissance*. Florence: Olschki, 1979.

Moli Frigola, Montserrat. "El ingreso de la future esposa el encuentro entre Venus y Adone o las bodas reales." In *Barocco Napoletano*, ed. Gaetana Cantone. Rome: Istituto Poligrafico e Zecca dello Stato, Libreria dello Stato, 1992.

Mols, Roger. "Population in Europe, 1500–1700." In *The Fontana Economic History of Europe*, vol. 2: *The Sixteenth and Seventeenth Centuries*, ed. Carlo M. Cipolla. London: Collins/Fontana Books, 1974.

Muir, Edward. "The Cannibals of Renaissance Italy." *Syracuse Scholar* 5 (Fall 1984): 5–14.

———. *Civic Ritual in Renaissance Venice*. Princeton: Princeton University Press, 1981.

———. *Ritual in Early Modern Europe*. 2nd ed. Cambridge: Cambridge University Press, 2005.

———. "The Virgin on the Street Corner: The Place of the Sacred in Italian Cities." In *Religion and Culture in the Renaissance and Reformation*, ed. Steven Ozment. Sixteenth Century Essays and Studies, vol. 11. Kirksville, Mo.: Sixteenth Century Journal Publishers, 1989.

Muir, Edward, and Ronald F. E. Weissman. "Social and Symbolic Places in Renaissance Venice and Florence." In *The Power of Place. Bringing Together Geographical and Sociological Imaginations*, ed. J. A. Agnew and J. S. Duncan. Boston: Unwith Hyman, 1989.

Mursell, Gordon. *The Theology of the Carthusian Life in the Writings of St. Bruno and Guigo I.* Analecta Cartusiana, no. 127. Salzburg: Institut für Anglistik und Amerikanistik, 1988.

Musi, Aurelio. *Italia dei Viceré. Integrazione e resistanza nel sistema imperiale spagnolo*. Cava de' Tirreni: Avagliano Editore, 2000.

———. *La rivolta di Masaniello nella scena politica barocca*. Naples: Guida, 1989.

———. "Le rivolte italiane nel sistema imperiale spagnolo." *Mediterranea Ricerche Storiche* 2:4 (August 2005): 209–20.

Muto, Giovanni. "Apparati e cerimoniali di corte nella Napoli spagnola." In *I linguaggi del potere nell'età barocca, 1: Politica e religione*, ed. Francesca Cantù. Rome: Viella, 2009.

———. "The Form and Content of Poor Relief in Early Modern Naples." In *Good Government in Spanish Naples*, ed. and trans. Antonio Calabria and John A. Marino. New York: Peter Lang, 1990.

———. "Gestione politica e controllo sociale nella Napoli spagnola." In *Le Città capitali*, ed. Cesare De Seta. Bari: Editori Laterza, 1985.

———. "Noble Presence and Stratification in the Territories of Spanish Italy." In *Spain in Italy: Politics, Society, and Religion, 1500–1700*, ed. Thomas James Dandelet and John A. Marino. Leiden: Brill, 2007.

———. "Il regno di Napoli sotto la dominazione spagnola." In *La Controriforma e il Seicento*. Vol. 11 of *Storia della società italiana*, ed. Giovanni Cherubini et al. Milan: Teti editore, 1989.

———. "Sacred Places in Spanish Naples." In *Frontiers of Faith*, ed. Eszter Andor and István György Tóth. Budapest: Central European University, 2001.

———. "Spazio urbano e identità sociale: le feste del popolo napoletano nella prima età moderna." In *Le Regole dei mestieri e delle professioni, secoli xv–xix*, ed. Marco Meriggi and Alessandro Pastore. Milan: FrancoAngeli, 2000.

Naddeo, Barbara. "Topographies of Difference: Cartography of the City of Naples, 1627–1775." *Imago Mundi* 56:1 (January 2004): 23–47.

Napoli, John Nicholas. "From Social Virtue to Revetted Interior: Giovanni Antonio Dosio and Marble Inlay in Rome, Florence, and Naples." *Art History* 31:4 (September 2008): 523–46.

Niccoli, Ottavia. "Images of Society." In *Early Modern History and the Social Sciences: Testing the Limits of Braudel's Mediterranean*, ed. John A. Marino. Kirksville, Mo: Truman State University Press, 2002.

Nigro, Salvatore. "Capaccio, Giulio Cesare." *Dizionario biografico degli Italiani*, 18:374–80. Rome: Istituto della Enciclopedia italiana, 1960–.

———. "The Secretary." In *Baroque Personae*, ed. Rosario Villari, trans. Lydia Cochrane. Chicago: University of Chicago Press, 1994.

Nora, Pierre. "Between Memory and History: Les Lieux de mémoire." *Representations* 26 (Spring 1989): 7–25.

———, ed. *Realms of Memory: Rethinking the French Past*. 3 vols. Trans. Arthur Goldhammer. New York: Columbia University Press, 1996–98.

Novellino, Paquale. "Il culto di Hebone: 'enciclopedia' classica e visibilità contemporanea ne *Il Forastiero* di Giulio Cesare Capaccio." *Res publica litterarum* 24 (2001): 106–36.

———. "Le filigrane culturali della 'fedeltà' nella storiografia napoletana tra fine Cinquecento ed inizio Seicento." *MEFRIM-Mélanges de l'école française de Rome: Italie et mediterranée* 118:2 (2006): 243–53.

Novi Chavarria, Elisa. "Un'eretica alla corte del conte di Lemos. Il caso di Suor Giulia de Marco." *Archivo storico per le province napoletane* 116 (1998): 77–118.

Nuti, Lucia. "I 'teatri' di città e l'Italia del secolo XVII. Il ruolo delle immagini." In *Cartografiques*, ed. Marie-Ange Brayer. Actes du colloque de l'Académie de France à Rome 19–20 mai 1995. Paris: Réunion des musées nationaux, 1995.

Olgier, P. Livarius. "Paolo Regio vescovo di Vico Equense, un agiografo dimenticato (1541–1607)." *Rivista di Storia della Chiesa in Italia* 1 (1947): 263–84.

O'Malley, John W. *Trent and All That: Renaming Catholicism in the Early Modern Era*. Cambridge, Mass.: Harvard University Press, 2000.

Orso, Steven N. *Art and Death at the Spanish Habsburg Court: The Royal Exequies for Philip IV*. Columbia: University of Missouri, 1989.

Pacelli, Vincenzo. "L'Ideologia del potere nella ritrattistica napoletana del Seicento." *Bollettino del Centro di Studi Vichiani* 16 (1986): 197–241.

Panico, Guido. *Il carnefice e la piazza. Crudeltà di Stato e violenza popolare a Napoli in età moderna.* Naples: Edizioni Scientifiche Italiane, 1998.

Parker, Geoffrey. *Philip II.* 3rd ed. Chicago: Open Court, 1995.

———. *The World Is Not Enough: The Imperial Vision of Philip II of Spain.* Charles Edmondson Historical Lectures, 22nd. Waco, Tex.: Baylor University Press, 2001.

Parlett, David. *The Oxford History of Board Games.* Oxford: Oxford University Press, 1999.

Passare il tempo. La letteratura del gioco e dell'intrattenimento dal XII al XVI secolo. Atti del Convegno di Pienza 10–14 settembre 1991. 2 vols. Rome: Salerno editrice, 1993.

Peters, Jane S., ed. *German Masters of the Sixteenth Century: Hans Rudolf Manuel (Deutsch), Tobias Stimmer.* In *The Illustrated Bartsch,* vol. 19, pt. 2, gen. ed., Walter L. Strauss. New York: Abaris Books, 1988.

Petraccone, Claudia. "Manifattura e artigianato tessile a Napoli nella prima metà del XVII secolo." *Atti dell'Accademia di Scienze Morali e Politiche* 89 (1978): 101–57.

———. *Napoli del Cinquecento all'Ottocento. Problemi di storia demografia e sociale.* Naples: Guida, 1975.

Petrarca, Valerio. "La festa di San Giovanni Battista a Napoli nella prima metà del Seicento: percorso machine immagini scrittura." *Quaderni del Servizio Museografico della Facoltà di Lettere e Filosofia dell'Università di Palermo* 4 (1986).

Pigler, A. *Barockthemen.* 3 vols. Budapest: Akadémiai Kiadó, 1974.

Piquard, Maurice. "Le livres du Cardinal de Granvelle a la Bibliothèque de Besançon." *Libri* 1 (1951): 301–23.

Pitt-Rivers, Julian. *The Fate of Shechem or the Politics of Sex.* Cambridge: Cambridge University Press, 1977.

Porter, Jeanne Chenault. "The 'Prophetic' Dozen: Jusepe de Ribera's Old Testament Figures at the Certosa di S. Martino in Naples." In *Parthenope's Splendor: Art of the Golden Age in Naples,* ed. Jeanne Chenault Porter and Susan Scott Munshower. Papers in Art History, vol. 7. University Park: Pennsylvania State University, 1993.

Propp, Vladimir. "Ritual Laughter in Folklore." In *Theory and History of Folklore.* Trans. Ariadna Y. Martin, Richard P. Martin, et al. Minneapolis: University of Minnesota Press, 1984.

Puppi, L. "Venezia tra Quattrocento e Cinquecento. Da 'Nuova Costantinopoli' a 'Roma altera' nel segno di Gerusalemme." In *Le città capitale,* ed. Cesare de Seta. Rome: Laterza, 1985.

Quinlan-McGrath, Mary. "The Italian City as a Living Entity." Paper presented at the Sixteenth Century Society and Conference, Pittsburgh, 1 November 2003.

Quondam, Amedeo. "Dal mannerismo al barocco." In *Storia di Napoli,* 5:337–640. Naples: Società editrice Storia di Napoli, 1972.

———. *La parola nel labirinto. Società e scrittura del Manierismo a Napoli.* Bari: Laterza, 1975.

Rabil, Albert, Jr., ed. *Humanism in Italy.* Vol. 1 of *Renaissance Humanism: Foundations Forms and Legacy.* Philadelphia: University of Pennsylvania Press, 1988.

Rak, Michele. "A dismisura d'uomo. Feste e spettacolo del barocco napoletano." In *Gian Lorenzo Bernini e le arti visive,* ed. Marcello Fagiolo. Rome: Istituto della Enciclopedia Italian, 1987.

————. *Napoli gentile. La letteratura in "lingua napoletana" nella cultura barocca (1596–1632)*. Bologna: Il Mulino, 1994.

————. "*Napoli no plus*. Cinque icone dell'immagine di Napoli nella letteratura in 'lingua Napoletana' fame, corpo, natura morta, specchio, sirena." In *Napoli Viceregno Spagnolo. Una capitale della cultura alle origini dell'Europa moderna* (sec. XVI–XVII), ed. Monika Bosse and André Stoll. 2 vols. Naples: Vivarium, 2001.

————. "Il sistema delle feste nella Napoli barocca." In *Barocco napoletano*, ed. Gaetana Cantone, 2:301–27. Rome: Istituto poligrafico e Zecca dello Stato, Libreria dello Stato, 1992.

————. "Lo squardo devoto." In Antonio Ermanno Giardino and Michele Rak, *Per grazia ricevuta: le tavolette dipinte ex voto per la Madonna dell'Arco. Il Cinquecento*. Naples: ci.esse.ti cooperative editrice, 1983.

Rapp, Richard Tilden. *Industry and Economic Decline in Seventeenth-Century Venice*. Cambridge, Mass.: Harvard University Press, 1976.

Rappaport, Roy A. *Ritual and Religion in the Making of History*. Cambridge: Cambridge Univesity Press, 1999.

Rebhorn, Wayne A. *Courtly Performances*. Detroit: Wayne State University Press, 1978.

Redigonda, A. L. "Alberti, Leandro." *Dizionario biografico degli Italiani*, 1: 699–702. Rome: Istituto della Enciclopedia italiana, 1960–.

Riccio, Luigi. "Nuovi documenti sull'incendio Vesuviano dell'anno 1631 e bibliografia di quella eruzione." *Archivio storico per le province napoletane* 14 (1889): 489–555.

Rivero Rodríguez, Manuel. "Doctrina y práctica política en la monarquía hispana; Las instrucciones dadas a los virreyes y gobernadores de Italia en los siglos XVI y XII." *Investigaciones Históricas* 9 (1989): 197–213.

Rosenthal, Earl. "*Plus Ultra, Non Plus Ultra*, and the Columnar Device of Emperor Charles V." *Journal of the Warburg and Courtauld Institutes* 34 (1971): 204–28.

Rosa, Mario. "L'onda che ritorna: interno ed esterno sacro nella Napoli del '600." In *Luoghi sacri e spazi della santità*, ed. S. Boesch Gajano and L. Scaraffia. Turin: Rosenberg & Sellier, 1990.

Rossi, Marco, and Alessandro Rovetta. "Indagini sullo spazio ecclesiale immagine della Gerusalemme celeste." In *"La dimora di Dio con gli uomini" (Ap 21,3). Immagini della Gerusalemme celeste dal III al XIV secolo*, ed. M. L. Gatti Perer. Milan: Vita e pensiero; pubblicazioni della Università Cattolica, 1983.

Rovito, Pier Luigi. *Il Viceregno Spagnolo di Napoli: ordinamento, istituzioni, culture di governo*. Naples: Arte Tipografica, 2003.

Rubinstein, Nicolai. "Vasari's Painting on the Foundation of Florence in the Palazzo Vecchio." In *Essays in the History of Architecture Presented to Rudolph Wittkower*, ed. Douglas Fraser, Howard Hibbard, and Milton J. Lewine. London: Phaidon, 1967.

Ryan, Mary. "The American Parade: Representations of the Nineteenth-Century Social Order." In *The New Cultural History*, ed. Lynn Hunt. Berkeley and Los Angeles: University of California Press, 1989.

Rykwert, Joseph. *The Idea of a Town: The Anthropology of Urban Form in Rome, Italy and the Ancient World*. London: Faber and Faber, 1976.

Sallmann, Jean-Michel. "Di Marco, Giulia." *Dizionario biografico degli Italiani*, 40:78–81. Rome: Istituto della Enciclopedia italiana, 1960–.

———. *Naples et ses saints à l'âge baroque (1540–1750)*. Paris: PUF, 1994.

———. "Il santo patrono cittadino nel'600 nel Regno di Napoli e in Sicilia." In *Per la storia sociale e religiosa del Mezzogiorno d'Italia*, ed. Giuseppe Galasso and Carla Russo. 2 vols. Naples: Guida editori, 1982.

San Juan, Rose Marie. *Rome: A City Out of Print*. Minneapolis: University of Minnesota Press, 2001.

Santoro, Mario. "Humanism in Naples." In *Humanism in Italy*, 296–331. Vol. 1 of *Renaissance Humanism: Foundations, Forms, and Legacy*, ed. Albert Rabil Jr. Philadelphia: University of Pennsylvania Press, 1988.

Schneider, Robert A. *The Ceremonial City: Toulouse Observed, 1738–1780*. Princeton: Princeton University Press, 1995.

Schumpeter, Joseph A. *History of Economic Analysis*. Ed. Elizabeth Boody Schumpeter. New York: Oxford University Press, 1954.

Schutte, Anne Jacobson. *Aspiring Saints: Pretense of Holiness, Inquisition, and Gender in the Republic of Venice*. Baltimore: Johns Hopkins University Press, 2001.

Schütze, Sebastian. "The Politics of Counter-Reformation Iconography and a Quest for the Spanishness of Neapolitan Art." In *Spain in Italy: Politics, Society, and Religion, 1500–1700*, ed. Thomas James Dandelet and John A. Marino. Leiden: Brill, 2007.

Schütze, Sebastian, and Thomas Willette. *Massimo Stanzione. L'opera completa*. Naples: Electa, 1992.

Scognamiglio Cestaro, Sonia. *Le istitutzioni della moda. Economia, magistrature e scambio politico nella Napoli Moderna*. Benevento: Edizioni Il Chiostro, 2008.

Seidel Menchi, Silvana. "Benincasa, Orsola." *Dizionario biografico degli Italiani*, 8:527–30. Rome: Istituto della Enciclopedia italiana, 1960–.

Sirri, Raffaele. *Bernardino Telesio e la cultura napolitana*. Naples: Guida, 1992.

Snow, Edward. *Inside Bruegel: The Play of Images in Children's Games*. New York: North Point Press; Farrar, Straus and Giroux, 1997.

Snyder, Jon R. *Dissimulation and the Culture of Secrecy in Early Modern Europe*. Berkeley and Los Angeles: University of California Press, 2009.

———. *Writing the Scene of Speaking: Theories of Dialogue in the Late Italian Renaissance*. Stanford, Calif.: Stanford University Press, 1989.

Sodano, Giulio. "'Sangue vivo, rubicondo e senza malo odore.' I prodigi del sangue nei processi di anonizzaione a Napoli nell'età moderna." *Campania Sacra* 26 (1995): 293–310.

Sparti, Barbara. "Breaking Down Barriers in the Study of Renaissance and Baroque Dance." *Dance Chronicle* 19:3 (1996): 255–76.

Starn, Randolph, and Loren Partridge. *Arts of Power: Three Halls of State in Italy, 1300–1600*. Berkeley and Los Angeles: University of California Press, 1992.

Stoll, A. "Napoli-Tarragona andanta e ritorno. Il *Burlador de Sevilla* percorre la cultura letteraria e política del viceregno spagnolo." In *Napoli Viceregno Spagnolo. Una capitale della cultura alle origini dell'Europa moderna (sec. XVI–XVII)*, ed. M. Bosse and A. Stoll. 2 vols. Naples: Vivarium, 2001.

Stratton, Suzanne L. *The Immaculate Conception in Spanish Art*. Cambridge: Cambridge University Press, 1994.

Strazzullo, Franco. *Edilizia e urbanistica a Napoli dal '500 al '700*. Naples: Arturo Berisio editore, 1968.

Strong, Roy. *Art and Power: Renaissance Festivals (1450–1650)*. Woodbridge: Boydell, 1984.

Strumwasser, Gina. "Heroes, Heroines, and Heroic Tales from the Old Testament: An Iconographic Analysis." Ph.D. dissertation, University of California, Los Angeles, 1977.

Sutton-Smith, Brian. *The Ambiguity of Play*. Cambridge, Mass.: Harvard University Press, 1997.

Tak, Herman. *South Italian Festivals: A Local History of Ritual and Change*. Amsterdam: Amsterdam University Press, 2000.

Tanner, Marie. *The Last Descendant of Aeneas: The Hapsburgs and the Mythic Image of the Emperor*. New Haven: Yale University Press, 1993.

Tanner, Paul. "Neue Künstliche Figuren Biblischer Historien zu Gotsförchtiger ergetzung andächtiger hertzen." In *Spätrenaissance am Oberrhein: Tobias Stimmer 1539–1584*. Basel: Kunstmuseum Basel, 1984.

Thompson, Stith. *Motif-Index of Folk Literature*. Helsinki: Suomalainen Tiedeakatemia, 1932. In Basile, *The Pentamerone of Giambattista Basile*, 2:305–19.

Toppi, N. *Biblioteca Napoletana et Apparato a gli huomini illustri in lettere di Napoli e del Regno*. Naples: Bulifon, 1678.

Torraca, F. "Sacre rappresentazioni del napoletano." *Archivio storico per le province napoletane* 4 (1879): 113–62.

Toscano, Tobia R. "Carlo V nella letteratura e nella publicistica napoletane (1519–1536)." In *Carlos V. Europeísmo y Universalidad*, ed. Francisco Sánchez-Montes Gonzalez and Juan Luis Castellano Castellano. 5 vols. Madrid: Sociedad Estatal para la Conmemoración de los Centenarios de Felipe II y Carlos V, 2001.

———. "Le Muse e i Colossi: apogeo e tramonto dell'umanesimo politico napoletano nel 'trionfo' di Carlo V (1535) in una rara descrizione a stampa." *Critica letteraria* 30:2–3 (2002): 377–410.

Toschi, Raolo, and Renato Penna. *Le Tavolette votive della Madonna dell'Arco*. Cava dei Tirreni-Naples: Di Mauro editore, 1971.

Tozzi, Simonetta. *Incisioni barocche di feste o avvenimenti giorni d'allegrezza*. Rome: Gangemi editore, 2002.

Trexler, Richard C. "Le célibat à la fin du Moyen Age. Les religieuses de Florence." *Annales, E.S.C.* 27 (1972).

———. *Public Life in Renaissance Florence*. Ithaca: Cornell University Press, 1980.

Tuck-Scala, Anna. "Caravaggio's 'Roman Charity' in the Seven Acts of Mercy." In *Parthenope's Splendor: Art of the Golden Age in Naples*, ed. Jeanne Chenault Porter and Susan Scott Munshower. Papers in Art History, vol. 7. University Park: Pennsylvania State University, 1993.

Turner, Victor. *The Ritual Process: Structure and Anti-structure*. Chicago: Aldine, 1969.

Ussia, Salvatore. "La festa delle Quarantore nel tardo barocco napoletano." *Rivista di Storia e Letteratura Religiosa* 18:2 (1982): 253–65.

Valerio, Vladimiro. *Piante e vedute di Napoli dal 1486 al 1599: l'origine dell'iconografia urbana europea*. Naples: Electa Napoli, 1998.

Varela, Javier. *La muerte del rey: el ceremonial funerario de la monarquía española (1500–1885).* Madrid: Turner, 1990.

Ventura, Piero. "Le ambiguità di un privilegio: la cittadinanza napoletana tra Cinque e Seicento." *Quaderni Storici* 89 (August 1995): 385–416.

———. "Governo urbano e privilegio di cittadinanza nella Napoli spagnola: leggibilità, validità, verifiche." *Etnosistemi* 2 (1995): 95–110.

———. "Il Linguaggio della cittadinanza a Napoli tra ritualità civica, amministrazione e pratica politica (secoli XV–XVII)." In *Linguaggi e pratiche del potere. Genova e il regno di Napoli tra Medioevo ed Età moderna,* ed. Giovanna Petti Balbi and Giovanni Vitolo. Salerno: Laveglia editore, 2007.

———. "Mercato delle risorse e identità urbana: cittadinanza e mestiere a Napoli tra XVI e XVII secolo." In *Le Regole dei mestieri e delle professioni. Secoli XV–XIX,* ed. Marco Meriggi and Alessandro Pastore, 268–304. Milan: FrancoAngeli, 2000.

Vernant, Jean-Pierre. *Myth and Society in Ancient Greece.* Trans. Janet Lloyd. Sussex: Harvester Press; Atlantic Highlands, N.J.: Humanities Press, 1980.

———. *Myth and Thought among the Greeks.* London: Routledge & Kegan Paul, 1983.

Vernant, Jean-Pierre, and Pierre Vidal-Naquet. *Myth and Tragedy in Ancient Greece.* Trans. Janet Lloyd. New York: Zone Books, 1988.

Veyne, Paul. *Did the Greeks Believe in Their Myths? An Essay on the Constitutive Imagination.* Trans. Paula Wissing. Chicago: University of Chicago Press, 1988.

Villari, Rosario. *La rivolta antispagnola a Napoli. I origini.* Bari: Laterza, 1973. Translated by James Newell as *The Revolt of Naples.* Cambridge: Polity Press, 1993.

Visceglia, Maria Antonietta. *La città rituale: Roma e le sue cerimonie in età moderna.* Rome: Viella, 2002.

———. "Nobiltà, città, rituali religiosi." In *Identità social. La nobiltà napoletana nella prima età moderna.* Milan: Edizioni Unicopli, 1998.

———. "Il viaggio cerimoniale di Carlo V dopo Tunisi." In *Carlos V y la quiebra del humanismo político en Europa (1530–1558),* ed. José Martínez Millán and Ignacio J. Ezquerra Revilla. 3 vols. Madrid: Sociedad Estatal papa la Conmemoración de los Centenarios de Felipe II y Carlos V, 2001.

Vitale, Giuliana. "La nobiltà di seggio a Napoli nel basso medioevo: aspetti della dinamica interna." *Archivio storico per le province napoletane* 106 (1988): 1–19.

———. *Ritualità monarchica cerimonie e pratiche devozionali nella Napoli Aragonese.* Salerno: Laveglia editore, 2006.

von Pastor, Ludwig. *The History of the Popes.* Trans. Ernest Graf. London: Routledge and Kegan Paul and Herder Book Co., 1952.

von Reumont, Alfred. *The Carafas of Maddaloni: Naples under Spanish Dominion.* London: Henry G. Bohn, 1854.

Weber, Max. *The City.* Ed. and trans. Don Martindale and Gertrud Neuwirth. New York: Collier Books, 1962.

Weissman, Ronald F. E. "The Importance of Being Ambiguous." In *Urban Life in the Renaissance,* ed. Susan Zimmerman and Ronald F. E. Weissman. Newark: University of Delaware Press, 1989.

———. "Reconstructing Renaissance Sociology: The 'Chicago School,' and the Study of Renaissance Society." In *Persons and Groups: Social Behavior as Identity Formation in Medieval and Renaissance Europe,* ed. Richard Trexler. Binghamton: SUNY Press, 1985.

———. "Taking Patronage Seriously: Mediterranean Values and Renaissance Society." In *Patronage, Art, and Society in Renaissance Italy,* ed. F. W. Kent and Patricia Simons. Oxford: Clarendon Press, 1987.

Whitfield, Clovis, and Jane Martineau, eds. *Painting in Naples, 1606–1705: From Caravaggio to Giordano.* London: Royal Academy of Arts; Weidenfeld and Nicolson, 1982.

Wilcox, Donald J. *The Development of Florentine Humanist Historiography in the Fifteenth Century.* Cambridge, Mass.: Harvard University Press, 1969.

Willette, Thomas, and Maria Ann Conelli. "The Tribune Vault of the Gesù Nuovo in Naples: Stanzione's Frescos and the Doctrine of the Immaculate Conception." *Ricerche sul '600 Napoletano* (1989): 169–213.

Woodward, David. *Maps as Prints in the Italian Renaissance: Makers, Distributors and Consumers.* 1995 Panizzi Lectures. London: British Library, 1996.

Zotta, Silvio. "Agricultural Crisis and Feudal Politics in the Kingdom of Naples: The Doria at Melfi (1585–1615)." *Melanges d'Ecole Française de Rome* 90:2 (1978): 715–96. Reprinted in *Good Government in Spanish Naples,* ed. and trans. Antonio Calabria and John A. Marino. New York: Peter Lang, 1990.

INDEX

Page numbers in italics refer to figures and tables.